Online Learning:
Personal Reflections on the
Transformation of Education

Online Learning:
Personal Reflections on the
Transformation of Education

Greg Kearsley
Editor

Educational Technology Publications
Englewood Cliffs, New Jersey 07632

Library of Congress Cataloging-in-Publication Data

Online learning: personal reflections on the transformation of education/Greg Kearsley, editor.
   p.cm.
   Includes bibliographical references and index.
   ISBN 0-87778-306-3
   1. Education -- Computer network resources. 2. Education -- Effect of technological innovations on. 3. Educational technology. 4. Internet in education. I. Kearsley, Greg, 1951-

LB1044.87.O44 2005
371.33'44678 -- dc22

2004053335

Printed in the United States of America.

Library of Congress Catalog Card Number: 2004053335.

International Standard Book Number: 0-87778-306-3.

First Printing: January 2005.

Acknowledgments

I owe a debt of gratitude to Marc Zolar for convincing me to do one final book. Thanks to Lawrence Lipsitz and Educational Technology Publications for recognizing the value of the book and being willing to publish it. And thanks to all the contributors for their great chapters and making this such a wonderful collection of stories about online education. I believe this book is a treasure trove of material that will greatly benefit the field.

The Contributors

Terry Anderson (terrya@athabascau.ca)
Professor and Canada Research Chair in Distance Education,
Athabasca University

Zane L. Berge (berge@umuc.edu)
Associate Professor, Dept of Education, University Maryland, Baltimore
County,

Alfred Bork (bork@uci.edu)
Professor, Information and Computer Science, University of California, Irvine

Betty Collis (collis@edte.utwente.nl) & **Jeff Moonen**
(moonen@edte.utwente.nl)
Professors, Faculty of Behavioral Science, University of Twente

Norman Coombs (nrcgsh@rit.edu)
Professor Emeritus, Rochester Institute of Technology &
CEO EASI: Equal Access to Software and Information

Chris Dede (Chris_Dede@harvard.edu)
Professor of Learning Technologies, Graduate School of Education,
Harvard University

Peter Fairweather (pfairwea@us.ibm.com) &
Mark K. Singley (ksingley@us.ibm.com)
Research Staff Members, IBM T.J. Watson Research Center

Diane Gayeski (gayeski@ithaca.edu)
Diane Gayeski, Professor of Organizational Communication,
Learning and Design, Roy Park School of Communications, Ithaca College

Chère Campbell Gibson (ccgibson@wisc.edu)
Professor, School of Human Ecology, University of Wisconsin, Madison

Peter Goodyear (p.goodyear@edfac.usyd.edu.au)
Professor of Education, Faculty of Education & Social Work, University of
Sydney

Judi Harris (judi.harris@wm.edu)
Professor and Pavey Chair in Educational Technology, School of Education,
College of William & Mary

Jesse M. Heines (heines@cs.uml.edu)
Associate Professor, Department of Computer Science,
University of Massachusetts Lowell

Beverly Hunter (bev@piedmontresearch.org)
President, Piedmont Research Institute, Amissville, VA

Annette Lamb (alamb@eduscapes.com)
Professor, School of Library and Information Science,
Indiana University-Purdue University at Indianapolis &
President, Lamb Learning Group, Livingston, TX

Robin Mason (r.d.mason@open.ac.uk)
Professor of Educational Technology, Institute of Educational Technology,
The Open University

T. Craig Montgomerie (craig.montgomerie@ualberta.ca)
Professor, Instructional Technology Group, Division of Technology in
Education,
University of Alberta

James L. Morrison (morrison@unc.edu)
Professor Emeritus of Educational Leadership, UNC-Chapel Hill

Frank Odasz (frank@lone-eagles.com) & **Dave Hughes** (dave@oldcolo.com)
Lone Eagle Consulting, Dillon, Montana

Jason Ohler (jason.ohler@uas.alaska.edu)
Professor, Educational Technology, University of Alaska

Thomas C. Reeves (treeves@coe.uga.edu)
Professor, Dept. of Instructional Technology, College of Education,
The University of Georgia

Margaret Riel (margaret.riel@sri.com)
Center for Technology in Learning, SRI, & School of Psychology and
Education, Pepperdine University

Alexander J. Romiszowski (ajromisz@syr.edu)
Research Professor, Syracuse University

Marlene Scardamalia (mscardamalia@kf.oise.utoronto.ca)
Professor, OISE/University of Toronto

Robert J. Seidel (bsseidel@att.net)
Research Chief, Emeritus, US Army Research Institute

Lorraine Sherry (sherry@rmcdenver.com**)**
Senior Research Associate, RMC Research Corporation, Denver, CO

Robert Tinker (bob@concord.org)
President, The Concord Consortium, Concord, MA

Preface

After being involved in online education for more than 25 years, I see a lot of naiveté from those who have just discovered the field — most of it is unbridled enthusiasm, but sometimes, unwarranted skepticism. Many people do not realize that there was online education prior to the Web. Indeed, online education existed back in the 1970s long before the emergence of the Internet. On one hand, early attempts at online education made use of rather primitive technology by current standards, but the pedagogy was often as good if not better than seen today. Most importantly, there is a rich and extensive body of research and practice to learn from.

Which brings us to the main point of this book — to present a comprehensive history of the field of online education as told by many of the pioneers who created it. In doing so, I hope that it fills in the background and provides a foundation for more recent efforts. Each of the contributors discusses their work in online education and presents a personal perspective of the field. Collectively, the chapters portray the major themes and issues that have characterized the past development of online education and will likely dictate its future.

Terminology

It may be useful to discuss a few terms that you will find in the subsequent chapters. Some of the contributors may define/use these terms somewhat differently, and if so, this is outlined in their chapters.

Online Education — Use of networked computers to learn or teach. The most common network these days is the Internet/Web, but it could just as well be a local network within a school or organization. Some authors use the term *telecomputing* to denote online learning.

Distance Education — Use of technology to deliver learning at a distance (i.e., the learner and teacher are physically separated). Computers are one form of technology used, in which case, distance and online education are synonymous. However, other technologies can be used, such as telephone, television, or print/mail.

Computer Based Education — Use of computers to learn or teach. If the computers happen to be networked, then computer based education is the same as online education. But if used as a stand-alone learning system (e.g., featuring content on CD-ROMs), it is not strictly online education. Most computer-based education systems involve networks of one form or another (even the early ones).

Blended or Mixed Mode Education — Combination of traditional on-site classes with online education, distance education, or computer based education. For example, computers could be used in a classroom to access online resources or do online group work. Also called "flexible learning" in Europe and Australia.

The word "training" is usually substituted for "education" in any of these terms when the teaching/learning domain is the business world rather than schools or academia.

There are dozens of variations on these basic terms, but the ones above present the important distinctions to be made — whether networks are involved, whether the technology is specifically computers, and whether classroom instruction is also involved.

While this book is about online education, you will find contributors discussing these related aspects too — most people who are involved with one tend to be involved in the others as well. And everything is ultimately connected.

Overview of the Book: Alphabetically

Here is an overview of the chapters, alphabetically by author:

Terry Anderson outlines his varied experiences with online discussions, beginning with initial use of Bulletin Board Systems, then organizing the first virtual conferences, followed by evaluation of conference transcripts, and current interest in Semantic Webs. Anderson concludes: "We need to critically discern where our own personal comfort level with technology, change, and diversity impairs our abilities to lead and to create new ways and means to enhance personal and social learning across our planet."

To *Zane Berge*, online education means: "A chance to reform what works in schools and organizations, a chance to refocus on what learners do instead of what instructors do, and a chance to redefine the roles and responsibilities of instructors, learners, and sponsoring organizations." He describes his work with scholarly discussion groups, a design model for online learning, research on barriers to distance education, and his conceptual analysis of the role of technology in educational change.

Alfred Bork discusses his work developing tutorial programs for science learning and its significance for distance education: "Distance learning with tutorial computer-based material allows us to reach all students, and so bring learning to people who do not have schools or universities. It allows learning at any time, at any place, in any language and culture." Bork feels that current efforts at online learning are not sufficiently interactive and individualized. He proposes large-scale experiments with computer-based learning on a global basis to demonstrate the practical impact.

Betty Collis and Jef Moonen conduct a conversation about technology and lessons learned based upon decades of work with online learning systems in the Netherlands. They describe the 4-E model (Environment, Effectiveness, Ease of Use, Engagement) which predicts the likelihood of technology use in learning. Their conversation emphasizes the balance needed between the human element and technology: "More technology is not necessarily better, as the human teacher still has an important role to play; certainly more automation is not necessarily better."

Norman Coombs describes how online learning and teaching can be a benefit to individuals with disabilities because it allows attention to individual needs: "Online, I can focus on a single student, but because it is asynchronous, the others do not have to sit idly by during this exchange. In short the technology lets me focus on a single student more than does the classroom setting. Instead of replicating the classroom, I realized that the goal should be to maximize the technology to enhance delivery of course content." Coombs discusses some of the design issues associated with providing a "level learning space" for all individuals and his involvement with the EASI program.

Chris Dede outlines the evolution of ideas about online and distance education over the years. Dede explains two principal themes: "The first challenge was to redesign the presentational instruction prevalent at that time to emphasize pedagogies in which students actively construct knowledge, using mediated interaction enabled by emerging technologies such as groupware and shared virtual environments. The second challenge was to conceptualize distance education and conventional face-to-face teaching not as a dichotomy, but as a continuum in which instructional design could develop various models for teaching/learning 'distributed' across space, time, and multiple interactive media."

Peter Fairweather and Mark Singley discuss the evolution of authoring tools for developing computer based learning programs with particular attention to prevailing instructional theories and cost considerations: "The different forms of computer-based instruction that have emerged since the early sixties mark pauses in a long, winding conversation between those trying to conceptualize what materials and systems for teaching and learning with computers ought to be and those seeking to build such things." Their survey includes Huntington II, IMSSS, Tutor/PLATO, TICCIT, frame-based systems, intelligent tutors, and the Web/HTML.

Diane Gayeski describes her odyssey with interactive multimedia spanning numerous technologies over two decades. She remarks: "Most of today's programs are no better than those from the early days of interactive video — in fact, they are worse...What we are now faced with is not primarily a problem of sorting out hardware devices: most online instruction can be delivered with a standard PC and an Internet connection. The dilemma now is understanding the various modalities of interactivity as they relate to a more constructivist learning model and a more results-oriented marketplace." An important contribution of her work is the analysis of what constitutes interactivity.

Chère Gibson recounts some of her experiences teaching online and their relationship to a humanist, constructive educational philosophy: "It's hard not to begin to really wonder about this environment for learning, this high tech world of words on a screen, often devoid of pictures but rich in emotions, both positive and negative. Questions emerged about the nature and role of emotionality in learning, the dynamics of online groups, and about perspective transformation." Gibson makes it clear that there is much research to be done in order to fully understand the rich and complex learning environment that constitute online communities.

Peter Goodyear devotes his chapter to an in-depth analysis of a single Master's degree program — the Advanced Learning Program (ALT) at Lancaster University in the UK. Goodyear discusses the many changes in technology, pedagogy, and the business climate that have occurred in the program since its first offering in 1989. He observes: "In my 15 years as an online teacher-researcher, the technology I have been using has moved from being strange, esoteric, and unreliable to a point at which it is central to life and work in all developed economies. The improvement of this technology is no longer the responsibility of a small and wayward cadre of technicians — many millions of users of online technologies now care about the quality of the facilities available to them. Moreover, the kinds of things I want to do as a teacher are the kinds of things everyone wants to do with this technology — share experiences, passions, and plans; stay in touch."

Judi Harris presents her perspective on the development of online learning by analyzing articles published in the ISTE magazine, *Learning & Leading with Technology* (previously called *The Computing Teacher*), over a period of 25 years. Her analysis suggests that current online teaching may be less ambitious than in the past: "Today, our more ubiquitous — but more pedagogically and structurally constrained — educational uses of online tools and resources demonstrate in a most powerful way a perpetual and pressing need for the creativity, innovativeness, and pioneering spirit that our pedagogical predecessors demonstrated in *Computing Teacher* articles more than 15 years ago." In other words, the technology may have improved dramatically, but online teaching skills may not have.

Jesse Heines provides an intriguing (and nicely illustrated) look at the history of computer-based learning, focusing on some of the earliest teaching devices and associated instructional programming. He finds current systems wanting in comparison: "It's as if the companies that develop these products simply hire programmers and tell them to start coding, without ever exploring the huge, existing body of knowledge on what's been tried before, much less look for solid theoretical ground on which to base their instructional designs." He suggests that system developers need to know more about the past history of the field and build upon it in their products.

Beverly Hunter describes her efforts to develop online learning communities over four decades: "I define an online learning community as a group of people who interact with each other through computer-based communications networks, learn from each other, and provide knowledge and information resources to the group related to agreed-upon tasks or topics of shared interest. A defining characteristic of an online learning community is that a person or institution must be a contributor to the evolving knowledge base of the group and not just a recipient or consumer of the group's services or knowledge base." She discusses a variety of projects at IBM, HumRRO, NSF, and many other organizations.

Annette Lamb examines online learning from a number of different perspectives including a resource-rich environment, a learning experience, an opportunity, and a lifestyle. She also considers the dynamic nature of online learning in terms of evolving needs, teaching styles, courses, communication, and relationships. In her view: "Learning is about conducting inquiries, making connections, and communicating understandings, not just listening to lectures and completing assignments. Over the past twenty years, this realization became even more apparent as I moved from teaching traditional face-to-face courses toward facilitating online learning environments."

Robin Mason describes the development of online learning at the world's oldest distance learning institution: the British Open University: "The new technologies also allow the OU to further remove the 'distance' from distance education, gathering together students from all over the world and bringing higher education to the doorstep of geographically remote students. However, the OU does not strive to become a totally 'online university.' The best outcomes for learning are usually achieved by striking a balance between using traditional and new media, individually selecting and developing the products that are best suited for each purpose." One of the significant aspects of online learning at the OU is the scale of their efforts — with classes involving hundreds or even thousands of students.

Craig Montgomerie discusses his involvement with computer-based education beginning with early time-shared minicomputers and mainframes, then stand-alone microcomputers, Internet networks and supercomputers, and two-way videoconferencing systems. He describes the capabilities of the various authoring and student management software associated with these different delivery systems. Montgomerie sums up his diverse experience: "Each instructional model and each technology works for some students, and fails for others. Similarly, each instructional model and each technology has proponents and detractors... I believe we are at a nexus in distant learning. Each of us needs to back up a little and look at the audience that needs to learn, the subject matter and level that are being taught and see which distance education technologies can be combined to give the students the best experience that is possible."

James Morrison provides an account of his experiences introducing information technology to graduate classes in education leadership — and the surprising reaction to his innovations: "In my enthusiasm to apply a constructivist perspective to teaching, incorporate requirements to use IT tools, focus on writing and presentation skills, and maintain the university grading standard, I violated faculty and student norms." While Morrison could foresee the need for IT skills and knowledge on the part of school administrators, neither they nor his faculty colleagues could do so until years later. In the meantime, Morrison founded two online periodicals (*On the Horizon* and *Technology Source*) that brought technology awareness to the entire educational community.

Frank Odasz talks about his Big Sky Telegraph project and other efforts to realize the potential of online learning and community networking in rural settings: "Human potential has never had such powerful enablers as we find at our fingertips today, but the art of developing social acceptance and best practices for leveraging these tools is still in its infancy...The global impact one creative individual can make applying these new capabilities is unlimited. The potential impact of empowering the majority of the world's population with such abilities is literally the task at hand." Much of Odasz's work has been with native peoples in remote locations, pushing the frontiers of cyberspace. The Odasz chapter features an Appendix written by David Hughes.

Jason Ohler discusses the emotional side of distance education in terms of the reactions that it often engenders: "While the educator in me has been attracted to distance education's contribution to teaching and learning for some time, the anthropologist in me has been equally fascinated by the cultural flashpoint it has created." Ohler addresses some of the social and psychological elements of distance education that are often overlooked or ignored.

Tom Reeves examines the evaluation methodology associated with online learning research, especially comparison studies that yield "no significant difference" results, and finds them wanting. Instead he calls for a different research paradigm: "Educational technology is a design field, and thus, our paramount goal of research should be solving teaching, learning, and performance problems, and deriving design principles that can inform future decisions."

Margaret Riel recounts her efforts to develop learning communities, initially at the K-12 level and, more recently, for graduate study. This includes the idea of "learning circles" intended to promote cross-classroom collaboration and provide a process for extending current curriculum activities. She concludes: "As technology becomes more portable and communication more pervasive, how we structure education will depend more on the social networks we create than on the forms of technology that supports them."

Alexander Romiszowski provides an analysis of the theory and research issues associated with the success and failure of online learning efforts. He suggests: "It is probably fair to say that the new information and communication technologies do not really offer any revolutionary new pedagogical innovations, but rather that they facilitate the re-discovery and cost-effective implementation of good teaching-learning methodologies that were known for eons, but largely ignored as impractical, or even forcibly abandoned (for practical and cost reasons) with the advent of the industrial revolution." Romiszowski discusses examples of past research relevant to online education and new developments that may or may not advance the cause.

Marlene Scardamalia discusses knowledge building environments (KBEs) including the initial CSILE system developed in the 1980s and the current Knowledge Society Network effort. She outlines the goals of a KBE: "The overarching goal is to transform education by shifting emphasis from staying abreast of information to contributing to the development of new cultural artifacts, from individual learning and achievement to the building of knowledge that has social value; from focus on tasks and activities to a focus on the continually improving ideas; from a focus on set course outlines to systems of emergence and self organization; and from a predominantly facilitator-directed discourse to distributed knowledge building discourses."

Robert Seidel describes some of the learning system projects conducted at HumRRO and ARI and related efforts at technology assessment. He presents two models that identify some of the variables involved in the successful implementation of technology. Seidel also discusses the major role that financial aspects play in technology adoption: "So the irony is that reform in training is taking place, not because of the promise of greater cognitive and skill achievement (which many of us old futurists contended), but because of the necessity of reducing costs."

Lorraine Sherry focuses primarily on the process of diffusing online learning and professional development programs for teachers and teacher educators within schools and universities, and within programs that are embedded in local, state, and national organizations. In doing so, she recounts her experiences with online learning encountered in various projects such as the Boulder Valley School District, Project WEB, and the Teacher Education Network: "At the beginning, the issues were all about getting the technology to work, designing an interface that was both functional and user-friendly, and persuading users that the new, online system was better than the status quo. Now, I see that the issues are not technological, but organizational in nature. They have to do with deep-rooted social and cultural issues, as well as epistemological issues that are far more difficult to deal with."

Robert Tinker discusses the ups and downs of developing and implementing online science learning materials at TERC for the K-12 setting. This includes the KidsNet project in collaboration with the National Geographic Society and the Global Lab project with NSF support. More recent efforts at the Concord

Consortium involve online teacher training for virtual schools. Tinker sees online collaboration as the critical element in all these projects: "Online collaborative courses represent one of the most exciting new educational resources created by technology. It appears that collaboration is central to the added value of online learning. Without collaboration, the social value of networking is lost and online courses become simply extensions of existing course formats."

Overview of the Book: Thematically

The Table below provides another summary of the chapters according to the major learning domains and issues they embrace:

Anderson	HiEd	conferencing; adoption
Berge	HiEd/K-12/Trng	organizational change; barriers
Bork	Science	interactivity; individualization
Collis & Moonen	HiEd	human/technology tradeoffs
Coombs	HiEd	disabilities, design
Dede	Research	social/technology interaction
Fairweather & Singley	Authoring	theory; implementation
Gayeski	HiEd/Trng	multimedia; interactivity
Gibson	HiEd	human element; emotions
Goodyear	HiEd	technology/pedagogy change
Harris	K12	teaching strategies
Heines	HiEd/Trng	system design; learning strategy
Hunter	Trng/K-12	learning communities
Lamb	K12	teaching strategies
Mason	HiEd	integration; implementation
Montgomerie	HiEd/K-12, Rural	technology; system design
Morrison	HiEd	pedagogical change
Odasz	Rural	community networking
Ohler	HiEd	social/psychological factors
Reeves	Research	evaluation; design
Riel	K-12/HiEd	learning communities
Romiszowski	Research	instructional theory and design
Scardamalia	K12/HiEd	knowledge building environments
Seidel	Trng	evaluation; implementation
Sherry	K-12	teaching strategies
Tinker	Science	collaborative learning

From the Table, we can see some common themes emerge across the book. A number of authors, such as Anderson, Berge, Collis & Moonen, Dede, Mason, and Morrison, are focused on issues related to technology adoption by individuals and successful implementation in organizations/institutions. Some have focused on specific learning domains or populations, such as Bork and Tinker (science), Coombs (disabled individuals), and Odasz (rural communities). Others, such as Gibson, Ohler, and Scardamalia, are specifically interested in the social, cultural, or psychological factors associated with online learning. Harris, Lamb, and Sherry are primarily concerned with teaching strategies in the K-12 setting. Hunter and Riel have devoted their attention to creating learning communities. Fairweather & Singly, Heines, Gayeski, Montgomerie, and Romiszowski address technology and instructional theory/system design questions. Reeves and Seidel explore evaluation and research design issues associated with online learning.

Many topics are addressed by a number of authors at different levels. For example, the nature of interactivity in online learning is an issue that is central to many chapters, particularly Bork, Gayeski, and Heines. Design and development considerations for online learning are also a common topic across chapters, especially Coombs, Fairweather & Singley, and Seidel. The chapters by Dede, Scardamalia, and Romiszowski examine trends and new directions for online education. Online teaching techniques are discussed in some detail by Gibson, Goodyear, Mason, and Morrison. And, online collaboration is a topic central to many of the chapters (e.g., Hunter, Odasz, Riel, Tinker).

Some contributors have presented a high-level perspective, whereas others have gone into considerable detail about specific programs or projects. Consequently this book shows different layers of the online learning endeavor, which together reveal the immense complexity of the education domain. In the final analysis, much of what has been written about in this book will be forgotten, but the overall transformation of how we learn and teach brought about by technology is real and will persist.

Greg Kearsley, August 2004

Contents

Chapter 1

Online Education Innovation:
Going Boldly Where Others Fear to Thread[1]

Terry Anderson

Terry Anderson is a Professor and Canada Research Chair in Distance Education at Athabasca University — Canada's Open University. He received his PhD in Educational Psychology with a specialty in Computer Applications from the University of Calgary in 1994. Since that time he has been involved in many research projects related to distance learning in Canada and was the Director of the Academic Technology for Learning unit at the University of Alberta from 1994 until 2001. He is the editor of the "International Review of Research on Distance and Open Learning."

In this chapter, I reflect on my experiences in the early days of online learning. I hope this more personal style will result in an appreciation for the diverse means by which innovations occur, synergies happen, and the capacity is shown for ordinary persons (like myself) to make contributions to the exciting world of teaching and learning in a networked society.

The chapter begins with a personal account of my first experiences being online and using these tools for educational activity. It then recounts the experiences I had organizing the first online or virtual conference that includes a brief note on subsequent development of this form of professional development. Next, I briefly overview my experiences and the results of a three year investigation focussing on developing tools and techniques for evaluation of computer conference transcripts from formal educational courses. Finally, it peers into the future, looking through a ball that is more foggy than crystal, with speculations and early development stories of the educational Semantic Web.

Early Networks on the Electronic Homestead

During the early 1970's I left my suburban home in a large Canadian city to become a "back-to-the land" homesteader on 160 acres of bush land in Northern Alberta. For part of that time, we lived with neither electricity nor telephone lines, so "online education" was a very long way from my thoughts or dreams. Most of my education in those days came from mastering the tools and techniques of food production, shelter construction, and the endless repair

---

[1] Editor's Note: Topics in discussion forums are divided into "threads." Starting a new thread shows a certain amount of initiative and audaciousness.

of old and often broken machinery. The birth of our first child inspired a move out of the wood shop and into the classroom. In this case, as a computer science instructor at a community college 20 miles from our farm. In 1982, I purchased, for the college, their first 300 BPS modem — complete with a cradle into which the telephone handset was inserted. I still remember the thrill as those first welcoming words streamed across the screen. Home access though was still problematic as we shared a party line with two other farm families. Fortunately, none of these folks had ever heard the squeal of a modem before and so assumed the line was broken, as I connected to the nearest host computer — some 200 miles away in Edmonton. The applications of online learning we worked on then focussed on accessing what was publicly available — in this case the Bulletin Board Systems (BBS)

FidoNet and early online communities
Every modern net user is indebted to the first community bulletin board owners for the techniques and community tools they developed and shared freely with all. These BBS operators provided public access to their machines (usually at no cost) to serve as repositories of programs (mostly games and utilities), forums for discussions, and to provide a home for a variety of special interest distributed communities (see www.fidonet.org). Beginning around 1984 these operators developed a series of exchange protocols and created the distributed FidoNet network — a reliable system for the free delivery of email and files around the world. The system worked by porting messages between nodes using dial-up telephone connections late in the evening. By 1989 over 5,000 machines were connected to the FidoNet network but by the mid-1990's access to the new Internet had made obsolete these telephone based systems. Also notable was the development of K12net, a network based on FidoNet technology that was used by teachers for discussion and the exchange of learning objects — though we certainly didn't call them that in those days.

Despite the demise of the FidoNet networks, many of us 'cut our teeth' on both the hardware and software of these first generation community based distributed systems. In that process we got to participate in our first flame wars sessions, received our first bad email jokes, and garnered a glimpse of life in a virtual and widely distributed community. Thank you BBS operators!

My personal life took a major turn in 1986, when I was appointed as the director of a new distance education network (Contact North/Contact Nord) located in Northern Ontario. This government-funded organization established over 60 distance learning classrooms in remote communities — each staffed by an often lonely and always isolated site coordinator. The primary delivery method for courses was telephone based audio conferencing. Building upon the experience of online communities that I had seen within the FidoNet community, I leased time on a computer conferencing system (CoSy) and soon each of the site coordinators had a dial-up distributed community of colleagues to lean on for support, technical or academic help, or just to have someone to whine with! Again I saw demonstrated the value of distributed communities — this time in a networked workplace.

How I Invented Virtual Conferences

By 1992, I was a PhD student in much reduced financial circumstances than those I had enjoyed as a professional distance education administrator. No longer did I have the money to fly to face to face (F2F) conferences that I had attended in the past. One of my favorites had been the tri-annual World Congress of the International Council for Distance Education (ICDE) that has, since the 1950's, sponsored three to four day conferences for distance educators. These conferences were usually held at exotic locations around the world. I believed that there were many other distance educators (and especially those in developing countries), who, like myself, might be interested in the conference, but who lacked the funds to participate. I thus conceived of the idea of sponsoring an online or virtual conference that would run parallel to the XVI World Congress of the ICDE in Bangkok, Thailand. I had (rather naively) thought that the virtual conference could be integrated with the F2F congress allowing remote participants to engage with F2F delegates and guest speakers, through terminals at the conference site. This endeavor evolved to become the first publicly accessible network-based online or 'virtual conference' (Anderson & Mason, 1993).

In those pre-WWW days, the major network technology available was a variety of email networks including the early Internet, Usenet, FidoNet, NetNorth, and BitNet and a few proprietary networks such as CompuServe, BIX, Genie, and the Well. This diversity of networks presented a great deal of organizational challenge and necessitated a means of 'porting' messages between networks. The hassle of those days makes me grateful for the ubiquity and standardization of the Internet today.

My first attempt to arrange for connectivity among the distributed participants was to gain the sponsorship of CompuServe or one of the other networks and persuade them to provide accounts for participants during the six weeks in which I planned to run the conference. However, they had no idea what a virtual conference was and my explanations rarely received more than a polite "no thanks." I was thus forced to recruit "porters" from each of the major networks. I reasoned that there already were discussion groups related to educational topics on most of these networks, and thus the largest audience could be reached if I could get someone to port messages (both ways) between these forums and a small email porters list that I established on the Internet. My recruitment strategy produced a group of porters who not only transported the postings from the conference, but also filtered them to eliminate overkill or items they felt would not be relevant to their audience.

The structure of the Bangkok Virtual Conference (VC) mirrored the structure of the F2F ICDE Congress by inviting speakers (some who were also speaking at the F2F congress) to compose opening (text-based) speeches or papers. These were followed by feedback, questions, and comments from the distributed audience. Since the interactions were mirrored over 25 different networks or private systems there was no way of calculating the actual number of participants. However, evaluation of the transcripts provided evidence that substantial debate and discussion could take place among a group of "virtual delegates" The most common complaint from participants was the sense of being overwhelmed by the volume of email. Can you still remember an era when 250 messages over six weeks seemed overwhelming? Hardly a week's worth of spam today!

A number of important lessons were learned from this pioneering experience. The first was that this form of professional development could be several orders of magnitude less expensive than F2F conferences. My expenses for running the VC consisted of a few faxes to Bangkok and a small gift to each of the keynote speakers. There was no charge for participation and the total cost to me was less then $100 at a time when the registration fee for the F2F Conference in Bangkok was $450 per person (not including transportation, lodging, meals, and entertainment costs). The second lesson learned was that timing is critical. The VC is often seen as competition by the organizers of the F2F conference and should not be scheduled so as to conflict and thus compete for delegates with the F2F conference. We also learned that one couldn't reasonably expect significant participation in virtual environments by F2F delegates who are immersed in the social and professional activities of the F2F conference. Finally, we learned that scheduling is critical even when using an asynchronous medium. We scheduled two topics to run simultaneously and found that participants had difficulty sorting through the various topic threads. Finally, I learned that it isn't that difficult to gain the participation of well-known education experts with global reputations — especially if they do not have to leave home and they have no idea what they are getting involved in!

By the time the next ICDE World Congress rolled around I was no longer a graduate student, but still not able (or to be honest, interested) in travelling half way across the world to attend a distance education conference — the irony of this favored practice of distance educators never fails to amuse my colleagues nor my wife! Having learned the lessons above, the second ICDE virtual conference grew beyond a horseless carriage type virtualization of a F2F conference (Anderson, 1996). Again, I organized six sessions, though they were run before the F2F Congress started. Each session featured a different learning activity (debate, dialogue, brainstorming, nominal technique, panel session, and an Open House at a MOO). By that period one could assume that everyone had either direct or automatic ports to Internet based email, so the conference was organized on dedicated email lists specifically created for the VC. A total of 554 persons from 35 countries subscribed to the list and 290 messages were posted during the three weeks of the conference. I gained a new appreciation for the MOO — a text based virtual reality environment, while relaxing with a beer in my living room, attending the end-of-conference party, and watching participants explode text-based fireworks!

Another positive outcome of this conference was my introduction to transcript analysis as Lani Gunawardena, Connie Lowe, and myself worked at developing a method for documenting the construction of knowledge that we witnessed during the debate session of the VC (Gunawardena, Lowe, & Anderson, 1997). This type of analysis became a research interest in subsequent years and is described later in this chapter.

Changing the Research University

My next adventure in academia included a seven year stint as director of an academic technology unit charged with professional development for faculty and the support of instructional technology use for both classroom and distance delivery in a major research university (Anderson, 1999). Although this period was both exciting and personally productive, I left with a sense that the culture of the research university is not adequately concerned with teaching and learning issues — either with or without technological assistance. Two academics from this University argued in their critique *No place to learn: Why universities aren't working* (Pocklington & Tupper, 2002) that the research university has abandoned its commitment to undergraduate education through its over-emphasis on research productivity. Despite a growing body of evidence illustrating the lack of relationship between either teaching and research productivity or quality (Gibbs, 1995; Hattie & Marsh, 2002), the myth that only good researchers are good teachers still pervades the culture and the reward system. It seems very unfortunate that large research universities cannot allow diversification and changes within the lifelong tenure of their professoriate to allow for and support the scholarship of teaching and learning within the disciplines.

Despite the challenges of these years, I was able to pursue my own research interests in computer mediated communications that are detailed in the next section.

Online Educational Conference Transcript Analysis

Much of the early literature describing computer conferencing (e.g., Feenberg, 1989; Harasim & Johnson, 1986) seemed to me to be full of exuberant claims for the tremendous pedagogical benefit of this new educational medium. Yet, in my own experience, I had as often been surprised by the banality and "chit-chat' nature of the discourse as revelations of profound learning experiences. I was seeking more empirical evidence to support or contradict the claims relating to the pedagogical value of this medium and, as important, I was looking for a tool that could be used to evaluate the impact of changes in instructional design made by course developers or teachers. This quest led to funding by the Social Science and Humanities Research Council of Canada for me and three colleagues at the University of Alberta — Randy Garrison, Walter Archer, and Liam Rourke.

Our first activity in this project was a review of the methodological issues raised in 16 transcript analysis studies found in the literature (Rourke, Anderson, Garrison, & Archer, 2001). Surprisingly, less then half of the studies reported reliability data, yet most made quantitative claims for the results. Further, we found that rarely did authors continue to develop content analysis over an extended research program (many were one-off publications) and finally that most researchers seemed to devise their own systems or make major revisions to existing analysis systems. This resulted in difficulty in comparing results and in gaining value from cumulative knowledge growth. Ironically, we fell into this same trap and also developed our own system. Unlike some of the previous empirical studies, ours was at least theoretically grounded upon a community of inquiry model. Our model (Garrison, Anderson, & Archer, 2000) focussed on three critical components of educational conferencing — social presence, cognitive presence, and teaching presence. We then developed techniques to identify indicators of each 'presence' in the transcripts and ways to reliably tabulate the number of such instances. We published a number of articles in which we documented the results of our work and the various ways we validated the results (see http://communitiesofinquiry.com). We've also been pleased with the evidence that scholars have picked up on our ideas and methods and continue to develop and validate the model and system that we developed (i.e., McKlin, Harmon, Evans, & Jones, 2002; Meyer, 2003; Shea, Pickett, & Pelt, 2003).

I've become less interested in transcript analysis lately, not because I think we have discovered all the secrets that these artifacts of online education can reveal, but because I think there may be easier and more meaningful ways of gathering evidence of the learning process. For example, we are now beginning a more phenomenological study focussing on learners' experience of knowledge creation and interaction with both other humans and agents in an online world. We are thus communicating directly with participants rather than extrapolating from the 'tracks' they leave on their educational journeys.

To end this personal narrative, I'd like to briefly discuss my recent interest in the emerging educational Semantic Web.

The Educational Semantic Web

Tim Berners-Lee's (Berners-Lee, 1998) proclamation of the next evolution of the WWW — named by him as the Semantic Web — has fuelled intense debate, activity, and construction of models and prototypes to instantiate this vision of an 'intelligent Web.' Although, not yet mainstream educational research, it is not difficult to see how an intelligent Web could be used to enhance both formal education and informal learning. The Semantic Web inherits and expands the affordances (Gaver, 1991) of the first Web. These are access to very large amounts of data and information; the support of asynchronous and synchronous communications among humans using a variety modalities; and the emerging capacity of autonomous agents to navigate, search, harvest, and make inferences relevant to the information they find (MIT, 2000). Although research in Semantic Web technologies is at present mainly focussed within the disciplines of information and computer science, we are seeing the first applications of teacher, student, and content agents dedicated to educational tasks (Hietala & Niemirepo, 1998; Johnson, Rickel, & Lester, 2000; Shaw, Johnson, & Ganeshan, 1999; Thaiupathump, Bourne, & Campbell, 1999; Thomas & Watt, 2002; Whatley, Beer, Staniford, & Scown, 1999). For example, Jim Greer and his colleagues at the university of Saskatchewan have developed the I-Help system that allows student users to configure personal agents based on the levels of expertise, willingness, and fees charged to help other students in large courses (2001). These agents can then search for expertise among other students, negotiate a price for the service, and instigate email connections between the two students.

Our own work has been more computationally modest and has focussed on the development of learning object repositories (see www.careo.org) and work at explicating emerging standards such as the IEEE LOM and IMS Learning Design. In particular we have been developing implementation profiles (www.cancore.ca) for tagging educational objects and a system of open source tools that allow for search and harvest of learning object metadata (www.edusource.ca).

The educational Semantic Web is a long term project that will evolve, likely at exponential speed (Kurzweil, 2001), over the next decade. It holds great promise but also is very threatening for formal educational systems. Increasingly sophisticated forms of learner-content and learner-learner interaction will be substituted for expensive and non-scaleable learner-teacher interaction (Anderson, 2002). And finally the monopoly on both content development, sequencing, and credentialing of learning will likely be broken as learners create their own learning paths through pedagogically structured learning portals. These developments will create an era of formal learning beyond the credentialed course.

Summary

In this chapter I've enjoyed a nostalgic trip through recollections of my personal involvement with online learning. The lessons learned are many, but focus predominately on the need for educators to boldly experiment with ideas afforded by developments in technologies and pedagogies. We need to develop new models of education that scale to support all humans on this planet — not just those from rich countries. We need to critically discern where our own personal comfort level with technology, change, and diversity impairs our abilities to lead and to create new ways and means to enhance personal and social learning across our planet.

References

Anderson, T. (1996). The virtual conference: Extending professional education in cyberspace. *International Journal of Educational Telecommunications*, *2*(2/3), pp. 121-135. Retrieved May 21, 2001, from the World Wide Web: http://www.ascusc.org/jcmc/vol3/issue3/anderson.html

Anderson, T. (1999). Using disruptive technologies in the Universities: Confessions of an Agent Provocateur. *Ed-Media 1999 World Conference on Educational Multimedia, Hypermedia and Telecommunications.*

Anderson, T. (2002). Getting the mix right: An updated and theoretical rationale for interaction. *ITFORUM , Paper #63* http://it.coe.uga.edu/itforum/paper63/paper63.htm

Anderson, T., & Mason, R. (1993). The Bangkok project: New tool for professional development. *American Journal of Distance Education, 7*(2), pp. 5-18.

Berners-Lee, T. (1998). Realizing the full potential of the Web. World Wide Web Consortium. Retrieved April 3, 2003 from http://www.w3.org/1998/02/Potential.html

Feenberg, A. (1989). The written world: On the theory and practice of computer conferencing. In R. Mason & A. Kaye (Eds.), *Mindweave: Communication, computers, and distance education* (pp. 22-39). Toronto: Pergamon Press.

Garrison, R., Anderson, T., & Archer, W. (2000). Critical inquiry in text-based environments: Computer conferencing in higher education. *The Internet and Higher Education, 2*(2-3), pp. 87-105.

Gaver, W. (1991). Technology affordances. *Proceedings of the CHI'91 Conference.* New York: Association for Computing Machinery. Retrieved March 28, 2003 from www.ics.uci.edu/~jpd/NonTradUI/gaver-aff.pdf

Gibbs, G. (1995). The relationship between quality in research and quality in teaching. *Quality in Higher Education, 1*(2), pp. 147-157.

Greer, J., McCalla, G., Vassileva, J., Deters, R., Bull, S., & Kettel, L. (2001). Lessons learned in deploying a multi-agent learning support system: The I-Help experience. AIED. Retrieved April 2, 2003 from http://julita.usask.ca/Texte/Aied01-camera.pdf

Gunawardena, C., Lowe, C., & Anderson, T. (1997). Analysis of a global on-line debate and the development of an interaction analysis model for examining social construction of knowledge in computer conferencing. *Journal of Educational Computing Research, 17*(4), pp. 397-431.

Harasim, L., & Johnson, M. (1986). *Educational applications of computer networks for teachers/trainers in Ontario.* Toronto: Queen's Printer for Ontario.

Hattie, M., & Marsh J. (2002). The relationship between productivity and teaching effectiveness. *Journal of Higher Education, 73*(5), pp. 603-641.

Hietala P., & Niemirepo, T. (1998). The competence of learning companion agents. *International Journal of Artificial Intelligence in Education , 9*, pp. 178-192. http://cbl.leeds.ac.uk/ijaied/abstracts/Vol_9/hietala.html.

Johnson, L.W., Rickel, J., & Lester, J. (2000). Animated pedagogical agents: Face-to-face interaction in interactive learning environments. *International Journal of Artificial Intelligence in Education, 11*, pp. 47-78. http://cbl.leeds.ac.uk/ijaied/abstracts/Vol_11/johnson.html

Kurzweil, R. (2001). The law of accelerating returns. *KurzweilAI.net,* http://www.kurzweilai.net/articles/art0134.html?printable=1

McKlin, T., Harmon, S., Evans, W., & Jones, M. (2002). Cognitive presence in Web-based learning: A content analysis of student's online discussion. *IT Forum.* Retrieved March 26 2002 from http://it.coe.uga.edu/itforum/paper60/paper60.htm

Meyer, K. (2003, October). The Web's impact on student learning. *T.H.E. Journal.* Retrieved Oct 1, 2003 from http://www.thejournal.com/magazine/vault/A4401C.cfm

MIT (2000). Software Agents Group. Retrieved May 21, 2001 from the World Wide Web: http://mevard.www.media.mit.edu/groups/agents

Pocklington, T., & Tupper, A. (2002). *On place to learn: Why universities aren't working.* Vancouver: UBC Press.

Rourke, L., Anderson, T., Garrison, R., & Archer, W. (2001). Methodological issues in the content analysis of computer conference transcripts. *International Journal of Artificial Intelligence in Education, 12*(1), pp. 8-22. Retrieved Feb 16, 2003 from http://cbl.leeds.ac.uk/ijaied/abstracts/Vol_12/rourke.html

Shaw, E., Johnson, W.L., & Ganeshan, R. (1999). Pedagogical agents on the Web. *Proceedings of the Third International Conference on Autonomous Agents.* Seattle: ACM Press. Retrieved June 28, 2002 from http://www.isi.edu/isd/ADE/papers/agents99/agents99.htm

Shea, P., Pickett, A., & Pelt, W. (2003). A follow-up investigation of teaching presence in the SUNY Learning Network. *Journal of Asynchronous Learning Networks, 7*(2). Retrieved Sept 17, 2003 from http://www.aln.org/publications/jaln/v7n2/v7n2_shea.asp#shea4

Thaiupathump, C., Bourne, J., & Campbell, J. (1999). Intelligent agents for online learning. *Journal of Asynchronous Learning Networks, 3*(2). Retrieved March 20, 2003 from http://www.aln.org/publications/jaln/v3n2/v3n2_choon.asp

Thomas, M., & Watt, S. (2002). Intelligent instant messaging agents to support collaborative learning. *Proceedings of the 16 British Human Computer Interface Conference.* London: British HCI Group.

Whatley, J., Beer, M., Staniford, G., & Scown, P. (1999). Group project support agents for helping students work online. Retrieved May 21, 2001 from http://www.isi.salford.ac.uk/staff/jw/HCII99.htm

Chapter 2

Taking the Distance Out of Distance Education

Zane L. Berge

Zane L. Berge is an Associate Professor, Instructional Systems Development Graduate Program at the University of Maryland System, UMBC campus. His scholarship in the field of computer-mediated communication and distance education includes numerous books, articles, chapters, workshops, and presentations. His book with Deborah Schreiber, "Distance Training: How Innovative Organizations Are Using Technology to Maximize Learning and Meet Business Objectives," was awarded the 1999 Charles A. Wedemeyer Award for Distinguished Scholarship and Publication by the University Continuing Education Association.

> What has been will be again, what has been done will be done again; there is nothing new under the sun. Ecclesiastes 1:9 (New International Version)

When I graduated from college in the late seventies, I went to work for a photofinishing division of a Fortune 1000 company in national marketing and sales. Later, the entrepreneurial spirit took hold of me. So, a partner and I bought our own, smaller, wholesale photofinishing operation and several retail camera stores. The recession of the early eighties, the 15 percent interest rates, and the Hunt brothers' desire to corner the silver market conspired to show me that there was not room for both my partner and me in our business. I sold my share of the enterprise to him and returned to my hometown of Lewisburg, Pennsylvania.

While there, I took a few statistics courses at Bucknell University, just to keep up to speed while I again tried to decide "what I wanted to do when I grew up." One can plan and one should plan. But the thing I have found is that no amount of planning can foretell several of the major turning points of a person's life. A door opens that you could never have anticipated. A door opens when you are in circumstances you would never have planned to be in, and leads to a place you may never have contemplated.

All this to say that when I started in the doctoral program at Michigan State University in education, I was a businessman. Except as a consumer for 16 or 17 years, I knew nothing of the field of education. I did not know who John Dewey was. In my first year as a Fellow with the Institute for Research on Teaching at MSU, I recall I would go to the library for every brainstorm I had about education — and I had quite a few. Not only would I find a book on the subject, or a shelf of books, I would find an entire section of the library on what I thought had to be an original thought of mine.

Building Perspective

In the early 90's, I was at Georgetown University as one of the directors of the academic computing center. I also founded the Center for Teaching and Technology. I was charged with building the international reputation of the Center and the University. One way I thought to do this was to start an online scholarly journal. In order to test this idea, find academics to serve as editors and reviewers, and to find potential contributors to the journal, I started a scholarly discussion group (SDG) —the *Interpersonal Computing and Technology* list (IPCT-L) (Berge & Collins, 1993). The founding of *IPCT Journal* occurred a year later in January of 1993. These efforts also led to the development of *The Moderators Homepage* — a resource that continues to serve scholars and moderators (see http://www. emoderators.com).

This SDG and *The Journal* shaped my research, writing, and thinking in many ways. It directly linked to my work and research on scholarly discussion groups. It also put me in contact with many scholars around the world, and especially introduced me to Mauri Collins, who was then at UNLV, and to the late Gerald M. Phillips (Professor Emeritus at Pennsylvania State University). GMP, as everyone online knew him, was the executive editor of the first seven books that I edited with Mauri Collins on computer-mediated communication (CMC) used in the service of teaching and learning. The first series was on higher and distance education, and the second series concerned CMC in elementary, secondary, and teacher education (Berge & Collins 1995, 1998). Taken together, along with the two case study books on distance training and education in the workplace (Berge, 2001; Schreiber & Berge, 1998), these books helped shape my perspective regarding online education.

Online Education

Online education is a form of distance education. I have been trying to take the "distance" out of distance education ever since I started exploring the field. It is not the delivery system that matters, it is the *education* that matters. However, the new delivery media have been a catalyst for educators to reevaluate and examine what constitutes "good education" in the early 21st century. It is this aspect that makes educational technology and online learning exciting to me. A chance to reform what works in schools and organizations, a chance to refocus on what learners do instead of what instructors do, and a chance to redefine the roles and responsibilities of instructors, learners, and sponsoring organizations.

Post Fordian Perspective

When it comes to education and training, our schools and workplaces were designed socially, politically, and technologically for the industrial era. Throughout history, new technology has ushered in new social, cultural, and political orders. Computers and telecommunication systems have changed the social order of the industrial era to the communication era. These changes need to be reflected in our schools. This will occur as educators design for diversity in students' needs and authentic learning activities. The type of cultural change technology is catalyzing necessitates changes to the roles and functions of students, teachers, the curriculum, and the educational institutions themselves (Berge, 1999).

The automotive industry is the model industry of modern times. The various forms of production adopted by automotive assemblers over the years "are the paradigms for production elsewhere in society. Fordist education emphasizes mass education, reduced student course choice, and increased divisions of labor" (Campion, 1990; Rumble, 1995).

What turns education on its head is that students have access to information. Teachers no longer need to be the sole or even primary source of information. For roughly the past 150 years, the command and control structure characterizing organizations was set to relay orders downwards and information upwards (Drucker, 1993). This breaks down once information technology makes information available to all persons.

In the industrial age, students went to schools. Today in the communication age, schools can go to the students (Norris & Dolence, 1996). It is for this reason that teaching and learning at a distance has rekindled the changes discussed here. The *distance* educators are speaking about change to the nature of schooling, and it is in this body of literature that I have found the most writing on the subject of technology-mediated learning and teaching in the post-Fordian society. Post-Fordism is characterized by a high level of labor responsibility, low division of labor, high decentralization, low mass marketing/production, and short product life cycles. Thus, academic staff must be rewarded for rapid adjustments to course curriculum and delivery as demanded by the changing needs of the students (Campion & Renner, 1992).

Since the time of Socrates, students who want to learn under a particular teacher's guidance have had to seek out that instructor and spend time in their presence — those in compulsory schooling have had little choice in the matter and, in post-primary grades, have been typically shuffled from room to room to sit in front of the "experts." Likewise, trainers in business and industry have typically taken students out of their workplace and gathered them into a central location. Teachers, professors, and trainers, using this mass production model, must pace the instruction within the confines of class periods/quarters/semesters, with little apparent regard for the time that *learning* can sometimes take. Today, adult students' life-styles place value on part-time study, and study when and where convenient for each of them. Business managers can no longer afford to have their employees leave for hours or days or weeks at a time for training at a central location. The training must go to the students, and arrive just-in-time (Edwards, 1993). For these and other reasons, demographics and competition will no longer allow educational institutions to unilaterally insist upon "my place at my pace." The pace of learning is hard to control, while the pace of teaching is much easier to control. What is needed is education to be available at a distance, or alternatively an implemented model of distributed or decentralized learning.

Formal educational experiences in the 21st century will not be confined to classrooms or corporate training rooms. We will find learning and training occurring everywhere and anywhere there are learners or trainees, just-in-time for the needs of those learners rather than just-in-case for the convenience of traditional educational institutions and corporate training departments. The necessary information resources to support learners are in diverse formats and, increasingly, as global in their distribution as the learners are.

Our traditional educational institutions are designed on the assumption that all students learn at the same pace and in the same place. The structure of the lecture hall typifies this assumption. It is designed for the rapid and efficient transmission of blocks of sequential information to relatively large groups of students in compressed time frames and assumes an expert at the front of the room and relatively passive learners ranged in fixed rows of seats. While such large groups may be efficient, the sheer number of students involved and the finite number of "contact hours" precludes discussion between the instructor and many of the students during class time.

Is there still a place for a Fordist education model? Some aspects may remain viable. After all, the industrial revolution did not replace farming, but it changed the way in which farming is done. Mechanization has reduced the number of farmers needed to feed the population from 85% of the workforce to less than 2% within a century (Jukes & McCain, n.d.). Yet, there is still a critical need for those 2% who plant and harvest. Many products are assembled efficiently and inexpensively on the Fordist production lines that replaced more costly individual craftsmanship, making more products available to more people. As technology has been a catalyst for changes in farming and production, so it has become a catalyst for change in education.

We can not imagine the completeness of changes to come — even though they will come. In many ways, the curriculum, the models of pedagogy used, the support given to students, and the way we manage the learning environment signal changes to the culture of higher education at a pace so quick and a context so complex that we can not see the end from when and where we begin the journey. Like the empty factories in the rust belt, the emptiness of our traditional institution of education will not please everyone. The gravest challenge for educators in the Communication Age may be to find better ways to plant the seeds in students that lead them to a harvest of greater knowledge.

Design Model for Online Learning

In my thinking about teaching and learning, I have been developing a framework that will allow me to speak about a wide range of learning models with different theoretical foundations. Simply put, the secret to designing successful learning is to align three elements: (1) learning goals, (2) learning activities, and (3) feedback and evaluation (see Figure 1) (Berge, 2002). This is true whether the instruction is designed and delivered from a constructivist or a behaviorist perspective or if the learning is done completely online, in-person, or in a blended environment. Blended or hybrid environments require careful attention to media characteristics and to the use of the most appropriate delivery system, including in-person if called for. The appropriateness of a delivery system is based on the benefits of each medium, the course content, and the needs of the learner, not on the convenience to the designer or instructor. This places the focus on learning and the learner, rather than on instruction or teaching. I encourage the reader to look elsewhere for an in-depth look at interaction from the instructor's perspective (McMahon, 1997; Northrup, 2001; Wilson, 1995).

Along with the three key elements shown in Figure 1, let me quickly note that the learning process occurs, among other things, within a particular infrastructure, it relies on support services from the organization, and exists within a learning environment created for the purpose of learning.

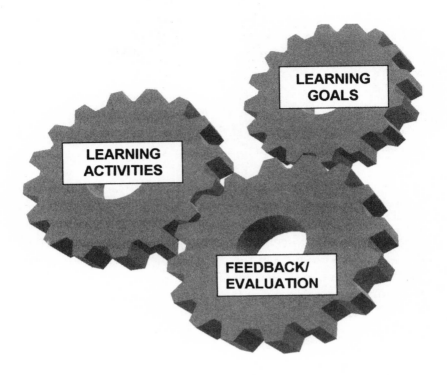

Figure 1. Secret of designing learning: Aligning learning goals, activities, and feedback.

Research

Analysis of the data of a recent literature review I conducted (Berge & Mrozowski, 2001) indicated that pedagogical themes, such as design issues, learner characteristics, and strategies for active learning and increased interactivity, dominate the research and appear to be increasing in recent years. Research in the areas of equity and accessibility, operational issues, and policy-and-management issues is less common. Three-fourths of the articles used descriptive research as their methodology. Experimental or correlational research was seldom utilized (<13% combined).

This report, along with earlier reviews of distance education research (e.g., Phipps & Merisotis, 1999), has shown gaps in what is being researched:

- The research has tended to emphasize student outcomes for individual courses rather than for a total academic program.
- The research does not adequately explain why the dropout rates of distance learners are higher.

- The research focuses mostly on the impact of individual technologies rather than on the interaction of multiple technologies.
- The research does not adequately address the effectiveness of digital libraries.

A widespread agreement on a research agenda for distance education could help point the way to removing these and other gaps that have historically been found in the early decades of research in distance education.

The methodology used in the Berge & Mrozowski (2001) study mentioned above is one way of analyzing and describing selected significant research that took place in the decade of the 1990's with regard to distance education. Is this the research that should have been conducted and published? Is more of the same research the best we can do in the future? The implications for the field of distance education cannot be weighed unless there is a research agenda — a vision for the future from which to judge the present and the past.

Barriers to Distance Education

An area of research that I have conducted the past five years involves the obstacles encountered when teaching and learning at a distance (Berge, Muilenburg, & Haneghan, 2002; see also "The Barriers Research" at www.emoderators.com). From the faculty perspective, the barriers to distance education can be viewed in ten categories (Muilenburg & Berge, 2001): administrative structure; organizational change; technical expertise, support, and infrastructure; social interaction and quality; faculty compensation and time; threats from technology; legal issues; evaluation/effectiveness; access; and student support services.

It appears that persons charged with implementing distance training and education within the organization need to recognize that it is common for the perceived barriers to be greater in the initial stages of organizational maturity in distance education and training. These normally abate as the organization matures. Secondly, it should be expected that the ranking of which obstacles are most important to solve will change as the organization gains experience with DE and as distance training and education becomes mission-critical within the organizational strategic planning. It is too early to tell the nature of student barriers, other than to say they will be different than the faculty perspective.

The Future

The business of education is changing (Berge, 2000). As the agricultural era gave way to an industrial society at the turn of the 20th century, so an information society is emerging as we move into the 21st century (Bell, 1976; Naisbitt, 1988; Toffler, 1980). With this shift in the means of production comes drastic changes to every segment of society — including higher education (Rowley, Lujan, & Dolence, 1997). New delivery systems that increase the effectiveness of learning at a distance, new organizations such as virtual universities, and other models of teaching and learning are forcing higher education to change the way they do business (Mangan, 1998; Oblinger, 1997; Selingo 1998).

Essentially, both the changes and the rate of change occurring in society are unprecedented in the past 100 years. What is unique is the increasing pace of change. We are seeing increasing global competition, increased customer expectations, and rapidly changing technology. These factors lead to a feeling of a crisis that will not go away. Can traditional organizations in higher education use similar responses to the changing environment similar to those that business has?

The mode of industrial production within our society is being replaced with models that rely on the rapid growth in technology, an increase in the accessibility of information, a more critically aware population, and a shift from the production of goods to a service economy (Merron, 1995). These factors are causing significant change in education as well. Technology is allowing non-traditional organizations involved in higher education to meet the curricular challenges many students are presenting (Whinston, 1994) including:

- the need to develop learning materials that can be easily updated and configured for the particular needs of students, and
- the capability of learning at any time and at any place.

Few organizations, including colleges and universities, change unless they feel directly threatened from outside the organization, often to the point their very survival is in question (Meyer, 1997). There are several factors making discontinuous change improbable within our traditional institutions of higher education. While not insurmountable, such issues as the promotion and tenure systems designed to reinforce and perpetuate the status quo are significant. What makes radical change improbable in higher education is that there are no mechanisms in place for such change. Secondly, the revolutionary change brought on by business process reengineering requires a different organizational and management structure and culture than found in traditional institutions of higher education. Additionally, the *purposes* for which people seek education are shifting and these needs are being supplied by emerging competitors that are different from the traditional university in essential ways.

The Roles of Teacher and Student Are Changing

In essence, technology needs to become as interwoven in institutional strategic planning and educational delivery as it is in society — to become an integral part of teaching and learning throughout the student's life-long learning environment. This change cannot be forced from the grassroots level by the student or individual faculty member or even a department or college. This use of technology as a strategy for learning needs to be part of the strategic plans within and among institutions of higher education. To do otherwise is to let the technology support the status quo. Is that what we want?

To work toward changing models of teaching and learning is important. It takes courage to move away from the idea of classroom lectures of stable content, delivered by expert teachers to students who are homogeneous, passive recipients and who work alone as they learn. Technology can provide networked access to worldwide information, collaboration with other people, multimedia, and powerful computer simulations and create learning environments where students are encouraged to explore and learn in teams, where there is sensitivity to the diversity of students, and which places teachers and other experts as mentors, guides, and collaborators in learning new and ever-changing content. Certainly there are barriers to technologically-rich learning environments: faculty reward structures, high front-end costs, training, equal access, student support, administrative and technical issues, copyright issues, and faculty resistance to name a few. But the major barriers to the use of technology involve the culture of our institutions and people within them. The type of structural changes required for facilitating changing roles are those most resistant to change. How will technology affect the changing roles of students, teachers, the curriculum, and our institutions of higher education? While we can't predict all these changes, we must surely have an influence upon them.

There are a number of significant factors driving change in the workplace and higher education. Contributing to the pressure to accelerate change in training and education are such things as the need for just-in-time learning, international competition for students, the fact that many parts of the world are saturated with technology, and communities filled with escalating expectations.

While it may be true that there is nothing new under the sun, certainly there are changes over time in the methods and types of learning we value and emphasize. Over the past two decades, constructivist learning is one set of principles that have become more valued. Thus, in the more learner-centric environment today, the roles and functions of both teacher and learner are very often different now than in the past. Some of the significant, emerging roles of faculty are listed here (Berge, 1995):

- from oracle and lecturer to consultant, guide, and resource provider
- teachers become expert questioners, rather than providers of answers
- teachers provide structure to student work, encouraging self-direction
- from a solitary teacher to a member of a learning team
- from having total autonomy to activities that can be broadly assessed
- from total control of the environment to shared learning with the student
- more emphasis on sensitivity to student learning styles
- teacher-learner hierarchy is broken down

The teachers today in the online classroom must be concerned about their function and role in at least four categories of the classroom: social, administrative, technical, and pedagogical (Berge, 1995). These roles could be called respectively: community leader, manager, technical consultant, and discussion leader/information resource (Brown, 2002).

Electric Lights Like Distance Education?

When Thomas Edison was asked his vision for electric lights his response is claimed to have been, "I shall make the electric light so cheap that only the rich will be able to burn candles" (Halgrim, 1993). I wonder if in 20 or 30 years when it is time for my grandchildren to go to college, will they go some*place?* Or will only the rich be able to afford a residential, post-secondary school experience? Emerging technologies may be beginning to be a factor in decreased demand for residential education (Smith & Webster 1997; Wheeler 2000). Would that shift be totally bad? After all, electric lights are convenient and probably safer than candles. The answer probably depends on whether we continue to pave over old cow paths, or use the emerging technologies to build new bridges to excite and motivate learning (Berge, 2003).

I wonder what changes will come. And since all things new are not good and all things old are not bad, regardless of whether my grandchildren go to college or not, will their education be better through the choices educators make between now and then?

Conclusions

Higher education institutions will need to transform their structures, missions, processes, and programs in order to be both more flexible and more responsive to changing societal needs (Hanna, 2003).

I am not sure, 20 years after starting down a path in educational technology, that much has changed or that I have changed much — other than I no longer chase after that which is new under the sun. That chase may be unwise given my miserable track record. Instead, I look for improvements, refinements, and different combinations of elements about which I think I know something.

References

Bell, D. (1976). *The coming of the post-industrial society.* New York: Basic Books.

Berge, Z.L. (1995). Facilitating computer conferencing: Recommendations from the field. *Educational Technology, 35*(1), pp. 22-30.

Berge, Z.L. (1999). Educational technology in post-industrial society. In J.G. Webster (Ed.), *Wiley encyclopedia of electrical and electronics engineering, Volume 6* (pp. 187-197). New York: John Wiley & Sons, Inc.

Berge, Z.L. (2000). Why not reengineer traditional higher education? In L.A. Petrides (Ed.), *Case studies on information technology in higher education: Implications for policy and practice* (pp. 209-216). Hershey, PA: Idea Group Publishing.

Berge, Z.L. (Ed.) (2001). *Sustaining distance training: Integrating learning technologies into the fabric of the enterprise.* San Francisco, CA: Jossey-Bass Inc., Publishers.

Berge, Z.L. (2002). Active, interactive, and reflective elearning. *The Quarterly Review of Distance Education, 3*(2), pp. 181-190.

Berge, Z.L. (2003). Click or brick colleges? And what ever happened to the *Saturday Evening Post?* Retrieved October 26, 2003 at http://www.globaled.com/articles/BergeZane2003.html

Berge, Z.L., & Collins, M.P. (1993). The founding and managing of IPCT-L: A listowners' perspective. *Interpersonal Computing and Technology: An Electronic Journal for the 21st Century 1*(2). [Online.] Retrieved November 22, 2003 at http://emoderators.com/papers/founding.html

Berge, Z.L., & Collins, M.P. (Eds.) (1995). *Computer-mediated communication and the online classroom. Volumes 1-3.* Cresskill, NJ: Hampton Press. *Volume 1 Overview and perspectives; Volume 2 Higher education; Volume 3 Distance learning.*

Berge, Z.L., & Collins, M.P. (Eds.) (1998). *Wired together: Computer-mediated communication in K-12, Volumes 1-4.* Cresskill, NJ: Hampton Press. *Volume 1 Perspectives and instructional design; Volume 2 Case studies; Volume 3 Teacher education and professional development; Volume 4 Writing, reading and language acquisition.*

Berge, Z.L., & Mrozowski, S. (2001). Review of research in distance education, 1990-1999. *American Journal of Distance Education, 15*(3), pp. 5-19.

Berge, Z.L., Muilenburg, L.Y., & Haneghan, J.V. (2002). Barriers to distance education and training: Survey results. *The Quarterly Review of Distance Education, 3*(4), pp. 409-418.

Brown, D.G. (2002). The role you play in online discussions. *Syllabus, 16*(5), p. 9.

Campion, M. (1990). Post-Fordism and research in distance education. In Terry Evans (Ed.), *Research in Distance Education 1*. Victoria, Australia: Deakin University.

Campion, M., & Renner, W. (1992). The supposed demise of Fordism: Implications for distance education and higher education. *Distance Education, 13*(1), pp. 7-28.

Collins, M.P., & Berge, Z.L. (1994). IPCT Journal: A case study of an electronic journal on the Internet. *Journal of the American Society for Information Science: Perspectives, 45*(10), pp. 771-776.

Drucker, P.F. (1993). *Post-capitalist society.* London: Butterworth-Heinemann.

Edwards, R. (1993). The inevitable future? Post-Fordism in work and learning. In R. Edwards, S. Sieminski, & D. Zeldin (Eds.), *Adult learners, education, and training.* New York: Routledge.

Jukes, I., & McCain, T. (n.d.) Shifting gears: Content to process. Retrieved from http://www.tcpd.org/tcpd/handouts.html

Halgrim, R. (1993). *Thomas Edison/Henry Ford winter estates*. Kansas City, MO: Terrell Publishing Co.

Hanna, D.E. (2003, July/August). Building a leadership vision. *Educause Review*.

Mangan, K.S. (1998, June 18). 'Corporate universities' said to force business schools to change their ways. *The Chronicle of Higher Education*.

McMahon, M. (1997). Social constructivism and the World Wide Web — A paradigm for learning. ASCILITE. December 7-10. Western Australia: Curtin University of Technology. Retrieved August 9, 2001 from http:www.curtin.edu.au/conference/ASCILITE97/papers/Mcmahon

Merron, K. (1995). *Riding the wave: Designing your organization's architecture for enduring success*. New York:Van Nostrand Reinhold.

Meyer, J.H. (1997). *Re-engineering the land grant college of agriculture*. Davis: University of California.

Muilenburg, L.Y., & Berge, Z.L. (2001). Barriers to distance education: A factor-analytic study. *The American Journal of Distance Education, 15*(2), pp. 7-24.

Naisbitt, J. (1988). *Megatrends*. New York: Warner Books.

Norris, D.M., & Dolence, M.G. (1996). IT Leadership is key to transformation. *CAUSE/EFFECT*, 19(1), 12-20. Also available online: http://cause-www.colorado.edu/information-resources/ir-library/abstracts/cem9615.html

Northrup, P. (2001). A framework for designing interactivity into Web-based instruction. *Educational Technology, 41*(2), pp. 31-39.

Oblinger, D.G. (1997). High tech takes the high road: New players in higher education. *Educational Record, 78*(1), pp. 30-37.

Phipps, R., & Merisotis, J. (1999). What's the difference? A review of contemporary research on the effectiveness of distance education in higher education. Institute for Higher Education Policy. Retrieved October 10, 2000 from http://www.ihep.com/difference.pdf

Rowley, D.J, Lujan, H.D., & Dolence, M.G. (1997). *Strategic change in colleges and universities: Planning to survive and prosper.* San Francisco: Jossey-Bass Inc., Publishers.

Rumble, G. (1995). Labour market theories and distance education III: Post-Fordism—the way forward? *Open Learning, 10*(3), pp. 25-42.

Schreiber, D.A., & Berge, Z.L. (Eds.) (1998). *Distance training: How innovative organizations are using technology to maximize learning and meet business objectives.* San Francisco, CA: Jossey-Bass Publishers.

Selingo, J. (1998, May 1). Small, private colleges brace for competition from distance learning. *The Chronicle of Higher Education,* pp. A33-35.

Smith, A., & Webster, F. (Eds.) (1997). *The post-modern university? Contested visions of higher education in society.* London: Open University Press.

Toffler, A. (1980). *The third wave.* New York: William Morrow.

Wheeler, S. (2000). The traditional university is dead: Long live the distributed university. Keynote speech delivered to the *European Universities Continuing Education Conference,* University of Bergen, Norway. May 4-7. Retrieved from http://www.fae.plym.ac.uk/tele/longlive2.html

Whinston, A.B. (1994, Fall). Reengineering education. *Journal of Information Systems Education, 6*(3), pp. 126-133. Retrieved from http://www5.pair.com/elicohen/JISE/Vol6/63/v63_1.htm

Wilson, B.G. (1995). Metaphors for instruction: Why we talk about learning environments. *Educational Technology, 35*(5), pp. 25-30.

Chapter 3

Distance Learning Today and Tomorrow

Alfred Bork

Alfred Bork is Professor Emeritus of Information and Computer Science at the University of California, Irvine. He has degrees in Physics from Georgia Tech and Brown University. Professor Bork directs the Educational Technology Center, a research and development group in technology-based learning. He is interested in effective use of highly interactive multimedia technology to make order of magnitude improvements in learning at all levels and has published hundreds of papers and books on the subject.

One of the problems in studying any development such as distance learning is to understand how far along we are at a particular time. There is a tendency to believe that at any one stage we are further along then we are, as seen in the light of later history. I intend to consider in this chapter that question with regard to the use of computers to aid in learning, particularly with regard to distance learning.

The history of mechanics in physics shows an example of this. At each stage developers of some new ideas thought they had reached an adequate theory of how bodies moved. But in our hindsight of today we can see that before Newton there was no adequate mechanics, in the sense of a successful, powerful predictive theory.

I argue that we have not yet reached the stage of adequate use of computers in learning, in any area. I begin this chapter with some personal history of my attempts to use computers in learning. Then I will discuss what is needed in learning, and then will suggest a new path for distance learning for the future.

This chapter is a much expanded version of an earlier paper delivered at an American Association of Physics Teachers meeting.

My Work with Computers and Distance Learning

Alaska and Reed College
I saw my first computer in 1958, an IBM 1620, while a faculty member in physics at the University of Alaska in Fairbanks. It came with the newfangled language called FORTRAN. In helping a graduate student, Harold Leinbach, on a research project, I noticed the drama of the results. Solar electrons were

entering the earth's atmosphere, and a group would watch with great interest to see how far each electron went. This encouraged me to use the computer in my own classes. That interest has continued to today, a span of more than 55 years. As I will indicate, my idea of how to use computers in learning has evolved in that time.

I was much concerned then, and still am, with the delays in learning physics at a reasonable level because of students' lack of mathematical background. It occurred to me that the fundamental equations of physics, differential equations and partial differential equations, that the student cannot be expected to solve analytically, could be solved numerically with the computer, even at an early stage of student development. Hence I began to use the computer to solve Newton's equations of motion and the Schrödinger equation. I even wrote a paper about this, but it received little attention. Someone in IBM later referred me to that paper! I continued this approach at Reed College, in a course for non-science majors, first with an IBM 1620 (Reed's first computer) and then with an IBM 1130.

Early Time at Irvine
Soon after this, while working on Harvard Project Physics, I first encountered timesharing computers, and I realized that the simulations I had used earlier are only one possibility for using computers in learning. When I came to the University of California, Irvine, in 1968, I was able to work in this new mode, with funding from the National Science Foundation. Again I tried to find where students were having learning difficulties that can be aided by the computer. The computer was a Scientific Data Systems Sigma 7.

The first program we wrote, working with Noah Sherman at the University of Michigan, was a program that allows students to prove the law of energy conservation, starting from Newton's laws. My idea was that students should prove or discover the important results of science, rather than just watching the instructors show them in a lecture or reading them in a book. An extensive early effort in this direction was the logic course constructed by Patrick Suppes at Stanford University; students proved, on the computer, many of the important theorems of logic.

Arnold Arons worked with me soon after in developing two dialogs about the phases of the moon. The strategy was to have students create a model to account for the known facts, and then use that model to make predictions. This collaboration continued with our work on the Scientific Reasoning Series, to be discussed later in this chapter.

The Beginning Physics Course at Irvine

Soon after that I became interested in a popular development of the time, a course based on the Keller plan or Personalized System of Instruction. The idea was similar to the concept of mastery; all students should continue to learn in a given area until they learned it well. Physics was in the forefront of this movement. We first ran a beginning physics course of this type with only a few computer aids in learning. But we and others had trouble with large classes, for reasons that I will not go into.

After discussing this problem, with Fred Reif at Berkeley, who taught a similar course, I decided that another approach might be better. A colleague, Stephen Franklin, had developed a mathematics course based on online testing. We decided to follow the same strategy for physics but to put much of the learning material within the quizzes. Joe Marasco worked with the two of us one summer in developing these quizzes.

There was a quiz for each unit of the work, typically about one week of student work. The quizzes contain problems similar to those that one would expect in a physics course. We never used multiple-choice, an inadequate tactic for learning. The problems on the quizzes all came from problem generators, so we never gave the same problem twice.

As soon as the student was in difficulty, we began to switch, with the student still on the computer, to a learning mode. It was possible for a student to learn just using the quizzes. If the student did not demonstrate mastery she or he would take the test over again after additional study. We offered this course for six years. Further details are in the papers describing the course. In addition to my own papers it was selected by Change magazine for one of its best physics courses. It was also described in the National Enquirer! This article stressed the idea that someone could learn without seeing a teacher, an important consideration later in this chapter.

The Scientific Reasoning Series

When personal computers were first developed, we saw new possibilities. Our work in this direction, supported by the National Science Foundation and the Fund for the Improvement of Postsecondary Education, led to a product called the Scientific Reasoning Series. This was initially developed on a computer called the Terak. IBM paid us to move it to their personal computer, and marketed it in their K-12 division for many years. The aim was to get students of about twelve years old to understand something of the processes of science, helping them to think like scientists. These well-evaluated units were discovery-based, in the sense of guided discovery.

There are 10 programs in this series, about 20 hours of student learning material for the 'average' student. The material is conversational in nature, resembling a conversation with a skilled human tutor, with questions from the computer and free-form answers from the student in English. We did experiments with this learning material to determine how many students should work together at the display, videotaping groups of students, and found that the best situation is to have three or four students there. The peer learning in such situations, focused by the computer material, is marvelous. Cooperative learning is a very important learning resource.

We discovered in testing these programs in public libraries that the maximum time between student inputs should be no more than 20 seconds, if we are to keep the interests of the students and help them to learn. In the library the student is free to leave at any time, so it is easy to find motivationally weak spots where many students leave, and improve them. With this level of interaction we can adapt the learning activities to each individual student. These programs can still be demonstrated today, and except for the rather old graphics they compare very favorably with many materials today, although they were developed fifteen years ago. They do not meet the standards discussed later, as they do not have voice input and do not run on the Internet, capabilities not available 15 years ago. We did have a graduate student who worked on converting the series to accept voice input, but he had to leave before the job was completed.

As an example, consider briefly the program Heat and Temperature. This is the shortest program in the Scientific Reasoning Series, about an hour for a typical student. The purpose is to let the student discover the concept of heat, often confused with temperature. It begins immediately by asking the student how to measure her or his body temperature. We look for the word 'thermometer,' in the student typing, a very simple analysis. Next we ask if the value is accurate if the thermometer is kept in the mouth for only a few seconds. The next question is how can we get an accurate value, and we look for things like 'leave it in longer' and 'keep it in for three minutes.' All this analysis of student input comes from the designers, to be discussed later.

If this material is moved to a different culture, an important step to attain global learning, we would need to change things a bit, as not all cultures consider it proper to put a thermometer in the mouth. With voice input we would not need to worry about misspelling words like 'thermometer.' The program proceeds in this questioning way for the hour it takes to complete it.

Several of the other programs in the Scientific Reasoning Series involve simulations. These were primarily programs in which the students were expected to discover important scientific results on their own. Some were based on earlier non-computer work from the Science Curriculum Improvement study (SCIS at Berkeley) and the Elementary Science Study (ESS at MIT), such as the module called batteries and bulbs, but we could offer detailed individual aid not possible in many classes. Another such program involved the students discovering the laws of genetics, using online genetic experiments. All students will be successful in these discoveries.

Simulations are only a small part of the code in these programs. We regard most simulations as naked simulations. There is no help given in how to use the simulation, and the program pays no attention as to whether the student is looking at critical cases or not, or is drawing reasonable conclusions from the evidence gathered. In our programs we watch carefully to see what the student is doing, and offer immediate help if necessary. We also ask questions about what the student has observed in the simulation, and may need to make suggestions here to guide the student in profitable directions. We still demonstrate these programs, as noted.

In spite of this success we found it increasingly difficult at this point to obtain funding in science. In particular, we could not find funding to modify these programs already developed, such as moving the physics course to personal computers or updating the Scientific Reasoning Series.

Understanding Spoken Japanese
Our next large project was an entirely different area. It was called Understanding Spoken Japanese, still highly interactive but using video prepared for us in Japan. Funding was from Japan, from Fujitsu and Nippon Television Network. The manager of the project was Rika Yoshii, now at California State University, San Marcos. We completed ten units, and were working on an additional ten when the Japanese economy took a plunge, ending the project. Each module was based on a video sequence. Because of our twenty second rule, we never played the full video sequence, except possibly at the end of the module at the student's choice. The target audience was United States university students learning Japanese. This project demonstrated that our system for producing highly adaptive learning units could be used in a very different area than that it was initially developed for.

A typical sequence in Understanding Spoken Japanese went something like this. We showed a small amount of video in Japanese, perhaps five seconds. Then the computer would ask what the people in the video were talking about. If the student knew, we would move to another question. If there were problems, we would move to a lower level, giving some help. We might even get down to individual words.

Another strategy used was to ask where the video was talking about something, such as horses. Simulated video controls would allow students to move around in a limited video sequence, and indicate when they found the desired item. Again help was given until the student could complete the task.

These strategies should be useful in a wide range of language learning, including English as a Second Language and for adult illiteracy.

Elearning
A common distance learning approach today is called elearning. I have not been engaged in developing and presenting elearning courses. This is a matter of choice on my part, because I do not regard current elearning as adequate.

The first problem with elearning as it exists now is that such courses are just imitations of what happens in class-based courses. They do not use the full power of the computer to assist learning. They use a variety of strategies, such as email and chat rooms, not developed for learning applications. As they are imitative of existing courses, they have all the problems of such classes, particularly the inability to consider and help with individual student problems. This is a major problem we can overcome with the type of highly adaptive distance learning discussed in this chapter.

In addition to the uniqueness of each student, another important problem not addressed by most current distance learning is that of numbers of students. I have emphasized that a critical factor of life on earth today is that we now have over six billion people. Current elearning classes are often restricted to 20 or 30 students, each with an instructor. So this strategy is not scalable to the entire earth. Too many teachers are needed, and the method is too expensive for global use.

If we are to overcome the major problems of the world today, such as water shortages and violence, we need to bring a high level of learning to all, starting with young children. There is a movement in this direction, called education for all. Elearning as it now exists will never do that, but highly adaptive tutorial learning through computers has a good chance. Now we discuss the nature of such learning. We will consider later experiments to show that this is possible and affordable.

> *I do not believe that the global education problem is solvable by conventional means: the building of classrooms in remote areas, and the preparation of a vast array of teachers. . . We have certainly come to the time when we need to entertain some new and creative thoughts about the total enterprise of education.*

Theodore Hesburgh, *The Human Imperative*, Yale University Press, 1974, p. 65.

What Is Needed for More Effective Learning?

In looking at what is needed in distance education we should consider the problems of learning today. Perhaps the major difficulty in our present learning systems is that many students do not learn, in schools and universities, or learn only poorly. We must ask why this happens. Another problem is that access to learning is not uniform, even in wealthy countries such as the United States; it is not a level playing field. Another problem is the cost of providing learning with today's methods. Finally, learning is not enjoyable for many students, essential for encouraging lifelong learning.

A major factor with the lack of success in classes is the inability to help all students individually. We know that every student is a unique individual, with different backgrounds and learning styles. We know that every student will have problems at some stages of learning, and that these problems will differ from student to student. Our current modes for responding to individual difference and treating student problems are inadequate both in classes and in distance learning environments. There are simply too many students in our classes to offer individualized attention, except for very few exceptional teachers. So some students do poorly, not receiving the personalized aid they need. We typically blame the students for poor performance, but it is the system, classes of 20+ students, that is responsible.

Tutors
There is a very successful traditional way of dealing individually with student problems. It involves human tutors working with each student. With a skilled tutor the results could be spectacular. Socrates is an early example. Late 19th-century England was an example. Every important physicist in England (including Maxwell) studied with the same tutor at Cambridge University,

Hopkins. Benjamin Bloom and his students showed, in the 1980s, with extensive experiments in the Chicago public schools, that almost everyone could succeed in learning with tutorial assistance.

The Computer as a Tutor

But human tutors, as Bloom realized, are much too expensive, particularly when we consider all levels of education. They are affordable only by the wealthy or in special circumstances. And we cannot find enough skilled tutors.

We can now achieve the benefits of tutors for everyone, highly adaptive learning, with the computer doing the tutoring. I am not using the idea of tutoring with the computer in the sense that has been discussed by artificial intelligence. This may eventually be possible, but is not practical today for very large numbers in all subject areas. Rather, what I am suggesting is economically and technically possible for very large numbers of students. By very large I am thinking of all the six billion people on this earth, soon nine billion. The Scientific Reasoning Series, mentioned above, is an example of what was possible more than fifteen years ago, with more primitive technology than we have now.

Interaction and Adaptability

Critical to this tutorial activity is the process of questions and answers already mentioned. It is these very frequent questions and replies, if carefully designed by the excellent teachers and researchers in the design groups (discussed later), which allow us to find individual student problems and so adapt the material to the needs of each student.

Since each student or small group of students can in this tutorial environment move at his or her own pace, students can continue until success is attained, as suggested by the Keller Plan. We may need different learning modes for different students. We can store and use records of past performance for each student, making the program even more responsible to student needs.

There is a different attitude in the Keller Plan than in the learning suggested here. In our Keller plan physics course the student sees the course as a series of tests, with built-in aid. In adaptive tutorial learning the tests are invisible, so the student sees the entire process as a learning experience. Testing and learning occur together in the tutorial environment, through the frequent questioning process. So the usual problems with testing are absent.

Another important aspect of adaptability is that we can always maintain a friendly attitude toward each student. We want to help students learn, not criticize them. The unfortunate threat of grades is no longer necessary, because all students will learn to the mastery level, in Bloom's sense. Everyone, or almost everyone, succeeds.

Voice

How are students to answer the questions? We require, as suggested, free-form answers in the student's native language. In our older programs, this was done by typing. Pointing and clicking is completely inadequate for the type of interaction needed for tutorial learning. Today there is a new technology which shows great promise in this direction. Students can talk to computers and the computer can identify what has been said, with commercially available software.

This is a much more natural way for conversational interaction between the computer and the student. Students have been talking and listening for most of their lives. The computer can speak too, so we can even help young students and illiterate students to learn. However, most educators do not understand the potential of voice input and output with computers for learning, and little material today uses voice. We stress that we do not require natural language recognition for this purpose. Simple string matching is sufficient. Current voice input software is adequate for the system being suggested.

Everywhere at Any Time

Distance learning with tutorial computer-based material allows us to reach all students, and so bring learning to people who do not have schools or universities. It allows learning at any time, at any place, in any language and culture, at reasonable cost. Again, the details are discussed elsewhere. But very little material of this kind exists now.

Shorter Learning Time

If learning is adapted to the needs of each student, we can expect that students will learn faster. This is valuable both for the student and for society. Costs of learning will be less if less time is required and students will become contributing members of society at an earlier age.

We estimate that most students could with adaptive tutorial learning complete 'school' in nine or ten years, with success. The possibilities are good that we will be able to deliver much better learning to far more students at a lower cost per student.

Next we consider the process for producing computer-based tutorial learning units.

Producing Highly Adaptive Learning Units

Perhaps the most important aspect of the work of the University of California, Irvine, group over 35 years was that we developed a system for producing such highly adaptive tutorial material. Initially we developed a methodology, beginning with our first work in 1968 with Noah Sherman, and then developed software to support that methodology. We believe that this is the only system developed particularly for producing highly adaptive interactive material, although it is possible in other systems.

The process we have developed for creating such material is fully documented in literature available. The most valuable source of information discussing all aspects of such materials, including costs, is a recent book by myself and Sigrun Gunnarsdottir, called *Tutorial Distance Learning*, available from Kluwer.

Design
The first stage of development, design, is critical in determining the quality of the materials. First we have in our process overall design, and then detailed design.

The first step in design is overall design, determining the outline of the course or segment to be developed. We begin with brainstorming, to develop ideas, and end with a one-page description of each module to be developed.

The next step is detailed design. The full details must be developed at this time, including the messages to students (vocal and text), the media needed, the analysis of student replies, the flow of control in the program, what student information is to be stored, and how this information is used in later student learning. The emphasis is always on helping students to learn.

Detailed design is done by excellent teachers and researchers, working in groups of about four, usually for a week, full time. They make all the decisions just mentioned. The designers do not need to know anything about coding, as their task is pedagogical. In a large project, many design groups are needed.

The visual document describing the design is called a script. We now have facilities for entering the script into a computer, developed by Bertrand Ibrahim at the University of Geneva.

Implementation

The next step is implementation. We move from the script to a running program. One step is programming. If the script is stored online, much of the program can be written by the computer, in any language desired. Some code will be written by hand, and the script editor aids with integrating this code with the automatically programmed code. Skilled programmers are needed here. To move to another platform, code appropriate to that machine can be generated. The stored script editor is independent of the target machine.

Experiments with interpretation directly from the script while the program is running are being done by Rika Yoshii at California State University, San Marcos. To move to a new platform, a new interpreter can be written.

A number of other specialists play a role in implementation. Graphic artists are responsible for deciding how the material is to appear on the screen, using what is known about reading text. Media specialists create the media specified by the designers. Evaluators play a role in beta testing, to assure that the program to be evaluated does not contain errors.

Evaluation

An important step is evaluation and improvement with large numbers of students. We recommend two cycles. No matter how good the designers are, they will miss some things. Much of the data is gathered by the computer as students run the program. As large numbers of students are involved, the data gathered will be extensive. Some professional evaluators will also interview students.

Both cognitive and affective issues are important for evaluation. We need to find if mastery is achieved at most points. Are all the questions understandable to the audience? Does the design miss some likely student inputs? We need to determine if the program holds the attention of the student for large periods of time. We need to find if students enjoy learning with this program.

Experiments

The critical ingredient missing at present, holding up progress, are full, extensive, professional experiments in using this technology with sizable groups of students, thousands. Such experiments should be done with several courses in different subject areas and different levels. If we are to have global education, as I think we must in the future, the experiments should involve several languages and cultures.

Perhaps the most important experiment is that concerned with young children, the beginning of establishing education for all. We are proposing an experiment of this type, with three components.

- **Scientific Literacy**. The audience would be elementary and middle school students and the emphasis would be on the nature of science. The Scientific Reasoning Series gives us an initial impetus. This experiment is proposed for five different languages and cultures, allowing us to see if essentially one development will work everywhere, with adaptations for each new culture. Further details, including the proposal itself, and moving materials to new languages and cultures, are available on request.

- **Reading and Writing**. We have suggested that this tutorial technology be used for helping students learn to read and write. This is a major problem in our society, both in the United States and in poor countries, because the illiteracy rate is unacceptably high. We plan to consider only English in the initial attack on this difficult problem, and go to other languages later.

- **Mathematical literacy**. A similar experiment, again in five languages and cultures, would be with beginning mathematics for young children. As with reading and writing, the recent publications of the National Academy Press offer excellent information for this development.

Although the languages would be determined in discussions with the funding agencies, the most likely languages for the initial experiment are Chinese, Spanish, English, an African language, and an Indian language. This experiment in elementary education would require about three years and 18 million dollars. Full proposals and budgets for each of these components in elementary learning are available from the author.

An interesting college-level experiment would consider the 25 courses which dominate our universities, the large beginning courses. These account for about 40 percent of the student hours. Many of them are very large lecture courses with limited help for students, and many students do not survive, or do poorly. We would not do all these courses at once, but rather select a few for the initial experiment. We could greatly improve learning, and, if used widely, decrease costs.

After the Experiments

The experiments are only the first stage in developing a new education system for the world. If these experiments are successful, we can proceed to full development. Both organizational structures and planning for the future are required.

Organizational Structures

Current organizational structures for education are unlikely to meet the demands of this new system. They do not have the flexibility needed for future learning.

We need to plan for continuing development of new learning units, in an ever widening circle of languages and cultures and ages. We also need to plan for and develop new hardware for future needs. Initially the learning material will run on existing personal computers and operation system. But such computers are too expensive for the developing world. A computer to run such learning units would cost much less than present machines, $50 or less, and would need a much simpler operating system than computers today, as it is not a general purpose computer. Solar panels would be needed for locations without power. We need an organization to develop such a system, after enough learning material is available to justify such development. Perhaps this would be planned about six years after the experiment or a bit more.

This organization, or another, would also need to consider how the learning units can reach everyone on earth. A variety of modes will allow us to reach more individuals, including CD ROM and the Internet. But these methods will still not bring learning everywhere. The most likely strategy for the future is a global satellite network to reach everyone. This probably will not be part of the current Internet, increasingly dominated by commercial forces, but a new network just for learning. Planning for this could begin about four years after the experiment with young children is completed.

An organizational structure will also be needed to let people know what is available. Part of this will be the job of the new operating system, based on stored information about what the student has already done. We also need to be concerned with planning future development. This implies some structure to carry out this work.

Research and evaluation also needs organizational guidance. We will have, for both, far more data available for analysis than with present research techniques.

Some of this will come from carefully designed experiments, some from general student use. This data will be publicly available for everyone. Data mining will probably be useful for analysis, given the large amount of data available. Perhaps we will soon have the powerful predictive theories for learning that characterize physics.

Planning for the Future

It will be possible to attain global education for everyone in a twenty year period with the approach proposed. The first task will be to expend the material developed in the experiment, both to later years and to more languages. By nine years after the experiment, we could have a full K-12 curriculum, with many options, and this could be extended to other languages and cultures. The satellite network and new computers can be widely deployed at this time.

We can then proceed to the undergraduate experiments. Thirteen years after the initial experiment with young children a full freshman and sophomore curriculum can be available, and we can begin on the upper division and lifelong learning courses.

Major Problems of the World

We also need to consider how we can use learning to help with major world problems. A problem that can be solved through education is violence. We need to begin with very young children, four or five, to solve that problem. The necessary learning material can be part of preschool learning, preparing for reading, writing, and arithmetic. Guidance can come from Gandhi and Martin Luther King, Jr. We could start the development process soon after the experiment is complete.

Another important early problem is health. This learning material should be developed initially for the very poor, but it would also be usable in the developed countries. The units would be part of the elementary curriculum, probably spread over many years. If people are to learn everything, they must be healthy.

Another problem that can be aided is that of water supply. Learning what water is drinkable, and how water can be conserved is part of the necessary learning in this situation.

Where Are We Now?

At the beginning of this chapter I raised the issue of how much we have to learn about computers in a learning process. We still have a long way to go to realize the full potential for the computer in learning, as seen in the last section. We need to stop imitating older non-adaptive ways to learn, such as the lecture, the book, and video. Much of what is today called online learning or elearning is in such imitative modes.

The computer gives us the possibility of adaptive leaning for all students, at all levels and everywhere. The prospects are exciting. We should begin at once.

We have the possibility of completely rebuilding our educational system, in a way that is both affordable and superior to present learning. Everyone on earth can learn to their full capability, in twenty years.

Note

Other related papers can be found at www.ics.uci.edu/~bork
The initial version of this paper was dictated using Dragon NaturallySpeaking Version 5.

References

Bloom, B. (1984, July). The two sigma problem: The search for methods of group instruction as effective as one-to-one tutoring. *Educational Researcher*.

Bork , A. (2000a, July/August), Interview: The future of learning. *EDUCOM Review*.

Bork, A. (2000b). Four fictional views of the future of learning. *The Internet and Higher Education, 3*.

Bork, A. (2000c, January/February). Learning technology. *EDUCAUSE Review*.

Bork, A. (2001). Tutorial learning for the twenty-first century. *Journal of Science Education and Technology*.

Bork, A. (2002). A story about learning. *Proceedings of ICCE 2002*, IEEE.

Bork, A., & Gunnarsdottir, S. (2001). *Tutorial distance learning: Rebuilding our educational system*. New York: Kluwer Academic Publishers.

Daniel, J. (1996). *Mega-universities and knowledge media: Technological strategies for higher education*. London: Kogan Page.

Chapter 4

Lessons Learned About Technology and Learning:
A Conversation

Betty Collis and Jef Moonen

This article is presented as a kind of dialogue between Betty Collis and Jef Moonen. They work at the Faculty of Behavioral Science (formerly Faculty of Educational Science and Technology) of the University of Twente in the Netherlands. Both have been involved with computers, and later, more broadly with ICT (information and communication technology) for several decades. In this article they tell a little about themselves as pioneers in the applications of computer-related technology for support of flexible learning (a term they prefer above others, such as online learning, or e-learning, or computer-based learning, because it focuses on a goal and not on technology), and then discuss five questions posed by Greg Kearsley, the editor of this book, to the authors.

About Betty, About Jef: Pioneers

Betty began as a mathematics teacher, in the US and Canada. She loved teaching, but had a problem: she is left-handed with a weird way of hooking her hand around a writing implement and thus had very poor skill at writing on the blackboard; graphing equations was a tedious and not very successful experience, yet she wanted to communicate to her students the joy of changing a coefficient and seeing the line or curve in question fly like a bird. In 1979 she had a life-changing day; she saw the Apple 32K microcomputer, running a program to graph equations in a variety of colors. This could solve her problem: she saw right away that she could use the computer in her classroom as a tool to extend her teaching by compensating for her poor equation-drawing skills. It also set the scene for a bottom line in her work: How to start from a need or enthusiasm of the teacher when considering technology support for learning. She started writing little BASIC programs, even one per day, to support her own mathematics teaching, usually to demonstrate something visually but also little games and lots of probability experiments. This approach took into account that she only had one computer (that she carried around with her along with a small monitor), a fully packed curriculum, and large classes. She rapidly developed these sorts of "extending the teacher" or "extending the textbook" ideas for other disciplines as well as her own mathematics, and began traveling around the world showing her little programs and big ideas. But she worried a lot, too, about the problems that would face teachers who were not likely to be writing little programs each evening or wanting to carry a computer and monitor up and down stairways and between buildings; would her enthusiasm mean anything to them? And what about students who started to respond with excitement to the use of the computer to support learning, but then lost this enthusiasm, and also even lost their enthusiasm for learning? What happens to them? What could she, and other computer-using pioneer teachers, do to help? Betty finished her PhD in this area in 1984, focusing on problems that serve as barriers to computer use in learning.

Jef, a Belgian, also started as a mathematics teacher, and also got involved early with computers to support learning, based, like Betty, on a problem in his own teaching. He moved to The Netherlands, at the University of Leiden in the 1970s, and developed a computer-based statistics program (at that time written in APL and later using the PLATO system) to support his own teaching of statistics to psychology students. This work was the basis of his PhD dissertation. While Betty was writing little programs on a portable computer, Jef was using a complex hardware and software system that had many of the attributes of complex learning-management systems today and also included communication support to extend the system to also include human interaction. He, and the PLATO system, were both very much ahead of their times. Jef went on to become more and more involved in policy and in the leadership of large-scale initiatives relating to computers in education in The Netherlands, and for most of the 1980s was director of the national computers in education centre as well as involved in many European projects relating to educational-software development. He, too, was traveling the world, focusing mostly on large-scale issues such as software-development methodologies, project management for large educational-software and multimedia projects, impact evaluation, and national policy.

Both came to the University of Twente in the late 1980s to work as professors in the Department of Educational Instrumentation, working on the design, development, implementation, and evaluation of ICT-based media. Jef's interests evolved towards the cost-effectiveness of using media and ICT in education and training and his time was divided between his research, his pioneer teaching with different forms of computer-related tools and systems, and being an administrator in the university: department head and dean of the faculty. Betty's interests stayed more with pedagogy and technology and helping the teacher and learner overcome barriers to learning as well as extending the good teacher and the good learning situation to make them even better. In terms of technologies both Betty and Jef evolved early into using ICT to support distributed learning via networked learning environments and Betty was one of the first people to use the World Wide Web as a collaborative-learning environment in her courses in 1994. Where she used to make little BASIC programs, she started making little HTML pages, then Web sites, then leading teams making Web-based systems. In this line of development, she and her team developed a specific Web-based course-management system in 1997 called TeleTOP which is now in use in many universities, schools, and the corporate sector. In 2001 Betty was appointed as the Shell Professor of

Networked Learning at the University of Twente. This special chair was created for her by Shell International Exploration and Production (SIEP), where she spends much of her working time supporting developments as team leader of research for the Global Learning & Leadership Development Organization of SIEP. Along the way, both Betty and Jef focused on a goal for technology use in learning: offering more options to learners, more flexibility, to increase the chance that learning will fit their needs and situations, extend their opportunities, and offer them efficient ways to carry out processes that accompany learning.

Betty and Jef started doing their respective traveling together, as they got married in 1990. Recently (2001) they wrote a book about their experiences with ICT and learning over the years. That book is built around 18 lessons that they drew from being involved in so many projects and through their own experiences as computer-using teachers. The lessons are given in Table 1. In this dialogue that follows, these 18 lessons will be a reference point around which the discussion centered on five general questions will be focused.

Table 1. The lessons learned by Betty and Jef (Collis & Moonen, 2001, pp. 2-3).

Lesson 1 Be specific	We need to define our terms and express our goals in a measurable form or else progress will be difficult to steer or success difficult to claim.
Lesson 2 Move from student to professional	Learning in higher education is not only a knowledge-acquisition process but also a process of initiation into a professional community. Pedagogy should reflect both acquisition and contribution-oriented models.
Lesson 3 You can't not do it	The idea whose time has come is irresistible, and conversely.
Lesson 4 Don't forget the road map	Change takes a long time and is an iterative process, evolving in ways that are often not anticipated.
Lesson 5 Watch the 4-Es	An individual's likelihood of voluntarily making use of a particular type of technology for a learning-related purpose is a function of four "E"s: the Environmental context, the individual's perception of educational Effectiveness and of Ease of use, and the individual's sense of personal Engagement with the technology. The environmental context and the level of personal engagement are most important.
Lesson 6 Follow the leader	Key persons are critical.
Lesson 7 Be just-in-time	Staff-engagement activities to stimulate instructors to make use of technology are generally not very effective: Focus on just-in-time support for necessary tasks.
Lesson 8 Get out of the niche	Most technology products are not used in practice beyond their developers. Keep implementation and the 4-Es central in choosing any technology product.
Lesson 9 After the core, choose more	Technology selection involves a core and complementary technologies. The core is usually determined by history and

	circumstances; changing it usually requires pervasive contextual pressure. The individual instructor can make choices about complementary technologies and should choose them with flexibility in mind.
Lesson 10 Don't overload	More is not necessarily better.
Lesson 11 Offer something for everyone	A well-designed WWW-based system should offer users a large variety of possibilities to support flexible and contribution-oriented learning not dominated by any one background orientation. If so, it is currently the most appropriate (core or complementary) technology for flexible learning.
Lesson 12 Watch the speed limit	Don't try to change too much at the same time. Start where the instructor is at, and introduce flexibility via extending contact sessions to include before-, during- and after aspects, with each of these made more flexible. Move gradually into contribution-oriented activities.
Lesson 13 Process yields product	Through the process of contributive learning activities, learners themselves help produce the learning materials for the course.
Lesson 14 Aim for activity	The key roles of the instructor are becoming those of activity planning, monitoring, and quality control.
Lesson 15 Design for activity	Instructional design should concentrate more on activities and processes, and less on content transmission and a pre-determined product.
Lesson 16 Get a new measuring stick	What we are most interested in regarding learning as a consequence of using technology often can't be measured in the short term or without different approach to measurement. Measure what can be measured, such as short-term gains in efficiency or increases in flexibility.
Lesson 17 Be aware of the price tag	It is not going to save time or money to use technology, at least not in the short term.
Lesson 18 Play the odds	A simplified approach to predicting return on investment (ROI) that looks at the perceived amount of relative change in the factors that matter most to different actors is a useful approach to support decision making or evaluation.

Now, to the dialogue…

Question 1: How have perspectives about online learning changed over the years (including yours)?

Jef: OK, Betty, I know that you are by nature a very optimistic and creative person; on the other hand over the last 20 years you have seen the evolution of many rounds of technology coming and going in education. How do you explain that you are still optimistic about online learning?

Betty: First, I am optimistic about the possibilities to extend and enrich learning as well as to make it more efficient by being more flexible. I am not particularly optimistic about any subset of this that may limit people's imagination about what they can do. For this reason, as you know, I never use terms like computer-based learning, Web-based learning, e-learning, or online learning, because each of them tends to bring along certain assumptions, such as only the computer and no teacher, or no face-to-face contact. You and I have seen several decades worth of attempts to equate computer support for learning with the idea of the computer doing everything, and in general the result is at best a niche solution that gets used in the context in which it was made (until the project funding runs out or the researcher moves on to something else). That is why our Lesson 8, Get out of the Niche, is a general phase of reference for me when I look at an idea for ICT-supported learning: Who is going to use this beyond the team that developed it? Many times, I can't really picture a broader uptake. You and I, together and separately, have been studying this for many years — in the 1980s, the terminology was how to make educational software portable; currently, the terminology relates to the standards and metadata needed for reuse of learning objects. In general, I believe that these efforts will continue to be limited at best, unless we change our focus from content delivery, to support for the processes of learning, such as collaboration, construction, contribution, finding, sharing, communicating. And these processes are not themselves located within a learning object, but in the way that the teacher and learner make use of learning objects. This is why our Lesson 15, Design for Activity, seems to me to be a key way of re-expressing the idea that was already expressed in 1980: the difference between seeing the computer as a tutor and as a tool (luckily, the third category, the computer as an object of study, is no longer a specific focus in itself).

But Jef, even though you tend to be more critical and less directly optimistic than me, I know that you have been more involved than me in developing and managing the use of authoring tools and systems over time. At one time, you felt this might be a solution to the not-invented-here problem: giving teachers the tools to write their own educational software. How do you see the evolution of teachers authoring their own online-learning materials? Do we need another round of authoring systems?

Jef: Certainly not. Assuming that in the long run people don't change, this means that the majority of teachers will do what they have done all along, which means using available textbooks or making handouts by cutting and pasting, from other materials or now, making PowerPoints, often also by cutting and pasting only now it is electronic. Looking back at the many examples of authoring systems and tools in all kinds of forms and formats, the potential of those tools has never been really used by teachers. (It is interesting now that a new terminology, learning-content management system, describes a form of authoring system, but those who sell them never refer to the previous history of such systems.) I remember a PhD dissertation I was involved in as a supervisor where we explored the possibilities of "adaptable courseware" using authoring tools in order to make the didactical fit between the teachers and the computer-based material as good as possible. Although the teachers very clearly indicated their support of this idea and responded well to workshop sessions, when we observed what teachers actually did with the tools in their own practice, we saw they were not used. My conclusion at that time was that the effort involved was too much for the teachers even though I remain convinced that what they want to do is still create their own material in their own ways and this has to be done in an easy way. The new potential of the Web as an endless source of resources is probably the right substitute or new version of the old cutting and pasting of existing printed material. At the same time, because of the enormous amounts of resources available, the selection is so much richer than was originally available. And because of the available technology, students can be included in the cutting and pasting, or more positively stated, in the construction of learning materials themselves that can be immediately shared by others. That is why I think that a (well-designed) Web-based course-management system is the new wave of authoring tool, and why I feel optimistic that this kind of system will be used by teachers. Your TeleTOP system is a good example; every instructor at the University of Twente uses it in some way, a take-up we never achieved with earlier authoring tools. We summarized this in our Lesson 11: Offer Something for Everyone. Tools such as TeleTOP let the teacher offer resources in whatever way he or she wants, but more than that, are used to support the processes of learning rather than to replace the teacher or textbook in terms of content delivery. This fits directly with what you said earlier…But before we talk too long on one question, we had better move on to the rest of the questions.

Questions 2 and 3: What are the primary factors affecting the development of online learning? What are the major obstacles to the growth of online learning?

Jef: Let's talk about these two questions together, because they are two sides of the same coin. And let's us substitute the term flexible learning for online learning, to match our usual way of talking and thinking. I know, Betty, that you have been thinking a lot for many years about a kind of theoretical or metaphorical framework to explain and get insight in a simple way into the complex question of factors that influence (positively or negatively) the likelihood that some aspect of technology-supported learning will be taken up in practice. You call the framework the "4-E Model," so please explain it.

Betty: Over the years, we have come to see four sets of factors as having a relationship with each other that we describe by the *4-E Model* (see Figure 1). This model says that an individual's likelihood of making use of a technological innovation for a learning-related purpose is a function of: ***Environment*** (the institutional context), ***Educational Effectiveness*** (perceived or expected),

Ease of Use, and *Engagement* (the person's personal response to technology and to change), each expressed as a vector.

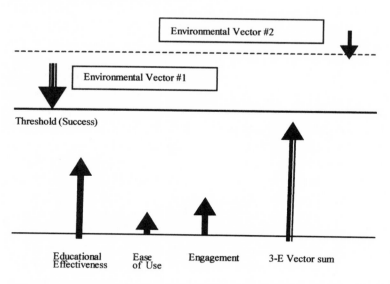

Figure 1. The 4-E Model as a heuristic to predict likelihood of use (in this case, use will be likely in Environment 1, and not likely in Environment 2) (Collis & Moonen, 2001, p. 25).

In the 4-E Model, the Environmental factor determines the level of the success threshold; a stronger environmental climate pushes the threshold lower so that the vector sum of the other three vectors does not have to be as high as when the threshold is associated with a weaker environmental vector. Figure 1 (from our book) shows a 4-E Model profile of an individual with a weak Ease of Use vector, a weak Engagement vector, and a moderately positive Educational Effectiveness vector. His vector sum is high enough in Environment Condition #1 to probably make use of the particular technology innovation in his teaching. In Environmental Condition #2, the push from the Environmental vector is too weak and thus the threshold is too far away; he is not likely to make use of the innovation. I see the 4-Es wherever I look. They are one of our major lessons (Lesson 5: Watch the 4-Es). They can be particularly helpful in guiding the implementation process, for example, giving guidance that relates to the vectors individually or in combination. Three of our lessons fit in this context: Lesson 4, Don't forget the road map; Lesson 6, Follow the leader; and Lesson 12, Watch the speed limit. The 4-Es provide the framework around which I would answer Greg's Questions 2 and 3 about factors that affect the development of online learning. Jef, from your administrator experience and also the many projects you have done with the Ministry with educational decision makers, do you see a major lesson relating to the development (or lack of) for online learning that you can interpret in terms of the 4-Es?

Jef: Oh yes. Talking from the Dutch perspective, it was very typical that when, in the beginning of the 1980s the microelectronics industry got momentum, reports began to appear about the impact of microelectronics on society, business, and education. The government in The Netherlands became convinced about the necessity of doing "something" about computers in education and from then on a well-funded policy was established to stimulate the use of computers in education. (This was when the National Computers in Education agency was formed that I headed from its start.) These types of initiatives were clearly an answer to the general feeling that you have to do this; in terms of the 4-Es, it was an attempt to influence the Environment as much as possible. This movement toward supporting the importance of ICT in education went on until not too long ago, when people and governments began focussing more and more on the real impact of using ICT in education, the "Effectiveness" part of the 4-Es, and it became clear that convincing answers were hard to find. The "you just have to do it" momentum faded and the Environment push was reduced. The main problem was that the "you can't not do it" push was not replaced by a clear and measurable goal that everyone bought into and that could be implemented in practice (our Lesson 1: Be specific). But then the Internet came along, with the stand-alone microelectronics (in the form of individual PCs) of the 1980s being replaced by the communication features provided by the Internet and the resources available via the World Wide Web. A whole new wave of "you can't not do it" is occurring in education, again stimulating another round of Environment push. In terms of the 4-Es, the first wave of barriers associated with the Ease of use of the technology has been reduced, but now problems even more difficult than installing a hard drive have replaced the earlier problems. Teachers have to deal with Spam, with virus problems, with copyright issues as their students use the Internet and Internet-related systems and tools; the technical problems are being replaced by other problems that are more difficult to handle. The feeling of "you can't not do it" is likely to fade with time, and administrators will again be looking for proof of the educational impact of using the Internet in education. This is why we included Lesson 3, You can't not do it, to point out that Environment pushes come, and go, in waves, and when the wave fades, then we need to be strengthening the other Es in order to go on. And for our discussion, let's go on to Greg's next question.

Question 4: What are the most important theoretical and research issues?

Betty: Jef, you have mentioned the need to supply decision-makers with documentation about the impact of flexible learning supported by ICT several times; do you see this as a major theoretical and research issue as well?

Jef: Yes, I do, and that is why three of our "lessons" relate to this (Lesson 16, Get a new measuring stick; Lesson 17, Be aware of the price tag; and Lesson

18, Play the odds). All along it has been clear that a main question for education is to illustrate the impact of the interventions and pedagogical approaches it is using. Technology is an intervention that needs to be associated with a pedagogical approach. The history of pedagogy has been paved with many, in themselves, very attractive ideas about how to teach and learn but for most of them the outcomes that they have led to have apparently not been convincing enough so that the new pedagogies and their associated technology are used widely. This may partially be because the way that impact is being measured doesn't capture what is really happening, so from a research point of view, much has to be done to translate Lesson 1 ("Be specific") into Lesson 16 ("Get a new measuring stick"). As we know from practice, learners in school and university mainly work to what is graded; as long as new pedagogies and new uses of technology are not translated into measurable "tests" that "count" in the formal school procedures, the results will not illustrate an impact of technology which will influence the opinions of administrators or skeptical teachers, which moves us into a vicious circle. So research about how to measure the impact of technology in education is a central issue. Research in this area should take into account that impact is a multi-dimensional concept, whereby short-term and long-term, tangible and intangible effects are all of importance. I try to capture these in my Simplified ROI (return on investment) Model, related to Lesson 18.

Betty: From the beginning, the theoretical issues that most interest me have related to the learning process. In particular, I am especially interested in the distinction between learning as acquisition of pre-determined material provided by an expert, and learning as participation and contribution, whereby the process of finding, creating, discussing, and designing can lead to new outcomes that were not pre-determined. You and I express this in terms of our "contributing student" terminology, and study it in various ways in our research and in that of the graduate students we supervise. The issue of how to reliably show impact, in ways that convince administrators, is particularly challenging here. But in particular, the role of the teacher in this sort of pedagogical shift is a major theoretical and research area. We discuss it in our Lesson 14, Aim for activity. We know from our own research, as well as more broadly, that teachers move slowly in terms of pedagogical change (unless the Environment forces them), and need support and help. When technology is involved, it is often seen more as something extra to learn rather than as a way to help you do what you want to do. That is why we and many others continue to study how best to support teachers in their new roles, and our Lesson 7, Be just-in-time, relates to our observations that the farther from the actual moment of using it, the less likely the intervention will help the teacher in practice.

I know that technology should not and does not drive an educational vision such as the Contributing Student, but I believe it can offer affordances that can invite teachers and learners to these new methods. Jef, how does this relate to your ideas about core and complementary technologies for learning as a major research theme?

Jef: Media selection as part of instructional design has been a research area for decades. However, if you analyze the reasons why certain technologies are chosen for a course or program, then it becomes clear that often rationality is not the basis for a choice but rather the context and the traditions of the environment. Therefore in our analysis we make the distinction between core and complementary technologies, whereby the core technologies are the major tools or methods ("artifacts") around which the course or lesson is planned and carried out. If those technologies are not available, there is a serious problem in going forward with the learning event. In the near-past and still in schools and higher education, the core technologies in the teaching- and learning-process are the face-to-face situation in the classroom with the teacher "giving the lesson," and the printed textbook as the other type of core resource. All of the other technologies being used (handouts, videotapes, WWW sites, PowerPoint presentations, educational software, etc.) are complements to the core technology. Nice to have, but not essential. Typically the individual instructor only has a choice about the complementary technologies (Lesson 9, After the core, choose more), as the core technology is mainly based on contextual and historical reasons. (Thus, the media-selection methods within traditional instructional design have had little meaning in practice, as they often are based on the assumption that the designer, in a logical way, can determine the core technology.) Now we see a movement, starting in higher education, where the core technology is gradually being replaced by networked systems such as course-management systems and tools that make use of the Internet and intranets. Finding a new balance between this new core technology and the already existing complementary technologies, and where the complementary technologies are more and more being integrated within the core technology electronically, is a new research area. For instance, how much video should be included within a course supported by a course-management system? Should the video be oriented toward knowledge transfer or emotional stimulation? In the corporate context, this integration of core and complementary technologies is occurring under the phrase "blended learning." But Betty, we are way over our word limit, so we better go on to the last question.

Question 5: What emerging trends do you feel will affect the evolution of online learning?

Betty: I think trends in higher education and also schools toward more and more use of the Web as a source of resources and contacts will help stimulate the shift from learning as acquiring pre-determined knowledge from carefully tailored resources, toward learning as creating, criticizing, and contributing. Our Lesson 13, Process yields product, can bring us to learner contributions as a major source of reusable learning objects. In the corporate context, the gradual movement toward a mix of the tools and resources in knowledge-management systems with the tools and resources of learners contributing experiences and artifacts from their own work experience, also fits within Lesson 13. If these trends grow as I hope they will, then we will really see an evolution in learning (in which technology will be an essential tool).

Jef: Yes, but…Having the availability of an enormously rich resource collection via the WWW can on the one hand be an enormous stimulus for the contribution approach, but at the same time can create the danger of an enormous overload. Think about a big buffet that is available during a dinner party; the invitation to eat a lot is clearly there but that does not mean it is healthy to do so. In a very comparable way, having the Internet and the WWW available is potentially good, but two issues should be taken very seriously. One of these is how to select resources, by what criteria, and secondly, how to evaluate their quality? These two important issues bring up the question of if the learner is able to be independent in his exploration of this resource base. Probably not. The learner cannot have the wisdom and the overview to deal with the overload in a sensible way. Therefore there will always still be the need for a teacher, to help the learner in these two issues of selection and quality control. This relates to an observation that I have been making for many years, that "more is not necessarily better" (Lesson 10, Don't overload). More technology is not necessarily better, as the human teacher still has an important role to play; certainly more automation is not necessarily better.

Betty: Maybe this is a good point to end…focusing on the human instead of the technology?

Jef: The human remains very important in learning, and focusing on the balance of when to apply technology, when to emphasize the human, and in what combination the technology can support the human, remains an important issue. In the past, trying to eliminate the human through things such as intelligent tutoring systems has had limited success. And yet, now we see this urge again, with new names such as Learning Management Systems, for an automated way to provide learning to the student, with metadata seen as the key. The whole metadata business is a potentially dangerous approach if people think that automation coupled with metadata can take over from the wisdom and experience of the good teacher.

Reference

Collis, B., & Moonen, J. (2001). *Flexible learning in a digital world: Experiences and expectations.* London: RoutledgeFarmer.

Chapter 5

Transcending Distances and Differences
with Online Learning

Norman Coombs

*Norman Coombs, PhD, is the CEO of EASI (Equal Access to Software and Information)
as well as professor emeritus from the Rochester Institute of Technology where he taught
history for 36 years. He pioneered RIT's distance learning program and was given Zenith's
"Master of Innovation" award for his uses of distance learning to mainstream students with
disabilities and also was chosen as New York State CASE (Council for the Advancement
and Support of Education) "Teacher of the Year" award in 1990 for using computers in
teaching. In 1998, he was selected for the Man of the Year Award by AHEAD; in 1999,
he received the Strache National Leadership Award from the CSUN Center on Disabilities;
and, in 2000, he was the recipient of the Francis Joseph Campbell Award of the American
Library Association for work in helping libraries to meet the needs of customers with
disabilities.*

When Being Blind Was an Advantage

What Does a Historian Want with a Computer?
When one of my colleagues kept nagging me to look at an Apple computer
with a speech synthesizer, I resisted as I couldn't see what a computer had to
do with studying cultural history. I finally complied with his demands only to
silence him. It took a very short time before I became addicted. I was already
a decent typist, preparing my own classroom materials and writing a book on
Black history. However, I had no way to know when I made mistakes or could
I correct those mistakes independently. Now, I realized that I could prepare
classroom materials myself; hear when I made typos; and correct them without
having to depend on anyone else. However, my printer was a nine pin dot
matrix printer, and I was told that making classroom copies on the copier
resulted in a blurred, unreadable product. Therefore, my secretary keyboarded
the materials I had prepared and printed, and she used her printer to produce a
higher quality product that could be copied. This duplication of input work
seemed a needless waste. I obtained a modem for myself and for the secretary
and sent her the document online. Almost immediately, I recognized that the
computer was a communication device.

Next, I realized that term papers being submitted in email could be read by the
computer, letting me avoid having to bother scheduling a human reader to read

the papers to me. Immediately, I recognized the potential that this would have in providing me with increased independence. One of the first students who volunteered to do this was a woman who was totally deaf. I graded the exams and returned the results by email the next day. Then she wrote with a question on the grade which I answered, and this was followed by still another question. When, on the third day there was still another email from her, I started to wonder what was this really about. The mail stated that this was the first time in her life that she had been able to talk with a teacher without a third party intervening between them. Not only was she deaf, but I am blind. The technology enabled us to transcend a double sensory barrier.

I say that being blind was an advantage for me because it positioned me back in the early 1980s to grasp the potential of the computer as a communication tool while few others recognized this potential. I recall a computer science faculty asking me for some information. When I offered to email it to him, after an awkward pause, he confessed he had never used email! For him the computer was not a communication device. Today, when anyone buys a computer, the software that comes loaded on it includes applications from several Internet providers like AOL. It comes ready to connect to the Internet and to use both email and the Web.

From Telecourses to Online Learning
The Rochester Institute of Technology had been delivering telecourses on local TV stations very early in the morning for some years. Typically these courses had little interaction between faculty and students. Paper mail usually took a week or more to turn around, which was long enough to discourage students from asking many questions of the teacher. The telephone was more immediate, but that usually resulted in a two-person game of phone tag, which became irritating to both student and teacher.

In the early 1980s, the telecourse office put out a request for a faculty person to experiment with using email and/or a computer bulletin board to encourage more frequent faculty/student interaction. I recognized that this was similar to what I was already starting to do with my classroom students, and I volunteered for the experiment. They were expecting an able-bodied engineer or computer science teacher and not a historian who is blind. However, they took what they got. This resulted in my having the excitement and frustrations of being one of the pioneers of distance learning as well.

This initial work was supported by a college faculty development grant which was mainly used to purchase a copy of DEC VAX Notes, which was the courseware system we adopted. (There were few choices at that time and all were command-line DOS-like interfaces.) In writing the final report for the college grant, I insisted that for online learning to succeed, every faculty would need a computer on his or her desk as handy to use as the telephone. The provost replied to me that this would never happen. As a historian, I could already recognize the inherent logical and impetus of the technology and was sure he was mistaken in his assessment.

This initial work based on the productivity grant was presented to the International Conference on Computer Mediated Communication held in 1988 at the Open University, Milton Keynes, England. "Using Distance Education Technologies to Transcend Physical Disabilities" is online at http://www.rit.edu/~nrcgsh/arts/open.htm.

Impact of Information Technology on Teaching and Learning

Replicating the Classroom Online
Like most others leaping into online learning with next to no background or experience to guide the way, I assumed that classroom teaching was the right way to teach, and online learning should do its best to copy its features. When, after teaching a class, I returned to my office, I took time to note what I had done in class the previous hour and sketch ideas of how to try and duplicate it in an online setting. At the end of the first online course, I was pleased that the students scored a better grade than those taking the same course on campus. I took this as evidence that I had done well in replicating classroom teaching online.

However, I quickly recognized that some things I did online, I could do even better than in the classroom and, similarly, other things worked better face-to-face. I came to think of an online classroom as functioning like a televised football game. The camera would show 22 men confronting each other waiting for the "snap" of the ball. Then, the camera tries to follow the ball as the focus of the main action. The play may end up being disputed as to whether or not the receiver landed with both feet on the playing field. The program producer then plays a recording of a shot from another camera which focuses on the one player, stops the motion at the moment the player's feet hit the ground and zooms in on one foot. Televised sports shifts between focus on the two teams and focus on one foot of one player. In the online classroom, I shift between focusing my attention on the group interactions and how well or poorly it is working. Then, I freeze my attention on a single student and on one statement that student has made. Shifting my focus between the group and the individual is something like the shifting focus in televised football games. If I do that in class, everyone has to sit and wait while one student and I have an interchange which may not relate to the needs of others. Online, I can focus on a single student, but because it is asynchronous, the others do not have to sit idly by during this exchange. In short the technology lets me focus on a single student more than does the classroom setting. Instead of replicating the classroom, I realized that the goal should be to maximize the technology to enhance delivery of course content.

Putting the Learner in the Driver's Seat

George Orwell's predictions for 1984 turned out to be mistaken in some crucial ways. While many still are concerned about the possible misuses of power by "big brother," most of the harmful and frightening hacking over the Internet has been done by "little brother," some student in high school or maybe a bright undergraduate student. The giant mainframe computers had given way to decentralized computing. In short there has been a shift of power and a decentralization of power.

In discussing the teaching and learning styles that emerge in distance learning, it has been a common saying to compare the classroom to having a "sage on the stage" and contrast to having "a guide on the side" in online courses. Many online teachers find that the technology places them increasingly in the role of a resource person and less in the role of distributor of the final truth. Asynchronous learning systems especially permit students to work in their own unique ways and at their own speed. Instead of the flow of ideas in a classroom marching on relentlessly controlled by the instructor or a few outspoken students, each student can connect and interact at any time of the day or night, skim the material or reread it several times slowly. The student can go back and reread something from the beginning of a discussion. In making a reply, the student may write it rapidly and spontaneously or write, pause, and rewrite something several times. Online learning lends itself to different working and learning styles. Increasingly, I designed my courses to more actively engage the student in the teaching and learning process. Sometimes, I felt that the student was robbed of some of my "pearls of wisdom," but it became obvious that the overall impact was that the student was actually learning more.

Ethnicity, Gender and Disability

While some people are genuinely alienated by online discussions and interactions, many find themselves free to interact in less inhibited ways than face-to-face. One shy girl in one of my courses that met both in the classroom and online commented that she was afraid to talk in class fearing what she called "a crazy look." Online, while her identity was still known by all, she talked freely. Apparently she had less fear of saying something that wouldn't sound right so long as she didn't have to watch their responses to her comments. I often say that, where there is no stage, there is no stage fright.

In the same course, an African American student commented that he liked the online discussion because he felt he was being judged by what he said rather than by his looks. He felt that no one cared whether he was male, female, Black, White, Red, Yellow, Deaf or Blind.

One Teacher's Reflections on Maximizing the Technology

Electronic Curb Cuts
Sidewalk curb cuts were designed for wheel chair users; most of the time they are used by people on skates or bikes; by people pushing strollers and heavy carts. What was created to meet the needs of those with disabilities has turned out to benefit the general public. In a similar way, design features that make accessing online information helpful for people who have a disability can enhance the learning for everyone.

How Do People with Disabilities Access Online Courses?
Before continuing to discuss general design principles that I have come to think are important and before I relate them to how they benefit users with disabilities, it may be helpful for me to parenthetically touch on how people with disabilities access online learning so that my accessibility comments will have a meaningful context.

Users with various motor impairments that prevent them from using the keyboard or the mouse have a variety of special software interfaces that still permit their operating a computer independently. Voice recognition is the best known of these applications. There are also on-screen keyboards where a cursor moves across the picture of a keyboard on the computer monitor. So long as the user can move a single muscle, the user can trigger a switch and the computer will input the key where it is positioned just as if the key on the physical keyboard was depressed. Another device is a sip-and-puff device which can be used to send morse code to the computer. The special software translates that into the equivalent of keyboard input. Probably the most important implication for designing online content is that these users usually will be using keyboard input instead of a mouse to navigate the course material.

Users with low vision will interface using software that will enlarge the text and images on the screen from two times to as much as 16 times the normal size. This means that only a small portion of the content is seen at any one time. Obviously, dense, complicated content becomes more confusing than does content that has blank spaces and which is laid out very clearly. Users with learning disabilities also frequently use this software. While they do not need the content enlarged to enable them to read it, enlarging it does limit how much is on the screen at once. This simplification can benefit some learning disabled users.

Users who are deaf usually only run into real problems when sound is added to course content. Audio will require a transcription, and videos will need streaming, synchronized captions.

Finally, users who are blind cannot see what is being displayed at all. Screen reader software is able to turn text into synthesized speech. The major problem becomes how it deals with pictures.

To summarize, users with disabilities have a variety of adaptive or assistive software that provides alternative input or alternative output giving them independent access to online course material. Still, content design can facilitate the interface with the specialized interfaces. Design choices can also either help or hinder the users comprehension of the content.

It's About People and not Technology
Information technology is both frustrating and seductive. In either case, it is all too easy to focus on the means and not the end. It is the mechanism to transmit content to students. The simpler the technology, the less it intrudes on the communication. While the information technology may be very rich and powerful, only use those elements that enhance the communication. Avoid using powerful and exciting tools merely to impress the student with your technical mastery. Communicating content to the student, and interacting with the students are at the core of what you should be doing. Although technically savvy students may be disappointed, they too will end up focusing on the content and not the technology. Students with disabilities, especially those using special assistive technology, may find the glamorous and new technological features are incompatible with their software blocking them from the actual content.

Where students with special needs require special attention to overcome some communication barrier, this can turn into a benefit for both the teacher and class. By giving careful attention to making communication very clear, it will be clearer for everyone. Teaching is communication, and whatever results in clearer communication will also result in better teaching.

In the early years of my online teaching, I was involved in several experimental pilot projects. While most went well and demonstrated that online learning did work, I participated in some projects that I considered at least partial failures. In every case, on examination, I realized that I had put my focus on the technology and as a result tended to neglect the students. I thought as a humanities person I was immune to technological seduction, but I was wrong. I had to remind myself repeatedly that the technology was the means and not the end.

Do not Replicate the Classroom

When people compare the classroom and online learning, most assume that the classroom is the ideal and that online learning should do the best it can to copy it or reach that standard. In truth, we all know how many dull classes we have endured. We all remember teachers who rambled and were disorganized. Others were so pedantic that it was difficult to stay awake. Some classroom experiences that we have had were awful, and other classes were dynamic and inspiring. In any case, the classroom need not be held up as the standard.

Keep It Simple and Modularize the Content

Studies of writing in email and in chat rooms have found that the style falls between traditional written language and traditional spoken language. Sentences tend to be shorter, more active, less complex. Paragraphs are shorter. The ideas may still be complex, but they are expressed in a more conversational and less pedantic tone. Besides being the way many of us do use computer communication, there are other advantages to the "keep it simple" rule. Few people like reading long documents online, but they frequently will read shorter discussions online. In asking questions or making comments about online material, it is easier to refer to a short, single-topic item.

It happens that this format is congenial for users with learning disabilities. Short sentences and short paragraphs helps them follow the flow of ideas.

People who are deaf frequently do not have English as their first language, as they primarily communicate with sign language. Just like the situation of foreign students, highly academic presentations can be bewildering for them, but straight-forward presentations are easier to comprehend. This is highlighted in the chapter written by Joseph Kinner and myself, "Computer Access for Students with Special Needs" published in *CMC and the Classroom* edited by Zane Berge and Mauri Collins (Hampton Press, 1995), which describes a pilot course with students from the Rochester Institute of Technology in New York State and students at Gallaudet University in Washington, DC. Most students were deaf, and they found the simpler language common in computer communications facilitated their learning.

For a blind user reading with a screen reader and speech synthesizer, it is easy to get lost in a large document but less so in reading a shorter, simple one. The same is true for a user with limited vision or a student with a learning disability using screen magnification software.

Use Redundant Communication Modes

I am aware that many graphic designers totally oppose this principle and say that nothing should be presented twice, such as in an image and with text. They want to have a very dynamic display that grabs attention in several ways. In listening to commercials on television, I am aware that frequently an important item is not verbalized. Sometimes, the product name is never spoken, and I am left not knowing what it is that I should purchase. Similarly, during broadcasts on all-news channels, while the anchor is reading a news item or a televised interview is happening, there is text crawling across the screen with totally unrelated news items in it. Multimedia frequently means having many messages being transmitted all at the same time using different communication modes.

In contrast, there is some evidence that, when presenting complex information to be studied and learned, that dual sensory input enhances learning. In classrooms, when a captioned video is being shown, students who are not deaf frequently learn better than when there are no captions.

The advantage of providing redundant information using different sensory modes is that the information will be available to people with different disabilities and to people with different learning styles. Some people without disabilities learn best from visual information, and some learn better from visual content.

A Level Learning Space

This is not the place to give a detailed discussion on details of providing maximum accessibility to online information. It is enough to admit that the wrong design choices can provide new and needless barriers to learning for students with disabilities. On the other hand, digital information is largely display independent and can be output to meet different needs of various disability groups. We already have created the most level learning space in the history of education. There is the potential to almost remove the barriers of traditional print disabilities. One radical change resulting from increased access to information is that libraries are increasingly becoming available for users with disabilities. This exciting breakthrough is discussed in two of my articles. "The Information Highway and the Print Disabled" is a paper I delivered at the International Federation of Library Associations conference in Istanbul, Turkey in 1995 (www.rit.edu/~nrcgsh/arts/istanbul.htm) and also in "Library Without Walls" presented with Richard Banks at the (CSUN) Technology and Persons with Disabilities Eleventh Annual Conference held in Los Angeles (www.rit.edu/~nrcgsh/arts/csun96bc.htm).

The use of adapted computers has been demonstrated to significantly increase the performance of students with disabilities. At the same time, by providing independent access to much course content, the support costs for a school have been significantly reduced. Purchasing specialized hardware and software will support many students. In contrast, providing a reader for a blind student has to be done for each student and provided over and over for every course.

The Explosion of Online Learning

The Rush to Online Learning

Today the number of colleges and universities with courses or parts of courses online are a vast majority of US schools. The numbers giving online degrees is growing every year. Frequently, administrators are looking to online courses to reduce costs and to bring in new and remote students. Faculty have found that online learning is time intensive, and they find it often takes more time and work than does the traditional classroom course. If the number of students in a course is continually increased because there is no physical limit, the result will be even worse than creating larger and larger lectures. Online student/teacher ratios are at least as important in the quality of teaching and learning as they are on campus. In 1996, I highlighted this in a conference at the State University of New York conference in Oswego, NY which included a number of administrators in a talk entitled: "Distance Learning: What University Presidents Need to Know."

With budget constraints, the staff support for computing and for online teaching are being reduced as the need is increased. Faculty are being propelled into teaching online with inadequate preparation. Instead of learning from those who have gone before, they are left to struggle on their own. At conferences on distance learning, presentations are reporting discoveries that were already made a decade or more before. The original pioneers were often forced to work in isolation or small cliques ignored by traditional faculty. Now online teachers are frequently unaware of all of this history.

Impact of Courseware Interface Changes

In recent years, the interface for online learning has become graphical. It looks and functions in ways that are very similar to all of the standard graphical software in today's computer world. Most are also Web-based and are accessed using one of the standard Web browsers. The student who is familiar with using a computer and who is familiar with the Web has only a small learning curve to master the online technology required for participating in the course.

The job of online faculty has been simplified even more than that of online students. At one point, faculty had to input content directly from the keyboard while online. In other cases, they had to learn the tricks of telnet or FTP to input content to the courseware. Now, courseware will let faculty cut and paste large blocks of content from their word processor into the online course. The systems also will permit the faculty to upload content from a variety of formats by merely selecting a courseware menu item. The courseware takes care of almost all of the technical issues for the faculty without their having to understand that technology.

The resulting content is usually more visually attractive. The content can be created on the faculty person's computer on the desk at work or home. It can be done at any time and done in several steps and only uploaded when there is a finished product. Less content is created on the fly. More of it is carefully organized, edited, spell-checked, and proof-read. Obviously, this has many advantages. On the other hand, it tends to remove some of the spontaneity and freshness from the communication. By the content being developed off-line and having it edited and edited, the resulting document now reads more like traditional print documents. Frequently it is more academic and literary and perhaps even more pedantic in its style. When this is the case, student responses will model themselves after what the faculty provides, and the online experience is in danger of losing some of the immediacy of the earlier online learning experiences. Long, carefully edited presentations, lengthy audio or video, or narrated PowerPoint presentations all put the teacher back in center stage and more in control of the exchange. For anyone who is uncomfortable with losing the position of power, these technical developments make it possible for an online teacher to oppose the decentralizing features of online learning.

Actually, some course content is better suited to group discussion than is other content. Some material needs to be explained and expounded in detail before there can be any useful discussion. Other content is suited to having the student learn details and does not lend itself to discussion at all. It may need questions and clarification but not actual discussion. To the extent that this is true, then the new interfaces are opening online learning to a wider array of teaching and learning situations that can reflect the preferences of a teacher, the preferences of a learner, and the requirements of different content. This makes it even more important that the specific online technologies being used be chosen to enhance the requirements of the specific content.

Where Are We Going?

Access to email and to the Web are becoming ubiquitous. Besides the rapid growth of laptop and notebook computers, wireless and other broadband access is becoming available from work, home, hotels, coffee houses, and more. Undoubtedly, computers will soon be able to access satellite broadband from absolutely anywhere. At the same time, more and more campus courses are putting some content online. The line between working on a computer and working on the Internet will disappear for functional purposes. The line between online and classroom courses will vanish. Cell phones and other hand-held devices will function more and more like an Internet-connected, broadband computer. Learning any time from anywhere will become normal. Where course content used to be confined to the class lecture, discussion and assigned text, Web browsers and ever improving search engines will remove any wall between course material and the content of the World Wide Web. Traditional, controlled, sequential learning of content is being threatened by a more chaotic and more organic approach to learning. Whether this change undermines real learning or creates an entire paradigm shift in our understanding of the nature of learning and knowledge is an important question at the heart of today's online learning.

EASI: Equal Access to Software and Information

EASI was established in the late 1980s to collect and disseminate current know-how for colleges and universities on how to make their computer and information technology systems accessible to students with disabilities. In 1988 I gave a presentation at EDUCOM on disabilities and distance learning. I was struck that other similar presentations were given by able-bodied people talking about helping people with disabilities. As a person with a disability using the technology, I stood out. I was approached by people from the newly-formed EASI program to join them. In 1993, I became the chair of EASI. In 2000, EASI became an independent non-profit organization. I found that I was gradually changing my major focus from history into educational technology with a special interest in accessible educational technology. In 1997 I retired from full-time teaching at the Rochester Institute of Technology and my work for EASI became my passion. In 1997 I co-authored a book providing an overview on providing accessible computer and information systems for colleges and universities: *Information Access and Adaptive Technology* written with Carmela Cunningham, published by Oryx Press.

I still teach at least one online course a year for RIT. With my background in distance learning, I took EASI into distance learning as the major way to provide training on accessible information technology for university staff including administrators, instructional designers, computer support staff, faculty, librarians, and more. EASI has provided online courses to well over 4,000 people in more than three dozen countries. EASI courses can provide continuing education units, and anyone taking five courses will earn the Certificate in Accessible Information Technology. EASI's Web site is http://easi.cc and its courses are at http://easi.cc/workshop.htm.

Resources for Creating Accessible Course Content

Every college or university will have an office for disabled students. The staff of the DSS office will help students but will also usually provide assistance to faculty in preparing accessible materials for their students. Sometimes the staff are trained in human support skills and are not trained in accessible technology, but they usually can help or point faculty to other resources.

There are a number of resources on the Web, and any search engine can turn up such Web sites.

The Federal Access Board has developed the specifications for the Section 508 legislation on accessible information technology, both for on-site technology and for Web resources. It is at http://www.access-board.gov

The World Wide Web's Web Accessibility Initiative has developed a set of Web accessibility guidelines, and these are available at http://w3.org/wai

EASI: Equal Access to Software and Information provides a Certificate in Accessible Information Technology based in a series of month-long, interactive online courses (see http://easi.cc/workshop.htm).

EASI also provides two monthly series of hour-long live, interactive Web conferences providing up-to-date information on accessibility topics (see http://easi.cc/clinics.htm).

Chapter 6

An Intellectual Journey from Distance Education to Distributed Learning

Chris Dede

Chris Dede is the Timothy E. Wirth Professor of Learning Technologies at Harvard's Graduate School of Education. He is also Chair of the Learning & Teaching Area in the School. His funded research includes a grant from the National Science Foundation to aid middle school students learning science via shared virtual environments with digitized museum artifacts, a grant from the Joyce Foundation to aid the Milwaukee Public Schools in implementing a knowledge portal for teacher professional development, and a grant from Harvard to explore applications of wireless handheld devices in higher education.

This brief chapter presents an "intellectual journey" tracing the development of my ideas about learning across distance and time from the late 1980's to the present. (I did some earlier work in educational television in the late 1970's, culminating in an invited speech to the Council of Chief State School Officers in 1979, but those models of distance education were severely constrained by the limits of information technology at that time.) Over the last couple of decades, my thinking has been shaped both by ongoing shifts in technology and society and by the progression of my pedagogical strategies in a course on distance education I've offered since the early 1990's. The historical sequence of my publications on distance education is the primary source on which this chapter draws; other publications relate the insights I have gained from the evolution of my own teaching over the past decade (Dede, Whitehouse, & Brown-L'Bahy, 2002; Dede, Brown-L'Bahy, Ketelhut, & Whitehouse, 2004). Hopefully, my reflections will help readers to see the interplay between shifts in the societal and technological context of education, personal insights from research and experience, and advances in the field of distance education.

Before the World Wide Web

In the mid- to late-1980's, I worked with NASA helping them understand the implications of emerging technologies for their practices in software engineering and in astronaut training. Hearing of these studies, Linda Roberts (then at the Office of Technology Assessment, U.S. Congress) commissioned a paper synthesizing ideas about distance education from me as background for a major study she was preparing on this topic. I later published articles related to that work (Dede, 1990; Dede, 1991). The abstract for the 1990 article captures the flavor of those studies:

This article describes how our present delivery of instruction over distance could become an even more powerful and useful educational medium through incorporating ideas from cooperative learning and computer-supported cooperative work. Advances in information technology that would enhance distance learning include collaborative mimetic interfaces, direct manipulation capabilities, telepointers, automatic electronic archiving, hypertext, and specialized software for different types of interaction. Through incorporating these functionalities, distance learning environments can be designed to have greater opportunities for students to interact than traditional single-classroom settings. By overcoming pupils' segregation into homogeneous enclaves, distance learning can enhance pluralism to prepare Americans for competition in the world marketplace. Eventually, all educational institutions will need to develop students' abilities in distanced interaction, for skills of collaboration with remote team members will be as central to the future American workplace as performing structured tasks quickly was during the early stages of the industrial revolution. However, whether technology-mediated interactive learning creates a global village or an unattractive world of weakened social relationships ultimately depends upon how carefully we think through our design decisions and monitor shifts in interpersonal interaction as they emerge.

Although much of this seems routine today, at the time it was prescient. For example, pre-World Wide Web not many people were thinking about hypermedia as a factor shaping distance education, yet as early as 1987 I was publishing articles about this topic (Dede, 1987). This work was shaped by my interactions with researchers in computer supported collaborative work and in hypermedia, both fields that held their initial national research conferences in the mid-1980's.

In this early work, I also began exploring the theme of how media shape not only their messages, but also their participants. As one illustration, in the 1990 article cited earlier I described potential advantages of mediated interaction from a teaching/learning perspective:

1. Students who are less adept socially can use the limited bandwidth of textual communications to interact more effectively with others.
2. Pupils who are shy can be more expressive, given the privacy and relaxed pace of mediated communication.

3. People who are less assertive or who are methodical can formulate responses at their leisure, rather than competing with others who jump in the instant a speaker has finished talking.

4. Students who are quite emotional can temper their immediate responses by waiting to send replies.

5. People who wish to skim the messages of others rather than read in detail can do so (saving considerable time over the forced listening to an entire communication that takes place in real-time verbal interaction).

6. All users can benefit by being able to communicate simultaneously, rather than being limited to the sequential "air-time" dictated by face-to-face interaction

7. All users will enjoy the comfort, convenience, and access of interacting from their individual environments, rather than gathering at a common place of minimum mutual inconvenience.

8. All users will maturationally benefit from exposure to a wider range of cognitive, linguistic, cultural, and affective styles than they would typically encounter from a purely local group of fellow students.

Studying the many subtle aspects of individual learning styles — cognitive, affective, and social — that shape learning across distance and time has proven a challenging and rewarding endeavor far from complete.

In the Early Years of the World Wide Web

In the mid-1990's, based on my publications and teaching, I was asked to keynote three major conferences on distance education. I deliberately developed a provocative speech challenging distance educators to reinvent the field in two ways. The first challenge was to redesign the presentational instruction prevalent at that time to emphasize pedagogies in which students actively construct knowledge, using mediated interaction enabled by emerging technologies such as groupware and shared virtual environments. The second challenge was to conceptualize distance education and conventional face-to-face teaching not as a dichotomy, but as a continuum in which instructional design could develop various models for teaching/learning "distributed" across space, time, and multiple interactive media.

These talks received so much attention that I was asked to write the core article for a special issue of the *American Journal of Distance Education* (Dede, 1996). I discussed my ideas; ten invited respondents presented their views on my perspective. Since about half of these respondents agreed and half disagreed with my formulation, I felt that my two challenges were well framed in encouraging debate.

In retrospect, many of the ideas in this core article were on target for the evolution of the field. For example, an excerpt from early in my article indicates:

> The 'information superhighway' metaphor now widely used to convey the implications of high performance computing and communications is inadequate. Such an analogy is the equivalent of someone in 1896 declaring that the airplane will be the canal system of the 20th century. Backward looking metaphors focus on what we can automate — how we can use new channels to send conventional forms of content more efficiently — but miss the true innovation: redefining how we communicate and educate by using new types of messages and experiences to be more effective. Since emerging forms of representation such as hypermedia and virtual reality are in their early stages of development, we are just beginning to understand how they shape not only their messages, but also their users.

> Many people are still reeling from the first impact of high performance computing and communications: shifting from the challenge of not getting enough information to the challenge of surviving too much information. The core skill for today's workplace is not foraging for data, but filtering a plethora of incoming information. The emerging literacy we all must master requires diving into a sea of information, immersing ourselves in data to harvest patterns of knowledge just as fish extract oxygen from water via their gills. As educators, understanding how to structure learning experiences to make such immersion possible is the core of the new rhetoric. Expanding traditional definitions of literacy and rhetoric into immersion-centered experiences of interacting with information is crucial to preparing students for full participation in 21st century society... Three forms of expression are shaping the emergence of distributed learning-through-doing as a pedagogical model:
> - knowledge webs complement teachers, texts, libraries, and archives as sources of information;
> - interactions in virtual communities complement face-to-face relationships in classrooms; and
> - immersive experiences in shared synthetic environments extend learning-by-doing in real world settings.
>
> We are just beginning to understand how these representational containers can reshape the content, process, and delivery of presentation-centered distance education.

For me, conceptualizing a "distributed learning" framework arose from the challenge every sector of society faces in using new technological capabilities not to automate conventional practices, but to innovate new models of effectiveness and quality. The subsequent development of distance education has borne out many of the ideas expressed in my provocative challenges from the mid-1990's.

Creating Technological and Human Infrastructures for Distributed Learning

In recent years, I have continued my exploration of emerging technologies for learning across distance (see http://www.gse.harvard.edu/~dedech for details) and my studies of how mediated interaction shapes teaching/learning. A third theme present in my work is the development of both human and technological capacity for reconceptualizing all instruction as an appropriately designed mixture of face-to-face and mediated interaction. The economic, social, and political issues involved in creating the human part of this distributed learning infrastructure lead to interesting dilemmas, which I had the opportunity to explore in a book chapter I wrote four years ago (Dede, 2000). This excerpt from a future scenario in the chapter captures some of the challenges and opportunities now facing the field:

...Across campus, two graduates of local high schools are waiting their turn for individual consultations at the Admissions Office. Both have equivalent, above-average transcripts and want to attend college in this city, but Nick has no money to offer beyond the minimum subsidy this State provides, while Elizabeth has $150,000 from her parents to use on her postsecondary education. Nick will be offered four years of predominantly large-group classes, most from other higher education institutions taught by lecture/discussion across distance or via computer-based training software. However, he will have some local seminar classes in his junior and senior year, this campus will arrange for an unpaid internship with a regional employer, and he will receive a degree from this university. In contrast, due to her financial contribution, Elizabeth will be offered mostly small-group classes, predominantly local (although many fellow students in those classes will attend across distance, as in Vesper's instruction [Vesper is a college instructor who is the protagonist in this vignette]). Elizabeth will also have a telementoring relationship with a nationally recognized expert in whatever major she chooses and a senior-year apprenticeship guaranteed with one of her five top choices of employers.

Down the hall, the university's president chairs a meeting on their forthcoming re-accreditation. Since the last accreditation a decade ago, major shifts have occurred. Many students who enroll in this university's courses live outside this region and will graduate from other colleges, while most local students take the majority of their courses across distance from other institutions, then have these counted toward their graduation from here. Due to excellent teaching, strong scholarly reputations, and distributed collaborations with industry, the faculty are better paid and have smaller classes—they command high fees in the competitive national market for distance course enrollments. However, determining "institutional quality" in this situation is a little confusing to the group preparing for accreditation: How does one describe this type of distributed virtual organization? Who counts as students? faculty?

Before walking down to the lab to join her students, Vesper decides to have a conversation with her colleague Dimitri. Both received notifications last week about next year's salary. Vesper got a 15% raise because the spirited bidding nationally for the limited distance-based enrollments in her classes drove up the university's revenue and thus the teaching part of her wages. Unfortunately, the opposite happened to Dimitri; his salary dropped 10%, as comparable faculty across the country showed greater increases in research visibility, student performance outcomes, and learners' ratings of teaching performance. All this led to reduced fees being paid by prospective applicants to his classes and lower wages for him. Vesper is trying to cheer up Dimitri by suggesting ways he can reverse this trend. Being this subject to the laws of supply and demand is upsetting to both instructors, but that is the price of progress…

Although four years has passed since publication of this study, some of these forecasts have not materialized. However, over the next decade I believe we will see many shifts in the field of distance education toward these predictions. The maturation of distributed learning will entail not only new models of teaching/learning based on the full capabilities of computers and telecommunications, but also new types of institutional structures and professional roles based on the evolutionary reinvention of schooling.

Conclusion: Where We Are in History

I hope this brief chapter has succeeded in tracing the development of my ideas about learning across distance and time, providing from my vantage point an historical perspective on the field's development. Ultimately, although the continuing advance of technology creates an exciting succession of opportunities, realizing these visions requires the difficult process of "unlearning" traditional ways of accomplishing distance education. As I wrote in my chapter four years ago and still believe today:

In this future, keeping a balance between virtual interaction and direct interchange is important. Technology-mediated communication and experience supplement, but do not replace, immediate involvement in real settings; thoughtful and caring participation is vital for making these new capabilities truly valuable in complementing face-to-face interactions. How a medium shapes its users, as well as its message, is a central issue in understanding the transformation of distance education into distributed learning. The telephone creates conversationalists; the book develops imaginers, who can conjure a rich mental image from sparse symbols on a printed page. Much of television programming induces passive observers; other shows, such as Sesame Street and public affairs programs, can spark users' enthusiasm and enrich their perspectives. As we move beyond naive "information superhighway" concepts to envision the potential impacts of knowledge networking and distributed learning, society will face powerful new interactive media capable not only of great good, but also misuse. The most significant influence on the evolution of higher education will not be the technical development of more powerful devices, but the professional development of wise designers, educators, and learners.

I'm looking forward to participating in the next chapter of distributed learning's evolution!

References

Dede, C. (1987, November). Empowering environments, hypermedia, and microworlds. *The Computing Teacher, 15*(3), pp. 20-26.

Dede, C. (1990, Spring). The evolution of distance learning. *Journal of Research on Computing in Education, 22*(3), pp. 247-264.

Dede, C. (1991, March). Emerging technologies: Impacts on distance learning. *Annals of the American Academy for Political and Social Science, 514*, pp. 146-158.

Dede, C. (1996). Emerging technologies and distributed learning. *American Journal of Distance Education, 10*(2), pp. 4-36.

Dede, C. (2000). Emerging technologies and distributed learning in higher education. In D. Hanna (Ed.), *Higher education in an era of digital competition: Choices and challenges*, pp. 71-92. New York: Atwood.

Dede, C., Brown-L'Bahy, T., Ketelhut, D., & Whitehouse, P. (2004). Distance learning (virtual learning). In H. Bigdoli (Ed.), *The Internet encyclopedia*, pp. 549-560. New York: Wiley.

Dede, C., Whitehouse, P., & Brown-L'Bahy, T. (2002) Designing and studying learning experiences that use multiple interactive media to bridge distance and time. In C. Vrasid & G. Glass (Eds.), *Current perspectives on applied information technologies. Vol. 1: Distance education*, pp. 1-30. Greenwich, CT: Information Age Press.

Chapter 7

Hammers in Search of Nails: The Interplay of Instructional Theories, Tools, and Costs

Peter Fairweather & Mark K. Singley

Peter Fairweather works in the Learning Research and Technologies Department at the IBM T.J. Watson Research Center, concentrating on adaptive learning and instructional support systems Upon completing a doctorate at Northwestern University, he joined the professoriate but was quickly seduced by more available resources in industry. He has held posts in learning technologies companies, developing intelligent device and process simulations and the software tools to create them. He has designed interactive elementary and middle school curricula offered by several publishers and has published over 60 papers, monographs, book chapters, and a book on tools and environments for computer-mediated learning.

Mark (Kevin) Singley is a cognitive psychologist with extensive experience in the design and evaluation of interactive learning environments, with an emphasis on intelligent tutoring systems. He received his PhD from Carnegie-Mellon University in 1987 and has worked for Bell Laboratories, Educational Testing Service, and most recently IBM Research. He is currently in the Learning Research and Technologies Department at the IBM T.J. Watson Research Center and is working on a system that performs automatic pattern detection and resource retrieval to support teacher planning in K-12 classrooms.

The different forms of computer-based instruction that have emerged since the early sixties mark pauses in a long, winding conversation between those trying to conceptualize what materials and systems for teaching and learning with computers ought to be and those seeking to build such things. As with our everyday conversations, economics has deeply colored this exchange, breeding tensions, forging alliances, and changing directions in sometimes surprising but usually revealing ways.

How to Begin

Our goal is to highlight the ways that conceptualizations of instruction and the structure of design and development tools shaped one another and how both created and responded to economic pressures. Milestone efforts that neither directly instructed nor evoked special tools or representations will be passed over, even though their freedom from standardization and their flexibility often enabled them to advance the frontiers of innovation. For example, one of us assisted with the operation of early simulative business games at

Northwestern's Kellogg School of Management that had marketing tyros joust with one another, pretending to be product strategists within competing corporations. The computer was used to gather their decisions regarding such things as budget allocations or target market definitions, then evolve the inter-company competition to a new state, providing quantitative results reflecting the consequences of the students' decisions. The students acquired experience — albeit simulated — involving marketing, finance, strategic planning, collaboration, and persuasion. Effective and intense as it may have been, the computer was not involved in instructional planning or delivery. No special tools were developed for these games, their implementers battling refractory FORTRAN compilers and juggling card decks alongside the urban planners, the physicists, or the demographers. Sadly, our retrospective must overlook them.

To track the co-evolution of tools and concepts, we establish a baseline between two points in the spawning grounds of computer-based instruction: the Huntington II project at SUNY Stony Brook and the Institute for Mathematical Studies in the Social Sciences (IMSSS) at Stanford University. The Huntington II simulations focused on accurately modeling the problem space in tasks such as the eradication of an infestation of screw-worm flies or the formulation of a defense budget. Even though vintage 1971 (Eisenhower National Clearinghouse, 2003), these simulations presciently foregrounded what later became known as "learning-by-doing" (Brown, Burton, & de Kleer, 1982) and at least some of the central themes of problem-based learning (Evenson & Hmelo, 2000).

Separating Learning and Instruction

Teaching programs like the Huntington II simulations kept their focus on material to be learned by iterating through three simple steps (see Figure 1):

(1) the presentation to the learner of the state of the simulation;
(2) the acceptance of input from the learner indicating changes to part of the simulation with an eye to reaching some goal or other (e.g., pest eradication or optimized allocation); and
(3) the re-computation of the state of the simulation in response to the learner's input.

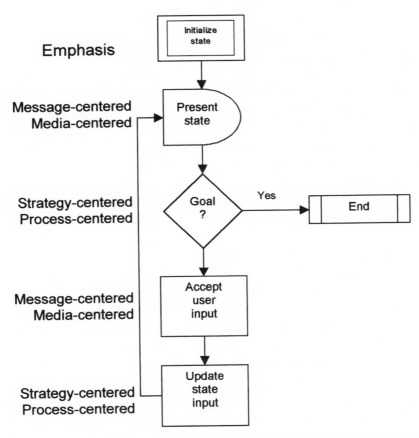

Figure 1. Early control structure providing points of emphasis for later development.

The stunning simplicity of the primitive control structure of Figure 1 seems to court the charge of banality, but we have included it as a sketch upon which to trace the major developments in the authoring of and the representational structure of computer-based instructional materials over the last forty years.

At the outset, this loop reflects the complete dissociation of the operations of teaching from those of computation, a separation illustrated by programs such as the Huntington II simulations. These programs simply avoided teaching altogether, applying computer resources instead to the representation of some process or other that the learner was to observe, test, change, and attempt to control. Instruction was left to a teacher, a manual, or, anticipating self-regulated informal learning on the Web some thirty-five years later, even to the learner.

Wrapping Learning with Instruction

Suppes and his co-workers at the Institute for Mathematical Studies in the Social Sciences at Stanford — IMSSS (Atkinson, 1968, 1972; Suppes, 1966, 1969) inaugurated a different perspective on computer use in learning, applying the computer resources to optimize the rate of learning of an individual or a class (Fletcher, 1979). By manipulating such things as task difficulty, number of practice trials, variety of feedback or session length, and experimenting across a range of candidate functions for optimization, from individual rates of skill acquisition to the utilization of expensive computer resources to even the variance of achievement test scores for a classroom, these investigators rated strategies manipulating observable, quantifiable, and behavioral attributes to best improve group and individual instruction.

Where Huntington II programs applied computers' analytical, arithmetic, and decision-making capabilities to the representation of a wide range of physical, biological, and social systems, IMSSS workers tried to represent the instructional environment in the behaviorist palette available to them. Disciplined models of instruction (and learning) of the day drew upon such notions as stimulus control, generalization, reinforcement scheduling, and interference, so they used these constructs to create representations that modeled a process, a goal they shared with the Huntington II workers. However, instead of having been drawn from the domains of physics or biology or social psychology, for example, this system was *instructional*. Moreover, where the Huntington II programs were evaluated in terms of their fidelity to the real world, the IMSSS programs attempted to optimize the system they represented. Their appearance inaugurated *strategy-centered* instruction that, because of the continuing assertiveness of the behaviorist paradigm in psychology, framed successful performance enhancement strategies in terms of observable behavioral and physical variables. (Later in the mid-eighties we will see other strategy-centered instruction, this time with a cognitive bent, which relies on the inference of a learner's progress instead of only on direct measurement.)

Factoring Common Patterns in Instructional Strategy

The scientific focus of the IMSSS work had been to identify and experimentally manipulate the salient variables that influenced students' rate of achievement in elementary reading and mathematics (Fletcher, 1979; Suppes, Fletcher, & Zanotti, 1975, 1976). Investigators there established the vivid metaphor of *trajectory* that led many to consider student achievement in almost physical terms so that knotty social engineering problems might be reduced to well understood problems such as the placement, timing, or positioning of forces to, for example, maximize the altitude reached by a projectile. This model thrived among those purveyors of computer-managed sequences of directed-instruction materials.

Seeking to generalize over the limited range of observable, directly measurable variables available to manage, early investigators factored out those elements needed to manage instruction in order to compare different instructional strategies, validating them against learner achievement data (see Figure 2). Behavior and system data types lent themselves to abstraction and standardization, given their invariance over different curriculum domains or learner characteristics. Time-on-task, elapsed time, proportion of errors, error rate, or problem difficulty level, to name a few, seemed important to the optimization of instructional strategies using computers no matter what the characteristics of the students and no matter what they were learning. Similarly, processes such as recording and retrieving score information, launching "lessons," or determining what problem the student should see next seemed to be necessary in almost all contexts.

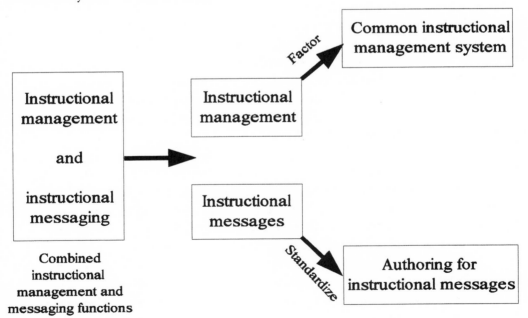

Figure 2. Abstraction and factoring of strategy and message functions.

Instead of expanding the experimental horizon for the investigation of instructional strategy, the creation of these rudimentary libraries of routines — Application Programming Interfaces (API) as we might term them today — partitioned instructional management and its optimal strategies from the content being managed: the presentation of problems, evaluation of student responses, or the presentation of feedback, for example. The list of packaged instructional management functions began to limit strategic innovation instead of supporting the development of new strategies. Freed from the problems of having to develop their own management routines with each piece of instruction, developers relied on what the toolkit offered them.

Separating instructional strategy into separate modules or libraries required that it feed on standard parameterized information about the student, the problem task, past history, and the current session, for example. The need for developers to program ways to manage instruction was transformed into the requirement that their programs communicate with a common library through this set of parameters whose channel capacity resembled a straw. Developers of created materials could count on receiving only a thin description of instructional history and context, consisting of little more than the learner's identity, directions for returning a set of scores, time and error limits to be observed, session history, or indicators of level of difficulty, for example. With such minimal information and with the realities of school settings that prevented experiments with, say, the differentiation of computer-time based on the rate of student achievement, innovative development and validation of optimal instructional management strategies withered.

The Message Becomes the Medium

Walling off instructional strategies beyond developers' bailiwicks set in relief their collective and repeated needs to compose, retrieve, display, or evaluate messages sent to or received from students using their materials. For example, developers needed to select feedback messages randomly from a pool or compose them to fit current student performance. Authors of mathematics curricula needed to generate sets of numbers with particular properties just as those in language-rich domains needed to identify correct responses independent of learners' non-standard punctuation or spelling. These common and repeated tasks related to the transaction of messages were met through the development of general subroutine or macro libraries that accepted lesson-specific content parametrically (see Figure 3).

```
LABEL:                          CALL INIT;
                           MSG = 'IN WHAT YEAR DID THE CIVIL WAR END?'
                                CALL ASK;

                           IF RES = '1861'
                                    THEN DO;
                                    MSG = ...
                                    ...
                                    GO TO _____;
                                    END;

                           IF RES = '1865'
                                    THEN DO;
                                    . . .
                                    GO TO _____;
                                    END;

                                CALL UNRECOG;
LABEL:                          CALL NEXT;
```

Figure 3. Example of a message-centered authoring template (after Meadow, Waugh, & Miller, 1968).

The dominance of message-focused development both fueled and was fortified by a proliferation of specially crafted computer languages that supported the management and manipulation of text (see Figure 4). The interpreters and compilers translating authors' directives to manage message transactions into actions or lower-level machine instructions were even supplemented by hardware, such as IBM's model 1500, a machine designed especially for the development and delivery of instruction (Szabo & Fuchs, 1999).

```
*START
T:
T: T:Please tell me your name?
A:$NAME
T:OK, $NAME, do you want to try to estimate the root?
A:
M:Y,y,Yes,absolutely,sure,OK
JY: *DOIT
J:*END
*DOIT C:#N = RND(9999)
T:The root is between 1 and 9999.
*L1: T:What is your estimate?
A:#G
T(G>N):Overestimated...
T(G<N):Underestimated...
J(G<>N):*L1
T:Your estimate equals the root.
:Try to converge on the root?
A:
M: Y,y,Yes,yes,OK, Why not
JM: *DOIT
*END T:Good-bye
E:
```

Figure 4. Example of Pilot authoring language statements (after Starkweather, 1977).

TUTOR (Sherwood, 1972), the language of the PLATO System (Wooley, 1994) not only sustained but extended the message-centered paradigm by enriching it with an unmatched armamentarium of media technologies, including what were for that era high-resolution plasma displays (512 x 512!) with touch panels and rear projection microfiche, programmable fonts, as well as provision to synchronously control external devices to deliver pre-recorded audio or slides.

While TUTOR promoted the development of message-centered materials, it provided for some innovative alternative formats as well. Masters of the TUTOR command set with its 400+ directives (Sherwood, 1972) created such sophisticated applications as a simulated fly breeding environment that demonstrated and required students to use of principles of genetics or a simulated titration procedure that enabled practice and review of a basic technique in analytic chemistry. Even rich, complex collaborative applications such as *Lotus Notes* germinated conceptually within the powerful *group notes* facility fashioned in TUTOR (University of Illinois, 1993).

However, the steep learning curve imposed by this complex language that, for most of its existence, could be learned deeply only on the steppes of central Illinois, limited most users' repertoire to less than five percent of the total command set. These included the directives necessary to position and write text, display graphics, ask questions, judge student responses, provide feedback, and jump to the next unit containing the next collection of message-handling commands. As a result, the TUTOR developer community was tiered into two layers. One tier comprised a score of artisans who invented powerful, novel learning environments, revered as classics over thirty years later. The other comprised legion journeymen developers responsible for implementing large sequences of material. Pressed to produce rapidly, they experimented little, learning what they needed to know to complete their assignments.

As TUTOR and its kin ebbed, with them died a particular genre of instructional interaction. TUTOR provided support for limited natural language interactions between the computer and the learner. Responses could be accepted and processed in various languages and echoed back to the screen with appropriate character representations. Authors could invoke what was then called "concept judgment" by specifying vocabularies of synonyms, indicating those words in student responses that could be ignored, or weighing the presence of words independent of syntactic form. Words in responses could be "stemmed" to their base morphemes and quantities and measurement units could be normalized to appropriately judge, for example, a response expected in miles that a student happened to express in furlongs.

Such constructed responses can communicate more than a key press or a touch panel input. Moreover, the availability of such tools profoundly influenced the kinds of questions computer-based materials could pose or the ways learners could direct an interaction. For example, consider the difficulty of assessing a learner's ability to plan a solution without verbal interaction. A response like, "I will save a part of the original sample for a confirmatory test and titrate what remains with a base indicator," reveals a great deal about a student's understanding of an analytical process and the ability to synthesize a sequence of steps to solve a problem. With touch panel inputs or single key responses, these sorts of assessments, if performed at all, take place while the learner performs the procedure which changes the nature of the information collected.

With tools like TUTOR removed from the workshop, costs to build such interactions from scratch led developers to abandon these kinds of interactions. It may be that today's powerful text analysis and natural language understanding tools will stimulate a recrudescence of this form of interaction.

Structure

TICCIT (Bunderson, 1974) was intended to counterpoint the laissez-faire culture of instructional development coalescing around PLATO by providing instruction informed by a rigorously articulated pedagogical strategy, Component Display Theory (Merrill, 1983). Apostles of this and other such instructional design methodologies often despaired of what they saw as the absence of structure in computer-based learning materials commonly labeled "tutorials" — the amorphous creatures defying classification that they saw teeming on PLATO. Champions of instructional theories believed that this lack of structure led benighted developers to pay too much attention to appearances that, while perhaps attractive and motivating, offered little more to positively affect learning. They denigrated the unschooled, suggesting that such developers "treated instruction as an intuitive, artistic affair" (O'Neal, *personal communication*). At the same time, they admitted that rigorously applied instructional design and development methodologies could not guarantee an interesting or attractive product, leading them to bemoan the dangers of "the seductiveness of PLATO" (Bunderson, *personal communication*).

Did TICCIT provide a structured representation whose execution invoked proper instruction leaving PLATO to stumble upon attractive but tawdry trinkets of learning? TICCIT did manage to demonstrate that exhaustive, resolute, and uniform application of an instructional strategy could be applied in the development of learning materials. However, neither the TICCIT system nor its development language, TAL (TICCIT Authoring Language) contained any constructs that represented components of the instructional strategy that differentiated TICCIT from PLATO or, for that matter, any other system. The instructional strategy, Component Display Theory, involved prescriptions about how particular classes of content, such as facts, concepts, procedures, and principles ought to be presented to learners. But because these constructs stood beyond the computational ken of TAL — it could not discern a statement of a concept from that of a fact, for example — alignment to the espoused strategy was accomplished by people rather than by computers.

Indeed, TAL strongly reflected and reinforced the message substrate of Component Display Theory. Teaching a principle, for example, called for the creation of an "expository generality," most often a textual statement of that principle. Certainly learners could be expected to induce a principle from a number of examples, but TAL itself did not support modeling of inductive reasoning. It supported only the presentation of the examples, generalities, and other message forms. Messages were developed before any instruction took place, so authors used TAL only to direct the presentation of the message. That TICCIT was to evaluate the use of video combined with computer technologies confirmed its focus on message management: video was shot and edited and referenced by TAL as something complete in itself.

The design of TAL was biased toward the management of text and video displays as well as audio messages as its power demonstrated. The element of analysis for this Component Display Theory was the presentation or, literally, the display and, while TAL's strengths made it ideal for message management, that focus left other capabilities fallow. As mentioned earlier, modeling a learner's inductive reasoning could never appear in TICCIT materials because of TAL's resolute focus on the display of prefabricated messages and the acceptance and evaluation of simple student responses.

Framing Instruction

As instructional languages made it easy to build transactions involving messages, developers found themselves repeating them in readily identifiable clusters to create menu choices, multiple choice or constructed response questions with feedback, or random selection from item pools with or without replacement, to name a few. In spite of the efficiencies of authoring languages, they offered too little to hold the costs to create computer-based learning materials at bay. As authors searched for even more productive ways to drive down costs, they seized upon the repeating clusters as a way to deal with larger functional assemblies and to reduce the complexity of having to string together individual language statements.

Tools such as Quest (Allen Communications, 2003), Authorware (Macromedia, 2003) or Toolbook (Asymetrix, 2003) enabled developers to think in terms of these clusters. For example, a "multiple-choice" frame could be filled in with the text and the graphics that formed the question prompt, the response choices accompanied by indicators of how they should be scored, and different anticipated and unanticipated answers associated with particular actions. With frame-based authoring systems, developers were relieved a bit from the error-laden chores of telling the computer *how* it should go about doing something to focus on telling the computer *what* to do instead. In other words, frame-based systems began to shift development tasks from the *procedural* domain to the *declarative*.

Frame-based authoring systems did not offer lowered development costs, reduced errors, and apparent increased productivity without exacting a price: freedom of choice. Alternatives for, say, the design of a multiple choice question or a path animation disappeared in a Hobson's choice enforced by authoring frame templates. Although most such systems did offer ways to program alternatives or additions to the basic frame catalog, they usually required someone with different skills than a typical curriculum developer.

As authors become expert with the frame set their systems offer, they begin to perceive solutions in terms of those choices. One of us worked in a learning technology company that had pioneered frame-based authoring, using it effectively in aerospace, military, and K-12 applications. We began to hear our designers express their ideas in terms of that authoring system, as if it had become a tool of analysis or, worse, a lens twisting their perception. Because most of the frame catalog within the tool addressed different forms of message transactions, the instructional materials these developers produced addressed the appearance of the objects of instruction rather than their behavior. For example, they would be able to quickly create materials targeting the name location and function of an avionics panel because their presentation and respond-by-point frames handled that sort of thing easily. Path simulations, those that interactively portrayed a panel's behavior if the student kept to a constrained sequence of responses, could be easily authored by chaining sequences of presentation and response frames together. Full state simulations, on the other hand, required experts outside the normal development staff to articulate the sophisticated control structures needed to implement them. Over time, we saw that we could not train frame-oriented curriculum developers to produce full simulations because of the sophistication of the software engineering skills they needed to build them.

Unsatisfied with the two-tiered development population, we extended the authoring system to respond to patterns in data so that simulation authors would not have to deal with such control structures involving iteration, recursion, co-routines, polling, or callbacks — the kinds of things often called for in full-blown avionics simulations. This scheme would allow authors to set up frames to be used when some event took place or the state of something changed without having to define how the frame was invoked. Moreover, authors could even work with classes of events so that they could avoid having to create anything that resembled a complex logical expression. They could, for example, specify something like "if any indicator on a panel exceeded its normal operating range then the annunciator associated with that panel should be activated." This way they could avoid having to describe events for each and every indicator.

Not one of these authors, each quite expert with sometimes more than one frame-based system, could ever build anything close to a full simulation, even after weeks of individualized training. Their difficulty seemed to be an extension of the "lexical loop" problem (Bunderson *et al.*, 1981) where the medium of instructional analysis intrudes into design and, sometimes, development. Bunderson and his colleagues noted that the text and static diagrams that gave form to instructional analysis spilled over into design, so that teaching a description of a procedure, for example, might substitute for teaching the procedure itself. Our developers had begun to perceive in terms of static frames — pictures, text, graphics, video, and audio — that proved to be a categorization inadequate to the task of representing the *behavior* of a system. Although we found it difficult to believe given their expertise with frames, these authors' perceptions interfered with acquiring different ways of thinking needed to build full simulations.

Strategy-Centered Instruction Continues

The intelligent tutoring movement contrasted with message-centered development by focusing on how learners, teachers, and domain experts thought and acted rather than what a computer and a learner might communicate back and forth. Like the early strategy-centered work begun at Stanford that emphasized the regulation of instruction, intelligent tutoring sought to exploit the calculation and decision-making capabilities that computers offered. However, instead of seeking to optimize learning by modulating the rate or duration of trials, errors, or sessions, for example, intelligent tutors decided how to conduct instruction based on the cognitive state of the student, additionally drawing upon resources such as a curriculum module, a student model, and a pedagogical tutor (Anderson *et al.*, 1990; Burns & Capps, 1988; Sleeman & Brown, 1982). Youngblut (1994) summarized intelligent tutoring efforts in military training, suggesting that their costs — roughly one million dollars per implementation — were high but justified by their unmatched effectiveness.

In spite of the long and successful history of intelligent tutoring, no set of common set of authoring tools has emerged. However, some of the ways these tutors commonly represent cognitive processes effectively shape the instructional materials developed as much as any authoring tools or development methodology considered thus far.

Although a variety of programming languages have been used to build intelligent tutors, the most frequently adopted mechanism across all of them — to realize models of learners, or domain and pedagogical experts — has been the production rule (Post, 1943):

IF any single sub-expression contains integers joined by an addition or subtraction operator
THEN make COLLECT-TERMS the current goal

Figure 5. Example of a production rule.

Production rules superficially resemble "IF-THEN" control structures in general purpose programming languages, composed as they are of *condition-action* sequences as shown in Figure 5, represented for convenience in something close to English. The power of production rules derives in part from the way their execution and data models depart from the conventional IF-THEN control structure. First, the pattern to be matched in the condition side of a production rule can be and usually is universally quantified. In other words, the pattern expresses something about *all* instances of a class of elements, not just one of them. General purpose IF-THEN or CASE control structures, on the other hand, test whether a particular element meets some condition.

Moreover, the execution model for production rule systems differs markedly from conventional programming languages. During execution, it may be that more than one rule will match parts of what is stored in memory, so the system determines which one to execute by applying a set of conflict resolution rules, "meta-rules," if you will, that help determine how regular rules will be applied. For example, if the condition patterns of two rules are such that one pattern is a subset of the other, the rule with the larger set will match more elements of the state of the system. If both are ready to "fire," the more specific one is selected for execution over the less specific candidate (unless that would violate some other, higher-priority conflict resolution rule).

This execution model enables the emergence and disappearance of data patterns to guide program execution, in contrast to imperative programming models that direct flow with sequences of control structures. Programmers do not have to deal with the problem of searching for patterns as that problem is taken over by the underlying production rule engine.

However, in spite of the ability of production rules to operate on general classes of data, the elements that are matched remain quite specific. Abstract constructs such as problems to be solved or goals to be accomplished ultimately are resolved down to small, concrete units. The algebra tutors developed at Carnegie-Mellon University (Anderson *et al.*, 1990) have emerged as a sort of reference architecture for production rule-based learning. They monitor what the learner does and bind specific actions at the user interface to rules that represent the model of a learner. What begins as, say, working through a multi-step word problem that requires the use of linear inequalities to achieve an optimal solution turns into a sequence of micro-operations such as "writing a 'greater-than' symbol" or "naming a variable." The tutor infers from, validates, and updates its model based on narrow, locally-scoped actions the learner performs with mouse and keyboard.

While the precision of the production rule is at least partially responsible for the effectiveness of such tutors, its fine-grained focus makes it a workable representation for only certain kinds of instructional tasks. For example, contrast this molecular perspective with the molar one needed to guide a reciprocal teaching session (Palincsar & Brown, 1984) aimed at developing emergent comprehension skills. An application of reciprocal teaching might involve a young reader acquiring comprehension strategies by directing a reading and discussion activity session. During the session, she asks students questions and evaluate their responses in ways that that require her to infer from the text they are reading. The form of the questions may range from evaluating the importance of information, to speculating about the writer's reasoning, to producing hypotheses about future plot elements or characters' behavior, or to locating evidence to justify claims. As these acts of planning, constructing, and posing questions become habitual and automatic parts of our student's reading repertoire, her inferential comprehension will improve.

Consider the difficulties presented if one tried to simulate reciprocal teaching sessions using the classic intelligent tutoring model presented earlier. Tutors of this type rely on a model of the learner to make predictions concerning the learner's next actions and then compare them with actual performance to confirm or adjust that model. To be computationally tractable, the set of next possible actions must be constrained. In the algebra tutors, for example, the learner is limited to a comfortably limited set of mouse selections and field entries. However, in reciprocal teaching sessions, "what happens next" commonly seems far less limited. For example, effective inferential comprehension requires not only the generation of predictive hypotheses but the rapid sloughing of those hypotheses that lack support. A tutor would not as effectively train these "hypothesis pruning" skills if it ignored unexpected hypotheses as it would if it could converse with the learner on issues of support and evidence. Because the production rule representation uses fine-grained descriptions of events to predict a learner's next actions in order to maintain the model of the learner's cognitive state, it would be difficult to use in situations such as reciprocal teaching where the catalog of such descriptions must be immense.

Farrell (2000) has pointed out that the equally well-known Lisp Tutor (Farrell, Anderson, & Reiser, 1984) proved most effective with *ab initio* training where learners' responses were constrained and predictable. With more advanced material, complex responses inevitably departed from the expected, rendering them devilishly difficult to recognize and to use as a basis for inferring what students knew how to do.

Putting Futurists Out of Work

The World Wide Web was conceived as a means to manage sharing of scientific documents, so its alignment with message-centered instruction should meet little argument. The principal representation used on the Web, HyperText Markup Language (HTML) was never intended to support instructional interactions beyond the presentation of information. The most-used method for Web communication, the HyperText Transfer Protocol, was first designed as a stateless communication medium, meaning that it interacted like a Karsakoff Syndrome patient incapable of remembering what just happened.[1] We would not expect a teacher who could not form memories of what happened in a classroom to be able to develop or pursue an instructional strategy, so when we hear the commonly-spoken phrase, "Web based instruction," we must be creative to connect it to its forebears of the sixties, seventies, and eighties.

The Web derives much of its message-focused flavor from the preponderance of learning materials it holds that were created as messages in the first place and, for that matter, often not for instructional purposes. Much of it has been produced with word-processors, spreadsheets, or presentation packages. These messages find their way into both formal and informal instruction in the form of materials for learners to read, critique, summarize, discuss, or reconstruct, for example. The management of this learning is increasingly handed over to the learners themselves, where possible and appropriate, or to Web-based instructional management systems that route learners through resources guided by occasional assessment.

Where "page-turning" was perhaps the most disparaging criticism that could be aimed at computer-based learning materials a decade ago, the Web has led "the page metaphor" to become firmly established, widely accepted, and intimately embraced by legions of instructional designers and developers as well as students. While experiments involving instructional effectiveness of such things as Web-based intelligent tutors continue, investigators now devote more attention to such things as how to effectively locate learning resources or to figure out if they can be usefully combined even though not originally designed to work together.

Despair or Delight

Looking back over the examples where tools influenced conceptualizations of instruction, where instructional theory informed tools, or where economics nudged both, we might be disappointed with the prospects of today's message-centered Web. When messages insinuate themselves too strongly, learning science and technology advances along some other front. If authoring comes to be largely replaced by assembly of re-usable components, will we have arrived there without having made concomitant progress with expertise location or the Semantic Web? We have already witnessed how the shortcomings of formal computer-based instruction helped to invigorate technologies for informal

---

[1]HTTP 1.1 provides for the directive to keep a connection between client and server open after the current request or response has completed. Most uses of the protocol do not exploit this feature, however.

learning, such as design collaboratories, expert proxies, or self-organizing knowledge-bases. Just as our technologies have led us to solidify current perspectives on instruction and learning, new technologies will lead us to refresh these and develop new ones.

References

Allen Communications. (2003). Retrieved from http:// www.allencomm.com /products/authoring_design

Anderson, J.R., Boyle, C.F., Corbett, A.T., & Lewis, M.W. (1990). Cognitive modeling and intelligent tutoring. *Artificial Intelligence, 42*, pp. 7-49.

Asymetrix Corporation. (2003). Retrieved from http://www.asymetrix.com

Atkinson, R.C. (1968). Computerized instruction and the learning process. *American Psychologist, 23*, pp. 225-239.

Atkinson, R.C. (1972). Teaching children to read using a computer. *American Psychologist, 27*, pp. 169-178.

Brown, J.S., Burton, R. R., & de Kleer, J. (1982). Pedagogical, natural language and knowledge engineering techniques in SOPHIE I, II and III. In D. Sleeman & J. S. Brown (Eds.), *Intelligent tutoring systems*, pp. 227-282. New York: Academic Press.

Brown, J.S. (1983). Learning by doing revisited for electronic learning environments. In M. A. White (Ed.), *The future of electronic learning*. Hillsdale, NJ: Lawrence Erlbaum Associates.

Bunderson, C.V. (1974). The design and production of learner-controlled courseware for the TICCIT system: A progress report. *International Journal of Man-Machine Studies, 6*, pp. 479-491.

Bunderson, C.V., Gibbons, A.S., Olsen, J.B., & Kearsley, G.P. (1981). Work models: Beyond instructional objectives. *Instructional Science, 10*, pp. 205-215.

Burns H.L., & Capps C.G. (1988). Foundations of intelligent tutoring systems: An introduction. In M.C. Polson & J.J. Richardson (Eds.), *Foundations of intelligent tutoring systems*, pp. 1-19. Hillsdale, NJ: Lawrence Erlbaum Associates.

Eisenhower National Clearinghouse. (2003). Retrieved from http://www.enc.org/ resources/records/0,1240,007567,00.shtm

Evenson, D.H., & Hmelo, C.E. (2000). *Problem-based learning: A research perspective on learning interactions*. Hillsdale, NJ: Lawrence Erlbaum Associates.

Farrell, R.G., Anderson, J.R., & Reiser, B.J. (1984). An interactive computer-based tutor for LISP. *Proceedings of AAAI 1984*, pp. 106-109.

Farrell, R.G. (2000). Personal communication.

Fletcher, J.D. (1979). The design of computer-assisted instruction in beginning reading: The Stanford projects. In L.B. Resnick & P.A. Weaver (Eds.), *Theory and practice of early reading instruction*, pp. 243-267. Hillsdale, NJ: Lawrence Erlbaum Associates.

Gibbons, A.S., & Fairweather, P.G. (2000). Computer-based instruction. In S. Tobias & J.D. Fletcher (Eds.), *Training & retraining: A handbook for business, industry, government and the military*. New York: Macmillan.

IBM (1976). *Coursewriter III, Version 3 Authors Guide*, pn:SH20-1009. Armonk, NY: IBM Corporation.

Macromedia Inc. (2003). Retrieved from http://www.macromedia.com/software/authorware.

Meadow, C.T., Waugh, D.W., & Miller, F.E. (1968). CG-1, a course generating program for computer-assisted instruction. *Proceedings of the 23rd ACM National Conference*. New York: ACM Press.

Merrill, M.D. (1983). Component display theory. In C. Reigeluth (Ed.), *Instructional design theories and models*. Hillsdale, NJ: Lawrence Erlbaum Associates.

Palincsar, A.S., & Brown, A. L. (1984). Reciprocal teaching in comprehension-fostering and comprehension-monitoring activities. *Cognition and Instruction,1*, pp. 117-175.

Post, E. (1943). Formal reduction of the general combinatorial decision problem. *American Journal of Mathematics, 65*, pp. 197-268.

Sherwood, B.A. (1972). *The TUTOR language*. Urbana, IL: CERL.

Sleeman, D., & Brown, J.S., (1982). *Intelligent tutoring systems*. New York: Academic Press.

Starkweather, J. (1977, April). Guide to 8080 PILOT, *Dr Dobbs Journal*.

Suppes, P. (1966). The uses of computers in education. *Scientific American, 3, (215)*, pp. 206-220.

Suppes, P. (1969). Computer technology and the future of education. In R. Atkinson, & H. A. Wilson (Eds.), *Computer-assisted instruction: A book of readings*, pp. 41-47. New York: Academic Press.

Suppes, P. (1979). Current trends in computer-assisted instruction. *Advances in Computers, 18*, pp. 173-229.

Suppes, P., Fletcher, J.D., & Zanotti, M. (1975). Performance models of

American Indian students on computer-assisted instruction in elementary mathematics. *Instructional Science, 4,* pp. 303-313.

Suppes, P., Fletcher, J.D., & Zanotti, M. (1976). Models of individual trajectories in computer-assisted instruction for deaf students. *Journal of Educational Psychology, 68,* pp. 117-127.

Szabo, M., & Fuchs, A. (1999). *The IBM 1500 System: Historical Perspectives.*[Online]. Available at http://www.quasar.ualberta.ca/ EDIT572/572h3.html.

Tonge, F.M. (1968). Design of a programming language for computer assisted learning, *Proceedings of the International Federation for Information Processing, Volume 2.* Dordrecht, Netherlands: Kluwer Academic Publishers.

University of Illinois (1993). Retrieved from http://www.cs.uiuc.edu/news /alumni/win93/iris.html.

Wiley, D.A. (2000).The instructional use of learning objects. Available at http://www.reusability.org/read/

Wooley, D.R. (1994). PLATO: The emergence of online community. *Computer-Mediated Communication, 1 (3).*

Youngblut, C. (1994). *Government sponsored research and development efforts in the area of intelligent tutoring systems.* Alexandria, VA: Institute for Defense Analyses.

Chapter 8

From Stir-fried Circuit Boards to Streaming Video: Perspectives from an Interactive Media Pioneer

Diane Gayeski

Diane Gayeski, PhD, is Professor of Organizational Communication, Learning & Design at Ithaca College in Ithaca, New York, and is CEO of Gayeski Analytics through which she assists clients in assessing and adopting new technologies and management systems for corporate communication and learning. She has designed and developed more than 100 interactive instructional systems since 1979. A frequent speaker, she is the author of 13 books on organizational media, new learning technologies, and management strategies for training and corporate communications.

I first encountered interactive media when I read a tiny ad in *Educational and Industrial TV Magazine* for a new video system that purported to combine the interactivity of computer-assisted instruction with the vividness of video. Interesting, I thought. Even more interesting was the fact that the company was located in Rochester, New York, about two hours away from my new home in Ithaca. Being a brand-new 25 year old professor, I was on the lookout for interesting guest speakers and this had a lot of promise. Little did I know that this technology would become the center of my professional life for the next two decades.

I called the company and was invited to a demonstration of interactive video. It was fascinating and powerful: the application they showed was created for the National Technical Institute for the Deaf and it enabled hearing-impaired students to practice their lip-reading skills. A man on videotape asked typical job interview questions, and the students responded to him via a keyboard. Somehow magically the system "understood" even rather complex phrases, the videotape shuttled to a new sequence, and the interviewer responded appropriately. The poor corporate trainers in the audience had no idea what they were seeing — I think they wondered what TV channel they were watching. The maze of wires and circuit boards that connected a refrigerator-sized mini-computer to a ¾ inch videocassette player probably took the demonstrator a day to set up. Although I couldn't understand exactly how this was all pulled off, I could see the potential in the technology and I not only invited them to make a guest presentation in my class, but I also started investigating who else was doing anything similar.

In 1980, under my direction, Ithaca College sponsored the first of what would become five annual Interactive Video workshops. This event brought out some other interesting devices, all of them rather hand-crafted systems that tied some sort of microcomputer, generally an Apple II, to either a VCR or slide projector. The next year, we got a glimpse of a prototype videodisc player from Sony. Subsequent years saw devices like the Sony Responder and the Panasonic Interactive Video System — specialized microcomputer response devices tied into videocassette players. Soon interface cards to manage the communication between a microcomputer such as an Apple II or the newly introduced IBM PCs came on the market. One year, we actually had a robot "guest speaker" that used voice recognition and speech synthesis to interact with the audience.

As I got more involved in writing and teaching about the technology, it seemed as though the world literally beat a path to my door at my house in the woods in upstate New York, where by this time I had established a little production and consulting company. People for all sorts of organizations — Xerox, the Ministry of Education of Turkey, Kodak, Troy State University, and even a psychiatric hospital in Helsinki — wanted a part of the excitement.

Exciting it was, to be sure. Interactive media was a cottage industry, made up of lots of people like myself who were concocting hardware and programs in their garages and basements. One popular card that interfaced Apple computers and VCRs was literally soldered in an electric frying pan! To be able to operate in this quirky new technological environment, one needed a lot of patience and persistence. I got to know the home telephone numbers and wives of most of the hardware and software developers because inevitably there were lots of nights and weekends struggling to complete programs for clients and demonstrations for conferences. It's a good thing that I *did* work from my own home; many a work day consisted of 21 hours, and I can vividly remember testing out a program by operating the keyboard with my toes so as not to spill my soup into the precious computer!

It's curious and somewhat sad for me to reflect on the great creativity and instructional effectiveness of many of the early programs. Few applications today match them. Many of them simulated interactive tutors who would literally talk to the learner — in response not just to simple multiple-choice questions, but to entire sentences and phrases. Probably the most creative system was the one developed by David Hon for the American Heart Association to teach CPR. It consisted of a CPR manikin, wired with all sort of sensors (many of which were parts to burglar alarms), hooked up to an Apple II computer, a videodisc player, an audiotape player, a computer monitor, and a TV monitor. A white-coated doctor on the TV monitor (coming from the videodisc) coached the learner in practicing compressions and breathing on the "dummy" — and the sensors were able to detect whether the breathing and compressions were timed and placed correctly. As the student practiced CPR, the doctor would continuously provide feedback (e.g., "that's good — the breathing is fine, but just place your hands a bit to the right").

Levels of Interactivity

The proliferation of devices and standards made the landscape of interactive learning systems in the 1980s very hard to navigate (Gayeski & Williams, 1980). Every manufacturer claimed that its system was the new standard, more powerful and easier to use than that of the competition. No two systems were compatible and all had different features. Understandably, potential adopters were confused by all of this and had no idea which system to purchase. In an attempt to make some sense of all of this, my colleague, David Williams, and I started to call all of these systems "interactive media," and we also developed a taxonomy called the "Levels of Interactivity" (Gayeski, 1985; Gayeski & Williams, 1985).

Figure 1 shows how different interactivity techniques or "levels" differ in terms of program designs that are possible as well as the hardware and programming (authoring) required. The levels start out with "direct address" in which any media program can generate an individualized and active response in the learner by merely asking rhetorical questions and thus engaging the learner in a mental "dialogue." The next level, "pause," extends this through program designs that ask the user to pause the video and then engage in some activity (such as doing some lab experiment) after which the video shows what the correct outcome should look like so that the learner can assess his/her own performance. Random access units on videotape and videodisc systems allowed users to control the flow of a video program, and directly access a certain segment by keying in a frame or segment number.

Responding devices are actually the first and lowest level of actual interactive video hardware devices. These were special-purpose units, like the Sony Responder and the Panasonic Interactive Video System, that shielded users from what were then seen as expensive and complex microcomputers while still enabling the user to respond to questions posed on a videotape. These systems consisted of two units: one for playback that consisted of a remote control-like device into which students could press a number in response to a question. The other part of the system was an authoring unit, somewhat like a videotape editing device, that the author used to mark segments and indicate where the tape should pause and where the tape should shuttle, depending on the user's response. The coding for this programming was recorded onto one audio channel of the videotape.

	Program Design	Hardware	Questions	Data Collection	Authoring
'intelligent' system	recursive	typical PC or specialized peripheral	natural language	data modifies program	sometimes AI languages
response peripheral	branching	specialized	motor responses evaluated	responses recorded and summarized	specialized programming
micro computer	branching	typical PC/ multimedia PC	constructed answers evaluated	responses recorded and summarized	authoring system / language
responding device	branching	remote controller or specialized player	multiple choice	may temporarily save last-use data	authoring device
random access	branching	remote controller	multiple choice	none	random access /remote controller
pause	linear	traditional media	self-evaluation	none	none
direct address	linear	traditional media	rhetorical	none	none

Figure 1. Levels of interactivity and interactive media.

Obviously, the types of interactions for responding devices was limited. Systems that incorporated microcomputers allowed for much more sophisticated programming, as well as open-ended user responses; for example, the learner could type in a word or phrase in response to a question. The computer programming for all of this was first done in languages such as BASIC or PASCAL, but soon specialized authoring languages and systems were developed that allowed non-programmers to create the branching and scoring required for interactive programs.

Building upon the ability of microcomputers to incorporate response peripherals other than keyboards, the next level of interactivity allows programs to respond based on motor responses of the learner. This could range from off-the-shelf devices like joysticks to specialized devices like data gloves or the

CPR manikin described above. The final level in our original levels scheme was artificial intelligence systems. In this level, programs could respond to open-ended questions through natural language programming, and programs could actually "learn" as they were used. For example, my company produced a training program for a bank. If, in responding to a question, a user typed in a word that the computer program did not "understand" (i.e., if that string of characters was not one that was programmed in as a match) rather than telling her that her response was incorrect, the program would come back with "I don't understand that word…could you use a synonym?" If the user then typed in one of the words that *was* in the original list of matches, the program would "learn" the new word. For example, if the user typed in the word "draft" instead of "check" the computer would ask to be taught the new word. If the user then responded that a "draft" was like a "check," the computer would add "draft" to its list of matches as a synonym for check, and subsequent users who typed in "draft" would then get the same response as if they had typed in "check."

Although most of the early interactive hardware devices no longer exist, it's informative to reflect back to the levels chart. Instructional designers still have a palette of interactive techniques with which to work, and some of the most powerful of these don't require any specialized programming or media at all.

The Teflon Factor

While thousands of programs were created and millions of dollars were spent on interactive media in the 80s, it seemed as though most of these initiatives never lived up to their promise. Most of my consulting work and research focused on the corporate training sector, and my observation was that training directors would be "sold" on an expensive and technically sophisticated program by a team of hardware vendors and production houses. They promised great return on investment by eliminating travel and classroom instructors, as well as great student satisfaction through the individualization of courses. What happened in most cases was that programs went over budget and beyond the deadline, and often by the time a program was ready to be deployed, either the hardware was "de-released" (talk about a euphemism!) or the content was obsolete — or both. When programs were finally distributed, more often than not the hardware failed and nobody knew how to put it back together. After the initial "Hawthorne effect" of the technology wore off, most learners found the programs to be boring. The touted interactivity was often limited to "great answer — let's proceed" or "you're wrong, try again."

To document my hunches, I conducted a study to follow up on some of the most publicized initiatives — programs that had won awards for technical or design excellence or those with big budgets that pushed the envelope of the technology. I also delved into organizations that had made a major commitment to interactive video in terms of buying hardware and gearing up their in-house training and media departments to make this a major training tool. Sadly, but not surprisingly, almost 80% of those big initiatives had stalled. Many organizations never got beyond their first videodisc. Many heads rolled in the corporate aftermath and it was very difficult to sell any type of interactive learning to those unsuccessful pioneers for years afterwards. I called the study "Videodisc and the Teflon Factor: Why Doesn't It Stick?" (Gayeski & Williams, 1989). As one of my clients quipped, "Resurrection is infinitely more difficult than birth."

The Breakthrough of the Web

In studying why most of the early interactive technologies failed, I found that the major factors were:

- Lack of standardization of hardware and programming that made it impossible for organizations to share programs or for vendors to create generic courses that could be sold to a mass market

- Inability of "ordinary people" (e.g., content experts and trainers) to produce programs themselves because of the expense of the equipment and complexity of video production and computer programming

- Difficulty in updating programs because programming was permanently "burned" into static media like videodiscs and then CD-ROMs, and because the computer programming was often very complex and not well-documented

- The "faux" interactivity of basic branching in response to simplistic questions was boring. There was no real instructor or students to clarify and discuss material.

The Internet, and specifically the World Wide Web standards, changed all of that. Finally, there was a simple, free standard for creating and distributing information and instruction. Although the first online instruction only consisted of text and rudimentary graphics, at least it could be updated, and it could be generated by "ordinary" people. Moreover, the Web allowed people to interact directly. Even simple e-mail suddenly opened the door to true collaboration. In the end, people want to interact with other people — and with those who have true subject matter credibility. All the talking "bots" and touch-screens and twirling animations can never replace that.

Where Are We Today?

The marketplace is still confused by online learning and its various terms and designs. I find that most people have formed their opinions about this technology through very limited experience with the possible instructional designs and techniques. Most of today's programs are no better than those from the early days of interactive video — in fact, they are worse. We still see too many textbooks or PowerPoint slide shows "ported" over to the Web, with a few links or silly questions inserted to make them "interactive." What we are now faced with is not primarily a problem of sorting out hardware devices: most online instruction can be delivered with a standard PC and an Internet connection. The dilemma now is understanding the various modalities of interactivity as they relate to a more constructivist learning model and a more results-oriented marketplace. Corporate training now requires programs not only to demonstrate Return on Investment (ROI), but also to support meaningful interactions that generate immediate impact on business projects. The fast-changing environment of the content of instruction, and the fact that there's often no one "expert" also requires a new approach.

I'm still developing "levels" — but in a new incarnation that my colleagues, J. Randall Nichols and Susanne Bruyere, and I refer to as "generations" of online learning (Nichols, Gayeski, & Bruyere, 2002):

The **first generation** of online experience in teaching could be characterized as a straightforward *information distribution* approach, in which the Internet allows a variety of forms of academic information to be distributed widely without regard to time or geography. The dominant educational **paradigm** of this generation is a traditional subject-matter delivery, "subject-to-consumer" approach.

The **second generation** of online experience builds on the first by adding an *interactive facility* through discussion boards and conferencing software, thereby introducing peer-to-peer communication and collaboration. The computer allows the delivery *both to and from* students of various educational resources, often in the pragmatic training mold, though still around what is usually a static or "textbook" approach.

The **third generation** of online experience incorporates the active utilization of the contemporary and ongoing workplace experience and context of the student as a source of essential data in the teaching-learning experience. The flow of workplace experience enters into reciprocal critical dialogue with relevant theory so that both are interactively critiqued and re-formed.

In 1980, I predicted that computers would become mostly communication and learning tools rather than calculating devices. Today, I predict that online learning will gradually fade away as we know it. That's not to say that we won't be doing a lot of learning that is supported by computers — quite the contrary. I see that this third generation of online learning will gradually predominate because it overcomes all the challenges that I found in the "Teflon factor" studies. Learning will assume a more natural and continuous activity, and rather than being separated from work, it will become a seamless part of work. What we now know and use as separate tools like groupware, knowledge management software, Web conferencing tools, courseware authoring programs, learning management systems, office productivity packages, human resources databases, online appraisal systems, and electronic performance support systems will exist in an integrated structure from technical, philosophical, and managerial perspectives (Gayeski & Brown, 2004).

What still matters — as it always did — are the factors that make interactive media so powerful: identification (the ability of the system to morph itself to individuals so that they feel that they are a part of the system) and attention (the program's ability to capture "mindshare" and make good use of the very scarce resources of time and brainpower in an environment of information overload).

Please excuse me … I've got to go check on a CD that's about to burn!

References

Gayeski, D. (1985). Levels of interactive video: Integrating design with hardware. *Journal of Educational Technology Systems, 13*(3), pp. 145-151.

Gayeski, D., & Brown, J. (2004, January-February). Online learning and groupware: Proposing a convergence. *Educational Technology, 44*(1), pp. 40-43.

Gayeski, D., & Williams, D.V. (1980, December). Program design for interactive video. *Educational and Industrial Television*, pp. 31-34.

Gayeski, D., & Williams, D.V. (1985). *Interactive media.* Englewood Cliffs, NJ: Prentice-Hall.

Gayeski, D., & Williams, D.V. (1989, June). Videodisc and the Teflon factor. *The Videodisc Monitor*, pp. 22-26.

Nichols, R., Gayeski, D., & Bruyere, S. (2002). "Third Generation" online education environments: A constellation of six critical issues in workplace-centered learning. *Proceedings of the Second International Conference on New Educational Environments.* Lugano, Switzerland: Eduswiss.

Chapter 9

Online Learning: From High Tech to High Touch

Chère Campbell Gibson

Chère Campbell Gibson is a Professor in the School of Human Ecology and faculty member in the graduate program in Continuing and Vocational Education at the University of Wisconsin-Madison. She brings over 25 years of experience in teaching and research on learners and learning at a distance, three national awards in distance education programming and international experience on the use of distance education for development. An author of numerous research articles on teaching and learning at a distance, she recently edited a book entitled "Distance Learners in Higher Education: Institutional Responses for Quality Outcomes."

"It was a dark and stormy night…." These seven words began each story composed by that intrepid beagle atop his doghouse in the Charles Schultz comic strip *Peanuts*. My story began about the same way.

Teaching in an inner classroom at the University of Wisconsin-Madison in the dead of winter was always an 'interesting' experience, particularly when I taught from 7:15 pm to 10:00 pm. You never knew quite what to expect when you left class and often it was a dark and stormy night! In the early 1990s I was teaching a course entitled "Designing for Distance Learning" and was teaching it face-to-face (what's wrong with this picture?) to a group of 12 advanced graduate students, all women. The gender, I'm embarrassed to say, was part of the circumstance that moved me towards teaching online. Over half of this class had to drive more than 90 miles to get home after class, often down rural roads that were windy and plowed irregularly. I worried about their safety and thought there has to be a better way than risk the lives of women in the dead of night in the winter for the sake of an education. Would I have thought the same thing, if the class were all men? I fear I wouldn't have given it another thought, to be honest.

Computers and Access to Education and Training

One solution to my dilemma was the computer. The primary focus of computers in the 1970s was on using computers in the classroom to enhance learning. In the mid-1980s the computer network environment had advanced sufficiently for postsecondary institutions to begin offering courses online, specifically via computer conferencing (Harasim *et al.*, 1995). I was personally aware of the work of those in adult education, specifically Lynn Davie at the Ontario Institute for the Studies in Education (see, for example, Davie, 1989) and Roger Hiemstra and Dan Eastmond's work at Syracuse (see for example, Eastmond, 1992). Graduate programs in adult education were often faced with practitioners who wished to gain competence in the discipline but needed time, place, and/or pace flexibility in order to balance responsibilities at work, in the home, and in the community. The computer provided one solution to enhance access to education. As a result, educators and institutional researchers explored the capability of the computer to facilitate learning and countless studies emerged focusing on the differences, or lack thereof, in accomplishments in the face-to-face environment when compared with the computer environment (see, for example, http://nt.media.hku.hk/no_sig_diff/ phenom1.html). The bottom line — I knew others had used computers to provide access to education with some success and I was determined to follow suit.

From Vision Toward Reality

Finding an instructional designer in the Computing Center wasn't that difficult surprisingly enough, but it went downhill from there. When asked if I was a facile email user, I noted I had successfully received email under our old system (whose name I never did know) but due to continual 'end of buffer problems' (whatever that meant), my success in sending was less than stellar. He now knew he had his work cut out for him. I at least knew what he meant by goals and objectives and even had some of each, for both content and process. I reminded him that not every faculty member who entered his office was perfect!

We talked about tools to make access to learning possible and initially that was my ultimate goal. Then recalling an early statistics course taught on a blue programmed learning machine when I was an undergraduate student at McGill University, a course I failed, I decided I had better consider both access and success. I felt a lot of hand holding was going to be necessary for my students and someone needed to hold mine too!

Beyond the usual instructional design discussion, we talked about tools. Frog Media was mentioned as a potential learning environment but I was told not to get my hopes up too high. They, of course, soared once I saw the tool and then we never purchased it on campus, a scenario that played out more than once for many. Our campus decided to use Eudora for Macintosh users and NuPop for the non-Mac users. We were beta-testing both as I recall. Another flag should have shot up but fools rush in where angels fear to tread. I had no idea what to even worry about. Students were to receive access to these two email tools first followed by faculty the next semester. I began my first online course with a 24K modem disguised as my sophomore son Scott in order to have access to the same tools as my students.

And so my first online class was launched. Entitled "The Adult Independent Learner" by my colleague Charles Wedemeyer, it was birthed as a listserv with the address: e-rita@students.wisc.edu. As you might guess, e-rita stood for *Educating Rita*, the old Michael Caine movie on the British Open University. It seemed apropos and I encouraged all of my students to rent the movie to get a feel for the distance learner. Little did I know how much 'feel' would begin to play into my future work.

Pre-semester I decided to go beyond my instructional designer (who had never taught online, I discovered) and found people who had actually done this sort of thing. Both Lynn Davie and Dan Eastmond provided as much counsel as they could, answering my questions and helping me discover others. I decided to work in weekly segments with a Topic Title, Overview, a listing of Readings, Actions to be taken (for example, join a listserv on distance education), and a Question to focus the initial discussion. The class would run Friday though Thursday to give my adult learners time to read on the weekend and post during the week. I doubled my reading packet to make sure students had something to read as I was not lecturing and I feared they would not be engaged in the content. Little did I know that online learners will get engaged and post on average 300 messages each in a 15 week semester!

A teaching assistant helped me throughout the course and provided computer support to the 13 students in the class. The computer center established the listserv and populated it with students, dealing early with forgotten passwords and software issues. Our 24/7/365 campus HELP line was birthed the same semester. We were all very busy and we learned a lot together.

Even before the online class was launched I had come to several new realizations — (1) faculty support, including instructional design assistance, was essential and (2) technical support was needed for both faculty and learners if we were going to provide not only access but success.

E-Rita Becomes a Reality

It was an interesting semester to say the least. An espoused humanist with a constructivist bent, I was a bit worried about this cold high tech environment. Couple my humanism with my techno-novice status and one might wonder why I even tried. But access to education was a key motivator and teaching a course on distance learners in the face-to-face classroom seemed odd at best. I needed to 'walk the talk.'

I did most everything wrong, but I was so excited, so motivated by this new adventure that I was not to be deterred. Eudora and NuPop (soon to be nicknamed NeverPop or NewPoop) remained a challenge throughout the semester although nothing insurmountable. After some degree of support, all my students were on the listserv and posting madly. I personally paid for the readers printed on campus and mailed them out to students. Checks were arriving in the return mail and we were off and running. Enter my first major faux pas — I typed the first several weeks' topic overviews in caps. Finally one student helped me understand the folly of my ways and Netiquette became part of my vocabulary. Of course emoticons arrived soon thereafter.

My greatest challenge was to sit on my hands and not respond to every posting. As a humanist I could certainly say 'guide on the side' but it seemed a bit more difficult to avoid jumping in and acting as the 'sage on the stage.' The challenge was not the computer but me! And, as a result, a community emerged, suggesting all the potential constructivists can hope for! While being a pioneer on campus as the first online class gave them a shared identity, each computer struggle, each answer to a fellow student's question, each posting in the Café about family and friends, brought them closer. Group cohesion, trust, and intimacy appeared to be growing over time in what I had first believed was a cold and impersonal environment. An oft quoted end of class posting from this first class says it all:

> *"One feeling I can't get over with this course — I feel like I have learned with my whole body....It's hard to explain, and I don't know what to make of it but when I think of this course my thoughts don't seem to come from my head. It's a physical feeling from my chest and my gut. I know it sounds dumb and it probably won't make any sense to anyone but it has been so strong and so strange that I wanted to share it. I guess I would describe it as learning with emotions as well. I have felt this course. I have given more of my inner self and revealed more of myself....If it strikes any cords with anyone I'd love to know I'm not crazy alone."*

And a response came back that said in part,

"This class has been very emotional for me — the highs and lows have been unbelievable, I think I have learned more about myself from this experience than any other class I have taken and certainly I think I can articulate ...what an adult independent learner is."

A clearer picture of these "highs and lows" hovered below the surface, a picture that I was only partially aware of in the first class I taught online. It wasn't until my next online class when I instituted a personal reflection paper focusing on comparing and contrasting learning strategies, practices, etc., in the face-to-face and online learning environments, that I came to understand the extent of these more submerged emotions. "On death and dying: A distance learner's reflections" — the title of a student's required reflective paper — certainly aroused my curiosity. What followed was one learner's reflections on learning online and her journey as a distance education student which, from her perspective, resembled Dr. Kubler Ross' (1969) stages of dying. These stages, as she reminded me in the paper, include denial, anger, bargaining, depression, and acceptance. What transpired between the first attempt at denial (that the online environment would be different than a face-to-face class) through the final stage of staring death in the face, represents, I believe, a transformational learning experience as defined by Mezirow (1991) as a result of a disorienting dilemma — that of being in the online classroom for the first time. While the flair for the dramatic was certainly unique to the writings of the learner quoted above, the journey was not. Others had traveled a similar path (Gibson, 2000).

Once more experience proved to be an excellent teacher. I began to understand the importance of learner support, not just the technical support learners and faculty may need, as alluded to earlier, but the emotional support. Helping learners learn to learn at a distance, including the assumption of new roles and responsibilities for teachers and learners, as well as learning with technology, seemed important. The process of learning loomed as a facet almost equal in importance to the acquisition of content and this process appeared to be infused with emotion.

I began to truly understand that the process of learning should engage learners both cognitively and affectively, help them see personal relevance in the content, and encourage them to develop a personal commitment and responsibility to learning in general and to the content in particular. Assisting learners to enhance their competence to engage in the content, to employ higher order thinking skills, to increase their confidence in their abilities to learn and to construct knowledge individually and in small groups all seemed critical and all were intertwined with emotion.

Emerging Research Questions

It's hard not to begin to really wonder about this environment for learning, this high tech world of words on a screen, often devoid of pictures but rich in emotions, both positive and negative. As Rowe (2003) notes, "…a review of the literature related to emotion and learning in general and emotion and *online learning* [emphasis in original] in particular, shows that both are under-researched and under-theorized topics in education" (p. 130). She continues, quoting Sylwester (1995), who asserts "Our profession [education] pays lip service to educating the whole person, but…focus[es] on the development of measurable, rational qualities" (p. 72). He later defines emotion as:

> "…*an unconscious body and brain system that alerts us to dangers and opportunities. It activates our powerful, multifaceted attention system in order to organize the myriad conscious and unconscious rational systems that our brain uses to solve the current challenge. Emotion and attention thus become pathways into all rational cognitive behavior.*"
>   (Sylwester, 1998, p. 35)

The last sentence immediately brings Gagné (1985) to mind and his Nine Events of Instruction, the first of which is Attention, which "determines the extent and nature of reception of incoming stimulation."

If emotion is important to learners and learning, countless research questions emerge related to the development and maintenance of a positive emotional climate in the online environment. But basic questions need to be answered first. What role does emotionality play in online learning? What are the interpersonal dynamics of online groups? How do learning communities emerge? How do communities create knowledge and what role(s) does emotion play in this construction? What about knowledge building discourse, the inherent emotions and the ability to foster community growth? Variables such as culturally diverse groups, group learning tasks, age, gender, and academic levels might be explored as they relate to emotional climate in online groups. What impact does a negative emotional climate have, if any, on learning in online groups and the social construction of knowledge? To what extent and in what ways are the dynamics of online instructional groups similar or dissimilar to those of a face-to-face instructional group? One might also ask, what roles facilitators and learners can play to enhance the development and maintenance of a positive emotional climate, of a learning community, etc.

General areas of research noted above and others that follow also need to consider race, class, and gender as additional overlays. Digital divides that disadvantage persons of color and those who might be considered belonging to lower socioeconomic groups need to be considered, as does gender in networked learning focused research. Research that considers these three variables is almost non-existent with few exceptions (for example, see Gibson, 2003).

The list of potential research questions could go on and on (and I do recognize we've begun to answer some of them), but first you need to have faculty teaching online to even have to worry about the answers and the faculty also need to be aware of and act on the findings of the research.

Obstacles to Online Teaching — Real or Imagined

Most faculty are unaware of the research, albeit limited, on teaching and learning online. Thus the lack of research to inform the practices of a would-be humanistic online facilitator would not be seen as an obstacle to many, but there are many other obstacles beyond the absence of research to inform practice.

Faculty members' lack of instructional system design (ISD) skills, as well insufficient faculty support for the development, implementation, and evaluation of online educational experiences are certainly considered major obstacles as others have already noted. Without ISD support from those with experience teaching online courses, faculty also find themselves with labor intensive designs. My early class provides a sad example. I can recall personally summarizing all the small group discussions at the end of every week to the delight of my learners in my first online class. It was their suggestion, and without the reflection it needed, I concurred. No one suggested that students can learn a lot if they not only take on the role of small group facilitator (requiring the posting of facilitation guidelines I might add as part of learner support) but also summarize the discussion on a block of content. No one suggested that small groups could complete, for example, the solution of a problem and a second small group could evaluate another small group's solution. In this way the learners get to revisit the content and their own understandings, identify strengths and weaknesses of the thinking of others, and convey their evaluation in a supportive manner, thus leaving the faculty member (I learned through experience) little to say once the feedback is shared between small groups.

But sometimes others have to learn for themselves. It has taken me five years to convince several colleagues who I team teach with that an online class of 30 engineering graduate students can be divided into small groups and that these small groups can engage in problem solving activities and provide feedback to other groups on their problem solutions. Part of the objection is the perception of appropriate faculty roles: learners do the work on the problems and faculty provide the feedback, especially in expensive graduate degree programs. While one can argue (and I have) that the above strategies potentially can enhance learning and decrease the amount of faculty effort, these strategies suggest new roles for teachers and learners. It is these new roles that provide one of the greatest challenges and perhaps obstacles to continued teaching AND learning online.

From early personal experience I would suggest that the greatest struggle for us all (both myself and my learners) occurred in the area of responsibility for learning and, as Mezirow (1991) might add, our personal habits of expectation. I struggled with my changing role. Initially trained as biological scientist, I'm quite at home lecturing and writing on the board, certainly more so than sitting on my hands reading learners' perspectives on the research articles of the week and their applicability to their world at large. I overstate the case perhaps, but trying to move from an espoused theory of constructivism (with a heavy overlay of humanism) to acting upon this theory is easier said than done. I did take heart as I read the following comedic but insightful comment from an online learner, "I think the most radical changes in roles occurs for the classroom leader or *The Artist Formerly Known as Teacher*." Someone appreciated my struggles.

A part of me is still the traditional teacher. Helping learners enter and examine a body of content is still my foremost agenda. For this particular class, I had a second agenda, positioning the learner in the environment of distance teaching and learning so they can live the content as I note in the syllabus. That content includes a focus on how people learn in general and at a distance in particular, with consideration given to the changing roles and responsibilities of teachers and learners.

And many of my graduate students are traditional learners, willing to take on the somewhat passive roles of information receptacles in contrast to assuming more active, time consuming roles as knowledge constructors. More questions than answers emerge in my mind. If we are to truly mine this online environment to enhance constructivist learning, how do we help the majority of learners beginning to question their conception of knowledge and their conception of learning? How do we support learners, both emotionally and cognitively, in this reflective process that often leads to perspective transformation? If learners come to understand their roles as creators of knowledge and facilitators of learning, how does this impact their learning processes, e.g., learning strategies they employ for this new networked learning? How do we help learners become more effective and efficient online group members and knowledge creators? What impact does this new understanding of roles and responsibilities have over time and across various teaching/learning experiences, including those face-to-face? The following quote gives me cause to believe that longitudinal research that begins to address these questions will be fruitful — "While these challenges (of online learning) create stress in the short term, I am certain that they are lessons I will remember in the long term."

And I had learned lessons that I will remember in the long term as well. These include the importance of faculty support, including instructional design support, as well as technical support for both teachers and learners. Learner support also emerged as important, not only netiquette and facilitator guidelines, but also helping learners develop group process and knowledge construction skills. Emotional and cognitive support to move learners into roles that may challenge their conceptions of both teaching and learning is also critical. The importance of both content and process seemed to loom large as well. Perhaps being an adult educator first and a distance educator second had ingrained in me the importance of lifelong learning and instilling in learners the skills to be independent and interdependent lifelong learners over time.

Continuing Trends

So, where to next? Dark and stormy nights will continue and access to education, either degree programs or certificate programs, will be essential for lifelong learners who hope to stay abreast or get ahead of a rapidly changing world. But will there be programs available to address the growing need for continuing education that affords learners time, place and/or pace flexibility?

One might worry about continuing growth of online teaching and learning given the lack of rewards and incentives at some institutions that may discourage those who are not innovators and early adopters (Wolcott, 2003). Urban legend suggests teaching online is very time consuming and the research to date is equivocal (DiBiase, 2000; Visser, 2000) to discourage yet others. Some faculty who have taught online have discovered that the online environment provides learners with additional access to faculty members, for better or worse, with learners more willing to let their feelings known related to content and/or process. Faculty also find it harder to maintain their usual roles in this highly interactive environment. The ability of learners to access courses from anywhere in the world has challenged faculty to learn to teach in culturally diverse classes. Many admit they are not equal to the task.

Institutions also struggle with the appropriateness of teaching and learning online for their institutional mission and vision. Private colleges who see their role as serving a unique geographically targeted audience have failed to embrace the online learning environment with its considerable upfront costs. In contrast, public institutions, especially community colleges and non-research focused universities, have embraced this new teaching medium. Some have even created free-standing online institutions as profit making arms of their publicly-funded institution. And many of these have disappeared from the higher education horizon, leaving some interested faculty with nowhere to teach, at least within their own institutions. The growth may not be sustainable.

On a more positive note, computers are becoming increasingly ubiquitous, wireless solutions are bringing connectivity to remote areas, and program designs are enabling access to education to those with disabilities. In addition, data trends show increased involvement in online learning by universities and business and industry, and increasing acceptance of online learning as research and evaluation demonstrates positive learning outcomes in terms of both content and process. The National Center for Education Statistics reported that, of those institutions, which offered distance education in 2000-2001 or planned to offer distance education courses in the next three years:

- 81% plan to use or increase use of asynchronous Internet courses
- 62% plan to use or increase use of synchronous Internet courses
- 40% plan to use or increase use of two way interactive video
- 39% plan to use or increase use of CD-ROM-based courses
- 31% plan to use or increase use of multiple mode packages
- 23% plan to use or increase use of one-way pre-recorded video

(Data source: National Center for Educational Statistics, July 2003, http://nces.ed.gov)

On the negative side, note that two of the three top trends are synchronous solutions to providing access to education. Synchronous Internet and two-way interactive video solutions will decrease learners' flexibility, in time and pace for the former, and time, pace, and place for the latter. These two solutions are non-solutions to many!

Learners will certainly continue to demand access to continuing education with flexibility in time, pace, and place, but yet another legend has emerged — learning online is a lot of work. Designs that engage learners in problem-based learning in small groups that are becoming increasingly favored by faculty do require more than one posting a week!

All in all, learners will demand access to education and the institutional support to help them move from access to education to success in learning. Faculty and their institutions that consider both access and success and provide a variety of support to make it happen will continue to thrive. That support will include not only cognitive support but also affective support and will recognize that an engaged learner is one who is engaged not only cognitively but affectively for deep learning. It's time to acknowledge the role emotions play in the education of the total person and the capability of computers to facilitate that individual and group growth!

References

Davie, L. (1989). Facilitation techniques for the online tutor. In R. Mason & A. Kaye, (Eds.), *Mindweave: Communication, computers, and distance education*, pp. 74-85. Oxford, UK: Pergamon Press.

DiBiase, D. (2000). Is distance teaching more work or less work? *American Journal of Distance Education, 14*(3), pp. 7-20.

Eastmond, D. (1992). Effective facilitation of computer conferencing. *Continuing Higher Education, 56*(1), pp. 23-34.

Gagné, R. (1985). *The conditions of learning* (4th ed.). Fort Worth, TX: Holt, Rinehart, and Winston.

Gibson, C. (2000). The ultimate disorienting dilemma: The online learning community. In D. Evans & D. Nation, *Changing university teaching: Reflections on creating educational technologies*, pp. 133-146. London: Kogan Page Publishers.

Gibson, C. (2003). Learners and learning: Theoretical foundations. In M. Moore & W. Anderson (Eds.), *Handbook of distance learning*, pp. 147-160. Mahwah, NJ: Lawrence Erlbaum Associates.

Harasim, L., Hiltz, S., Teles, L., & Turoff, M. (1996). *Learning networks: A field guide to teaching and learning online*. Cambridge, MA: The MIT Press.

Kubler-Ross, E. (1969). *On death and dying.* New York: Macmillan Publishing Co., Inc.

McDonald, J., & Gibson, C. (1998). Interpersonal dynamics and group development in computer conferencing. *The American Journal of Distance Education, 12*(1), pp. 7-25.

Mezirow, J. (1991). *Transformative dimensions of adult learning.* San Francisco, CA: Jossey-Bass.

National Center for Educational Statistics (2003). Accessed August, 2003 at http://nces.ed.gov

Rowe, J. (2003). *What do I do with my anger and fear? A narrative inquiry toward understanding emotion in online teaching and learning.* An unpublished research proposal. University of Wisconsin-Madison.

Sylwester, R. (1995). *A celebration of neurons: An educator's guide to the human brain.* Alexandria, VA: Association for Supervision and Curriculum Development.

Sylwester, R. (1998). Art for the brain's sake. *Educational Leadership, 56*(3), pp. 31-35.

Visser, J. (2000). Faculty work in developing and teaching Web-based distance courses: A case study of time and effort. *American Journal of Distance Education, 14*(3), pp. 21-33.

Wolcott, L. (2003). Dynamics of faculty participation in distance education: Motivations, incentives, and rewards. In D. Moore & W. Anderson (Eds.), *Handbook of distance education,* pp. 549-565. Mahwah, NJ: Lawrence Erlbaum Associates.

Chapter 10

The Emergence of a Networked Learning Community: Lessons Learned from Research and Practice

Peter Goodyear

Peter Goodyear is Professor of Education and co-director of the CoCo Lab at the University of Sydney, Australia. CoCo's research program focuses on collaborative learning and the co-construction of knowledge, supported by computer and communications technology. Formerly he was Professor of Educational Research and founding director of the Centre for Studies in Advanced Learning Technology (CSALT) at Lancaster University in the UK. He has been active in research and postgraduate teaching in the field of technology in higher education since 1980. Peter is editor of the international journal "Instructional Science."

Background

Fifteen years ago I began teaching on what I believe is the world's longest continuously-running online Master's program. This is the *Advanced Learning Technology* program — the ALT program — run by Lancaster University in the UK. In its first four years, the ALT program was a retraining course for people intending to move into the technology-based training (TBT) industry. Subsequently it became a professional development program for people working with advanced learning technologies who wanted a better grounding for their professional work and/or a formal qualification.

I was the founding director for the program from 1989 until 1994 and have taught on the program every year since it started. Other programs may have similar claims to longevity, though I have yet to hear one that beats us. Our colleagues in the Management School at Lancaster began their online Master's program in Management Learning at the same time, but for a while they had to give up the online mode (Hodgson & McConnell, 1992). Jean Hartley and her team at Birkbeck College in London launched their online Master's in Occupational Psychology a year before us, but found the online mode too demanding of tutor time (Tagg & Dickinson, 1995). Looking further afield one could, of course, find earlier pioneering efforts in online education, and we were influenced by people like Margaret Riel, Jim Levin, Linda Harasim, Robin Mason and Tony Kaye (Harasim, 1990; Mason & Kaye, 1989; Riel & Levin, 1990). However, as far as I can discover, none of this early innovation took the form of an ongoing postgraduate level program continuing through to the present day.

As well as being an innovative teaching program, the ALT program has been the site for several research and evaluation projects, including the European Union funded JITOL and SHARP projects. Early accounts of the program can be found in Steeples, Johnson, and Goodyear (1992) and Goodyear (1994, 1996). Students' accounts are also available (e.g., Nicholson, 1994; Watson, 1991). Papers arising from research studies based on the program include work on online teachers' beliefs and actions (Goodyear, 2002), competencies for online tutoring (Goodyear *et al.*, 2001), design intentions (Jones, Asensio, & Goodyear, 2000), the nature of just-in-time support for professional learning in distributed communities (Goodyear, 1995; Goodyear & Steeples, 1993) and the use of multimedia representations of working practices in distributed collaborative professional learning (Goodyear & Steeples, 1998, 1999).

This chapter falls into three main parts. In the first, I sketch the initial version of the ALT program (1989-1993), attempting to capture some of the distinctive qualities of online education as we then experienced it. In the second, I describe the ALT program ten years later, highlighting shifts in pedagogy and technology but also some of the special features of working with the ongoing learning community we helped create. In the third and final section I take a dangerous step and speculate about future directions.

The Lancaster interpretation of online education has been quite distinctive. Pedagogically, there are strong roots in student-centered education and open learning, and a high value is placed on learning through collaboration and dialogue — especially where the learners are experienced professionals and much of the most valuable knowledge in their field is embedded in innovative working practices. Technologically supported interaction between people has always been more important to us than (say) access to online learning materials. Our preference has been to call this style of education *networked learning* — learning in which technology is used to promote connections: between one learner and other learners; between learners and tutors; between a learning community and its learning resources (Steeples & Jones, 2002).

The ALT Program 1989-1993

The initial version of the ALT program was designed and developed by two academics (Robin Johnson and myself) and an administrator (Alison Sedgwick) in less than four months. At the time, the dominant model for creating distance learning courses was that used by the UK Open University, which was reputed to take five years to prepare a new program and another eight to recoup its investment. We were funded by a UK government department to demonstrate that it was possible to take a more flexible and timely approach to the creation of distance learning courses using new technology. This was seen by the government as of strategic national importance, given much that was then being proclaimed about the emergence of the knowledge economy, the dwindling half-life of professional knowledge, the need for regular retraining, etc. The Open University was master of the use of text and TV and used large multidisciplinary course teams — and the BBC — to produce very high quality learning resources. Our alternative approach involved reducing the upfront development time and costs by at least an order of magnitude and shifting resources into providing higher levels of tutorial support for the students during the period of their study. This tutorial support would be provided by email and would capitalize on peer support provided by the learners themselves. We produced almost no learning materials of our own. Instead — for good and bad reasons — we insisted that the students read material from the emerging research and professional literatures, supplemented with one or two textbooks that covered some of the more established areas of learning theory, instructional design, software design, and project management.

The first cohort of students began the program in October 1989. The UK government funding given to the program — part of the High Technology National Training scheme (HTNT) — was intended to allow us to recruit unemployed graduates and train them to work as instructional designers in the fledgling TBT industry. The course was one year full-time and included a four month 'industrial placement' during which the student would work in a TBT company or in the TBT branch of a major corporate or public sector organization. Prior to the launch of the Lancaster ALT program, it was almost impossible to get a postgraduate-level qualification in the field of instructional design and development in the UK. There was no equivalent of the Masters programs in ISD found at universities in North America.

Students came from a variety of backgrounds. Many had never touched a computer before. Their ages ranged from mid 20s to late 50s. Almost half of the students were women (compared to 13% female on the HTNT schemes nationally). The government funding rules were meant to ensure that the students' chances of completing the program would not be affected by their income levels — all the additional costs of participating in the program had to be covered by us as program providers. We loaned each student a Macintosh computer, printer, modem, all the software needed for the course, and a collection of course readings and text books. We covered their dial-up phone bills and the costs of the travel to Lancaster. The key points to make here are that we were working with students who:

(a) were out of a job and typically had no money beyond the small weekly allowance provided by the government; they were all from time to time affected by major distractions and disruptions — from family crises to problems with landlords; and

(b) had little technological experience, no direct experience of the industry for which they were being trained, no exposure to learning theory, instructional design, or courseware authoring skills, little experience of collaborative learning and no experience of learning online; at this time (late 80's early 90's) it was rare to meet a student who had ever used email, let alone one who could immediately see how email might be of some use in tertiary education.

The students were recruited from all parts of the UK and spent most of their study time at home. The main period of their study was broken up into five-week study blocks, each of which was preceded by an intensive residential study week at Lancaster. (We did not know it at the time but we were pioneering 'blended learning'.) In their first residential study week with us — the first week of the course — we had to get them to a point of technical self-sufficiency such that, when they got home, they would be able to assemble their hardware, make a dial-up connection through to the Symmetry (the central Unix computer at Lancaster), and send an email to the tutor team. Once they could do that, we could help them.

The technical support available to new computer users 15 years ago was generally very poor. Campus-based users in universities could call on a central helpdesk or support system, but to the home-based user very little help was available. There were few books or magazines. The culture was not imbued with computer technology. Very few homes possessed a computer. Very few of our ALT students had used a computer in school. There was no World Wide Web, only a rudimentary form of the Internet, no ISPs, no retailers with a strong interest in educating a mass market of potential computer purchasers.

In addition, networking and email connectivity was still rudimentary, as were the software applications available for email and computer conferencing. Not until 2-3 years into the program (around 1992) did I have email on my desktop. To communicate with my students I had to walk to a shared terminal room and log in to the Symmetry. If I wanted to print an email, it appeared on line-printer paper that I had to collect from the University's computer center. The students were in a rather more luxurious position — in the sense that they had email to their desktops and had local printers — though they rarely had a quiet or convenient space to work at home.

Although the Macs had a windows-icons-mouse interface, email had to be done in 'terminal' mode. To summarize the online environment then:

(1) emails could not be prepared off-line but had to be written while connected to the Symmetry;

(2) emails had to be composed using a line editor interface — you could edit the current line but there was no easy way to 'scroll back' to change earlier lines in a message;

(3) the connection with the Symmetry was unreliable — a connection lasting more than 30 minutes was rare;

(4) even when the connections were working they were very slow (300 baud or about 200 times slower than a 56k modem line); and

(5) the number of connections into the Symmetry proved a serious bottleneck, even for students used to working through the night; it would often take 10-20 attempts to dial in before a connection was achieved.

What did this configuration of technologies afford? Unsurprisingly, students did not engage in leisurely construction of long, considered messages. When they managed to get online, they would focus on priority communications, determined to catch up on emails from their peers, and important announcements from the course team, before losing their connection.

During the five-week-long home-based study periods, students were required to use email at least once a week. As a minimum, they had to let us know they were still alive and thinking. The role of email in the success of the program is still quite hard to unravel. In designing the course, we had imagined that the main purposes of email would be:

(a) to allow students to ask tutors for specific help and guidance, e.g. in clarifying the meaning of something in the reading materials;

(b) to allow us to hold 'electronic seminars,' as a substitute for face-to-face discussions on campus; and

(c) to facilitate communication about administrative matters, e.g., arrangements for forthcoming residential study periods.

In actuality, uses (a) and (b) proved much rarer than we anticipated. Use (c) on its own probably paid for the costs of setting up an ICT infrastructure in the first place. But the most highly valued contribution of the email network was for *moral support* among the student group (Watson, 1991). Home-based study gave all of them a great amount of flexibility in how they organized their work, and this flexibility was essential for many of the students. (For example, it was the main factor enabling women on our program to make the transitions from raising children to studying to getting a job.) However, one of its costs was the deep sense of isolation felt by many of the students, especially when the going got tough on an into-the-small-hours programming assignment. At such times, email messages from colleagues arrived as if from a comforting 'voice in the dark' (as it came to be known among the students). The system we set up made it relatively easy for students to send private or group messages to each other, without the staff being able to see what was being said. This private channel did a great deal to build group solidarity and help individual students air their problems and give shape to their worries and grievances (Watson, 1991).

Although the email system was used less than we anticipated, and in different ways, we — and the students — were completely convinced that the program would have foundered without it.

On most indicators, this early version of the program would be judged a success. We recruited a full cohort each year, and had to turn away between five and ten applicants for each place. Of the 74 students who passed through the program, 65 graduated, 14 with a distinction. External examiner's reports were full of praise. The sponsor's target of 80% in relevant employment or further training was met each year. Staff enjoyed teaching on the program, though signs of fatigue began to show by the fourth year.

What of the student experience? There is no denying that the full-time version of the ALT program was a tough course. There were 14 pieces of assessed work — three in the first six weeks. The varied nature of the modules meant that students had to acquire and integrate skills and knowledge of many different kinds and from many different sources. Flexibility was highly valued, but brought isolation and made huge demands on students' powers of self-motivation, organization, persistence, and ability to solve problems for themselves. Those who learned to succeed on the course demonstrated these attributes very clearly. Most of the negative feelings that students expressed about the course came at the second residential study period; that is, after the first five-week period of home-based study. By this point, most of the students were emerging from shock and realizing that not all of their problems stemmed from their own inadequacy; many were intrinsic to the program and to distance-learning more generally.

Specific and recurring problems tended to be focused around the intellectual demands of the course, the difficulty of some of the original reading matter in the study packs (notoriously, the tortured language used by some American instructional design experts), and unreliable technology. The evaluation session in the second residential week normally took one and a half full days. It proved crucial in establishing a shared set of understandings and expectations among students and staff.

The strongest *positive* feelings were expressed in the first month of their industrial placement — after 25 weeks or so of full-time study. Many of the students were surprised to discover that much of what we had been teaching them was actually applicable in the workplace. They spoke of 'everything coming together' — the many separate elements of the taught program beginning to cohere and links strengthen. They also reported on the almost universal absence of formal qualifications among their workmates; the lack of a principled underpinning to much of the work that was going on around them; the ad-hoc and inefficient methods being used, and the tendency for projects to be driven by technological possibilities rather than learning needs. (Most of the students were smart enough not to voice these feelings in the workplace. Email communications between them, during the industrial placement, were important in sharing startled insights into the TBT industry.)

As for the students' working practice, and especially those connected with the online aspects of the program, I would single out the following:

1. Students would use email on at least a daily basis. Catching up with the general mails and with messages from friends on the course was a routine practice; important in helping the student develop and maintain their sense of themselves as active and engaged participants who were coping with the demands of the program.

2. This regular use of email enabled the course team to make email the standard method of communicating course requirements to students; arrangements for upcoming residentials, specifications for assessment tasks, information about industrial placements, etc. This clearly distinguished the program from contemporary distance learning programs that relied on postal correspondence from center to periphery and that provided little by way of peer or informal interaction.

3. Email sustained and strengthened individual and small group relationships during the five-week home-based study periods; relationships that developed during, and gave character to, the intense one-week residential study periods at Lancaster.

4. In managing their email correspondence, students did not spontaneously value question-asking or opinion-sharing initiated by their peers. On one interpretation, these 'self-indulgent' emails were seen as distractions from the main online tasks involved in 1-3 above. That is, they got in the way of the main business, which was either administrative or social. Managing relationships, attending to your identity and sense of self within your network of relationships, ensuring that you do not miss important course announcements or assessment requirements are much more important than (perhaps) learning something by reading the comments or questions of your peers.

5. Online discussion of course content *did* take place, but not spontaneously. It certainly happened when the students thought they were being assessed on their contributions to online seminar-type discussions and where a clear task-structure was provided for the students. Such situations would generate more than a ten-fold increase in

the volume of student contributions (see Goodyear, 1996, for a detailed analysis).

6. Did students routinely use online information resources? No. This was the world before the Web. Their use of online technology was restricted entirely to human-human communication. Surfing was something the Beach Boys sang about.

I now want to track forward to the ALT program ten years later. The first students joined this part-time, professional development version of the program in January 1992, and it is this date which marks the real beginning of an extant online learning community. From the outset, students could join the program at any one of six starting points each year. Since they typically take 2-3 years to complete the program, this means that the small number of new students joining the program at any point are greatly outnumbered by students who have been involved in the program for a year or more — the new students are inducted into the life and study practices, the culture and expectations of an established community.

The ALT Program at the Turn of the Century

Employers began to show interest in having their *current* employees benefit from some systematic training, so in 1992 we began offering a part-time version of the ALT program. Like the full-time program, this led to an M.Sc. degree. Most of the study was done at home (or, more rarely, at work) in modules lasting 12 weeks. Each also involved two days of intensive residential study at Lancaster. The part-time program underwent radical overhaul around 1998-9 and I will focus here on the program as it runs currently.

A major change in our pedagogical approach was necessitated by the shift from training new recruits for industry to the provision of professional development opportunities for experienced workers. Underpinning the new approach was our conviction, mentioned above, that much of what is worth learning in a rapidly changing field of practice already exists as 'working knowledge' embedded in the working practices of professionals in the field. Research-based knowledge still plays a role. Our intent was to move away from a notion of theoretical understanding preceding, or being privileged over, practical knowledge. We wanted to facilitate the sharing of working knowledge within what might optimistically be described as a community of practice and to help improve the quality of working practices through — among other things — a serious and ongoing conversation with research-based knowledge.

Figure 1 helps convey the spirit of our pedagogical intentions. There is nothing new about the idea of a learning cycle or of personal development as something which could be imagined as taking a spiral trajectory. We were well aware of the work of Kolb and others (e.g., Kolb, 1984). Nor did we make any original claims about the power of reflection as an aid to the improvement of professional practice. But the following, we can reasonably claim, are distinctive features of the approach we have sought to implement.

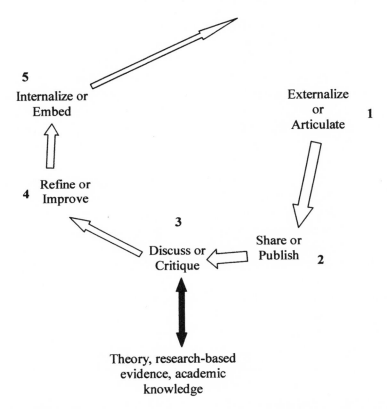

Figure 1: The Professional Development Cycle in a Distributed Learning Community.

First, we need to describe the cycle. The point of departure is some area of working practice. Professional knowledge is both situated and distributed. The process starts with someone constructing a shareable representation of a working practice, and of the knowledge embedded in it. This is no easy matter. It involves careful and honest self-observation and an attempt to articulate the tacit knowledge of practice. Keeping the focus tight and the objects of concern quite concrete helps enormously. A simple attempt by a worker to describe 'how we do things here' (in our company or in our team) — in relation to a small and well-bounded area of practice — is the starting point. In general, the description has to be rendered as text — as a written description of context, problem, solution, rationale, etc. Production of this representation of practice must give enough of the context to render the representation comprehensible to others working in the field, but it must also involve enough abstraction for them to recognize the problems faced, or solutions used, as being similar to things which preoccupy them in their own work. The representation is created so that it can be shared within the learning community. If it exists as text then it is a simple matter to make it available as (say) an entry on a web-based discussion board.

The third step is for members of the community to discuss and critique what is captured in the representation. This can be for one of several purposes: to improve their own understanding of what has been written, to make comparisons with their own practices (or practices of which they know), to bring in new ideas, question or evaluate, or suggest better ways of doing things or better conceptualizations of a problem. But discussion and critique are not enough. The cycle moves back towards the field of practice. The fourth step involves an effort to refine or improve the working practice initially represented. The fifth involves embedding improved working methods — or new 'working knowledge' — back into the field of practice. A common way of doing this, in the ALT program, is through the creation of a new tool of some kind. That is, the practitioner(s) who are most involved with the practice that is in focus develop some kind of performance-support tool or procedural aid that can be used in their workplace. New or improved working knowledge becomes recontextualized and becomes physically and socially situated once more. Naturally enough, we see this as a process which may pause or change focus, but not stop — hence the notion of a professional development cycle or spiral.

The second aspect of Figure 1 that needs explanation is where we, as academics, add value to the process. This happens in two main ways. We help structure the discussion and critique phase of the learning cycle so that participants draw on relevant areas of theory or research evidence in making their contributions. At a micro level, this promotes a 'conversation' between theoretical ideas and evidence (on the one hand) and working knowledge and practice (on the other). At a meso level, we learn from the field of practice and construct abstractions about working methods and working knowledge — we theorize practice and help systematize elements of the knowledge base for practice.

How does this work out in actuality? The technology we have been using since the mid 90s is based on the Lotus Notes platform and most students favor use of the Web interface to Notes. We start one new Notes database with each new course module; students can read the databases from previous generations of the module if they wish. Some program-wide databases are also maintained (such as a Café for general social discussions, etc). A team of two or three tutors manages a module. They have responsibility for designing a set of tasks for the students. These tasks will map onto one or more steps in the learning cycle depicted in Figure 1. For example, a task set for the first week will often be to write a definition of a key concept from the intellectual space covered by the module and situate that definition in the student's own work context. ('What do you mean when you talk about "learning" in your workplace? How do you know that learning has happened?') Or, to take another example, a task may require each student separately to write a description of how the evaluation tools used in their organization embody a particular interpretation of learning or competence. Students will then be asked to read all the descriptions, identify similarities and differences, evaluate strengths and weaknesses, etc. Later in the module, when students are turning to their main, assessed, task, they are likely to take on a project which involves a change to working practices, such as the construction of a performance support tool along the lines described above.

Student contributions to the online space are much more frequent and extensive than we saw with the full-time course ten years previously. Increased reliability and speed of communications and better software are part of the story. At least as important is the fact that the learning community has established a set of expectations about participation, and these expectations are passed on (made visible) to new students. The unasked question is, 'if you aren't going to contribute to the online space, why have you come here?' To give some sense of the scale of contribution, students will typically be submitting the equivalent of 500-1000 words a week and often more. This is without *any* additional tutor input (other than the initial set of task specifications). This contrasts sharply with experiences in many other online courses, where tutors report having to use grades to encourage students to contribute to online discussions, or having to spend unsustainable amounts of their own time and energy trying to stimulate and manage discussions.

Although there is always a sense that things can be improved, the ALT program in its current state seems to embody a number of characteristics of success. Students recognize and respond to the underpinning pedagogical approach. They engage very actively and constructively with the online tasks we set. They tell us that what they learn is highly relevant for their own professional practice and for that of their workmates and employing organizations. External examiners report that the academic quality and vocational relevance of the program mark it out as the best in the country. Students and tutors have created between them an ongoing networked learning community, capable of sustaining itself over time and passing on a positive set of values and practices with respect to productive online learning.

Ten Years After

Assessing what we have achieved on the ALT program, I am struck by how sharply it contrasts with what might be regarded as 'mainstream' practice in online education — particularly in the field where teachers, trainers, and managers have rushed to adopt the terminology of e-learning and the technology of Virtual Learning Environments or Learning Management Systems. The ALT program can be viewed as successful but in a small and distinctive niche. Critics claim it is not scalable and that mass e-learning in higher education requires the whole panoply of managed learning, reusable learning objects, standards, content management tools, remote students, casualized (adjunct) teachers, and a general shift from "bricks to clicks." So where do I expect the ALT program to be a decade from now?

I will start with technology and will assume that the main positive change in this direction will be the ability to deal effortlessly with multimedia communications. When talking about the creation of shareable representations of working practices, above, I mentioned that the main representational form was text. Text has many virtues, but it is an awkward thing with which to represent practice. In recent research projects we have experimented with using digital video and audio to create shareable representations of practice (for use in the kind of learning cycle depicted in Figure 1). It turns out that professionals working in the ALT/TBT field need combinations of audio, video, and text to create and discuss such representations efficiently. We have produced some assessments of the affordances of various kinds of multimedia representations (see, e.g., Goodyear & Steeples, 1999). What becomes clear from this work is that limitations in the currently deployed technology are serious impediments to the use of multimedia representations of practice and to proper exploitation of the pedagogical model to which we subscribe. Of course one *can* share photographs, sound files, and videoclips in emails or on the Web. But that is different from being able to work as effortlessly in an asynchronous multimedia conferencing environment as one can, currently, in a text-based asynchronous conferencing environment. I will assume that, over the next ten years, the tools for digital video/audio capture will become cheap enough to be virtually ubiquitous and that we will have an asynchronous multimedia conferencing platform that will be robust and easy to use. If so, then I do not see our pedagogical intentions changing dramatically. After all, we were first captivated by notions of sharing representations of practice, and creating reifications of working knowledge, during our experiments in the JITOL project back in the early 90s. Pedagogy moves more slowly than technology.

How widely our vision will be shared by others is not a question I approach with any great optimism. There are powerful forces at work shaping contemporary visions of e-learning. Companies with e-learning products to sell have a vested interest in marginalizing pedagogies that demand functionality their products don't provide. Managers in companies have eyes on the bottom line; on the reduction of training costs rather than enhancing the quality and relevance of learning — slippery benefits whose presence is hard to prove. Managers in universities have one eye on costs and another on accountability — on quality audits and QA protocols. Both sets of managers have bought into e-learning with an appetite never previously seen in the field of educational technology and one wonders about the size of the backlash when they realise this was not a one-time investment.

But I will try to end on a positive note. In my 15 years as an online teacher-researcher, the technology I have been using has moved from being strange, esoteric, and unreliable to a point at which it is central to life and work in all developed economies. The improvement of this technology is no longer the responsibility of a small and wayward cadre of technicians — many millions of users of online technologies now care about the quality of the facilities available to them. Moreover, the kinds of things I want to do as a teacher are the kinds of things everyone wants to do with this technology — share experiences, passions, and plans; stay in touch. The companies and managers who are currently promoting distorted, half-baked visions of learning, as something which can be commodified and 'delivered,' will recognize their mistakes as inexplicable, transient aberrations…and the moon will turn out to be made of green cheese.

Acknowledgment

Work on this chapter has benefited from the support of an internal research grant from the University of Sydney's Sesquicentenary fund. The research projects and teaching innovations on which this chapter draws have been funded from a range of sources, but especially from the European Commission and from various agencies of what is now the UK Department for Education and Skills. I have been very lucky to work closely with a band of online learning pioneers and would especially like to thank Christine Steeples, Chris Jones, Viv Hodgson, Bob Lewis, Mireia Asensio, David McConnell, Robin Johnson, Mike O'Donoghue, Alison Sedgwick, and Alice Jesmont for all their help, encouragement, and stimulating company over the years. They do not share all my views and I take full responsibility for what is written here.

References

Goodyear, P. (1994). Telematics, flexible and distance learning in postgraduate education. *CTISS File (Journal of the Computers in Teaching Initiative Support Service)*, *17*.

Goodyear, P. (1995). Situated action and distributed knowledge: A JITOL perspective on electronic performance support systems. *Educational and Training Technology International, 32*(1), pp. 45-55.

Goodyear, P. (1996). Asynchronous peer interaction in distance education: the evolution of goals, practices, and technology. *Training Research Journal, 1*, pp.71-102.

Goodyear, P. (2002). Teaching online. In N. Hativa & P. Goodyear (Eds.), *Teacher thinking, beliefs, and knowledge in higher education* (pp. 79-101). Dordrecht: Kluwer Academic Publishers.

Goodyear, P., & Steeples, C. (1993). Computer-mediated communication in the professional development of workers in the advanced learning technologies industry. In J. Eccleston, B. Barta, & R. Hambusch (Eds.), *The computer-mediated education of information technology professionals and advanced end-users* (pp. 239-247). Amsterdam: Elsevier.

Goodyear, P., & Steeples, C. (1998). Creating shareable representations of practice. *Association for Learning Technology Journal, 6*(3), pp. 16-23.

Goodyear, P., & Steeples, C. (1999). Asynchronous multimedia conferencing in continuing professional development: Issues in the representation of practice through user-created videoclips. *Distance Education, 20*(1), pp. 31-48.

Goodyear, P., Salmon, G., Spector, M., Steeples, C., & Tickner, T. (2001). Competences for online teaching. *Educational Technology Research & Development, 49*(1), pp. 65-72.

Harasim, L. (1990). *Online education: Perspectives on a new environment.* New York: Praeger.

Hodgson, V., & McConnell, D. (1992). IT based open learning: A case study in management learning. *Journal of Computer Assisted Learning, 8*, pp. 136-150.

Jones, C., Asensio, M., & Goodyear, P. (2000). Networked learning in higher education: Practitioners' perspectives. *Journal of the Association for Learning Technology, 8*(2), pp. 18-28.

Kolb, D. (1984). *Experiential learning.* New York: Prentice Hall.

Kollock, P. (1999). The economies of online collaboration: Gifts and public goods in cyberspace. In M. Smith & P. Kollock (Eds.), *Communities in cyberspace* (pp. 220-239). London: Routledge.

Mason, R., & Kaye, A. (Eds.). (1989). *Mindweave: Communication, computers, and distance education.* Oxford: Pergamon.

Nicholson, A. (1994). The MSc in Information Technology and Learning at Lancaster University: A student perspective. *CTISS File, 17.*

Riel, M.M., & Levin, J.A. (1990). Building electronic communities: Success and failure in computer networking. *Instructional Science, 19*, pp. 145-169.

Steeples, C., Johnson, R., & Goodyear, P. (1992). The rationale and design of the MSc Information Technology and Learning course. In G. Holmes (Ed.), *Integrating learning technology into the curriculum* (pp. 13-17). Oxford: Computers in Teaching Initiative.

Steeples, C., & Jones, C. (Eds.). (2002). *Networked learning: Perspectives and issues.* London: Springer.

Tagg, A., & Dickinson, J. (1995). Tutor messaging and its effectiveness in encouraging student participation on computer conferences. *Journal of Distance Education, 2*, pp. 33-55.

Watson, J. (1991). *An evaluation of a distance learning course: The Lancaster MSc in Information Technology and Learning.* Unpublished MSc, Lancaster University, Lancaster.

Chapter 11

Curriculum-Based Telecomputing:
What Was Old Could Be New Again

Judi Harris

Judi Harris is the Pavey Family Chair in Educational Technology in the School of Education at the College of William & Mary in Virginia. Her scholarship and service focus upon curriculum-based telecomputing, telementoring, and authentic professional development. Judi directs "The Electronic Emissary" (http://emissary.wm.edu), a K-12 curriculum-oriented telementoring service and research effort, and was the founding director for "WINGS Online" (http://wings.utexas.org), a suite of online support services for novice teachers at the University of Texas at Austin. Her "activity structures" method of designing and implementing curriculum-based telecollaborative, telecooperative, and teleresearch learning activities, first published in 1993, is used by K-12 teachers and teacher educators worldwide. She received her PhD from the University of Virginia.

We need to haunt the house of history and listen anew to the ancestors' wisdom.
Maya Angelou

For more than 30 years, the International Society for Technology in Education (ISTE) and its parent organizations, the International Council for Computers in Education and International Association for Computing in Education, have been assisting elementary, middle-level, secondary, and teacher educators to use educational technologies to support and transform students' learning. ISTE's premier publication for practitioners, *Learning & Leading with Technology (L&L)*, formerly *The Computing Teacher* and *Oregon Computing Teacher*, is one of the oldest educational technology magazines read and used by classroom teachers, technology specialists, and teacher educators worldwide.

L&L has published my articles for educators regularly since May 1988, and my work supporting K-12 curriculum-based telecomputing since August 1992. (For a list of selected educational telecomputing publications, please see the bibliography at the end of this chapter.) I have been helping students to learn with computers since 1980 — first as an elementary school teacher, adding part-time graduate-level instruction in 1983 — then as a full-time university faculty member in curriculum and instruction beginning in 1990. I have been teaching with online tools and resources since 1981, first with elementary and middle-level students, then as a teacher educator. My predominant interest during all of these years has been integrating use of educational technologies— especially those available via networks— into K-12 curricula.

During the 15+ years that I have been working with *L&L*'s editorial staff as a contributing author, much has changed in educational computing. A recent examination of some specific patterns within that change, though, revealed some surprises — and, in turn — a worthwhile way to connect what educational telecomputing pioneers did more than a decade ago to where curriculum-based telecomputing should be going in the next decade.

Since December 1978, *L&L*'s authors have been sharing ideas about how to use online tools and resources to assist students' learning. What kinds of curriculum-based, Internet-enriched learning activities have been introduced in this venerable publication during the past twenty-five years? More importantly, what can we learn about the future of curriculum-based telecomputing by examining the patterns of its past?

Today's Telecomputing

Today, 94-99% of elementary, middle-level, and secondary students and teachers in Australia, Canada, the United Kingdom, and the United States have instructional access to online tools and resources at school, with an ever-growing majority also using the Internet at home. In a 2002 study sponsored by the Pew Internet & American Life Project, students were asked to describe their educational uses of the Internet. The study's researchers reported that:

> *Virtually all use the Internet to do research to help them write papers or complete class work or homework assignments. Most students also correspond with other online classmates about school projects and upcoming tests and quizzes. Most share tips about favorite Web sites and pass along information about homework shortcuts and sites that are especially rich in content that fit their assignments. They also frequent Web sites pointed out to them by teachers—some of which had even been set up specifically for a particular school or class. They communicate with online teachers or tutors. They participate in online study groups. They even take online classes and develop Web sites or online educational experiences for use by others.*
>
> (Levin & Arafeh, 2002, p. ii)

The contents of volume 30 of *L&L* — with issues published from August 2002 through May 2003— reflected this prevalent use of the Internet for school-related learning and teaching. Almost half (44 of 103) of the articles published during this academic year focused in some way upon curriculum-based learning activities that made significant, and often predominant, use of Internet tools and resources. Other articles in Volume 30 addressed teachers' use of the Internet for different types of professional development.

At first, it seems that we have come a very long way in a relatively short time. In terms of technological accessibility, we have. Just ten years ago, for example, only 35% of public schools in the U.S. had Internet access, and less than 10% of the instructional areas in those schools were configured for curriculum-based Internet use. During the last decade, access at home and at school for many students and teachers worldwide has improved dramatically.

Yet as educators, we must ask an important question about these statistics: what are students and teachers *doing* with this online access in support of curriculum-based learning and teaching? Comparing answers to this question in 2004 to its responses during the first decade of educational telecomputing yields some interesting patterns that might give us pause.

Earliest Uses

In December 1978's *Oregon Computing Teacher*, readers learned of Judy Edwards's Educational Telecommunications Project for Alaska, which stated as one of its four purposes that it was funded:

> *...to design and use practical rural secondary school curriculum and instruction using modern telecommunications to mediate instruction in the necessarily existent one, two and three teacher isolated schools in rural Alaska.* (NWREL, 1978, p. 4)

In February 1982, Robert Hilgenfeld suggested to *Computing Teacher* readers that online resources could bring valuable information resources into the classroom:

> *Data bases like the UPI Wire Service and the New York Times Consumer Data Base make up-to-date information instantly available to teachers and students. Contemporary research projects can be designed for students to explore the wide range of topics available in the news, as well as to monitor events in all aspects of the world community.* (p. 18)

In April 1986, Dan Lake explained the then-rarely-used "wire service" feature of the popular educational software package, *Newsroom,* which allowed his students to combine their writing with that of students in five other school districts to produce a common document. A year later, in April 1987, *The*

Computing Teacher presented its first special issue on telecommunications in the classroom, which contained six articles that described curriculum-based projects that encouraged students to write for real audiences: their peers in other geographic places.

This spring 1987 issue of *TCT* marked the beginning of a two-year spate of published works on educational telecomputing in *TCT*. In November 1987, educators from the New Jersey Institute of Technology described a project in which they were assisting middle school science teachers statewide to communicate with each other using NJIT's computer conferencing system, the Electronic Information Exchange System (EIES). The teachers created and completed data-based science learning activities with their students on EIES, including the following examples.

- Data were collected on amounts and pH of precipitation in northern and central New Jersey. The compiled data were available on EIES for each school to study and analyze.
- Students used EIES, short-wave radios, and chronometers to determine the longitude and latitude of their schools and shared their findings with other students over the network. (p. 37)

In May 1988, Vicki Baer described a year-long online "information exchange between two middle schools" (p. 20) in two different parts of Maryland, during which participating students researched and shared information about their regions' geography, culture, notable citizens, and more. In the same issue of *TCT*, Lynne Schrum, Kitty Carton, and Steven Pinney described two very successful curriculum-based telecommunications projects: the science-focused Plant Growing Contest and the The Great Pumpkin Letter Writing Campaign in language arts.

In October 1988, Marianne Handler described how second graders communicated online with children's book author Beverly Major, using the Student Forum on CompuServe. In December/January 1988/89, Dan Lake reported on early curriculum-based projects that were part of Margaret Riel's first "learning circles" online: round robin stories and a simulated bicycle trek in New York state.

Look Again

What can these articles about the earliest curriculum-based educational telecomputing projects teach us, 15-25 years later? In just eight issues of the *(Oregon) Computing Teacher,* published over a 10-year period, *eleven different types* of curriculum-based educational telecomputing learning activities — what I call telecollaborative/telecooperative /teleresearch *activity structures* and *activity purposes* — were shared. (For more information about the 24 different curriculum-based telecollaborative/ telecooperative/teleresearch activity structures and purposes, first published in 1993, please see Tables 3 and 4 at the end of this chapter.) All of these activities were conceived and carried out long before the multimedia version of the World Wide Web was available for use, and most were completed before teachers and students had access to what we now call the Internet. Truly, the educators who contributed these articles were both technological and pedagogical pioneers.

Why is this so remarkable and instructive in 2004? In Volume 30 of *Learning & Leading with Technology,* in which *all* of the issues included multiple articles describing curriculum-based uses of Internet tools and resources to educators in countries such as Australia, Canada, the United Kingdom, and the United States, in which close to 100% of schools have Internet access — *there were fewer different types of curriculum-based Internet learning activities described* than in the 13 articles published in 1978-1988 and depicted in Table 1. In Volume 30, learning activities based upon only *nine* different telecomputing activity structures or purposes were presented to *L&L's* readers in almost *four times* as many articles.

Table 1: Activity structures and purposes represented in *OCT/TCT/L&L* articles.

December 1978-December 1988	September 2002-May 2003
Keypals	Global classrooms
Global classrooms	Telementoring
Electronic appearances	Question-and-answer activities
Telementoring	Information searches
Information exchanges	Telefieldtrips
Electronic publishing	Electronic publishing
Pooled data analysis	Telepresent problem solving
Parallel problem solving	Simulations
Sequential creations	Explore a topic/answer a question
Simulations	
Explore a topic/answer a question	

This startling pattern is similarly evident in my observations of and conversations with K-12 teachers at professional conferences, in workshops, in university courses, and in service work done with school districts. It is triangulated by an analysis of curriculum-based telecomputing projects shared online by classroom teachers during 2003.

Hilites is a well-established, moderated, K-12 classroom project announcement list sponsored by the Global Schoolnet (http://www.gsn.org). The Global Schoolnet's founders have been supporting project-based use of online tools and resources in K-12 classrooms for more than 20 years. Any teacher can post his/her classroom project announcement to the *Hilites* list, and teachers from all over the globe do so regularly.

I examined the 383 project announcements that were posted to the *Hilites* list during 2003 — all of the recent project postings available in the *Hilites* online archives at the time that this chapter was written. I analyzed these postings to determine the full range of telecollaborative/telecooperative/teleresearch activity structures and purposes present. Only 16 of 24 possible activity structures or purposes—listed in Table 2 below — were represented in *Hilites* list distributions during 2003.

Table 2: Activity structures and purposes represented in *Hilites* List Messages.

January - December 2003
Keypals
Global classrooms
Question-and-answer activities
Impersonations
Information exchanges
Telefieldtrips
Electronic publishing
Pooled data analysis
Information searches
Peer feedback activities
Parallel problem solving
Sequential creations
Telepresent problem solving
Simulations
Social action projects
Explore a topic/answer a question

Unfortunately, archives of postings to FrEdMail, *Hilites'* predecessor in the 1980's, were not available online to review and analyze, so we can't know for sure whether Global Schoolnet's older projects, like the earlier *L&L* articles, were more varied in their structures and purposes than more recently shared telecomputing activities. Still, since I first developed the activity structures and purposes in 1993, having regularly examined curriculum-based telecomputing activities posted to FrEdMail and *Hilites* since 1981, I think that it is reasonable to assume that the variety of *Hilites* projects, like the range of educational telecomputing ideas published in *L&L,* has probably decreased over time.

Egad! Why?

Our instructional access to and educational use of Internet tools and resources in K-12 classrooms has grown quite dramatically during the past 25 years. At the same time, though, the variety and creativity of our instructional designs for that educational use may have decreased — if we can assume that the topics for articles published during the past 25 years of *Oregon Computing Teacher, The Computing Teacher,* and *Learning & Leading with Technology* are representative of what has been happening with telecomputing in elementary, middle-level, and secondary classrooms around the world. Why might this have happened?

A definitive answer to this question is probably not possible to derive. Yet there are clues to some of the probable causes of this perplexing pattern in the nature of the telecommunications technologies that were and are available to us 25 years ago and today. From 1978 through 1988, not only classroom-based *access* to telecommunications was dramatically less than today; so was the range of *tools* and accompanying uses that could be employed online. In that decade, the few teachers and students who had access to online tools used email and electronic bulletin boards — early predecessors to today's Web fora — primarily (and often exclusively). A few teachers and students used realtime text chat and even fewer retrieved information from text-based information databases that were generally difficult to find and often expensive to use.

This more limited set of online tools and resources, compared to what the World Wide Web offers learners and teachers today, was decidedly text-based and communication-focused. The amount of searchable information freely available online in 1988 was minuscule compared to what is accessible via the Web today. So, curriculum-based uses of Internet tools and resources in 1978-1988, understandably, emphasized students *writing* for and with others in different geographic locations: writing to share what they were learning and to learn from what others were sharing. Telecollaborative educational ventures, in which, through ongoing exchange, students and teachers collaborate at a distance on a project that cannot proceed until each group contributes — and cannot succeed without communication among groups — were proportionally much more common fifteen years ago than today. This is probably because the text-based and communication-oriented tools available to students and teachers then suggested, through their particular technological affordances and constraints, such online collaborations.

Contrast those characteristics with what is available *and most often used* on the Internet today. Since approximately 1995, by which time a critical mass of schools in North America, Western Europe, and Australia had gained Internet access, the great majority of curriculum-based educational uses of online tools and resources involved finding and using — but not necessarily discussing or analyzing with remote learning partners — information; activities that I label generally as *teleresearch*. You can see this teleresearch emphasis in students' reports of schoolwork-related Internet use presented in the 2002 Pew study that was cited near the beginning of this chapter.

Indeed, only nine of the 44 articles in volume 30 of *L&L* that depicted curriculum-based uses of online tools or resources described telecollaborative or telecooperative learning activities. (Telecollaboration requires students to work together online to complete a learning activity; telecooperation involves sharing information with others online, but does not require the processing of that information for the learning activity to succeed.) Compare that with 12 of the 13 *L&L* articles published in the first 10 years of educational telecomputing's presence in the magazine that presented telecollaborative or telecooperative ideas. It seems probable that collectively we have forgotten about the rich telecollaborative possibilities of email and computer conferencing in our fascination with online information-seeking and use. It may be, as Thoreau once cautioned, we have unwittingly "become the tools of our tools."

What to Do?

Why should the advent, expansion, and refining of the World Wide Web's services and resources preempt telecollaborative and telecooperative educational uses of email, Web boards, instant messaging, and videoconferencing? The answer is simple: it shouldn't, and it doesn't have to continue to do so. How do we reverse this trend? We must consciously and continuously examine the *full range* of learning activity types that are supported by the *full range* of telecommunications tools and resources available. This is precisely what the activity structures and purposes mentioned earlier were designed to help educators to do.

Taking our instructional design cues from online tools' attributes, rather than from the ways in which those tools can be used to serve educational ends, limits pedagogical possibilities, which, in turn, limits the depth, richness, and efficacy of students' learning. As Margaret Riel sagely stated in the April 1987 special telecommunications issue of *The Computing Teacher,*

> *Trying to determine the educational potential of computer networks is a bit like trying to assess the educational value of a film projector. Unless you know something about what is to be projected and the educational context that will be created around it, the project is not useful. Educators need to look past networking as the goal in itself and ask the more serious question of how activities that include the interaction of participants in other locations help students and teachers achieve important educational goals. ... Like other educational media, the way computers and networks are used is crucial.* (p. 30).

Or, as Emerson said almost 160 years ago,

> *It is a lesson which all history teaches wise men, to put trust in ideas, and not in circumstances.*

Today, our more ubiquitous — but more pedagogically and structurally constrained — educational uses of online tools and resources demonstrate in a most powerful way a perpetual and pressing need for the creativity, innovativeness, and pioneering spirit that our pedagogical predecessors demonstrated in *Computing Teacher* articles more than 15 years ago. Let's learn from their designs and their initiative, adding back the telecollaborative and telecooperative activity types that seem to be disappearing from our instructional repertoires. In doing so, we will serve even better the learning needs of our students. What was "old" (at least in "Internet years") could — and should — be new again.

Table 3: Telecollaborative and telecooperative activity structures.

Genre	Telecollaborative /Telecooperative Activity Structure	Description
INTERPERSONAL EXCHANGE	Keypals	Students communicate with others outside their classrooms via email about curriculum-related topics chosen by teachers and/or students. Communication are usually one-to-one.

	Global Classrooms	Groups of students and teachers in different locations study a curriculum-related topic together during the same time period. Projects are frequently interdisciplinary and thematically organized.
	Electronic Appearances	Students have opportunities to communicate with subject matter experts and/or famous people via email, videoconferencing, or chatrooms. These activities are typically short-term (often one-time) and correspond to curricular objectives.
	Telementoring	Students communicate with subject matter experts over extended periods of time to explore specific topics in depth and in an inquiry-based format.
	Question & Answer	Students communicate with subject matter experts on a short-term basis as questions arise during their study of a specific topic. This is used only when all other information resources have been exhausted.
	Impersonations	Impersonation projects are those in which some or all participants communicate in character, rather than as themselves. Impersonations of historical figures and literary protagonists are most common.
INFORMATION COLLECTION AND ANALYSIS	Information Exchanges	Students and teachers in different locations collect, share, compare, and discuss information related to specific topics or themes that are experienced or expressed differently at each participating site.
	Database Creation	Students and teachers organize information they have collected or created into databases which others can use and to which others can add or respond.
	Electronic Publishing	Students create electronic documents, such as Web pages or word-processed newsletters, collaboratively with others. Remotely-located students learn from and respond to these publishing projects.
	Telefieldtrips	Telefieldtrips allow students to virtually experience places or participate in activities that would otherwise be impossible for them, due to monetary or geographic constraints.
	Pooled Data Analysis	Students in different places collect data of a particular type on a specific topic and then combine the data across locations for analysis.
PROBLEM SOLVING	Information Searches	Students are asked to answer specific, fact-based questions related to curricular topics. Answers (and often searching strategies) are posted in electronic format for other students to see, but reference sources used to generate the answers are both online and offline.

	Peer Feedback Activities	Students are encouraged to provide constructive responses to the ideas and forms of work done by students in other locations, often reviewing multiple drafts of documents over time. These activities can also take the form of electronic debates or forums.
	Parallel Problem Solving	Students in different locations work to solve similar problems separately and then compare, contrast, and discuss their multiple problem-solving strategies online.
	Sequential Creations	Students in different locations sequentially create a common story, poem, song, picture or other product online. Each participating group adds their segment to the common product.
	Telepresent Problem Solving	Students simultaneously engage in communications-based realtime activities from different locations. Developing brainstormed solutions to real-world problems via teleconferencing is a popular application of this structure.
	Simulations	Students participate in authentic, but simulated, problem-based situations online, often while collaborating with other students in different locations.
	Social Action Projects	Students are encouraged to consider real and timely problems, then take action toward resolution with other students elsewhere. Although the problems explored are often global in scope, the action taken to address the problem is usually local.

(Dawson & Harris, 1999, p.2)

Table 4: Teleresearch activity purposes.

Genre	Teleresearch Activity Purpose	Process Description
TELERESEARCH	Hone information skills	Practicing information-seeking and information-evaluating skills.
	Explore a topic or answer a question	Exploring a topic of inquiry or finding answers to a particular question.
	Review multiple perspectives	Discovering and investigating multiple beliefs, experiences, etc., upon a topic.
	Generate data	Collecting data remotely.
	Solve problems	Using online information to assist authentic problem-solving.
	Teleplant/telepublish	Publishing information syntheses or critiques for others to use.

References

Angelou, M. (1991, August 25). I dare to hope. *The New York Times.*

Baer, V.E. (1988). Getting to know the neighbors: An information exchange between two middle schools. *The Computing Teacher, 15*(8), pp. 20-22.

British Educational Suppliers Association. (2002). Information and communication technology in UK state schools: 2002 summary edition. Retrieved on April 20, 2003 from: http://www.besanet.org.uk/ict2002/summary/s-ch4.pdf .

Dawson, K., & Harris, J. (1999). Reaching out: Telecollaboration and social studies. *Social Studies and the Young Learner, 12*(1), pp. 1-4.

Emerson, R.W. (1844). "War," published in *Essays: Second Series.* Retrieved on April 20, 2003 from: http://www.walden.org/thoreau/default.asp?MFRAME=/contemporaries/P/Peabody_ElizabethP/04_War.htm.

GDSourcing.com (2000, September). Canadian Internet stats pack. Report #3. Retrieved on April 27, 2003 from http://www.gdsourcing.ca/StatsPack3.pdf .

Global SchoolNet (2004). *Hilites* list archives. Available at http://www.gsn.org/lists/hilites.html).

Handler, M. (1988). Meeting an author online. *The Computing Teacher, 16*(2), pp. 17-19.

Hilgenfeld, R. (1982). Education — Online. *The Computing Teacher, 9*(6), p. 18.

Moursund, D. (2002). History of *Learning & Leading with Technology.* Retrieved on October 19, 2003 from http://www.uoregon.edu/~moursund/dave/history_of_llt.htm

International Council for Computers in Education. (1987, April). *The Computing Teacher, special issue: Telecommunications, 14*(7).

Kimmel, H., Kerr, E. B., & O'Shea, M. (1987). Computerized collaboration: Taking teachers out of isolation. *The Computing Teacher, 15*(3), pp. 36-38.

Lake, D. (1988-89). Two projects that worked: Using telecommunications as a resource in the classroom. *The Computing Teacher, 16*(4), pp. 17-19.

Lake, D. T. (1986). Telecommunications from the classroom. *The Computing Teacher, 13*(7), pp. 43-46.

Levin, D., & Arafeh, S. (August 14, 2002). The digital disconnect: The widening gap between Internet-savvy students and their schools. Washington, DC: Pew Internet & American Life Project. Retrieved on April 20, 2003 from http://www.pewinternet.org/reports/pdfs/PIP_Schools_Internet_Report.pdf

National Center for Educational Statistics. (Fall 2002). NCES fast facts: Internet access. Retrieved on April 20, 2003 from http://nces.ed.gov/fastfacts/display.asp?id=46

Northwest Regional Educational Laboratory. (1978). Alaska telecommunications program. *Oregon Computing Teacher, 6* (2), pp. 3-4.

Riel, M. (1987). The InterCultural Learning Network. *The Computing Teacher, 14*(7), pp. 27-30.

Schrum, L., Carton, K., & Pinney, S. (1988). Today's tools. *The Computing Teacher, 54*(8), pp. 31, 34-35.

Statistics Canada. (2002). Information and communication technology: Access and use. *Education Quarterly Review, 8* (4). Retrieved on April 20, 2003 from http://www.statcan.ca/english/indepth/81-003/feature/eqar2002008004s0a03.pdf

Victoria Commercial Teachers Association. (April 2003). Staffroom news: Did you know? Retrieved on April 20, 2003 from http://www.vcta.asn.au/html/staffroom/staffroom_news.htm

Selected Bibliography (presented in reverse chronological order)

Harris, J. (in press). *Virtual architecture: Designing and directing curriculum-based telecomputing* (2nd ed.). Eugene, OR: International Society for Technology in Education (ISTE).

Harris, J. (2003). Generative connections: An Internet-supported response to standards schizophrenia. *Learning and Leading with Technology, 30*(7), pp. 46-49, 59.

Harris, J., & Reifel, S. (2002). Children should be seen *and* heard on the Web. *Learning and Leading with Technology, 29*(7), pp. 50-53, 59.

Harris, J. (2002). Wherefore art thou, telecollaboration? *Learning and Leading with Technology, 29*(6), pp. 55, 57-59.

Harris, J. (2001). Telecollaborators wanted: More than seek & find. *Learning and Leading with Technology, 28*(8), pp. 46-49.

Harris, J. (2001). Teachers as telecollaborative project designers: A curriculum-based approach. *Contemporary Issues in Technology and Teacher Education*, [Online serial], *1* (3). Available at http://www.citejournal.org/vol1/iss3/seminal/article1.htm

Harris, J. (2000-2001). Structuring Internet-enriched learning spaces. *Learning and Leading with Technology, 28(4)*, pp. 50-55.

Harris, J. (2000). An illusory dilemma: Online to learn or in line with standards? *Learning and Leading with Technology, 28(3)*, pp. 10-15.

Harris, J. (2000). Taboo topic no longer: Why telecollaborative projects sometimes fail. *Learning and Leading with Technology, 27(5)*, pp. 58-61.

Harris, J. (1999). First steps to telecollaboration. *Learning and Leading with Technology, 27(3)*, pp. 54-57.

Harris, J. (1999). Curriculum-based opportunities for Internet-supported learning. *Syllabus High School Edition, 1*(1), pp. 18-20.

Harris, J. (1999). "I know what we're doing but how do we do it?" Action sequences for curriculum-based telecomputing. *Learning and Leading with Technology, 26*(6), pp. 42-44.

Harris, J. (1998*). Design tools for the Internet-supported classroom*. Alexandria, VA: Association for Supervision and Curriculum Development (ASCD).

Harris, J. (1998). *Virtual architecture: Designing and directing curriculum-based telecomputing*. Eugene, OR: International Society for Technology in Education (ISTE).

Harris, J. (1998). Educational teleresearch is a means, not an end. *Learning and Leading with Technology, 26*(3), pp. 42-48.

Harris, J. (1998). Activity structures for curriculum-based telecollaboration. *Learning and Leading with Technology, 26* (1), pp. 6-15.

Harris, J. (1997-98). Wetware: Why use activity structures? *Learning and Leading with Technology, 25*(4), pp. 13-17.

Harris, J. (1997). Content and intent shape function: Designs for Web-based educational telecomputing activities. *Learning and Leading with Technology, 24* (5), pp. 17-20.

Harris, J. (1996). *Teaching & learning with the Internet: Facilitator's guide.* Alexandria, VA: Association for Supervision and Curriculum Development (ASCD).

Harris, J. (1995-96). Telehunting, telegathering, and teleharvesting: Information-seeking and information-synthesis on the Internet. *Learning and Leading with Technology, 23*(4), pp. 36-39.

Harris, J. (1995). *Way of the ferret: Finding and using educational resources on the Internet* (2nd ed.). Eugene, OR: International Society for Technology in Education (ISTE).

Harris, J. (1995). Organizing and facilitating telecollaborative projects. *The Computing Teacher, 22*(5), pp. 66-69.

Harris, J. (1994). *Way of the ferret: Finding and using educational resources on the Internet.* Eugene, OR: International Society for Technology in Education (ISTE).

Harris, J. (1994). "Opportunities in work clothes:" Online problem-solving project structures. *The Computing Teacher, 21*(7), pp. 52-55.

Harris, J. (1994). Information collection activities for students of the Information Age. *The Computing Teacher, 21*(6), pp. 32-36.

Harris, J. (1994). People-to-people projects on the Internet. *The Computing Teacher, 21*(5), pp. 48-52.

Harris, J. (1993). Using Internet know-how to plan how students will know. *The Computing Teacher, 20*(8), pp. 35-40.

Chapter 12

Technology for Teaching:
Past Masters Versus Present Practices

Jesse M. Heines

Jesse M. Heines is an Associate Professor of Computer Science at the University of Massachusetts Lowell. He specializes in the implementation and evaluation of interactive, user-centered programs with rich graphical user interfaces (GUIs), particularly those employing Dynamic HTML, JavaScript, Java, C++, and XML and XSL and their related technologies. Prior to joining the UMass Lowell faculty, Jesse spent ten years with Digital Equipment Corporation, where he founded the Computer-Based Course Development Group and developed a large variety of CBT courseware. He earned an EdD in Educational Media and Technology from Boston University.

Blended Learning?

Google is an amazing resource. No matter what your question, Google can find you an answer. The answer may not be correct, of course, but you can rest assured that even in the relatively short existence of the Web, someone, somewhere, has posted something pertaining to your question.

Thus, it never ceases to amaze me how often I hear a company claim that its new instructional technology product incorporates some radically new approach to teaching. Don't they talk to educators before they make such claims? Don't they ask someone who has studied instructional technology if such a thing has ever existed before? Don't they even bother to do a Google search to see if anyone else has taken a similar approach?

I guess not. A couple of years ago I was invited to address educators at E-Learn 2002 (Heines, 2002), which was billed as a "World Conference on E-Learning in Corporate, Government, Healthcare, and Higher Education." Pretty impressive. As I considered what I would say, I scanned the conference's list of topics identified under "Strategic Focus," and one in particular caught my eye: "Blended Learning." "Hmm," I thought, "I wonder what that is?"

Enter Google. A search on "blended learning" turned up some amazing statements. First, I found a news article on a relatively reputable site, that of the American Society for Training & Development. Jennifer Hoffman (2001) posted an article there that stated:

> Every few months a new trend hits the training industry. One of the latest trends revolves around the application of blended learning solutions. *The idea behind blended learning is that instructional designers review a learning program, chunk it into modules, and determine the best medium to deliver those modules to the learner.* [Emphasis added by JMH.]

Hmm. Didn't Robert Mager (1967, 1999) do pretty well back in the 1970s teaching corporate trainers how to "chunk" instructional material into modules? Isn't determining "the best medium" for delivering instruction the very essence of instructional technology design that's been taught in colleges of education for years (Moore & Kearsley, 1996)? This doesn't sound like a very new trend to me.

But the fact that something isn't new never stopped anyone from claiming they own it and, more importantly, trying to sell it! Google found a company that referred to "blended learning" as "our approach" and claimed it as a service mark (EpicLearning, 2001):

> *Our Blended Learning^{SM} approach is the real difference.* No other learning option combines the synergy of live instructor-led classes and live online coaching with proven self-study programs, hands-on labs, and a network of outside resources. This approach promotes greater retention and accommodates differences in learning styles. [Emphasis added by JMH.]

Promotes greater retention *than what?* They don't say. (Sigh.)

Google also found one refreshingly honest reference to blended learning (Smith, 2001):

> *Blended learning is a fairly new term in education lingo, but the concept has been around for decades.* Essentially, blended learning is ... a method of educating at a distance that uses technology (high-tech, such as television and the Internet, or low-tech, such as voice mail or conference calls) combined with traditional (stand-up) education or training. [Emphasis added by JMH.]

Ah, finally, a bow to past masters. "On the shoulders of giants..." "Those who do not learn from the past are destined to repeat it..." Etcetera. It's been said many times in many ways, but people continue to reinvent the wheel and believe that their applications of instructional technology are totally new.

How About Computer-Based Instruction?

I attended a session at a conference in 1998 in which the speaker asked the audience when they thought the first CBI program had been written. [CBI stands for "computer-based instruction," but various researchers and marketeers refer to sister technologies designed for other target populations as CAI (computer-assisted instruction), CAL (... learning), CBT (... training), CBI, and CBL.] The first respondent shouted "1981." Another called out "1976." Someone guessed "1969." I responded "the early 60s or late 50s." To that the speaker said, "Whoa, can you give me a reference?"

I couldn't quote chapter and verse off the top of my head, but I remembered reading an interview with Ivan Sutherland, an early pioneer of computer-controlled cathode-ray tubes, in which he described a program written by a colleague "in the early days of computer graphics" to help his daughter with math. The computer presented the child with an arithmetic problem and a face on a display screen. If the girl entered the correct answer, the face smiled. If she entered an incorrect response, the face frowned. Successive wrong answers caused the face to cry.

Once home I checked a paper I wrote in graduate school in 1974 and found the interview had been published in *Computer Decisions* magazine in 1971. "The early days of computer graphics" to which Sutherland referred were indeed the early 1960s or even the late 1950s, when he developed the Sketchpad interactive graphics system as a graduate student at the Massachusetts Institute of Technology. Readers may also remember that PLATO was in widespread use at the University of Illinois by the late 1960s (Bitzer & Skaperdas, 1970) around the same time that C. Victor Bunderson was developing the TICCIT system at Brigham Young University (Bunderson, 1973, 1974).

Sidney Pressey and Thorndike's "Miracle"

Sutherland's colleague may have written the first real CAI program, but it certainly wasn't the first instructional application of technology. It wasn't even the first mechanical instructional application. That honor goes to Sidney L. Pressey, who realized a vision expressed by Edward L. Thorndike way back in 1912:

If, by a miracle of mechanical ingenuity, a book could be so arranged so that only to him who had done what was directed on page one would page two become visible, and so on, much that now requires personal instruction could be accomplished by print.

Pressey realized Thorndike's "miracle" in 1926, when he exhibited the machine shown in Figure 1. This device presented multiple choice questions one at a time by rotating a cylindrical drum on which the questions were printed under a glass window. Students indicated their responses by depressing one of the four keys that corresponded to each choice in the question. In the test mode, no indication of the correctness of the student's response was supplied. In drill mode, all keys except the correct one were locked.

Figure 1. Pressey's 1926 device (Lumsdaine & Glaser, 1960).

One exciting feature of Pressey's 1926 device was that it automatically recorded all responses. Pressey claimed that he used this information (an item analysis of sorts) to revise his lecture plans, spending more time on concepts that were consistently missed and less on those easily grasped. In a much later paper (1964), Pressey noted that an attachable mechanism existed for the 1926 device that would give the user a candy lozenge when a programmable number of correct responses had been made. This feature is especially interesting because it predates B. F. Skinner's writings on machine reinforcement by almost 30 years. In 1927, Pressey refined the drill mode of his original machine to omit successive presentations of questions which had been correctly answered twice in succession (Figure 2). Skinner adopted a similar contingency in 1958.

Figure 2. Pressey's 1927 device (Lumsdaine & Glaser, 1960).

As one looks at these devices, one really has to ask how much further have we come with instructional technology in 78 years. We have larger and networked item banks these days, and we have graphics that Pressey couldn't produce on his cylindrical drum, but how many of today's technological programs use more sophisticated instructional strategies than Pressey's devices? Few, I daresay. And fewer still give teachers the level of feedback provided by Pressey's devices.

Pressey discontinued much of his research in 1932 due to a lack of funds (he sponsored most of his work out of his own pocket), but before he did he wrote of a coming "industrial revolution" in education and publicized yet another two contributions to the technology of mechanized testing during that same year (Pressey, 1932). The first of these was a generalized answer unit consisting of a 3x5-inch card with numbered answer boxes that students would mark with their responses. By placing a transparent window over the students' cards, the teacher could easily distinguish correct responses from incorrect ones.

Pressey's second 1932 invention was more elaborate. The student's answer cards were pieces of cardboard with 30 rows of five circles each (Figure 3).

Students marked their answers by punching through a circle. The card was then inserted into a machine consisting of 150 holes in the same configuration with spring-loaded pins in the correct answer positions. The device sensed the pins that protruded through the correctly punched holes, printed the number of correct responses on the answer sheet, and kept a running tabulation of the number of correct responses to each item — all at a rate of one answer sheet per second! The tabulated results could be read directly from the back of the machine to provide an instant item analysis to guide class discussion. If produced in modern form today, this device might seriously compete in the classroom market!

Figure 3. A 1950s version of Pressey's 1932 punchboard (Lumsdaine & Glaser, 1960).

Early Research on Instructional Technology

One of the first research studies to investigate the effects of these early testing devices was conducted by James Little in 1934. Using Pressey's 1926 drill device and 1932 test scorer, Little found a significant difference between the final exam grades of students who were immediately informed of their results on preliminary exams and those of students who did not have this feedback. He also found that drill and the use of preliminary exams significantly improved final exam grades. It is interesting to note that Little found drill and immediate feedback to be of greatest benefit to students in the lower half of the scholastic distribution, while Reed, working in 1961, found programmed instruction to be most effective with students in the upper portion of the distribution (see discussion in Saettler, 1968). Little concluded that mechanical test scoring and drill devices have practical applications in the classroom due to their convenience, speed, and possibilities for immediate reinforcement.

Another significant piece of research on mechanized testing during the 1930s was that of John and Hans Peterson, who developed "chemosheets" that students could mark with a damp swab. Correct answers turned blue, while incorrect answers turned red. In 1931, John Peterson published the results of an investigation into the use of the "Self-Instructor and Tester" (chemosheets) in a class in introductory psychology. He used several control and experimental groups which all employed a multiple-choice test as a pretest, posttest, and study guide. The only difference in the groups was that the experimental group used chemosheets to accompany their study guides for reading assignments while the control group used only untreated answer sheets. He found the improvement of the experimental groups' posttest scores over their pretest scores to be significantly greater that the corresponding improvement for the control groups.

The Age of Skinner

It would be impossible to discuss all the various learning devices that were developed throughout the first half of this century. Ibert Mellan reported in 1936 that over 600 inventions had already been patented as educational aids; the earliest on record was by H. Chard, who called his 1809 device a "Mode of Teaching to Read." While a great deal of ingenuity was exhibited in the design of these early testing and teaching machines, it appears they were used only nominally. Widespread acceptance of mechanized testing and teaching in public education would not occur until after World War II.

The beginning of contemporary educational technology is generally agreed to be B. F. Skinner's historic 1954 paper, "The Science of Learning and the Art of Teaching." It can be seen, however, that a great deal of work set the stage for the acceptance of Skinner's approach to education, including Sidney Pressey's, who was 30 years ahead of his time when he began experimenting in the 1920s.

Skinner's first machine, introduced in 1954, grew out of his desire to allow students to construct responses rather than simply select the correct statement in a multiple choice fashion (as in Pressey's devices). This machine displayed questions on a tape, the bottom section of which was hidden from students and contained the answer coded by a series of punched holes. Students indicated their responses by positioning slides on the machine's front panel to appropriate letters or numbers.

After the slides had been set, the student turned a crank. If the response was correct, the machine advanced to the next question. If incorrect, the crank would simply not turn. Thus, knowledge of results and reinforcement (the positive movement of the crank) were both immediate. One version of this machine (circa 1960) is pictured in Figure 4.

Figure 4. A 1960s version of Skinner's 1954 teaching machine (Lumsdaine & Glaser, 1960).

A typical set of frames that might have been used with such a machine to teach a third or fourth grade student to spell the word "manufacture" is shown in Figure 5.

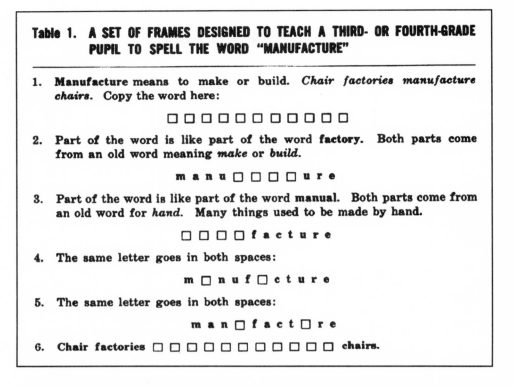

Figure 5. A typical set of frames for Skinner's 1954 teaching machine intended for use with third and fourth grade students (Lumsdaine & Glaser, 1960).

The shortcomings of this machine were quickly apparent. While the device seemed to function well for short answers, it did not allow complex responses. Skinner introduced another device in 1958 that addressed this problem (see Figure 6). This machine consisted of a large disk covered by a panel with two windows and a lever. A question was presented in one window, and students wrote their responses on a blank part of the disk exposed through an open slot in the other window. When they moved the lever, the correct answer was revealed in the question window while the response just written was moved under a transparent shield so that it could be read but not changed.

An adaptable feature of Skinner's 1958 machine then came into play: the *students themselves* decided whether their responses were correct by comparing them to the printed answers. If they judged their responses correct, they moved the lever horizontally, causing a hole to be punched in the disk. This hole would cause the question to be skipped on subsequent revolutions of the disk. When the disk turned freely, students knew that they had answered all of the questions to their own satisfaction. This machine was very similar to

Pressey's 1932 testing device, except that the responses were constructed rather than multiple choice and evaluated by the students rather than the machine.

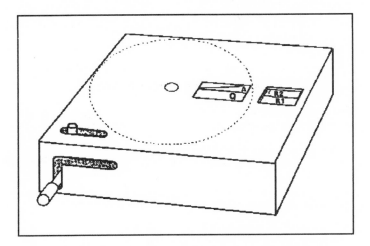

Figure 6. Skinner's 1958 improvement over his 1954 device (Lumsdaine & Glaser, 1960).

Skinner concentrated very heavily on the construction of learning programs for his machines. His aim was to teach and question in such small steps that the learner would be led smoothly to complex behavior through carefully conditioned responses. Part of a sample program to teach high school physics students about the emission of light from an incandescent source is shown in Figure 7.

Intrinsic Programming

Despite the improvements in Skinner's 1958 machine over his 1954 device and the care with which he tried to program his instruction, many problems still existed. For example, while students were rewarded for correct responses, they received no feedback or explanation when their responses were incorrect. This may have served satisfactorily with the minute steps of the 1954 machine, but the open-ended nature of the 1958 device led to problems in interpretation.

Norman Crowder (1960) attempted to remedy this shortcoming with a technique he called "intrinsic programming." The basic premise of this approach was that students' responses should determine what material is presented next. The device Crowder used was simply a textbook in which material was presented a paragraph or so at a time. At the end of each discrete section, a multiple choice question was presented with a page number following each choice. Students turned to the pages that corresponded to their choices. If they were correct, new material was presented. If incorrect, review or reinforcement material was found. This scheme was used throughout the entire book, which Crowder termed a "TutorText." [It has also been called a "Scramble Text" elsewhere in the literature.]

Table 2. PART OF A PROGRAM IN HIGH-SCHOOL PHYSICS

The machine presents one item at a time. The student completes the item and then uncovers the corresponding word or phrase shown at the right.

SENTENCE TO BE COMPLETED	WORD TO BE SUPPLIED
1. The important parts of a flashlight are the battery and the bulb. When we "turn on" a flashlight, we close a switch which connects the battery with the _____.	bulb
2. When we turn on a flashlight, an electric current flows through the fine wire in the _____ and causes it to grow hot.	bulb
3. When the hot wire glows brightly, we say that it gives off or sends out heat and _____.	light
4. The fine wire in the bulb is called a filament. The bulb "lights up" when the filament is heated by the passage of a(n) _____ current.	electric
5. When a weak battery produces little current, the fine wire, or _____, does not get very hot.	filament
6. A filament which is less hot sends out or gives off _____ light.	less
7. "Emit" means "send out." The amount of light sent out, or "emitted," by a filament depends on how _____ the filament is.	hot

---

Figure 7. A program for Skinner's 1958 device designed to teach concepts in high school physics (Lumsdaine & Glaser, 1960).

Crowder not only developed a random-access film reader to automate his TutorText by presenting pages of text stored on 35mm film, he also developed a variety of instructional strategies dealing with the sequence in which material was presented to help people understand how to use TutorText effectively. Figure 8 shows a simple sequence in which single alternative frames exist to reinforce concepts that seem difficult to some students. Figure 9 extends this approach to alternative sequences consisting of multiple frames. Figure 10 depicts a simple "wash-back" sequence, in which students struggling with a concept are routed back to earlier parts of the program for review. Figure 11 is just the opposite: a "wash-ahead" sequence that moves students along faster if they grasp concepts quickly. Finally, Figure 12 diagrams a complex strategy in which incorrect answers are weighted for seriousness and the student may be "washed back" one, two, or three steps depending upon how he or she answers.

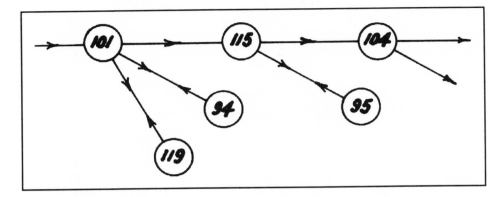

Figure 8. A simple intrinsic programming sequence in which single alternative frames exist to reinforce concepts that seem difficult to some students (Crowder, 1960).

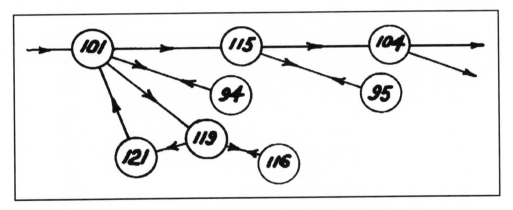

Figure 9. Alternative intrinsic programming sequences consisting of multiple frames (Crowder, 1960).

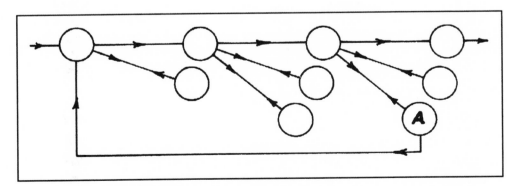

Figure 10. A simple "wash-back" sequence in which students struggling with a concept are routed back to earlier parts of a program (Crowder, 1960).

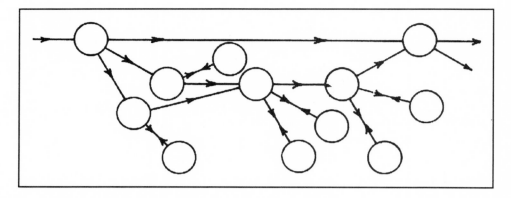

Figure 11. A "wash-ahead" sequence that moves students along faster if they grasp concepts quickly (Crowder, 1960).

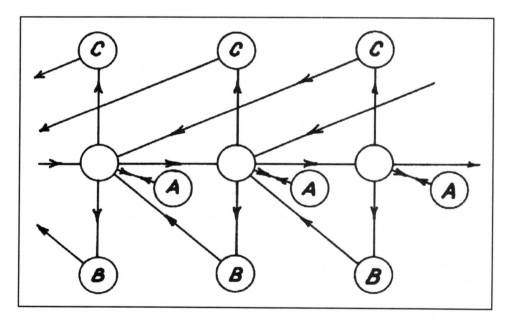

Figure 12. A complex strategy in which incorrect answers are weighted for seriousness and the student may be "washed back" one, two, or three steps depending upon how he or she answers (Crowder, 1960).

The main advantage of intrinsic programming was that it does not waste the time of the fast learner with unnecessary repetition. Its disadvantage was that it required a large textbook to present even a relatively small amount of material. With computers, of course, such size considerations are not an issue. One simply has to be willing to invest the effort to implement alternative paths through the material, a feature built in to virtually all authoring systems but often unused by developers. I can only guess that this is because they do not understand the principles, do not have the training to use the authoring system's advanced features, or are simply under too much time pressure to implement alternative paths.

Today's Technology for Today's Instruction

Given the perspective of these pre-computer-age teaching devices — their grounding in instructional theory as well as the cleverness of their implementation — educational technology newcomers may better understand why some of us old-timers continually encourage developers to "put the C back in CBI" (Heines, 1988). It is common to hear us lament that while today's programs can present beautiful multimedia programs that we didn't even dare dream of back in the days of PLATO and TICCIT or the early days of the PC, at their instructional heart these programs are little more than electronic page-turners.

In a recent conversation with a representative of one of the leading CMS vendors about their testing subsystem, I asked about the system's capability to analyze the data it stored and present it to teachers. [CMS stands for "course management system," another new term applied to a capability that's been around for years.] I was told that the system can show the teacher each student's response to every question. OK, I responded, but can a busy teacher see a summary of that data so that s/he can see trends and identify widespread class misunderstandings? The representative didn't know. He said something about computing an average, but he was not familiar with the terms "item analysis," "difficulty index," "discrimination index," and "standard deviation." (Sigh.)

Today's computers are of course much more capable than the machines of Pressey's, Skinner's, and Crowder's days, yet many systems don't even store all the response data needed to do a complete item analysis, much less use this data to adapt the program to students' individual backgrounds and abilities in real time. None lead developers through the implementation of sound instructional strategies anywhere near as sophisticated as those implemented by Crowder with film readers over 40 years ago. Microsoft PowerPoint provides an "autocontent wizard" that asks me for the *type* of presentation I want to create ("employee orientation," "project overview," etc.), the *style* I wish for that presentation, and what *options* I desire. I have yet to see a test item banking program that enforces even the most basic, long-established rules of good test construction.

It's as if the companies that develop these products simply hire programmers and tell them to start coding, without ever exploring the huge, existing body of knowledge on what's been tried before, much less look for solid theoretical ground on which to base their instructional designs. No wonder so many teachers choose to "do their own thing" when they try out these products and so quickly uncover their limitations and shortcomings.

Of course, it's easy to criticize. It's easy to sit here before my word processor and espouse the need for more sophistication in vendors' instructional products. But as Pressey wrote at the conclusion of his 1932 paper, "The writer has found from bitter experience that one person alone can accomplish very little." Product commercialization is needed to have any real impact on our vast, amorphous educational system, and the cost of developing *and marketing* commercial products today is so huge that they must often cater to the lowest common denominator in an effort to appeal to the widest possible audience. Economic pressure drives many technological advances, and the sorry state of educational financing makes it extremely difficult to find funding for efforts that only address the needs (or desires) of a few sophisticated teachers and/or students.

Therefore, we need to work with commercial vendors to show them how to expand their products' capabilities to provide creative instructional strategies based on solid theory and proven practices. One approach is to adopt the "plug-in" strategy used in so many products today, from Web browsers to Microsoft Excel to computer program development environments. Only such extensibility provides hope that we will one day see a computer-based testing subsystem that implements algorithms such as Ferguson's 1971 Bayesian decision analysis model (based on work done by Wald in 1947) to quantify the probability that a student has mastered a given body of knowledge (see also Emrick, 1971; Ferguson & Novick, 1973; and Millman, 1974). Given such a system, a teacher could adjust those probabilities to ensure that important tests such as final exams have a small probability of false positive errors (saying a student *has* learned something when s/he *hasn't*) while perhaps allowing a slightly higher probability of false negative errors (saying a student *hasn't* learned something when s/he *has*) (Heines, 1979).

Regardless of the sophistication one manages to implement, however, educational technology will never fully supplant caring, dedicated teachers. The magic of human interaction simply cannot be duplicated, just as film has not succeeded in supplanting the thrill of live theater, and even crystal clear digital CD sound can never evoke the emotion of a live concert. Technology is most effective when used *in partnership* with personal tutoring. Yes, that's true "blended learning." The catchword may have been dreamed up by some advertising firm, but the concept was first expressed by Edward L. Thorndike in 1912 when he wrote, "The best teacher uses books and appliances *as well as his own insight, sympathy, and magnetism.*"

Note

All figures are reproduced with permission of the National Education Association.

References

Bitzer, D.L., & Skaperdas, D. (1970). *The design of an economically viable large-scale computer-based education system.* Proceedings of a Conference on Computers in Instruction: Their Future for Higher Education. Santa Monica, CA: The Rand Corporation.

Bunderson, C.V. (1973). The TICCIT project: Design strategy for educational innovation. In S. A. Harrison & L. M. Stolurow (Eds.), *Productivity in higher education.* Washington, DC: National Institutes of Education.

Bunderson, C.V. (1974). The design and production of learner-controlled courseware for the TICCIT system: A progress report. *International Journal of Man-Machine Studies, 6*(4), pp. 479-491.

Computer Decisions magazine (with no byline, 1971, Feb). Decision maker: Ivan E. Sutherland. *Computer Decisions, 3*(2), pp. 46-47.

Crowder, N.A. (1960). Automatic teaching by intrinsic programming. In A. A. Lumsdaine & R. Glaser (Eds.), *Teaching machines and programmed learning: A source book* (pp. 286-298). Washington, DC: National Education Association of the United States.

EpicLearning (2001). Statement posted at http://www.epiclearning.com/BL_approach.htm, accessed October 2002, no longer available.

Emrick, J.A. (1971). An evaluation model for mastery testing. *Journal of Educational Measurement, 8*, pp 321-326.

Ferguson, R.L. (1971). *Computer assistance for individualized measurement.* Pittsburgh, PA: University of Pittsburgh Learning Research and Development Center.

Ferguson, R.L., & Novick, M.R. (1973). *The implementation of a Bayesian system for decision analysis in a program of Individually Prescribed Instruction.* Research Report No. 60. Iowa City, IA: American College Testing Program.

Heines, J.M. (1979). *The use of interactive, computer-managed instruction to control the quality of self-paced training.* Doctoral Dissertation, Boston University School of Education.

Heines, J.M. (1988). *Let's put the "C" back in CBI.* Honorary Dean Lecture, 30th International ADCIS Conference, Philadelphia, PA.

Heines, J.M. (2002). *Creating and Maintaining Data-Driven Course Web Sites.* Invited paper, AACE E-Learn 2002 Conference, Montreal, Canada.

Hoffman, J. (2001). *Blended learning case study.* Article posted at http://www.learningcircuits.org/2001/apr2001/hofmann.html, accessed December 2003.

Little, J.K. (1934). Results of use of machines for testing and for drill upon learning in educational psychology. *Journal of Experimental Education, 3.*

Lumsdaine, A.A. & Glaser, R. (Eds.). (1960). *Teaching machines and programmed learning: A source book.* Washington, DC: National Education Association of the United States.

Mager, R.F. (1999). *Making instruction work.* Atlanta, GA: Center for Effective Performance.

Mager, R.F., & Beach, K.M., Jr. (1967). *Developing vocational instruction.* Palo Alto, CA: Fearon Publishers.

Mellan, I. (1936). Teaching and educational inventions. *Journal of Educational Experimentation, 4.*

Millman, J. (1974). Sampling plans for domain-referenced tests. *Educational Technology, 14*(6), pp. 17-21.

Moore, M.G., & Kearsley, G. (1996). *Distance education: A systems view.* Belmont, CA: Wadsworth Publishing Company.

Peterson, J.C. (1931). The value of guidance in reading for information. *Transactions of the Kansas Academy of Science, 34.*

Pressey, S.L. (1926). A simple apparatus which gives tests — and teaches. *School and Society, 23*(586), pp. 373-376.

Pressey, S.L. (1927). A machine for automatic teaching of drill material. *School and Society, 25*(645), pp. 549-552.

Pressey, S.L. (1932). A third and fourth contribution toward the coming "industrial revolution" in education. *School and Society, 36*(934), pp. 669-672.

Pressey, S.L. (1950). Development and appraisal of devices providing immediate automatic scoring of objective tests and concomitant self-instruction. *Journal of Applied Psychology, 29.*

Pressey, S.L. (1964). Autoinstruction: Perspectives, problems, and potentials. In E.R. Hilgard (Ed.), *Theories of learning and instruction* (Sixty-third Yearbook of the National Society for the Study of Education, pp. 355-356). Chicago, IL: The University of Chicago Press.

Saettler, P. (1968). *A history of instructional technology.* New York: McGraw-Hill, Inc.

Saettler, P. (1990). *The evolution of American educational technology.* Englewood, CO: Libraries Unlimited.

Skinner, B.F. (1954). The science of learning and the art of teaching. *Harvard Educational Review, 24*(2), pp. 969-977.

Skinner, B.F. (1960). Teaching machines. *Science, 128.*

Skinner, B.F. (1968). *The technology of teaching.* New York: Appleton-Century-Crofts.

Smith, J. (2001). *Blended learning: An old friend gets a new name.* Article posted at http://www.gwsae.org/ExecutiveUpdate/2001/March/blended.htm, accessed December 2003.

Thorndike, E.L. (1912). *Education.* New York: The MacMillin Company.

Wald, A. (1947). *Sequential analysis.* New York: John Wiley and Sons.

Chapter 13

Learning, Teaching, and Building Knowledge: A Forty-Year Quest for Online Learning Communities

Beverly Hunter

Beverly Hunter is President of Piedmont Research Institute in rural Rappahannock County, Virginia. She currently specializes in Geographic Information Systems (GIS) applications in education, community development, and environmental conservation. She is author or co-author of over 25 books and 100 articles or book chapters on applications of advanced technologies to learning and teaching. Since the 1960's, she has served as principal investigator, manager, project director or grant officer for projects involving computer and communications technologies in education and training, with schools, private industry, universities, government agencies, and research institutes.

Introduction

I define an online learning community as a group of people who interact with each other through computer-based communications networks, learn from each other, and provide knowledge and information resources to the group related to agreed-upon tasks or topics of shared interest. A defining characteristic of an online learning community is that a person or institution must be a contributor to the evolving knowledge base of the group and not just a recipient or consumer of the group's services or knowledge base. Members and the community as a whole take advantage of information technologies, telecommunications, and organized collections of information for these purposes, in addition to face-to-face interactions they may have. The notion of "learning" means a mutual knowledge-building process is taking place. Members learn both by teaching others and by applying to their own situations the information, tools, know-how, and experiences provided by others in the Virtual Community. Hence, the knowledge base/resources of the entire community are advanced, as well as that of the individual members.

Over the past forty years, in many different groups and institutional contexts, and through technological revolutions of timesharing, microcomputers, digital databases, computational tools, Internetworking, and the World Wide Web, I have sought this "Holy Grail" of collaborative online learning communities. In this chapter I highlight some of the conceptual milestones that I experienced, and a few of the many projects and people I have learned from. I share here some of the lessons I have learned about the political and institutional contexts for online learning communities, the participants in the communities, the content, and the technologies.

I. 1960's: Computer-Telecommunication Networks for Instruction

In the 1960's, there were not very many computers and almost no one interacted with them in real time. As a computer programmer, my interactions with computers were in batch mode — through stacks of punched cards and program code printouts. However, one computer application at the time that did require something approaching "real time" interaction with a computer was computer-assisted instruction.

Collaborative Knowledge-Building in IBM's Field Engineering Nationwide CAI Network

In 1965 I was a rookie Systems Engineer with IBM in Arlington Virginia. My assignment, according to my manager, was to become "IBM's East Coast expert in CAI." No one in my office knew what "CAI" stood for, but I had the good fortune to have as my mentor Harvey Long in the IBM Poughkeepsie New York office, who had set up a nationwide online learning system to train IBM's Field Engineers (FE's). The system in Poughkeepsie was based on an IBM 1440 mainframe with 48,000 bytes of core memory, using local and remote 1050 teletypewriters. Field Engineers throughout the country interacted through the telecommunications system (via an acoustic coupler and a telephone line at 300 bits per second) and could be tracked on their progress through the programs.

The ability to interact with a computer at all, much less from a remote site (before the widespread implementation of timesharing operating systems) was in itself pretty exciting, but what inspired me was the collaborative knowledge-building that took place in this system. The training materials were developed at the central office in Poughkeepsie, using the Coursewriter software system. FE's learned from the interactive courses how to install and maintain various IBM products at their local customers' installations. However, each customer's equipment configuration was somewhat different, so individual FE's had learned from experience some of the idiosyncracies of the interaction of the various devices. The FE's could send comments about their own field experience back to the system to the course authors. The authors then would update the course content and make it available to everyone in the system. In this way, the FE's were able to share their own field experiences and teach each other. In a precursor to email, the programmer developed a facility allowing you to exit Coursewriter and enter APL, execute an APL program, and return to Coursewriter. Messages could be sent out to students or have customized text inserted into their courseware, thus customizing their material.

1965 Demo for the Federal Communications Commission

In 1965, IBM was operating under a "consent decree" from the U.S. Department of Justice, which was investigating IBM for its potentially monopolistic practices in the computer industry. One of the ways in which the federal government was attempting to constrain the power of IBM was to prohibit it from using telephone lines in connection with computers. (At that time telecommunications was the regulated monopoly of AT&T.) In an attempt to convince the FCC that telecommunications was an essential component of computing, IBM set up a huge, multi-floor collection of demonstrations of computer applications in a hotel in Washington, DC. In partnership with my mentor, Harvey Long, I set up a demonstration of computer-assisted instruction at this exhibit, connected to a remote computer in Poughkeepsie. At that time it was technically challenging to make the thing work at all, but the important lesson to me as a rookie professional was that public policy would greatly affect the future of online learning communities.

I think that the cumulative weight of all the various application demos at that exhibit did in fact persuade the FCC that telecommunications could not, in the interest of the nation, be uncoupled from computing.

Early Economic and Conceptual Barriers to Developing Online Communities

By the time I got to IBM in 1964, scientists and engineers at IBM Research Center had been conducting research and developing computer-based instructional systems for several years. Research was also underway at System Development Corporation (SDC), Bolt Beranek and Newman (BBN), the University of Illinois, and several other institutions, largely with funding from military R&D programs. At that time, there were both economic and conceptual barriers to using computer networks for building online communities.

The economic barrier was real, since computers were very expensive and there were very few of them. Nearly all of these researchers in the field of education and training in the 1960's and 1970's viewed computer communications networks and time sharing the computer as an economical means for enabling one-on-one interaction between a person and a computer. For instance, Herbert Teager at MIT at a 1961 conference on programmed learning and computer-based instruction (Coulson, 1962) stated, "Time sharing can be justified purely on grounds of cost per unit capacity...a human-machine system must allow the human partner time to think and consider his next action. Unless the machine can be doing something else during this period, there will be a loss of potentially usable machine time" (Teager, 1962).

The conceptual barrier was that the researchers focused exclusively upon *individualized* instruction in which the individual learner interacted with a computer; therefore human-human interaction was irrelevant. This conceptual barrier was more profound in the long run than the economic one, and slowed the development of learning communities mediated by computer networks. Donald Bitzer of the Coordinated Science Lab at the University of Illinois, at the same conference in 1961, described the important feature of PLATO II in the following way: "Each student may proceed through the material in a manner and at a speed of his own choosing" (Bitzer, Braunfeld, & Lichtenberger, 1962).

Licklider's "Ultimate Purpose of a Computer Communications Network":
Maximum Interaction Between People

The visionary J.C.R. Licklider (BBN and then MIT) was an exception to the dominant paradigm in educational computing. He influenced and inspired me in those formative years. He said in 1974:

> *The ultimate purpose of a computer-communications network in our times is to provide a creative environment for people to interact in. By "creative" I mean a network which has great diversity and thus allows for freedom of choice and which generates a maximum of interaction between people and their intellectual surroundings.*   (Greenberger et al., 1974)

The Importance of Interdisciplinary Teams for Creative Problem Solving
in a Technological Environment

In 1966 I left IBM to join an interdisciplinary group at George Washington University's Human Resources Research Office (HumRRO), organized by Robert J. Seidel to conduct research and development of computer-based learning environments. Our group was called IMPACT — Instructional Model Prototypes Attainable in Computerized Training. Funded by DARPA and the Army Institute for Research, we assembled a stellar group of engineers, research psychologists, mathematicians, and computer scientists, and we were able to experiment with the latest state-of-art in input/output devices such as graphic display devices, computer-controlled slide projectors, joysticks, and handwriting tablets. These were all connected to a timesharing IBM 360 mainframe outfitted with the Coursewriter instructional programming language along with several other languages including COBOL, which was the subject being learned by our military trainees. My task was to implement the pedagogical experiments and instructional designs through programming and testing. COBOL, of course, was a batch processing system at that time, so one of the greatest technical challenges was to find ways to integrate the learner's experiences of writing and testing COBOL programs into the conversational interactions in the Coursewriter tutorials. I wanted the learner to have the full power of computer-based tools at his fingertips throughout the training program. The operating system architecture of the IBM 360 made this impossible at the time, but the goal became a central component of my vision of online learning.

I never was convinced that the pedagogy of tutorial CAI was the most important goal for educational computing, because human collaboration was so much more powerful than the limited tutorial logic we could build into the software. The brilliant and creative collaborations within our face-to-face interdisciplinary team were a daily reminder of this fact, and I vowed that someday we would be able to integrate the power of human collaborations with the power of computer-based tools into an online system for learning and teaching.

II. Early 1970's: Computer Networks as a Means of Sharing and Improving Learning Materials

By the early 1970's considerable investment had been made in developing computer-based learning materials in the U.S. The U.S. Office of Education alone spent an estimated $161 million between 1964 and 1969 for the use of computers in education (Grayson & Robbins, 1972, cited in Hunter *et al.*, 1975). The National Science Foundation under the leadership of Dr. Andrew Molnar supported the development of computer-related innovational projects in education with about $40 million between 1965 and 1971 (Hunter *et al.*, 1975). Roughly $142 million was spent in higher education on instructional computing in the year 1969-70. Private industry was also investing millions in the development of computer systems and associated curriculum materials at that time.

Given the accelerating investment in the development of such materials and systems, a central concern at that time was how to provide students with access to the computer in order to use the materials. An equally major concern was how to "transport" the educational software from one machine to another, given the plethora of unique and incompatible operating systems and programming languages. Thus, in the early 1970's Andrew Molnar at the NSF funded our group at HumRRO to study the problem and propose national strategies for developing and disseminating computer-based learning materials. In the book that we wrote to document the study's findings, we devoted an entire chapter to "ways of achieving more widespread benefit from computer-based learning materials" and another chapter to examining alternative means of providing computer services to individuals and institutions (Hunter *et al.*, 1975).

Participant Contributions to a Learning Community's Online Resources: The Lister Hill Network

Dozens of physical and organizational networks were emerging in the early 1970's, such as the NSF-sponsored Regional Computing Networks, commercial time-sharing services, ARPAnet, and several discipline-based networks. One of the most influential to my ideas about how to build online learning communities was the educational network sponsored by the Lister Hill Center. The Lister Hill network provided educational services to a variety of institutions in the health professions, including medical schools, nursing schools, and hospitals. The network used the Biomedical Communications facilities of the National Library of Medicine. These facilities were furnished by a commercial time-sharing corporation, Tymshare, which had a nationwide hook-up of leased line facilities. In order to become an operational user of the network, an institution had to agree both to evaluate existing curriculum materials and to contribute to the expansion of these materials. The user institutions were required to add to the repertoire and quality of materials available from the service providers. For example, the University of Illinois Medical Center provided the CASE program, which simulates a clinical encounter. The user institutions were required to submit additional medical case histories to expand the range of experiences the students could obtain. The Director of the Lister Hill network, Dr. Harold Wooster, believed that user-developed materials were a key to the long-term success of the network. The biggest problem in sustaining that network at that time was the cost of telecommunications, which was about 40 percent of total system costs (Hunter *et al.*, 1975).

Removing Social Barriers to Collaboration: PLATO in the 1970's

By the 1970's, PLATO had evolved into a nationwide network for educational computing. At HumRRO, down the hall from my office we had some PLATO terminals (plasma display devices) connected via modem and telecommunications to the PLATO mainframe at the University of Illinois. Thousands of people — mainly college students and faculty — used PLATO and its telecommunications network to create and use computer-based learning materials and to play collaborative interactive games and simulations. I used to take my daughter Cynthia and son Gregory Shawn to the office with me and let them play on the PLATO terminals. My son Shawn, at the time about nine years old, came into my office one day with a quizzical — almost guilty — look on his face. "Mom," he said, "a college student on PLATO is teaching me how to play this complicated spaceship game. He thinks I am another college student." Pause... "Is that ok? Should I tell him I'm just a little boy?"

That brief query from my "little boy" gave me a powerful insight about possibilities in online learning communities. The modern-day expression is, "On the Internet, no one knows you are a dog." The lack of visual and auditory cues in an online environment made it possible to filter out cultural cues about age, gender, race, culture, and status that often create barriers to collaboration in face-to-face settings.

III. Early 1980's: Using Microcomputers to Build the Foundation for Computer Literacy and Data Sharing

The advent of stand-alone microcomputers in the late 1970's resulted in a few years' hiatus in the efforts to build online community. However, this period of experience with micros laid important groundwork for later online learning communities of people who were computer-literate, had access to personal computers, and were able to build knowledge from data.

Building Understanding of Computer Tools and Applications into School Curricula

By 1980, a few dozen microcomputers had already made their way into scattered classrooms in Montgomery County Maryland when my HumRRO colleague Carol Kastner and I began collaborating with teachers and administrators at Montgomery County Public Schools in a computer literacy project. Bev Sangston, Director of the Instructional Computing department at the schools' central office was an incredibly able and devoted administrator who made such innovation possible within the school bureaucracy. We were swept up in the excitement of integrating these low-cost machines and associated software tools into the curriculum so that kids could have the power of computers in their own hands. It was a heady time, because stand-alone machines meant freedom from the bureaucracies who controlled mainframe computers, and freedom from the very high costs of telecommunications lines.

The early 80's were a critical period for building a broad base of computer-literate teachers, students, and administrators. Sangston, Kastner, and I worked with over 200 local teachers and administrators and hundreds of children, as well as national leaders in elementary education to create a comprehensive and classroom-tested K-8 curriculum called *My Students Use Computers* (Hunter, 1983). Written for school board members, administrators, curriculum coordinators, principals, teachers, library media specialists, computer coordinators, teacher educators, and parents, this book provided a comprehensive guide to the pedagogical and curricular applications of procedural thinking; software tools such as word processors, data bases, spreadsheets, and simulations; and programming languages at each grade level from kindergarden to eighth grade. Fundamental concepts about computers, appropriate applications, and ethical and social implications formed important parts of the curriculum.

Building the Foundation for Sharing and Interpreting Data

I always felt that shared access to data was an essential element in an online community focused on knowledge-creative collaborative projects. So in the late 1970's I went to a conference of the Information Industries and talked with providers of online data bases to seek their interest in having school children use their online services. I spoke with a salesman for LEXUS/NEXUS, the premier provider of online legal and news database access. He laughed at me, saying school children would *never* be able to afford these expensive services which ran into hundreds of dollars per hour! Then, he proceeded to tell me the story of his own son, aged nine, who had used LEXUS to research the status of the black-footed ferret, an endangered species, and how impressed his kid's teacher was when this child was able to write about the latest court cases involving the protection of this species. It infuriated me to think that a handful of privileged children such as his son (and mine) would have access to such powerful data services but the mainstream of children would not. So I thought, "Some day, the cost of accessing online data will be much lower than it is now. I will build smaller electronic databases, designed to fit into the curriculum, and put them on floppy disks for the Apple microcomputer, and then kids and teachers can begin learning how to create knowledge out of data."

I found a data file software program called "PFS: File" that was the first database program for Apple II. I remember the day it arrived at my home. I sat up all night building a data base about insects. Over the next few years, my colleagues and I built data bases about everything we could think of that might be relevant to school curricula and interesting to kids: trees, insects, rocks, inventions, weather and climate, mythology; the U.S. Constitutional Convention; Presidential elections, U.S. federal budgets. With colleagues from around the country in science education, social studies education, and literature, we created step-by-step lessons for the classroom showing how to use these little files (Apple floppies only held about 30,000 bytes at the time, as I recall) to explore data, test hypotheses, and create investigations. Over several years in the mid-1980's, Scholastic published dozens of these data bases and lesson plans.

Direct Computer-to-Computer Networking

My curriculum database co-authors and I were in Virginia, California, Michigan, New York, and a few other locations as we developed the Scholastic curriculum database packages in the mid-1980's. We exchanged manuscripts and datasets directly among our microcomputers by dialing up each others' Apple II microcomputers through Hayes modems. It wasn't really a very efficient network, but it kept us inspired for the collaboration potential at a future time when telecommunications networks would become more user-friendly.

DBKids: My First Online Community of Teachers

A couple hundred teachers around the country were very excited about the Scholastic curriculum databases, and sent me letters about how they and their students were using them in their classrooms. I published a paper newsletter called *DBKids* to share these teachers' ideas plus news about data bases. Then, a few of us started discussing these topics in a threaded discussion board we called DBKids on the dial-up network service CompuServe. This was my first attempt to create an online community of teachers. I wanted to share this online experience with inservice teachers in a graduate course I was teaching at the University of San Francisco with Mary Furlong, one of my co-authors for the Scholastic data base project. However, the University did not have any telephone lines in their classrooms. So I copied the dialogue from the threaded discussions onto floppy disks and had my teachers at the university read the discussions in word processors on stand-alone microcomputers.

Online Searching in the Curriculum

By the late 1980's, school library media specialists were becoming interested in providing access to online databases in their schools, and the data base service providers were beginning to offer more affordable contracts for schools. Library media specialist Erica Lodish from Montgomery County Maryland was one of these pioneers. She and I wrote *Online Searching in the Curriculum: A*

Teaching Guide for Library/Media Specialists and Teachers (Hunter & Lodish, 1989). In the introduction, we said,

> *Hundreds of large databases are available online through telecommunications and on CD-ROM. These databases are the doorway to vast stores of knowledge in bibliographies, full-text articles, and statistical data. These large databases provide learners and teachers with a rich environment in which to formulate problems, think critically and creatively, analyze and organize information, and collaborate with others. Online databases provide diverse perspectives and a broad array of information — heretofore unavailable for the vast majority of high school students. Electronic information will become the great equalizer for our schools: Rural students will be able to tap the world's information as readily as students from large metropolitan areas. To take advantage of such resources, learners must acquire and practice skills in problem solving and information handling.*

We laid a pedagogical foundation in this book for the future integration of databases into learning communities:

> *In our highly technological Information Age, many skills, abilities and points of view are needed in order to accomplish a task or solve a problem. This means we need to learn how to collaborate with other people. A major purpose of this book is to help both students and teachers improve their skills in collaboration and teamwork.*

IV. Late 1980's: Pioneering Online Learning Communities

By the late 1980's, several pioneering projects were trying out different ways of organizing online "electronic communities" for educational purposes. TERC's LabNet for teacher enhancement; FrEdMail for group projects among classrooms and teachers via dial-up mini servers; AT&T's Long Distance Learning Network, and Big Sky Telegraph were a few of the ground-breaking attempts at organizing online learning communities.

Collaborative Learning Communities: Kids Network

In 1987, the National Science Foundation initiated funding of a grant of $2,617,140 to TERC and the National Geographic Society for a project called *Kids' Network*. The abstract for the first grant included the following description:

> *The National Geographic Kids Network Project is a series of exciting, flexible elementary science units featuring cooperative experiments in which students in grades 4-6 share data nationwide using telecommunications. Topics will involve students in issues of real scientific, social, and geographic significance. Combining*

*basic content from typical school curricula and guided inquiry learning, the Network
Project can be used to supplement textbooks and existing materials or to form
complete year-long science courses. Technical Education Research Centers will
produce six units and software for sending, processing, and displaying data. The
National Geographic Society will develop at least four additional units, publish all
the materials, and provide teacher development assistance. Materials and
telecommunications will be designed for practicality in partnership with
experienced classroom teachers and administrators. The telecommunications
will be software-controlled for ease of use and reliability.*

The Kids' Network was extremely important to me for many reasons.
Fundamentally, it became an existence proof of the possibility of online
learning communities that were project-based, collaborative, data sharing, and
knowledge-building. Over several years, I used Kids' Network as an example
in many presentations and papers aimed at informing policy makers about the
importance of computer-communications networking in education.

Understanding Participant Structures in Online Learning Communities

In 1988, Margaret Riel, then at the AT&T Learning Network, provided what
was for me an important conceptual step forward in thinking about online
learning communities. I saw a draft of a paper she had developed for the
California State Educational Technology Committee in 1988. As Associate
Editor for the International Journal *Education & Computing*, I asked Margaret to
submit an updated version for the Journal, which she did (Riel, 1989). Riel
compared four educational network communities: AT&T's Long Distance
Learning Network, FrEdMail, McGraw-Hill MIX, and National Geographic's
Kids Network. In so doing, she created a conceptual framework for describing
the participant structures of these networked communities. She described each
community in terms of four participant structures:

- Organization of the network group: its size, common knowledge,
  interests, past experiences, and the physical locations of the
  participants.
- Network task organization: the types of activities that participants
  engage in over the network.
- Response opportunities and obligations: ease of access to the
  interaction, including social and technical resources for sending and
  receiving messages, and the tacit or formal requirements for
  responding.
- Coordination and support: the structures for facilitating group
  interaction, support for technical and curriculum development on the

network, and means of assessing the quantity or quality of the
exchanges on the network.

Riel's conceptual framework for the participant structures of an online learning
community immediately became part of my considerations when designing and
developing similar communities and projects.

Understanding Moderator Roles in Online Communities:
TERC's LabNet for Teacher Enhancement

Comparable in importance to Riel's analysis of participant structures in
advancing my understanding of online learning communities was the
experience and analysis of moderator roles in TERC's LabNet. Starting in 1989,
the TERC LabNet Project, funded by the NSF for six years, provided teacher
enhancement and support for high school science teachers. The LabNet
project aimed to motivate and support teachers to teach science in a more
experimental, collaborative, and in-depth, project-enhanced approach, using
technological tools where appropriate. The project was designed as a
community of practice, connected mainly by a telecommunication network.
The LabNetwork, carried on America Online (AOL), provided a meeting place
for over 700 teachers to support each other in experimenting with new
teaching strategies, reflect on their teaching experiences, problem-solve, share
resources, and build collegial connections with their peers. AOL provided the
necessary (and very user-friendly) software free of charge for the most
commonly used school computers, and offered extensive user support,
competitively priced rates, experience in serving over 1,000,000 users, and a
commitment to building easy-to-use interfaces to new features such as Internet
services. The LabNetwork provided *message boards* (where members can initiate
and carry on extended, public dialogues), *file libraries* (with science materials and
project database), online *chat areas* (for real-time conferencing), and a private
email system (which supports an Internet gateway and easy computer-computer
transfer of all kind of files). The network was designed for and with teachers,
and its evolution was linked to teacher contributions. Teacher-moderators help
to initiate, contribute, moderate, and sustain dialogues, and help to link
reflection on the network with action in the classroom.

LabNet in its second three year project of National Science Foundation
funding, expanded the networked community of practice to a total of 1,500
teachers of high school physics, chemistry, biology, and other sciences, and also
added educators who teach science to younger children (Spitzer *et al.*, 1994).

V. Early 1990's: National Science Foundation and the National Research and Education Network

In 1990, I was a Program Manager for the Applications of Advanced Technologies program in the Science Education Directorate at the National Science Foundation. One day, the Director of the Elementary and Secondary Education Division to whom I reported, asked me whether I thought the NSFNet, also known then as the National Research and Education Network (precursor to what we now call the Internet) might have any implications for science education. "YES!" I replied, emboldened by what I had been learning since the mid-1960's about the possibilities of online learning communities, and the existence of the inspiring models of the late 1980's.

What struck me immediately was that *all* of NSF's educational programs — in educational research, instructional materials development, teacher preparation and enhancement, undergraduate curriculum, systemic change, informal science education, and so forth — would be far more powerful, and have a vastly greater impact, if they all were interconnected through the Internet and created virtual communities among their diverse participants and constituent institutions. At that time, only a handful of NSF's educational projects took advantage of the combination of computers and telecommunications networks. Immediately, I began work on creating a new program initiative to encourage research, development, and implementation of science education projects that would take advantage of the Internet.

With the support of the NSF administration and the enthusiastic participation of pioneering educators and technologists, we first initiated a series of studies and stakeholder workshops in 1990 and 1991. One outcome of these forums were proposals for projects we called "Testbeds" to generate and test out ideas about how to take advantage of Internetworking to support educational reforms at all levels of education and across various types of institutions (Hunter, 1992). This initiative was later formalized as the National Infrastructure for Education programs under the leadership of Nora Sabelli, who replaced me in 1993 at the NSF when I left to join TERC and then BBN in Cambridge, Massachusetts.

Investigating Local Infrastructures to Support School Internetworking
One of our first small studies was funded through a Small Grant for Exploratory Research (SGER). At this point in time, we did not have World Wide Web browsers, so one of the major concerns was the design of user interface software to enable users to access resources on remote computers.

Title: Investigations of Local Technological Infrastructures for School Communications
Start Date: May 1, 1991
Investigator: Denis Newman dnewman@bbn.com (Principal Investigator current)
Sponsor: BBN Laboratories Inc.

Little is known about how students and teachers can get high quality and equitable access to the educational and scientific resources that are becoming available on the Internet. With the proposal of a new NSF program that will develop resources and virtual communities on Internet to support the widespread implementation of advanced technologies and curricula in science, math and engineering education, our lack of understanding of local communication infrastructures becomes an urgent concern. This project will examine the technological and pedagogical infrastructures that are required for teachers and students to make optimal use of these resources. The exploratory research will investigate:
1) the major issues schools and materials developers will face in implementing programs making use of the Internet,
2) models that are currently available for providing access,
3) the current resources, capabilities and mechanisms of the Internet, and
4) new developments and approaches that are most likely to provide maximum leverage in obtaining educational advantages from Internet resources.

This study, along with several others, helped to lay the foundation for the NSF's National Infrastructure for Education (NIE) program, and also led to the project National School Network Testbed discussed below in section VI.

Telecommunications as a Tool for Educational Reform

Another of our early projects to engage potential stakeholders in considering how the Internet could be used for improving and reforming education was a series of workshops sponsored by the Aspen Institute.

Title: Linking for Learning: Telecommunications as a Tool for Educational Reform
Start Date: August 1, 1991
Investigator: Charles M. Firestone
Sponsor: The Aspen Institute

This project will examine the integration of telecommunications technologies into the science and mathematics educational reform process. We propose to address a particular educational goal or strategy in order to examine the process of translating a strategy into practice through the lens of telecommunications. Through commissioned papers and seminar discussions in roundtable format among visionaries, experts, critics, educators, and other participants in the educational process, the project will produce guidelines and recommendations, for both the National Science Foundation and other key leaders and organizations, of necessary actions in linking online learning to the science and mathematics educational reform process.

Discipline-Based Online Communities

One key idea that came out of the Aspen Institute study was that discipline-based communities of learners and teachers would be able to focus in a deeper and more detailed way on the needs and opportunities for reform than would projects that addressed a wide spectrum of subject matters. One of the participants in this workshop was Eugene Klotz, a mathematics educator at Swarthmore College. One of the outcomes of the workshop was a project he proposed, called the Geometry Forum.

Title: A Computer-Communications Forum for Geometry
Start Date: June 15, 1992
Investigator: Eugene A. Klotz klotz@forum.swarthmore.edu
Sponsor: Swarthmore College

We propose to create the Geometry Forum, which will consist of the following three elements:
1. an electronic database containing a great deal of useful information on geometry in all its aspects — its teaching, modern research questions, information on mathematics education projects, records of student interactions and questions;
2. a community consisting of the many satisfied users of the database (often conducting their own private electronic mail correspondence on the side): high school and college students, high school and college teachers, pure and applied research geometers, developers of materials, and researchers into geometry education;
3. especially user-friendly software for creating, maintaining, and accessing the electronic database, which allows sophisticated techniques for browsing and searching, uses symbols and diagrams, and implements hypertext features.

In effect, we will be creating a dynamic geometry journal, together with a large and diverse group of readers/contributors. Users will have their own personalized electronic journal, with immediate access to all previous material, and easy means of making their own contributions.

Our Forum will contribute both to new telecommunications technology, and to education. We will expand the possibilities for student learning via telecommunications, and also increase the geometry resources available to teachers (including such personal resources as support groups). Our Forum should also make it possible for the geometry research community to become meaningfully involved with the education of school students.

The success of the Geometry Forum led directly to development of the Math Forum in the mid-1990's:

Title: Mathematics Education and the World Wide Web
Start Date : October 1, 1995
Investigator: Eugene A. Klotz klotz@forum.swarthmore.edu
Sponsor: Swarthmore College

The Math Forum will be a virtual mathematics education and technology-transfer center that brings together four critical elements that must be integrated in order to realize the promise of the WWW for math education: teacher support and networking, math resource development, a well-designed WWW focal point for math education, and development of necessary WWW tools. Built on knowledge gained in the successful Geometry Forum project, the Math Forum will use the power of the WWW to weave public discussion forums, teacher education, interesting mathematics, and sophisticated archives into a productive community. New tools modeled on our existing software will be employed to create collaborative environments that enable public discussion with the full set of resources available on the Internet. Through interactive projects and facilitation of special topic discussions, students, mathematicians, and math educators will contribute to each other's work and provide the rich input, networking, and support sought by teachers for their ongoing professional development. Through the process of archiving and summarizing the activity of online communities and teacher groups, the Math Forum will build a collaborative math educational materials library. The Math Forum will collaborate with existing publishers and curriculum groups, such as those working on NCTM Standards materials, so that educators and students can participate effectively in the curriculum development process and the products can meet the needs of real classrooms. In the course of this effort many more well-developed curricular resources will become available online. In order for the archives to be useful and for math educators to make effective use of the WWW the Math Forum must adapt and create software tools and Web site designs to meet their specific needs. Forum programmers will produce subscription software, evaluation tools, and structured resources that enable users to make sense of the overwhelming information on the Internet. These tools will make it possible for participants to filter and evaluate resources and to move more directly to the task of constructing the environments they wish their students to explore. Furthermore, the Math Forum will develop interactive math projects that take advantage of the WWW for presenting engaging mathematics. Many of the experiments conducted here will have immediate and wide applicability in other areas of education and use of the Internet. A careful program of evaluation and outreach will bring regular reports to the broader educational community. Hired netsurfers and online support staff will keep the Forum on top of new developments and gather relevant resources while publicizing the Forum and establishing the resourcefulness of this pivotal venture.

Early 1990's Testbed Projects Funded by NSF

By 1992 at NSF we were receiving hundreds of preliminary proposals for educational projects to take advantage of telecomputing and Internetworking. Through NSF's peer review system, several testbed projects were funded, and several of these projects created models that have spread throughout education.

Title: Computer-Based Networks for Teacher Education: Science and Mathematics Teaching Teleapprenticeships
Start Date: September 15, 1992
Investigator: James A. Levin j-levin@uiuc.edu & Michael L. Waugh
Sponsor: U of Ill Urbana-Champaign

The proposers have developed a model for improving teacher education called Teaching Teleapprenticeships. Using this model, teacher education students and practicing teachers learn about teaching and learning by participating in electronic network-based activities with K-12 students and teachers and university-based scientists and teacher educators. They will implement and evaluate this model as a means of improving the preparation of science and mathematics teachers. To support this model, they will develop, evaluate, and disseminate communication tools that allow these Teaching Teleapprenticeships to be practiced widely in a diverse set of science and mathematics educational settings.

Title: The Weather Underground: Application of Computer Technology to Science in Michigan Secondary Schools
Start Date: August 1, 1992
Investigator: Perry J. Samson samson@umich.edu (Principal Investigator current)
Sponsor: University of Michigan

The scientific community is challenged by the need to reach out to students who have traditionally not been attracted to engineering and the sciences. This project would provide a link between the University of Michigan and the teachers and students of secondary education in the State of Michigan with an initial emphasis on southeast Michigan, through the creation of a range of computer services which will provide interactive access to current weather and climate change information. Taking advantage of a unique computer network capacity within the State of Michigan named MichNet which provides local phone ports in virtually every major city in the state, and the resources available to the university community via the University Corporation for Atmospheric Research (UCAR) UNIDATA program, this project would provide secondary schools with access to a state-of-the-art interactive weather information system. The real-time data available via the system, supplemented by interactive computer modules designed in collaboration with earth science teachers, will provide animated background information on a range of climate and weather related topics. While the principal objective of this project will be to provide educationally stimulating interactive computer systems and electronic weather and climate modules for application in inner city Detroit and its environs, the unique nature of the available computer networking will allow virtually every school system in the state to have access. Subsequently successful completion of this project could eventually make the same systems available to other cities and states.

Title: Common Knowledge: Pittsburgh
Start Date: January 1, 1993
Investigator: Robert D. Carlitz (Principal Investigator current)
      Ralph Z. Roskies (Co-Principal Investigator current)
      Michael J. Levine (Co-Principal Investigator current)
      Stanley J. Herman (Co-Principal Investigator current)
Sponsor: MPC Corp.

This project establishes an educational networking testbed to test conjectures about major changes in the teaching environment of the Pittsburgh Public Schools made possible through the installation of an electronic data network that will ultimately be available to all students and teachers in the school district. The proposed network will be novel in its distributed architecture and distributed administrative structure. Teachers and students will use the network to access information and people outside of their classrooms. These new resources will be incorporated into curriculum reform efforts, and the network will be used as a tool for the development, implementation, evaluation, and dissemination of new curriculum components. The project will develop a set of network-based activities and provide a framework in which such activities can be implemented throughout the local school system, tested, evaluated and made available to other school districts around the nation. The project is a joint effort of the school district, the University of Pittsburgh, and the Pittsburgh Supercomputing Center, which itself was jointly founded by the University of Pittsburgh, Carnegie-Mellon University, and the Westinghouse Electric Corporation. The proposed activities will build coalitions involving these groups and many others across the local community.

Within the school district the project involves cooperative activities which include students, teachers, instructional specialists, administrators and the Pittsburgh Federation of Teachers. The proposed network is the key element which will allow these groups to work together efficiently and smoothly. It is also the key to significant changes in the structure and quality of education in the Pittsburgh Public Schools and, by extension, in other school districts across the country.

1993 Breakthrough: Mosaic & the World Wide Web

Up until 1993, a substantial proportion of our educational networking projects' resources were necessarily devoted to finding or developing software to enable user-friendly interface for Internet resources and interactions. The critical technical breakthrough was Mosaic, developed at the National Center for Supercomputer Applications at the University of Illinois. The following brief history helps to provide the context in which we were operating at this time.

In 1985 with the creation of the National Science Foundation's Supercomputer Centers program, NSF created NSFNET, a network that connected the five supercomputer centers (including NCSA) and provided a network for research and education. Based on the ARPANET protocols, the NSFNET created a national backbone service. At the same time, regional networks were created to link individual institutions with the national backbone service. NSFNET grew rapidly as people discovered its potential and as new software applications were created to make access easier.

The software program that effectively opened the Internet to millions was CERN's World Wide Web hypertext protocol, first invented by Tim Berners-Lee. A team of researchers at NCSA picked up on Berners-Lee's idea and developed NCSA Mosaic. In 1993 the National Science Foundation's Computer Science Division awarded a grant to the NCSA to further develop Mosaic. The award abstract read as follows:

> This award will support further development of the Mosaic software and related activities such as workshops, documentation development, and Internet standards activities. Mosaic was developed by the National Center for Supercomputing Applications at the University of Illinois Urbana/Champaign, building on the World Wide Web software kernal. Mosaic is client/server software which enables dynamic browsing, retrieval, and display of multimedia data over the Internet using Unix, Macintosh, or PC computers, using hypertext to allow English documents to contain words or images as direct links to additional information. Clicking on linked words or images retrieves and displays new files and information transparently. Retrieved files in turn contain links to other databanks, creating a global Web of information. Mosaic has rapidly grown to be very popular; over 300,000 copies of the software have been distributed to date, with thousands more every month. (NSF 1993).

In 1993, Mosaic became the first popular graphical Web browser and was offered free to the general public from NCSA's Internet site. By 1994, Mosaic had a user base of several million users worldwide. In addition, NCSA developed WWW server software (originally called httpd—made commercial as Apache), which is now used in about 66 percent of all Web servers.

This technology was quickly transferred to the private sector when Marc Andreessen and several other developers of NCSA Mosaic left the center to form Netscape. In addition, more than 100 companies licensed the Mosaic software through Spyglass, Inc., including Microsoft, which led to the development of Microsoft Internet Explorer.

As the use of Mosaic and browsers based on Mosaic continued to bring educators, business, and government to the Internet, NSFNET continued to expand. Corporations such as Sprint and MCI began to build their own networks, which they linked to NSFNET. As commercial firms and other regional network providers began taking over the operation of major Internet arteries, NSF began to withdraw from actively managing the backbone. Yet, it was the NSF's initial investment in a high-speed link and for research centers that put in place the backbone of what is now the commercial Internet. (For

more detailed history of Mosaic see http://www.ncsa.uiuc.edu/Divisions/
Communications/MosaicHistory/history.html)

Pioneering Collaborations Inventing New Ways to Offer Educational Opportunities

One of the pioneering projects funded by the NSF's National Infrastructure for
Education program was the Science Learning Network.

Title: The Science Learning Network
Start Date: October 1, 1994
Investigator: Stephen H. Baumann baumann@fi.edu (Principal Investigator current),
Wayne E. Ransom (Co-Principal Investigator current), Paul M. Helfrich (Co-Principal
Investigator current)
Sponsor: Franklin Inst Science Museum

 The Franklin Institute proposes to establish the Science Learning Network (SLN), a unique
online collaborative of science museums, industry, and schools to support the teaching and
learning of science, mathematics, and technology (SMT) in grades K-8. The SLN will
integrate the educational resources offered by science/technology centers with the power of
telecomputing networking to provide powerful new support for teacher development and
science learning. By December 1997 the SLN will develop and evaluate the following:
UniVERSE — an online SMT database and software package which will provide interactive
capabilities to actively and intelligently assist K-8 classroom teachers in their Internet
explorations, much like an electronic "librarian." Online Museum Collaborative — a national
consortium of science museums (The Franklin Institute, the Exploratorium, Oregon
Museum of Science and Industry, Museum of Science, Boston, and Science Museum of
Minnesota) that will pool their resources and expertise to create online assets and provide
ongoing professional development on telecomputing networking for precollege SMT
teachers. Online Demonstration Schools — a network of K-8 schools, working in
collaboration with consortium museums and Unisys Corporation volunteers as
demonstration sites for online teaching and learning in SMT.   Over the course of three
years, the SLN will provide direct support to 180 teachers and 3,000 K-8 students in the
online demonstration schools. Through existing teacher networks, each museum will offer
professional development for an additional 200 teachers each year. The Urban Systemic
Initiatives in Philadelphia and Miami offer the potential for broader, systemic impact in
those cities.   By the end of the grant period, the SLN will provide field-tested models of a
new kind of online SMT community through the collaboration of science museums with
industry and schools. The sustainable impact of the SLN will be assured by UniVERSE's
status as a publicly accessible database and software package and the development of the
national consortium of online museums, whose network resources will be made available on
an ongoing basis to educators. The three-year formative development of the online
demonstration schools will contribute vital data to precollegiate school reform in SMT,
showing how schools build capacity to become members of the online community and
demonstrating how teaching and learning are enhanced by online resources. Unisys
Corporation has pledged its support to this project and will provide matching funds for up
to 40% of the total NSF award.

The Science Learning Network was a seminal effort by science museums to bring the resources of these centers of informal learning to millions more people by taking advantage of Internetworking. One of the greatest challenges to the SLN was to invent ways of collaborating among the six premier science museums. I had the privilege of serving as an advisor to this project, and so had the opportunity to learn about the myriad obstacles to multi-institutional collaborations. The dedication of the leaders of this effort is reflected in the fact that it succeeded in creating many new ways to offer science museum experiences to millions of learners of all ages. By 2004, the SLN has matured and expanded to include several international museums. See http://www.sln.org.

VI. Mid-to-Late 1990's: Towards Universal Participation in Online Learning Communities

In the mid-1990's, the challenge I wanted to address was not whether and how to create such communities (this had been done successfully in the 1980's), but whether, given ubiquitous access to the Internet, such communities could be created on such a large scale that they could actually play a central role in the restructuring and reform of regular educational practices (e.g., Hunter, 1992). Educational virtual communities in the 1980's and early 1990's were pioneering efforts that attracted visionary innovators and early adopter teachers and their students.   To make a real difference in educational practice, however, we would need to engage a dramatically broader base of stakeholders from participating institutions. For educational reforms and innovations to take hold and become institutionalized, *all* learners and teachers and other stakeholders needed to participate. A useful conceptual framework for understanding such a shift both in virtual communities and local educational institutions is the well known *Technology Adoption Life Cycle* proposed by Geoffrey Moore in *Crossing the Chasm* (Moore, 1991).

Crossing the Chasm in the National School Network Testbed (BBN et al.)

One of our NSF networking Testbed projects, the National School Network Testbed led by BBN was ideally suited to address this challenge.
In 1993, the National School Network Testbed (NSNT) posed the following question for communities in the United States:

> *Can we construct and manage communications networks and*
> *information services to support educational innovation on a local level in such*
> *a way that taxpayers, governments, and private industry will view their*

benefits as warranting the investment needed to support them on a large scale? (Toward Universal Participation in the NII, 1994, p. C5)

Between 1994 and 1998, over 450 local communities and institutions in the NSNT were building local information infrastructure while inventing new roles and educational services that take advantage of the technologies. (Hunter, 1995) The NSN members included a wide range of the kinds of institutions that are a part of the educational system — State Education Agencies, universities, school districts, individual schools, museums, research organizations, private corporations. Our theme of user-constructible networking went to the heart of educational reform groups who were looking for a new generation of school technology that better maps onto their constructivist ideas about learning and a project-based curriculum. A typical NSNT organization was in the process of moving from a host-terminal mode of internet access to a full IP connectivity and client/server mode (Hunter, 1995b).

Our vision at this time was that Internetworking provides us with new choices about the extent to which we merge activities, roles, and institutions previously separated in time and space — activities such as learning, teaching, working, playing, collaborating, and governing (Hunter,1997a). With benefit of experience and data from testbed virtual community efforts of the past decade (Hunter 1993, 1997b), we were by the end of the 1990's in a position to understand the interactions between learning in virtual communities on the one hand and changes in local communities on the other. With benefit of survey data and a period of analysis and reflection, we could in retrospect see what the organizers of the NSN could not have understood at the time. They faced two major challenges that were not then understood or even formulated. First, the NSN sought to facilitate learning about emerging new modes of teaching, learning, professional development, and community interactions that are made possible through Internetworking. An assumption was made that since the innovators and early adopters of telecommunications networks in education had been involved in virtual communities, that such practices would become widespread across a school once the enabling technical infrastructure was built and more users came on board. However, the majority of the people newly adopting the use of the Internet in the member institutions were not (yet) very much interested in these educational innovations. In other words, the nature of change within member institutions was different from the predicted changes. Secondly, the NSN sought to facilitate learning and collaboration across institutions through a virtual community. However, the majority of the people in the member institutions were not (yet) participating in *any* virtual communities. Therefore, as the use of the technology moved beyond the innovators and early adopters to the majority, it became less likely that these new users would contribute their voices, agendas, and experiences to the learning collaborative of the NSN.

Pioneering individuals (the Innovators and Early Adopters of Geoffrey Moore's framework) can benefit from participating in Virtual Communities relevant to their learning needs, almost irrespective of the local conditions in which they live and work. By definition they are willing and able to overcome all sorts of obstacles in order to try out new practices that appear promising to them. If we are to place a high priority on offering these new learning opportunities to *all*, then local educational institutions and communities need to change along with the evolution of virtual communities. The culture and skills of collaboration are the *sine qua non* of virtual communities and need to be fostered within the local organization. This means that the designers and implementers of new virtual communities for learning need to work hand-in-hand with leaders in the local institutions that are the everyday worksite for the potential members of the virtual community. Some policies and procedures typical of traditional educational institutions will need to change if they are to cross the chasm between the early adopters and the majority. For instance, support and incentives for teachers' ongoing professional development need to be in place and regularized. Management and the allocation of time within a school needs to become more flexible, to enable teacher collaborations locally as well as in the virtual community. Technology initiatives will be tied more closely to school improvement priorities and associated budget opportunities. Conversely, the virtual community needs to stay closely attuned to changing priorities, agendas, capacities, and participant groups from the local communities (Hunter, 2002).

Designers and leaders of online learning communities will need to continue providing appropriate social organization, technical tools for communication and information management, and content within the networked social space of a Collaboratory. However, they must also help the local institutions and communities to change in ways that enable everyone to benefit (Hunter, 2002).

VII. Early 2000's: The Challenge of Implementing Innovative Online Communities "In the Trenches"

By the year 2000, the technological and experiential foundations had been laid within the R&D community, for all the major components needed to build online learning communities, and there were numerous "existence proofs" of the feasibility of such communities. The key components that were in place included the following:

- nearly ubiquitous telecommunications networking in homes and schools via the Internet;
- user-friendly software interfaces such as WWW browsers;
- online access to shared digital data bases on all imaginable topics via the Internet;
- powerful computer-based tools such as Geographical Information Systems for manipulating and visualizing data;
- software environments for structuring online discussion and organizing knowledge;
- know-how about structuring and facilitating online communities (e.g., Riel, 1989; Spitzer *et al.*, 1994); and
- a wealth of prior research and experience in teachers' professional development (e.g., Loucks-Horsley *et al.*, 1998).

Projects such as those mentioned in earlier sections of this chapter had demonstrated the feasibility of creating and sustaining online learning communities. However, these projects had been carefully built and nurtured by people and organizations whose primary mission is advancing the state of art and practice — that is, the R&D community. Could that foundation now be applied to projects led by people outside of the R&D community?

Project VISIT: Implementing Online Communities in the "Real World" of Schools, Colleges and Local Government Agencies

Project VISIT (Virtual Immersion in Science Inquiry for Teachers) is a professional development program for teachers in grades 5-12, supported by a grant in 1999 from the National Science Foundation's Teacher Enhancement program. Between January 2000 and August 2003, 215 teachers, 31 teacher leaders, and experts in GIS participated in the VISIT online Collaboratory. The purposes of this activity included the following:

- advancing teachers' understanding of geospatial data and information systems (GIS);
- applying these tools and applications in their classrooms and curricula; and
- conducting real-world investigations that take advantage of these technologies.

Participants included teachers of chemistry, physics, earth science, geography, history, environmental science, biology and life sciences, mathematics, technology, Integrated Natural Science, social studies, library/media, and English. The discussions among these participants resulted in a collection of over 11,000 messages, in addition to products such as a structure for collaborative discussions, a one-semester syllabus, lesson plans, hands-on tutorials, data sets, documented investigations, technical manuals, assessment rubrics, and a guide to sources of geo-referenced data. These products are available for anyone to use, at the VISIT Web site at http://ceita.emich.edu/visit .

The VISIT Collaboratory has been a fruitful learning community in many ways, both for individual participants and for the group as a whole. However, it almost did not survive its first year of existence. Although, as I said above, the groundwork for most of the pieces of this effort had already been laid in terms of the state-of-art, this project faced an additional and nearly insurmountable challenge. Most of the successful online communities that I was aware of had been designed and developed by teams of people from organizations such as TERC, BBN, University of Illinois, University of Michigan, SDC, and Northwestern University, who devote their professional lives to creating innovative projects in education. But now that the pieces were in place in the state-of-art and infrastructure, could such online communities be designed and developed by a team that was led by regular academic teaching faculty, practicing scientists, and classroom teachers, all of whom were outside of the educational R&D business and had no prior experience in building online communities? Simply stated, the answer was "no." The Core Team that originally was to design and develop the Collaboratory included (besides the Principal Investigator Dr. Yichun Xie and myself, the co-PI), three university faculty members in a school of education, six applied scientists from a County department of environment, and six high school teachers with prior experience in using GIS in the classroom. While each individual potentially had something important to contribute, they simply would not work in cyberspace.

The project was saved by a change in leadership. We replaced the original Core Team with classroom teachers who are already Teacher Leaders either within their discipline or region and who really wanted to learn how to collaborate and facilitate professional development in cyberspace. We found Al Lewandowski, a teacher with experience in using GIS in the classroom and with an interest in online learning communities, who served as the "leader of leaders." Al and I coached these teacher leaders over two years with some of the know-how about online moderators that had been learned in LabNet and elsewhere, and codified in a book by Collison *et al.* (2000). In the end, we had a very effective leader team with diverse skills, knowledge, and personalities.

Another type of obstacle that plagued this project involved institutional operations and administration. It proved to be nearly impossible to establish and regularize the administrative functions needed for an online program that had requirements for online recruiting, registration, record-keeping, awarding credits, paying moderators, and so forth that were different from the normal university operations with on-site students. A large proportion of participants and leaders left the project in frustration over these operational and administrative hurdles.

Equally daunting was the challenge of building quality assurance into the project operations. In an online community, especially one focusing on highly technical content such as GIS, there are a myriad of technical pieces that have to work properly and in a way that participants who are not fluent in the technology can use them reliably in cyberspace. In a professional R&D center professional staff and numerous mechanisms are built into the team's development processes to ensure quality of products and services for the projects. In a typical university operation involving face-to-face classroom instruction, there are not such team-based quality assurance mechanisms. My continual efforts to build quality assurance processes into the project operations were repeatedly dismissed as "outside interference" in university operations. VISIT participants were constantly battling technical glitches in the online registration forms, the GIS instruction, the procedures and instructions for downloading of data sets and lessons, and so forth. Many teachers were simply unable to work around these problems, and just dropped out of the program before they really got started.

Despite all these obstacles, a great deal was learned in VISIT, especially about the kinds of help and support teachers need when they are learning highly technical subjects, and also about the ways in which communities of teachers can contribute to each others' learning given appropriate structures, pedagogy, and facilitation.

Summary and Conclusions

I have shared here some highlights of my personal experience in a 40-year quest for online learning communities.

Through a variety of contexts and projects, the following have been some of the key learnings.

Learnings About Political and Institutional Context
- Institutional policies, and politics at all levels, constrain or enhance the possibilities for online learning communities.
- Grant support for innovative, pioneering projects that take advantage of emerging technologies, such as projects supported by the National Science Foundation over the years, is critical to the evolution of new models of learning, teaching, collaboration, and knowledge-building in society.
- Local communities and institutions need to change (or new ones need to be invented) in order for online learning communities to meet the needs of a broad spectrum of people within those institutions.
- There are many conceptual barriers to creating effective online learning communities.

Learnings About Participant Structures
- Teamwork is as hard to create and sustain in cyberspace as it is in physical space.
- There are ways in which we can reduce social barriers to collaboration in cyberspace that are harder to overcome in face-to-face settings.
- Access to personal computers, and fluency in the use of associated software tools, is a prerequisite to participating in online communities.
- Participant structures need to be consciously designed to meet the needs of the particular online community and its purposes, and these structures must be revised as the community grows and learns.
- Although much is known about the roles and techniques of effective moderators or facilitators in online learning communities, personality characteristics and motivations to work in cyberspace must also be taken into account in selecting people for these roles.
- Learning communities comprised of innovators and early adopters are different from learning communities that attempt to serve the majority of people.

Learnings About Content
- Sharing, interpreting, and building knowledge from data is an essential component of an online learning community.

- The most successful online learning communities provide a wide range of structures, tools, incentives, practices, and facilitation aimed towards helping individual participants contribute to the knowledge base of the overall community.
- Participants in online learning communities are more dependent upon a reliable technological infrastructure, quality software tools, and polished instruction than are participants in a comparable face-to-face group setting. Therefore, quality assurance processes are more critical in building online communities than in conventional classroom instruction.

Learnings About Technology
- The technological infrastructure available at a given time constrains the ways in which participants interact with each other and the kinds of tools they have for building knowledge individually and together. However, beneficial collaborations can take place through creative use of relatively primitive tools.
- If something is worth doing, you can find a way to do it even if the tools are not perfect.

The Next Forty Years?

Over the past forty years, a great deal has been learned about how to build, nurture, and sustain online learning communities. And, at least in the U.S., we have practically ubiquitous access to the Internet, databases, and computing machines, with user-friendly software to perform a wide array of information-handling, knowledge-building, and collaboration activities.

The greatest obstacles now are institutional and political. The traditional institutions that control and operate elementary, secondary, and higher education evolved in a paper-pencil world that required face-to-face interaction for teaching, learning, and collaboration, as well as for administration of the enterprise. Attempting to graft productive, creative online learning communities that can benefit everyone onto the routine practices of these institutions could well take another forty years. It will likely require invention of new institutions of education, designed for the contemporary world, in order to take advantage of the special opportunities offered through online learning communities as well as their connections with local communities.

References

Bitzer, D.L., Braunfeld, P.G. & Lichtenberger, W.W. (1962). Plato II: A multiple-student, computer-controlled, automatic teaching device. In J. Coulson (Ed.), *Programmed learning and computer-based instruction.* Proceedings of the Conference on Application of Digital Computers to Automated Instruction. New York: John Wiley & Sons.

Collison, G., Elbaum, B., Haavind, S., & Tinker, R. (2000). *Facilitating online learning: Effective strategies for moderators.* Madison, WI: Atwood Publishing.

Coulson, J. (1962). *Programmed learning and computer-based instruction.* Proceedings of the Conference on Application of Digital Computers to Automated Instruction. New York: John Wiley & Sons.
Grayson, L., & Robbins, J. (1972). *U.S. Office of Education Support of Computer Projects, 1965-1971.* Washington DC: U.S. Government Printing Office.

Greenberger, M., Aronofsky, J., McKenney, J., & Massy, W. (1974). *Networks for research and education.* Cambridge, MA: MIT Press.

Hunter, B. (1983). *My students use computers: Learning activities for computer literacy.* Reston, VA: Prentice Hall.

Hunter, B. (1992). Linking for learning: Computer-and-communications network support for nationwide innovation in education. *Journal of Science Education and Technology, 1(1).*

Hunter, B. (1993, Oct.). NSF's networked testbeds inform innovation in science education. *T.H.E. Journal.*

Hunter, B. (1995a) Learning and teaching on the Internet: Contributing to educational reform. In B. Kahin & J. Keller (Eds.), *Public access to the Internet.* Cambridge, MA: MIT Press.

Hunter, B. (1995b). Internetworking and educational reform: The National School Network Testbed. Paper presented at the 1995 INET Conference in Hawaii. Available at http://www.isoc.org/HMP/PAPER/065/html/paper.html

Hunter, B. (1997a). Learning in an Internetworked world. In *The Internet as paradigm*. Aspen Institute Annual Review of the Institute for Information Studies.

Hunter, B. (1997b). Fostering collaborative knowledge-building: Lessons learned from the National School Network testbed. In B. Collis & G. Knezek (Eds.), *Teaching & learning in the digital age: Research into practice with telecommunications in educational settings*. Eugene, OR: ISTE. Presented at the Annual Telecommunications in Education (TelEd) Conference. Austin, TX. Available at http://www.gse.uci.edu/Ravitz/Hunter_TelEd98.html.

Hunter, B. (2002). Learning in the virtual community depends upon changes in local communities. In K. Renninger & W. Shumar (Eds.), *Building virtual communities: Learning and change in cyberspace*. Cambridge, UK: Cambridge University Press.

Hunter, B., Kastner, C., Rubin, M., & Seidel, R. (1975). *Learning alternatives in U.S. education: Where student and computer meet*. Englewood Cliffs, NJ: Educational Technology Publications.

Hunter, B., & Lodish, E. (1989). *Online searching in the curriculum: A teaching guide for library/media specialists and teachers*. Santa Barbara, CA: ABC-Clio, Inc.

Licklider, J.C.R. (1974). Potential of networking for research and education. Chapter 5, In M. Greenberger *et al.* (Eds.), *Networks for research and education*. Cambridge, MA: MIT Press.

Loucks-Horsley, S., Hewson, P., Love, N., & Stiles, K.. (1998). *Designing professional development for teachers of science and mathematics*. Thousand Oaks, CA: Corwin Press.

Moore, G. (1991). *Crossing the chasm: Marketing and selling high-tech products to the mainstream customers*. New York: HarperCollins Business.

Renninger, K., & Shumar, W. (2002). *Building virtual communities: Learning and change in cyberspace*. Cambridge, UK: Cambridge University Press.

Riel, M. (1989). Four models of educational telecommunications: Connections to the future. *Education & Computing, 5*(4), pp. 261-274.

Spitzer, W., Wedding, K., & DiMauro, V. (1994). Fostering reflective dialogues for teacher professional development. Available at http://www.terc.edu/papers/labnet/Guide/Fostering_Refl_Dialogues.html

Teager, H. (1962). Systems considerations in real-time computer usage. In J. Coulson (Eds.), *Programmed learning and computer-based instruction.* Proceedings of the Conference on Application of Digital Computers to Automated Instruction. New York: John Wiley & Sons.

Chapter 14

From Potential to Prosperity:
Twenty Years of Online Learning Environments

Annette Lamb

Annette Lamb has been an elementary library media specialist, computer teacher, and Professor of education. She is currently a Professor at Indiana University - Purdue University at Indianapolis (IUPUI) teaching online graduate courses for librarians and educators. As president of Lamb Learning Group, she also writes, speaks, and conducts professional development workshops, presentations, and keynotes throughout North America focusing on ways to more effectively integrate technology into the classroom. Annette received her PhD in Educational Technology from Iowa State University.

Beware. This chapter contains shocking revelations from a teaching and learning addict. Although I considered dozens of careers, I was born to be an educator. As a child I corralled my siblings, cousins, and neighbors in the basement turning them into my students. I assigned math problems from old textbooks, directed elaborate skits, and even created a library complete with card pockets and Dewey decimal labels made with masking tape.

Whether educating young children or adults, I soon discovered the key to effective teaching and learning is motivation and meaningfulness. Learning is about conducting inquiries, making connections, and communicating understandings, not just listening to lectures and completing assignments. Over the past twenty years, this realization became even more apparent as I moved from teaching traditional face-to-face courses toward facilitating online learning environments.

It's easy to translate the informational aspects of a course into an electronic form. Selecting books, articles, video clips, Websites, and visual resources is time-consuming, but not difficult. The tough part is translating the less obvious roles of the teacher as mentor, facilitator, nurturer, and promoter. In other words, when students are feeling lost, how does an online instructor provide a virtual hand of support? How does a teacher convey the love of content, enthusiasm for learning, and other elements that motivate learners? These are the difficult parts of being an online educator or any teacher concerned with making effective use of online resources.

This chapter explores the options for online learning. Then, it examines the dynamic nature of these learning environments. It concludes with challenges for online teaching.

Online Learning As...

From information access to communication options, distance learning environments provide many opportunities for educators and students. No longer are classes made up of students who live in the same location or share similar backgrounds. Promoting cultural understanding, global awareness, and international perspectives, this diverse environment reflects a range of cultures, opinions, and ideas. In addition, flexible course scheduling, independent study, and varied communication channels can often address the barriers of time, distance, and physical disabilities (Lamb & Smith, 1999).

Online learning can be viewed as a resource-rich environment, a learning experience, an opportunity, and a lifestyle.

Online Learning as a Resource-Rich Environment
The Web is woven by people who are willing to openly share their knowledge and expertise with others.

When microcomputers were first introduced in schools, educators developed computer literacy curriculum and separate computer courses. Many computer curricula focused on technology as an object of instruction rather than a learning tool and resource. In a 1995 article titled "Driver's Education for the Information Highway: Teaching Information and Ideas, not Internet," I expressed concerns about how the Internet was being used in schools. Rather than focusing on the technology itself, I emphasized the importance of integrating the Internet as an information and communication tool (Lamb, 1995). Rather than pressuring teachers to go online, I asked them to consider their content needs and decide whether it was worthwhile to use Internet resources. Instead of abandoning books, videos, and hands-on experiments, I encouraged teachers to focus on the unique attributes of the Internet and add these resources to enrich learning.

Information Resources
Over the past decade, the Web has become a huge information resource. As a result, the need for careful selection of online resources has become even more important. Whether creating entire online courses or individual lessons that

incorporate Web resources, evaluating and integrating online resources is time-consuming, but necessary.

An increasing number of Web portals have provided starting points and pathfinders for educators. While some early innovators have either folded or shifted to subscription services, others such as Kathy Schrock and her Guide for Educators (http://school.discovery.com/schrockguide) have survived the demands of ongoing Website revision and need for sponsor support (Johnson & Lamb, April 2003).

Since 1999, our 42explore project (http://42explore.com) has provided quality Web-based thematic resources for over 300 popular K-12 topics across subject areas. Each 42explore page begins with a basic and more in-depth description of the topic, four good starting points, a variety of activities, and many student and teacher Website resources (Lamb & Johnson, 2001).

Information-Rich Learning
Developing a resource-rich learning environment involves combining a wide variety of materials. Teachers are increasingly integrating online materials along with trade books, videos, and other resources. By drawing on the natural relationships among subjects and connecting to authentic resources, students can see how the curriculum connects to the world around them. The Internet provides a worldwide audience for sharing, along with resources for better connection between the curriculum and the "real world" (Lamb, 1999).

Until the late 1990s, a majority of Web-based activities focused on low-level, scavenger hunt types of activities. Frustrated by this poor use of online resources, many educators began to develop strategies that would emphasize higher-level, inquiry-based activities. For example, since Bernie Dodge developed the WebQuest concept in 1995, thousands of teachers have developed these authentic, technology-rich environments for problem solving, information processing, and collaboration.

Today rather than creating a WebQuest from scratch, teachers are able to use or adapt existing resources already available online. For example, a teacher might add resources at different reading levels, incorporate new content, identify multiple perspectives, or locate different channels of communication such as audio or video.

Some teachers still have difficulty seeing the role of online resources in their traditional curriculum. In the book *Newberys and the Net: Thematic Technology*

Connections, Nancy Smith and I explored ways to encourage teachers to connect literature, reading, and online resources (Lamb & Smith, 2000a). Our project began by identifying Web-based resources and activities to enrich the exploration of 150 Newbery award-winning children's books. The appeal of this approach is reflected in the popularity of our Literature Ladders Website (http://eduscapes.com/ladders). For example, the page providing Web-based resources on the book *Holes* by Louis Sachar receives over 10,000 hits per month.

Teachers may begin by simply enhancing their traditional lessons with Web-based resources. As they gain confidence, they may try other strategies, such as literature-based WebQuests that use a book(s) as a focal point for the reading-centered, online learning activities (Teclehaimanot & Lamb, 2004).

Online learning begins with carefully selected, quality Web resources followed by meaningful, engaging experiences.

Online Learning as a Learning Experience
Remote learning technologies provide teachers with exciting ways to engage their students in real-time, real-world science and cultural experiences.

During the 1990s, I was involved with a number of US Department of Education Technology Challenge Grants that provided opportunities for students of all ages to participate in exciting, innovative applications of online technology. For example, pre-service teachers acted as online mentors for elementary children, middle school students conducted interviews with experts thousands of miles away, and high school students accessed and applied science data from ongoing, real-time projects.

In Project Whistlestop, students and teachers in schools surrounding the Truman Presidential Library were involved with developing online materials based on the Truman presidency. Their goal was to provide an online learning experience for millions of students who could not to travel to Missouri to visit the library (http://www.trumanlibrary.org/kids/index.html). Their online lessons, adventures, activities, and WebQuests promoted their own understanding of curriculum content as well as the learning of others.

"Flat Stanley" by Jeff Brown is a children's book about a boy who is flattened by a falling bulletin board and is able to fit in an envelope and travel around the world. Since the 1960s, teachers have used this book as the basis for activities related to geography, culture, and travel. Today, thousands of classrooms around the world participate in these formal and informal virtual adventures (http://flatstanley.enoreo.on.ca). For example in 2003, I hosted a Flat Stanley project as part of a trip to China, Japan, and South Korea. Children from around the world emailed me their questions and requests for information and photographs. As I visited each location, I posted ideas, photographs, answers to questions, and insights.

A growing number of teachers see the Internet as a tool for building rich learning experiences for children. For example, each year Joan Goble's (http://www.siec.k12.in.us/cannelton) third grade class gains global experiences by interacting with children from places such as Japan, The Netherlands, and Australia. They've written animal diaries, shared information about endangered animals, and saved local historical sites through Web-based activities. As a teacher and technology coordinator, Susan Silverman's (http://kids-learn.org) online projects have focused on ways to share experiences among teachers and students. Projects like Bunny Readers, Kidspired Frosty Readers, Graph Goodies, and Orphan Trains ask students to share their understandings of the world around them by posting projects online.

While these teachers make effective use of Internet resources, they also value online collaboration with other teachers and focus their efforts on ways to involve their students with knowledge construction. By actively involving their children in using technology as a tool for creating meaningful communications and products, students gain valuable experiences and view learning as an opportunity.

Online Learning as an Opportunity
Regardless of whether the student is five or ninety-five, the online learning environment has something to offer.

In the early 1990s, online learning was viewed as special and separate from other programs. It required its own department, committees, and facilities. Specially trained instructional designers and faculty taught courses that appeared in course catalogs under "distance education." Because many learners didn't have access to email or video conferencing facilities, they often came to campus to access the computer labs that were in heavy demand for face-to-face classes. Thus defeating the purpose of the "anywhere, anytime" idea. By the mid-1990s, some universities began offering blended or hybrid courses that combined online and face-to-face learning (Lamb & Smith, 1999).

As educational institutions at all levels began searching for ways to reduce budgets while maintaining support, many campuses recognized the need to merge service units. As a result, many campuses have experienced a convergence of departments and resources related to academic technology and specifically distance learning (Johnson, Lamb, & Teclehaimanot, 2003).

By the turn of the century, distance learning was viewed as a legitimate option, rather than a replacement or substitute for a face-to-face classroom. Online learning was simply a different type of course delivery.

Some students hate it and others love it. In the same way, some teachers view it as restrictive and isolating, while others find teaching through the Internet exciting, stimulating, and expansive.

Online Learning as Lifestyle

Internet-based resources and communication provide access to "anywhere, anytime" teaching and learning. Students don't need to drive hours to a campus and faculty aren't required to reside where they teach.

As a graduate student in the early 1980s, I taught enthusiastic teachers about the future of email using BITNET. Although we only communicated with other universities, educators could already see the potential of bringing the outside world into their classroom.

However as a doctoral student driving two hours each way to attend courses in the mid-1980s, I quickly became frustrated by the lack of telecommunications technology in K-12 schools. Although computer applications such as word processing and graphics packages were available on microcomputers where I taught, email and network assignments had to be completed on the college campus.

By the late 1980s, dial-up connections and bulletin board systems began making telecommunications projects possible at all levels. As a new faculty member at the University of Toledo, I coordinated online discussion groups for teachers interested in integrating telecommunications projects into their classroom. We began encouraging teachers to join national projects such as JASON (http://jasonproject.org) and Journey North (http://www.learner.org/jnorth/).

Online forums, email, and Internet resources became a regular component of on-campus courses in the early 1990's. However, most on-campus and distance learning courses fit into the traditional structure of the university. Rather than holding class on Monday evening, I sat in my office and communicated with students through chats, forums, and email communications. As time passed, I wondered about the purpose of a university office and traditional schedule. I also considered the time wasted driving to campus and sitting in committee meetings. As my students became accustomed to communicating over the Internet, fewer students chose to meet face-to-face.

Over the past decade, I began taking the "anywhere, anytime" philosophy to heart. Eliminating all required, synchronous class meetings from my syllabus and shifting to paperless courses was just the beginning. In my case, distance learning has provided a freedom to live and work where and when I wished. It's become a way of life.

As I sit in a lawn chair with my wireless laptop in the mountains or near a beach, it's hard to imagine those long commutes to teach or take classes. With increasing pressures at home and work, many students are finding that online learning provides access to learning opportunities that wouldn't be possible in the traditional time and place specific university.

One of the goals of education is to help students become independent, life long learners. Online courses demand students take control of their own learning, ask questions, seek answers, set their own schedule, and take responsibility for their work. For many, learning becomes part of their lifestyle.

Dynamic Learning Environments

Online learning environments are alive. While this dynamic environment can make materials development time-consuming, it also makes teaching refreshing and learning exciting. Distance learning is the ongoing process of connecting learners with remote resources as primary or secondary means of learning (Lamb & Smith, 1999).

In our 1994 article "Cowboys and media specialists: Educators, technology, and change," Larry Johnson and I discussed the importance of keeping pace with rapid changes in technology and educational opportunities. This continues to be true a decade later.

Because of the ongoing changes in technology and information resources, needs, teaching styles, assignments, courses, communications, and relationships are constantly evolving.

Evolving Needs
Having worked with distance learning programs in high schools and universities, a key to success is whether online learning addresses a specific need.

With a growing emphasis on the importance of information fluency in our technology-rich society, educators have increasingly considered the information needs of their students. A paper dictionary can be more efficient than an electronic dictionary. The library is filled with interesting books at the reading level of second graders. However students wishing to gather the latest census data or track a hurricane will find the Internet to be the most efficient and effective tool.

Many teachers are adding online reading experiences to their curriculum. For example, students might read historical accounts using primary resources available on the Internet. As students read the books and online resources, they generate questions about the historical aspects of the readings. The Internet is a perfect tool to address these questions, because it provides access to information not available through traditional sources (Teclehaimanot & Lamb, 2003).

During the mid-1990s schools around the world began developing "virtual high schools" and "online courses." Since that time, some programs have become successful, while others have been dropped. Although much of the success can be attributed to course content and instructor quality, in many cases it comes down to need.

While working with the Digital Dakota Network, our planning committee found that the most useful online programs were those that wouldn't be available without the network. For example in rural areas, qualified teachers are often not available in every content area. Distance learning provided students with a variety of quality course offerings.

By working together, many small rural schools are able to keep their independence. For example, the three high schools in the East Porter Indiana School District are able to offer advanced high school courses in English, Science, and Social Studies by sharing teachers and offering courses over their two-way video network.

Evolving Teaching Styles
It's easy to spot a good teacher. Although their knowledge of content is critical, their passion for facilitating, guiding, nurturing, encouraging, and engaging makes them special.

Having spent over 20 years observing new educators, a passion for teaching is easy to identify. Yet as I began developing distance learning courses, I was apprehensive about whether my passion for teaching and learning could be conveyed at a distance. Would the energy and dynamic personality that was reflected in my teaching evaluations be lost in the world of cyberspace?

As an animated teacher, I was always concerned about whether my personality would come through online. It took a while to figure out that a combination of approaches worked best for me. At first, I thought video was the answer, but I soon found that "talking heads" were deadly. Next, I tried live chats. However, many students found them difficult to follow and the lack of keyboarding skills frustrating. In the end, a combination of approaches seemed to make the most sense.

At first I feared that I wasn't "teaching" if I wasn't talking to my class as a group. Soon I found that conversations were often richer when I wasn't leading the discussion. Projects were better when I provided one-on-one assistance rather than whole-class lectures.

Currently, I do everything asynchronously. In surveys, students have indicated that one reason they like online learning is because they never have to be at a particular place at a specific time. Although personal chats or telephone calls can be arranged, I find that email works great for most interactions. Being online most of the time, email is almost synchronous most of the time anyway. One advantage of email is the archive that's generated and easy to organize. I can easily go back and review conversations before addressing questions or examine a series of email communications to identify a reoccurring problem or concern. Because of these archives, I find students are much more thoughtful and reflective in online courses.

Not all course content works well in an online environment. For example, many virtual high schools have found that mathematics courses are particularly difficult to teach online because of the need for individual tutoring. Although teachers have tried fax communications, electronic white-boards, and video conferencing, they have not yet found effective ways to translate their teaching methods to the online environment. As technologies evolve and teachers gain more experiences and develop additional resources, more effective online teaching techniques will be developed.

Evolving Assignments
As new online resources and tools are identified, many teachers are rethinking their assignments and redesigning their assessments.

In the 1980s and 1990s, educators promoted the development of technology-rich projects. Unfortunately, these time-consuming activities often involved students in low-level thinking activities such as "copying and pasting" information from the Internet.

During the past several years, many educators have sought ways to improve their assignments and assessments. In 2000, I participated in a North Central Regional Education Laboratory committee charged with developing an instrument to evaluate student projects (see http://www.ncrtec.org/tl/sgsp/index.html).

Since that time, I've been encouraging educators to design learning environments that ask students to take on new roles. They may be asked to collaborate with an organization promoting native plants, collect local folklore for an online museum, or participate on a global issues forum. Rather than simply being a student in a class, the learner becomes a scientist, historian, or citizen of the world through meaningful assignments that use online resources and communication tools. Collaborative, generative, and interactive projects challenge students to seek out new ideas, build content connections, collaborative with others, and develop flexible communications (Lamb, 2003).

Evolving Courses
Before online learning, it was easy for a faculty member to avoid course revision. Simply write a lesson, place it in a notebook or better yet, laminate it. The same lecture could be used for an entire teaching career.

Whether planning online learning experiences for children or adults, instructional design is critical. For over twenty years, I've been preaching about the importance of instructional design. Yet in a face-to-face class, it was easy to repurpose old lectures and limp through the semester with little new planning. The flexible nature of the online environment demands constant attention as Website locations change, new articles appear, and innovative ideas are generated by students.

By encouraging students to suggest changes and contribute ideas, courses are constantly revised through the ideas of colleagues, students, and even outsiders who stumble upon my online courses while surfing the Web.

I find that updating my online materials as I work through a course has been difficult, but essential. When I see that several students have the same question, I immediately review my online materials, identify where they got confused, and make revisions. As I grade projects or review threaded discussions, I consider how I could provide more effective guidelines to lead students in the right direction to facilitate their learning.

In a constantly changing world, the flexibility of online course content is an important element of online learning. In the mid 1990's, many schools and universities employed professional Web developers who monitored all Internet postings. The process of posting or updating a Web page could take numerous communications with the Webmaster.

Today, faculty can make course revisions immediately and students can easily share their projects online. Forums and email provide a fluid environment where the content of the course evolves with each posting.

Evolving Communication
When teaching traditional face-to-face courses, I found class discussions frustrating. The prepared students excelled, the insecure learners looked to the instructor for answers, and a majority of the class avoided conflict in favor of nods or doodling.

The prospect of online discussions offered the opportunity for total class involvement. Rather than being concerned about any one student dominating the conversation, online forums can provide multiple discussions and many perspectives. Students have a chance to think about their postings, seek supportive evidence, and reflect on the comments of others. Some of the best conversations occur late at night or early in the morning well outside the traditional "school day."

Creating quality online discussion environments takes time. During my first experiences using forums in the mid 1990's, I relied on "read the article and discuss it" types of activities. However, I found that these conversations were not always enlightening or insightful.

As I began analyzing student discussions, I found that the best conversations came from case studies and real-world dilemmas that asked students to share experiences and examples as well as professional theories and literature.

In the past several years, my use of discussion forums has expanded to include many kinds of interactions and discussions. Flexible discussion areas have been used for students sharing project ideas, conducting peer reviews, and collaborating in cohort groups.

Evolving Relationships
I can be closer to my students by being far away.

An advantage of online learning is the ability for teachers and students to develop an ongoing relationship rather than the week-to-week connection that occurs with traditional classes.

It wasn't until I began to teach at a distance that I really began to know my students. After many years of teaching, I'd grown accustomed to introducing myself at the beginning of the semester and patiently listening as students went around the room and told about their families and careers. After the first night, this information was often stored away as the important task of learning began. With only three hours per week together, we rarely spent time to learn who liked romantic comedies and who vacationed in the mountains. It didn't really seem that important when compared to the important learning theory, management approach, or technology skill I was trying to teach.

However, when I began teaching online this all changed. I found that my courses weren't just "classes" that met once per week. Instead, they were learning communities full of drama, frustration, excitement, and anticipation. After helping a student with breast cancer, it occurred to me that, statistically, five of my 40 students could get breast cancer. This semester, Lisa has painful kidney stones, David is excited about his new job, and Suzanne is planning her wedding. This may not seem relevant to a graduate course, but it's amazing how this knowledge can impact student learning.

Rather than chastising Carla for a less than stellar forum posting, I wonder whether her daughter is feeling better and provide useful feedback that might trigger a more in-depth discussion on the next activity. She may still lose a point on the activity, but I have a better insight into why. Often my words of encouragement diminish stress and increase performance.

The key to building teacher-student relationships is developing a comfort level with students. In a face-to-face class or online course with video communication, the instructor can use facial expressions and voice inflections to convey an idea or gain information from students.

As email and forum discussions gained momentum in the 1990s, faculty and students found ways to simulate the facial expressions and voice inflections found in visual and auditory communication. Most students quickly caught on to the different kinds of writing necessary for an online communication. For example, formal writing was needed for professional communications and Web page development. On the other hand, forum discussions often included informal kinds of short cuts such as emoticons like smiley faces :-) and .... for pauses. People wrote LOL (Laugh Out Loud) or (teehees) to convey smiles and giggles. Over the past decade, these small elements have helped students become more comfortable.

The recent emphasis on multiple intelligences and differentiated instruction has encouraged many educators to include more varied channels of communication to address individual differences. For example, I have included personal photographs in my regular communications and developed short video clips for students to view online on a wide range of topics. These clips are intended to increase the comfort level of students, provide course content, and help students get to know my teaching style. As indicated in course evaluations, students feel comfortable e-talking with me about their concerns and frustrations after gaining a little insight into my personality through the videos.

Today, these written, video, and auditory communications are all put together in regular ongoing communications with students. These weekly updates provide professional news, course information, deadline reminders, project ideas, personal information and photos, links to videos, as well as other tidbits that keep students motivated and on-track. Reminders to keep smiling and email if they have questions are repeated in different ways each week.

Some skeptics might wonder why I bother. How does forming personal and professional relationships with students increase their success? First, I find that my drop-out rate has been dramatically reduced. When I first taught online courses, I found students often fell behind and eventually dropped out. Students no longer procrastinate. They know me and I know them. I feel comfortable sending a personal reminder as well as extending deadline when someone has a personal need. I have a better handle on the temperament of the class when I get to know them individually. This is very difficult to do when you only see your students once per week. Second, I can help students learn much more effectively if I can relate the course materials to student experiences and interests. It's much easier to suggest motivating research topics when I have a feeling for the student's background and personality. Third, the level of interaction depends on the needs of individual students.

With over fifty students in a class and 3000 forum message to read, teaching could be overwhelming. However since each student is different, they need support at different times during the semester. While some students seem to need reassuring email practically every day, others only need an occasional question answered.

The Challenge
Virtual learning environments allow students the flexibility to learn when they have the time, where they need to be, and how they learn best.

Whether planning a middle school WebQuest or a graduate level online course, the mission is the same. Educators want to develop quality online materials that will help all students be successful. In the article "Top Ten Facts of Life for Distance Education," William Smith and I identified ten tips to keep in mind when teaching and learning at a distance. These include (Lamb & Smith, 2000b):

1. Students are individuals.
2. Technologies change and evolve.
3. Technology fails.
4. Planning shows.
5. Students procrastinate.
6. Track them or lose them.
7. Students appreciate feedback.
8. Technology takes time.
9. Active learning is critical.
10. Students have great ideas.

Online learning environments require thoughtful planning, flexibility, and ongoing attention. Even experienced teachers find developing and delivering online materials and courses a challenge. Each situation has unique problems and frustrations. To build effective, efficient, and appealing online learning environments, teachers must make adjustments in student-teacher communication, class preparation, and many other things easily taken for granted in a traditional classroom.

Over the past twenty years, educators have just begun to experience the potential of effective online learning environments. The key to future prosperity lies in discovering innovative ways to enrich the learning experience through the use of these resources and technologies.

References

Johnson, L., & Lamb, A. (2003, April). Portals: Rabbit holes to grand gateways. *DataBus, 2*, pp. 8-9.

Johnson, L., Lamb, A., & Teclehaimanot, B. (2003, Fall). Academic technology: the convergence of diverse disciplines. *College and University Media Review.*

Lamb, A. (1989, Summer). Microcomputers in the media center. *The Ohio Media Spectrum, 41(2)*, pp. 6-11.

Lamb, A. (1992). Multimedia and the teaching/learning process in higher education. In M. Albright & D. Graf (Eds.), *New directions in teaching and learning: Instructional technology.* San Francisco, CA: Jossey-Bass, Inc.

Lamb, A. (1994, Spring). Getting started: Taking the multimedia leap. *Minnesota Journal of Educational Technology.*

Lamb, A. (1995, September). Driver's education for the information highway: Teaching information and ideas, not Internet. *SACE (Saskatchewan Association for Computers in Education) Bulletin*, 11-15 (Invited).

Lamb, A. (1998). *Spinnin' the Web: Designing & developing Web projects.* Emporia, KS: Vision to Action.

Lamb, A. (1999). Literature ladders. Website at http://eduscapes.com/ladders

Lamb, A. (2001, Jan./Feb.). Literature ladders. *Tech Trends, 45(1)*, pp. 40, 42.

Lamb, A. (2002a). *Catching the best of the Web: Practical ideas for internet integration.* Emporia, KS: Vision to Action.

Lamb, A. (2002b). *Building treehouses for learning: Technology in the classroom (3rd ed.).* Emporia, KS: Vision to Action.

Lamb, A. (2003, July-Aug.). Extreme thinking: Transforming traditional student projects into effective learning environments. *Educational Technology, 43(4)*, pp. 31-40.

Lamb, A., & Johnson, L. (2001). *42eXplore: Thematic Internet integration.* Emporia, KS: Vision to Action.

Lamb, A., & Johnson, L. (1994, Summer). Cowboys and media specialists: Educators, technology, and change. *Indiana Media Journal, 16(4),* pp. 91-106.

Lamb, A., & Smith, W.L. (1999). *Virtual sandcastles: Teaching and learning at a distance.* Emporia, KS: Vision to Action.

Lamb, A., & Smith, N. (2000a). *Newberys and the net: Thematic technology connections.* Emporia, KS: Vision to Action.

Lamb, A., & Smith, W.L. (2000b, Feb.). Top ten facts of life for distance education. *Tech Trends, 44(1),* pp. 12-15.

Teclehaimanot, B., & Lamb, A. (2004, March/April). Reading, technology, and inquiry-based learning through literature-rich WebQuests. *Reading Online.* Website at http://reading.org

Chapter 15

The Evolution of Online Education at the Open University

Robin Mason

Robin Mason is a Professor in the Institute of Educational Technology at the UK Open University. She received her PhD in Educational Technology from the Open University in 1989 and since that time has worked with many course teams in the design, tutoring, and evaluation of online courses. Her research interests center around cultural issues in online courses, assessment methods using the Web, and the globalization of education through new technologies.

Introduction

The UK Open University (OU) began using computer conferencing in 1988 and now has over 160,000 students online, either studying courses that require networking or accessing a range of administrative, social, and additional course resources. The University has always been a mass distance teaching institution focused primarily on working adults for whom flexibility of access to higher education opportunities is paramount. The OU continues to develop its e-learning activities, in line with advances in technology and increasing public access to personal computers. The new technologies also allow the OU to further remove the 'distance' from distance education, gathering together students from all over the world and bringing higher education to the doorstep of geographically remote students. However, the OU does not strive to become a totally 'online university.' The best outcomes for learning are usually achieved by striking a balance between using traditional and new media, individually selecting and developing the products that are best suited for each purpose.

This chapter documents some of the ways in which the OU has been transforming itself to meet the higher education demands of the 21st century, in particular, the ways in which its use of communications technologies have brought about an evolution from distance teaching to online education. I will highlight key points along the way and describe the problems and barriers which marked this journey. My own career as an academic is directly mirrored in this journey of the OU, as I was employed in 1986 to work on the University's first use of computer conferencing in mass distance education. My perspectives about online learning have also evolved over this period and I will indicate some of the milestones in this evolution.

First Use of Computer Conferencing

Following small-scale trials of the use of electronic mail on two courses and after an evaluation of a range of conferencing systems, the OU purchased the CoSy conferencing system from the University of Guelph, Ontario in 1986. Its principal use was for the proposed course *An Introduction to Information Technology: Social and Technological Issues*, for which nearly 1400 students registered in its first year of presentation. The largest portion of this course, as with all major OU courses to date, was the print component of seven 'blocks' of material. These were enhanced by a Course Reader, audio, and broadcast media, and other supplementary materials. However, in addition to these standard presentation media, this course was one of the first to require all students and tutors to have an IBM computer in order to gain practical experience of the social and technological issues discussed in the written material. Computer conferencing along with word processing, database management, and spreadsheet analysis, made up the practical component of the course, which accounted for about 20% of the students' study time. Consequently the conferencing element was a very small part of the whole.

Integration of the Communications Medium

A number of steps were taken to prevent this small communications element from being perceived by students as an added extra, which could be ignored if necessary. As OU students resemble many other students in tending to be 'assignment driven,' and being distance learners, feel isolated from an academic environment, the obvious uses of the conferencing system were as a means of tutor and peer support and as an integrated component of the assessment system. Consequently, about half of the face-to-face tutorials were replaced by online interaction with the tutor in small tutor group conferences (one tutor and 25 students) and in larger, plenary conferences for discussion of general course issues. In addition, the main use of conferencing in the assessment of the course was for the final double weighted essay in which students were expected to write an evaluation of computer-mediated communication, based on their experience of it during the course, on the textual material presented in the units about conferencing, and on the reactions of their fellow students. The latter information was to be drawn from a database formed by all students uploading answers to two detailed questionnaires concerning their use of the conferencing system during the course. Students were expected to download data and combinations of data from this remote database, present it in graphs and tables using the various software packages provided, and write an assessment of some aspect — social, educational, or technological — of computer conferencing.

Problems and Successes in the Early Implementation

I carried out extensive evaluation and analysis of students' and tutors' use of the conferencing system as part of my PhD, which was a case study of this first use of the medium at the OU (Mason, 1989a). Through survey questionnaires, telephone interviews, and on-site visits of students and tutors in their homes, I gathered detailed accounts of the problems and successes which characterized this first implementation.

Technical problems in logging on from home plagued the early implementations of computer-mediated communications, although not to the extent that the pessimists had predicted. The University provided a telephone help service and online support conferences, and the course team prepared extensive training materials including an audio tape to talk students through their first log-on. Eventually nearly all 1400 students managed to log on, but many fewer became competent and confident users. The social barriers to use were, as usual, much greater than the technical barriers.

The variability of tutors' input to their small group conferences was another problem. Many of the 70 tutors gave unflaggingly of their time and energy in contributing to the conferences, while others put in an opening message and expected their students to get on with discussions themselves. It soon became clear that tutors who continued to put in messages — cajoling, informative, chatty, or substantial — produced the most interactive groups. These were the tutors who enjoyed the medium, both as a communications tool or as a new piece of educational technology.

Similarly, about a third of the students immediately gravitated to the medium with comments like the following:

> *I have used the conferencing, conversation and mailing facilities almost every day from the beginning of the course until the end and have found the system an invaluable tool in helping with the course work, overcoming initial technical difficulties and discussing the arguments surrounding the study of IT.*   (quoted in Mason & Kaye, 1989, p. ix)

Many other students complained about how time consuming it was to find useful information on the system — for every gem of a discussion, there were too many irrelevant or chatty messages. Reluctance to input messages led to desultory conferences or to dominance of the active discussions by the most frequent and confident users. Nevertheless, the computer-generated statistics showed that well over 50% of students were reading the active conferences and reported that they felt very much less isolated on this course than they ever had as distance learners.

Barriers to Use

Despite the undoubted problems of the first large-scale implementation, the enthusiasm of a significant number of students and tutors, added to the obvious potential which the course team could see for this medium, led to immediate refinements and requests by other faculties to use conferencing. One of the main barriers to widespread take-up of conferencing was in fact the cost of telephone charges, or to be more accurate, the perceived cost of them. This was an issue I investigated in some depth in my interviews with students and in my analysis of the user statistics.

Partly because of the relatively high cost of telephone charges in the UK, compared with North America, and partly, perhaps, to cultural differences, the UK could be described at that time as 'telephone shy.' The absolute costs of online connections over the whole nine months of the course were between £5-10 for the majority of students — not more than a couple of evenings in the pub, as one student pointed out to me. However the complaints about the costs and the accusations that the OU was transferring costs to students were out of all proportion to the actual costs incurred by students. It is ironic that with the UK deregulation of the telecom industry in the 90s and the subsequent explosion of the mobile phone phenomenon, the UK has suddenly become one of the least telephone shy nations in the world!

However, in addition to this early barrier of 'quantity,' there was an equally strong barrier around the issue of quality. Many users turned away from the medium as being a poor investment of their precious study time — there was too much chat, too many messages in the wrong place, and not enough structure to the discussion.

The conclusion I drew from my research on this first use was:

> *This model of a very small exploitation of the medium amongst a plethora of other teaching tools can not be recommended for other applications and indeed, was responsible in great part for the little use made of it by the majority of students. Some of the frustrations experienced by tutors and students alike would be considerably reduced if conferencing formed a more significant role in the teaching and delivery of a course. Tutors would have to receive proper recognition for their role in the presentation of the course and all students would be obliged to log on frequently to take the course. The life-blood of a conferencing system is the contributions and interactions of its users. It can integrate with and enhance other teaching media, particularly print, but not when relegated to a 5% stake in a course.*

(Mason, 1989b, p. 143)

Early Research

While the OU was the first large-scale user of conferencing in higher education, there were many institutions which had been using the medium before the OU. We decided to hold a face-to-face conference at the OU in 1988 to bring together researchers who already had experience of the issues we had just met on our first implementation that year. Over 200 people attended from Europe and North America, and from the keynote presentations and other papers, we produced one of the first books on computer conferencing, entitled *Mindweave: Communication, computers, and distance education.* It soon sold out even of its second reprint and when the copyright reverted to us, we made it available electronically through our International Centre for Distance Learning at http://icdl.open.ac.uk/mindweave/mindweave.html. It continues to be cited regularly and chapters from the book have been used in innumerable courses about conferencing around the world.

Despite this early recognition abroad, I must note that we extended invitations to attend the conference free of charge to anyone and everyone at the OU who had any input to our use of computer conferencing. Less than ten people came and then only to the odd session. The medium had a few champions at the OU, but was regarded with suspicion by most academics and certainly most computer staff who saw communications as a poor use of computing power.

Hindsight Reflections

It is remarkable to me looking back at this early implementation with over ten years of refinement and the development of new technologies, how many issues are still with us and yet how much the OU got right first time.

- The socio-psychological support side of the medium continues to have important implications for a distance teaching institution.
- The integration of the medium with student assessment continues to be a focus of development, experimentation, and innovation.
- The collaborative nature of the project and other activities designed for the first presentation were bold and innovative for their time and have been built on in all subsequent courses.
- The combination of small tutorial groups plus larger conferences for discussion of the main course themes continues to be the framework for subsequent uses, although there has been considerable experimentation and elaboration on courses across the disciplines.
- The issues which continue to cause the most difficulties are: tutor and student workload; getting all students to participate actively; reluctance of a minority to take part in collaborative work; and students' lack of time to participate as much as they would like.

The problems which, fortunately, have faded into the background are: costs of connecting (although not costs of the initial pc); training students and tutors to use a conferencing system (command-line CoSy was incredibly daunting compared to current systems); messages in the wrong place; and the 'gee whizz' nature of the early interactions when the medium was so novel to most users.

Research and Development

Following this initial large scale use of the medium, a range of early adopter courses in the OU began to introduce conferencing as a partial replacement for face-to-face tutoring. Various kinds of collaborative activities were designed and integrated with assignments. One example is the following:

> *An area on the system is allocated to groups of between ten and twenty students, and discussion of the assignment question lasts for anything up to three or four weeks. Students then select some of their messages to submit for assessment and the criteria for marking include such items as:*
> - *the extent to which the student has used the issues raised in the course material to develop their arguments;*
> - *the way in which the student's messages build on and critique the ideas and inputs of other contributors to carry the discussion forward;*
> - *the succinctness with which the student's arguments are conveyed.*

(Mason, 1995, p. 213)

Group projects, common enough in campus-based education, could now be used in distance education, and we experimented with various combinations of individual and group work, such as an individual introduction and conclusion to the assignment with a common core produced jointly. On another tack, we began to develop a system for the electronic submission of assignments, in order to improve turnaround time. Other courses used the conferencing system to provide access to previous assignments, examinations and databases of 'best answers'.

My own research turned to the issue of analyzing the content of educational conferences, as a way of understanding how to improve the value of conferencing for students. I argued for a qualitative approach against what I saw as the prevailing quantitative and systems-based approach in which messages were counted and message maps created to look at who sent messages to whom — as if the amount of interaction indicated the amount of learning taking place:

I have attempted to draw up a typology of conference messages related to the educational values they display. This method involves a thorough reading of a set of messages with a view to discovering what, if any, skills and abilities the participants are displaying or developing. Some of the questions the educational analyst would want to bear in mind during such a process are:

- *Do the participants build on previous messages?*
- *Do they draw on their own experience?*
- *Do they refer to course material?*
- *Do they refer to relevant material outside the course?*
- *Do they initiate new ideas for discussion?*
- *Does the course tutor control, direct or facilitate discussion?*

This kind of questioning would lead to a typology of messages which focuses on the independence and initiative of the student, and would provide a means by which evidence of these attributes in students can be sought in the conferencing medium. By using other educational goals, such as collaborative learning, critical thinking, deep understanding of course material, or broad awareness of issues, and by breaking these down into examples of behavior or written work which display these characteristics, it is possible to analyze conference content and draw conclusions about the educational value of the particular online activity. Quantitative data can be used to show to what extent all students took part, or what percent of the total activity the educationally valuable interactions represent. By using a strategy such as the one suggested here, we can, as a community progress beyond description to analysis. We should not be afraid of making value judgements about what is educational interaction. The educator/ evaluator can go beyond description and explanation of conferencing interactions, and actually interpret them according to educational criteria. This stance represents a view of evaluation as 'construction' of knowledge rather than 'discovery' of knowledge.   (Mason, 1992, pp. 114-115)

Throughout the 90's, a large research program in telematics was funded by the European Commission and this launched a whole series of investigations, experiments, and developments in the use of computer conferencing across Europe. The OU was the lead partner in one of these projects and as a result hosted an international conference on site about computer conferencing in 1994. Only about 25 places were available for OU staff, and as one of the organizers, I experienced every form of arm-twisting and down-right abuse from colleagues trying to secure a place, so great was the demand to attend. Six years on from our first conference, the medium had certainly come of age at the OU.

Turning Points

During the early 90s, there were three major turning points at the OU which account for this transformation of interest in computer conferencing. The first was the arrival of our new Vice Chancellor, Sir John Daniel, in 1990. He already had some acquaintance with CoSy and quickly threw his weight behind electronic communication generally, both for staff and students. A program of funding was set up as 'seed-corn' money to encourage electronic tutoring initiatives across the university at grass-roots level. He installed a Pro-Vice Chancellor with a specific brief to develop and manage the OU's use of electronic media. His leadership of the transition of the OU from a print-based university to an electronic university has been unflagging and whole-hearted, and his own research and public addresses have been a significant encouragement (Daniel, 1996 and http://www.open.ac.uk/vcs-speeches).

A second turning point has been brought about by technology developments: the advent of another Canadian conferencing product, FirstClass, which the OU adopted following trials conducted as part of its European funded research project. FirstClass was so much more intuitive a system than CoSy that much of the effort for staff in preparing training materials and for students in trying to apply them to their system at home, became a thing of the past. Training could now focus on more significant issues of how to use the system educationally. By the mid-90s, we had nearly 50,000 students online, about half studying courses which required computer conferencing and the rest using it optionally for contact with their tutor and other students. FirstClass, as robust and well supported software, facilitated this growth in numbers and allowed academics to adapt conferencing more fully to the demands of their curriculum. We combined conferencing with CD-ROM material for resource-based learning (Alexander & Mason, 1994), ran a Virtual Summer School (Issroff, 1994), and branched out with other models of course design (Mason, 1998a).

The other technology development at this time was of course the Web. Contrary to the practice of many institutions rushing to become electronic, the OU did not see any value for its students in 'putting all its courses on the Web.' It was evident to us from experiments with CD-ROM as a delivery medium for course content, that students prefer to print out materials for study, partly because they are not accustomed to learning from a screen, but also because of their need to study at times and places where a computer is not available (journeys to work, holidays, etc). Our printed materials are of a very high quality and it would be using technology for its own sake rather than for any educational benefit to put materials written and designed for the print medium onto the Web. Nevertheless, we have found that a wide range of administrative uses of the Web are transforming the University into an e-university far more effectively than mere course delivery could. Apart from the obvious facilities of registration, student records, and submission of assignments, we have begun an ambitious program of putting 'course tasters' on the Web to help new and continuing students make the right course choice. Pre-course materials in mathematics and computer literacy and in study and essay writing skills, and counseling and careers advice are all being offered on the Web for students who need extra support in preparing to study. Whereas in the first years, it was a considerable investment for distance students to buy their own pc for one course, now there are a whole range of benefits that the University can offer to justify the expense. We currently have 100,000 students online and the day when all 250,000 students will be required to have access is within sight.

Teaching Online

During the early 90's, I began to design and tutor online courses myself. In the Institute of Educational Technology we ran a series of professional development courses using CoSy and soon FirstClass, and right from the beginning, these courses attracted students from all over the world. With the advent of the Web, we wanted to integrate online course material and links to the many relevant Web sites at other institutions, with the online discussions. FirstClass was slow to develop an integrated system and we tired of sending out FirstClass disks around the world with all the attendant problems this caused. We developed our own system in-house which had many of the best features of FirstClass but was fully available from a Web browser. Based on our experiences from the short professional development courses, we initiated a Masters Program, taught online to a global student body of 150 students.

One of the courses, *Applications of Information Technology in Open and Distance Education*, provided me with the opportunity to implement the ideas and conclusions I had come to as a PhD student and subsequent researcher of online interaction:

- the need to reduce the course content if students are to make a major contribution to online discussion and group collaborations;
- the need to structure online interactions if all students are to feel comfortable about taking part; and
- the importance of valuing online discussion by encouraging students to use extracts in their assignments.

We began experimenting with smaller group sizes and with set activities, giving everyone a specific task and an area of the system in which to discuss their findings. In addition, we allowed those with the time, access, and enthusiasm to participate across any of the sub groups if they wanted. We developed the concept of an online debate, choosing carefully a polemical statement which contests central course issues, which has good resources available to substantiate both sides of the argument, and which is significant enough to warrant discussion over a three week period. We assigned specific roles to each person in the group such as: moderator of the discussion, proposer of the motion, opposer of the motion, documentalists (who summarize relevant ideas from the set readings), reseachers (who go and find relevant papers and resources on the web), commenters (whose specific task is to discuss the ideas put forth by the opposer and proposer), and finally rapporteur (who is responsible for summarizing the discussion at the end of three weeks).

The first four months of the course are based on collaborations of this sort and have two supporting books and a short Web study guide, but the last four months have more printed materials and more individual work. What we have found is that this mixture of intense collaboration tailing off into traditional, more independent study works very well.

The students, many of whom became total converts to the value of collaborative learning in the early stages of the course, were definitely flagging by about four months into the course. The term 'collaboration fatigue' was coined to express their combination of appreciation but overload with the demands of collaborating online. The problems are:

- that the structure and timetable imposed by collaborative learning makes the course very much less flexible than traditional distance education;
- that the schedules of busy professional people who are attracted to this program mean that holidays, family crises, and sudden job commitments are a major hindrance to regular, sustained participation in group activities; and
- ironically, that students definitely experience more guilt and stress about failing their colleagues in collaborative work than their tutors in individual work!

Collaborative work is definitely more time-consuming, more stressful, and less flexible than individual work. However, in many ways it is more rewarding. The benefits of collaborative activities as the core content of the course are:

- that students can engage in authentic tasks directly relevant to their work, in this case as educators and ICT specialists;
- that the whole, usually in the form of a group report, is more than the sum of the parts which are the individual contributions;
- that the individual expertise of the students is brought into the teaching/learning environment to the benefit of all concerned;
- that larger, more comprehensive tasks can be undertaken through the combined efforts of a group;
- that the burden of supporting and motivating students can be shared by all the students, not just the tutor. (Mason, 1999, pp.7-8)

In 2002 I began to turn my attention to designing shorter learning opportunities which built on what we had learned from this course, but presented the content in a more accessible and flexible form. Along with two colleagues in IET, I developed a new course for the Masters Program entirely in learning objects (Weller, Pegler, & Mason, 2003a). Called "Learning in the Connected Economy," the course focuses on the ways in which learning has been impacted by the Internet — both in the content of what is learned and the ways in which it is learned. This new course is run on a platform designed specifically for learning objects and one of our interests in this method of presentation is the ease with which we have already been able to reuse and reversion the materials for other courses for different levels and markets.

The OU as a Global Educator

Throughout the 1990s, the OU has systematically changed itself into a global institution. It has probably invested more than any other established university, certainly in the UK, to re-engineer itself for the challenges of the new educational market, and has transformed itself into a global education provider using new technologies and a range of methods for operating in different countries:

- It has an extensive network of partners in Asia, Africa, Eastern Europe, and South America.
- It offers courses throughout Continental Western Europe and Ireland, using its own study centers and tutors.
- It leads a number of aid-funded projects in various countries (e.g., Ethiopia, Eritrea) where western business and management methods are in great demand.

While it is undoubtedly the case that telecommunications technologies are an essential component of this global activity, they are all means to an end. The OU has become one of the most prominent examples of an institution enshrining access to educational opportunity and openness to students of all backgrounds, not only into its name and mission statements, but into the very heart of the organization: its preparation of course materials, its enrolment procedures, its tutorial support provisions, and its commitment to helping similar, developing organizations around the world.

A Large-Scale Online Course

While our Masters Degree developed the first online, Web-based course in the OU, it remains small and hand-crafted by OU standards. The first large-scale undergraduate course delivered entirely on the Web was offered in pilot form to over 800 students in 1999. It was so successful that over 12,000 students signed up for the course in 2000.

The course is innovative for the OU in the following ways:

- the course is supported entirely online and there are no face-to-face tutorials;
- the course content, apart from several set books, is entirely on the Web; and
- the combination of teaching information and communication technology (ICT) to complete beginners, using online group work and very large-scale online delivery is unique in the OU and probably the world.

Along with the course team chair, I carried out an evaluation of the first presentation of the course. It was not without its problems and obviously with such large student numbers, some were disappointed with the content and approach of the course. In our evaluation paper, we wrote:

> *There has been a good deal of evaluation of the use of computer conferencing as a means of interaction between students and tutors on distance education programs over the last ten years. One way of characterizing its use as an educational medium is to say that its strengths are also its weaknesses:*
>
> - *it doesn't require fixed times for study, but consequently other demands on one's time easily take precedence;*
> - *it maintains a record of all interactions — but this makes many people wary of committing their ideas to such a public forum;*
> - *it allows everyone to be 'heard,' but this leads to an overload of messages which many find completely overwhelming.*
>
> *One of the paradoxes of this medium which is very apparent in the student feedback of this course lies in the disparate perceptions that on the one hand, there were too many messages, or that, on the other, there was too little participation. For example:*
> *"I couldn't have coped without the conferencing."*
> *"Because of the mix of people, there is a lot of self-help."*
> *"I wouldn't have understood nearly so much of the course if there hadn't been the support conferences."*
> *But also*
> *"I felt intimidated by the level of knowledge some people displayed in the conferences."*
> *"I found the online conferencing unusable. I tried a few times to get into the discussions, but without success. I would have had to be logging in everyday for it to work and this was impossible."*
> *"The most disappointing thing about the course was the lack of participation in the conferencing."*
> *"Most people seem to be too busy to contribute to the conferences and this is a real pity."*
> (Mason & Weller, 2000)

Despite all the improvements in computer conferencing systems, the huge benefits of the Web, and the increase in our understanding about how to design online courses, it remains the case that these comments by our students in 1999 are virtual replicas of feedback from students on our first-ever use of the medium over ten years before. However, so integrated is online teaching in the way the OU operates now, and so positive are the enthusiasts and our huge student association, that we are committed to developing our online capacity, while maintaining traditional print-based methods for those who prefer this style of learning.

Recent Research

One of the many lines of research being pursued at the OU in support of online teaching, is that of real-time learning opportunities using streaming technologies on the Web. We have been convinced of the value of real-time interaction among students and tutors right from the inception of the University. In fact, in my opinion, we are more aware of the benefits than campus-based universities, which squander precious time together in the same room by lecturing at students! Our Knowledge Media Institute has developed software for running large-scale events on the Web. One example of this is the Virtual Graduation Ceremony we ran for the first graduates of our Masters Degree in March 2000 (http://kmi.open.ac.uk/projects/vdc). Other software has been developed for holding small real-time tutorials using multi-way audio and a shared screen. This has tremendous potential for us in terms of student-initiated real-time interaction, student presentations, real-time debates and discussions, problem-solving tutorials, second language practice, and so on.

The taste of working with a global student body led me to a major new research program — the globalization of education (Mason, 1998b), and in particular, the cultural issues one encounters in online interactions, assessment and collaborative activities when students not only are working in their second language, but in an adopted and unfamiliar educational paradigm.

An Emerging Trend

One of the most 'talked about' trends in e-learning now is the concept of learning objects and repositories for their reuse. My approach to this contentious issue is probably colored by my position in a very large university which has an extensive repository of not-very-reusable teaching material. Reuse of teaching materials across faculties within the University is highly desirable, but requires the material to be conceived in short 'stand alone' learning episodes rather than in a highly cross referenced and linked narrative. We are just beginning an extensive evaluation of the learning outcomes from our course designed in learning objects. We developed our own version of learning objects based on the pedagogy of action learning: a discursive overview of the issue, a set of resources and further reading, and an activity which may be individual or collaborative (Weller, Pegler, & Mason, 2003b). The initial findings from students' engagement with the course are very positive, and we are convinced that the learning object approach does not inevitably have to be reductive. We have observed deep level approaches to learning and reflective engagement with course issues by our first cohort of 55 students.

Conclusion

Many things have changed or developed since we first implemented CoSy in 1986. The OU has adopted e-learning as a medium for social, educational, and administrative interaction, and has supported all three directions through research, evaluation and start-up funding. Nevertheless, it has listened to the students who cannot afford access, who do not want to collaborate with other students, or who do not want to learn online. The vast majority of our courses are not delivered on the Web, and conferencing and online access are optional on many courses. The business of encouraging people to learn is delicate, artful, and evolutionary.

Note

Parts of this chapter were originally published in the *Internet and Higher Education, 3*, 1-2, pp. 66-74, under the title, "From Distance Education to Online Education."

References

Alexander, G., & Mason, R. (1994). *Innovating at the OU: Resource-based collaborative learning online.* CITE Report No. 195. Institute of Educational Technology. Milton Keynes: The Open University.

Daniel, J. (1996). *Mega-universities and knowledge media.* London: Kogan Page..

Issroff, K. (1994). *Virtual summer school evaluation.* CALRG Report 144, Institute of Educational Technology. Milton Keynes:The Open University.

Mason, R. (1989a). *A case study of the use of computer conferencing at the Open University.* PhD dissertation. Institute of Educational Technology, The Open University, CITE Thesis no. 6.

Mason, R. (1989b). The evaluation of CoSy on an Open University course. In: Mason, R. and Kaye, A. (Eds.), *Mindweave: Commmunication, computers, and distance education.* Oxford: Pergamon.

Mason, R. (1991). Analyzing computer conferencing interactions. *International Journal of Computers in Adult Education and Training, 2(*3), pp. 161-173.

Mason, R. (1995).Using electronic networking for assessment. In F. Lockwood, (Ed.), *Open and distance learning today.* London: Routledge.

Mason, R. (1998a, October). Models of online courses. *Asynchronous Learning Networks Magazine, 2(2)*. Available online at http://www.aln.org/publications/magazine/v2n2/mason.asp

Mason, R. (1998b). *Globalising education. Trends and applications*. London: Routledge.

Mason, R. (1999). *IET's Masters in Open and Distance Education: What have we learned?* CITE Report No 248, The Institute of Educational Technology, The Open University, Milton Keynes. Available at http://iet.open.ac.uk/pp/r.d.mason/downloads/maeval.pdf

Mason, R., & Kaye, A. (1989). *Mindweave: Commmunication, computers, and distance education*. Oxford: Pergamon.

Mason, R., & Weller, M. (2000). Factors affecting students' satisfaction on a Web course. *Australian Journal of Educational Technology, 16(2)*. Available at http://www.ascilite.org.au/ajet/ajet16/mason.html

Weller, M., Pegler, C., & Mason, R. (2003a) Putting the pieces together: What working with learning objects means for the educator. *Paper presented at the E-LearnInternational 2003 Conference*, Edinburgh, Feb. 2003. Available at: http://iet.open.ac.uk/pp/c.a.pegler/ukeu/edinburgh.doc

Weller, M., Pegler, C., & Mason, R. (2003b) Working with learning objects — some pedagogical suggestions. *Proceedings of the ALT-C conference*, Sheffield, September, 2003. Available at http://iet.open.ac.uk/pp/c.a.pegler/ukeu/ATLC_2003.doc

Chapter 16

Flight of an Academic Magpie:
From Face2Face to Virtual Presence

T. Craig Montgomerie

T. Craig Montgomerie is a Professor of Instructional Technology, Department of Educational Psychology, University of Alberta. He is the principal investigator on the Rural Advanced Community of Learners (RACOL) project, developing a model of teaching and learning that exploits the potential of broadband networks and advanced digital technologies. He received his PhD in Educational Administration from the University of Alberta.

Introduction

This is a different experience for me. I am essentially a quantitatively oriented scientist who respects and admires those with a more qualitative bent. I have practiced the concept of the disinterested, rational scientist when I write about my research. This book is different. We've been asked to write about and describe our professional life work. As such, what you'll read is a personal reflection. As many qualitative researchers have found, my research is based upon what worked for me at the time I was doing it. So this chapter describes where I came from, who has influenced my work, what I have done, what I'm doing now, and, probably most importantly, where I think the application of technology will take education in the near future. As you'll quickly see, it takes a lot to hold my interest for a long time, and I have spent a lot of time working in many different areas. But being an academic magpie sometimes isn't a bad thing. You gain a lot of knowledge in a lot of areas, and eventually a time comes when you can pull it all together into something that is really special.

Time Before Teaching

My first job when I graduated engineering in 1967 was as one of three systems analysts working on an IBM 1800 — a real-time process control computer. Each morning one of us had to toggle in about 80 16-bit commands to bootstrap the computer. The specifications for the IBM1800 were very similar in terms of memory, address space, machine cycle time, and disk size to the Apple II computer which was produced a couple of decades later. One major difference was the IBM 1800 was about $750,000 while the first Apple II was marketed for about $2,838 (Apple Computer, 1977). I remember thinking longingly of Arcadia Darrel's transcriber — a machine that you spoke into and which would "spell and punctuate correctly according to the sense of the sentence" (Asimov, 1953, p. 81). Science fiction is one of the great idea generators for any scientist and Asimov was one of the best. This was the earliest time I can remember thinking that the real breakthrough in computers was just around to corner — when we would be able to converse with computers in natural, spoken English and they would understand and respond appropriately. Of course, Arthur C. Clarke's famous HAL-9000 computer in Stanley Kubrick's film *2001 A Space Odyssey* (1968) released the next year brought a slightly more sobering picture of computers that could interact with humans using natural language, but then began to reason for themselves.

While we were waiting for delivery of the IBM 1800, we found out that an IBM 1500, a computer using the same CPU and operating system as the IBM 1800, had been purchased by Dr. Steve Hunka in the Faculty of Education at our university. Dr. Hunka offered us the use of this system to practice configuring our system, and to debug our software while we waited for the IBM 1800 to be delivered.

As a brand new chemical engineering graduate, I remember being intrigued that the same computer system that we were using to do real time process control of chemical processes was being used two blocks away to provide direct, interactive instruction. This really brought home to me the concept that the digital computer was a general-purpose machine, and that the future uses of computers would only be limited by the imagination and abilities of humans.

Programming a process control computer was completely defined by developing efficient code. Everything had to be done within very tight time constraints. This meant that we were developing assembler-level and even machine-level code. The wonderful Fortran II compiler that we had received with the IBM 1800 made code production faster, but the code produced was inefficient and, eventually, deemed to be unusable. As a "people person" I found it extremely frustrating to have my working day circumscribed by trying to make one machine control another machine. When this was combined with the fact that the IBM 1800 and our computing group were located in a brand new, otherwise unoccupied, building that had no heat, I decided that I needed some human interaction. I applied for a job teaching mathematics and scientific computing at the Northern Alberta Institute of Technology, and when I got back from the interview, there was a message waiting offering me the job if I could start in one week. I accepted.

Stand and Deliver — My First Teaching Experience

Teaching in an institute of technology was an interesting experience. Even though we prepared students in a number of different programs, I found myself teaching essentially two courses: an introduction to calculus and an introduction to Fortran. Once I had taught the courses once, I thought I had caught on to what I was doing. The second time through I think I fixed up most of my previous errors, and generated a pretty good set of lesson plans. The third time through, I had all my handouts completed. We worked on a quarterly system, so I hadn't even finished my first year and I was pretty comfortable that those two courses were as good as I could make them. Somewhere in the second year of teaching the same courses, repetitively, I began to realize that some of my lectures weren't nearly as good as the same lecture had been the last time I taught that concept (or the second last time, or maybe it was five times ago).

I remember vividly the day I decided I had to stop teaching this way, in this environment — a rather nice student asked a question that indicated a lack of comprehension of a basic principle. I found myself thinking "I told you this last year, I told it to you the year before, and I told it to you the year before that, don't you ever learn?" Within a week I had made application for leave to go back to graduate school. I intended to become an educational administrator and help change the system.

The Early Days — Aspiring to Replace the Teacher

I returned to the University of Alberta and even though I was studying to be an educational administrator, I found myself drawn back to Steve Hunka and his group that were working with the IBM 1500 computer assisted instruction system. I took a couple of courses from Steve and learned CourseWriter II, the language used to write CAI on the 1500. Steve used Hicks and Hunka (1972) as the text for the course, but he felt so guilty about it that he reimbursed each of us 25¢, his royalty.

In the early 1970s we were trying to develop computer programs that could "replace the teacher." We tried to develop courseware that was very comprehensive and which collected as much information as possible to allow the instructor to develop algorithms that diagnosed what particular problem a student was having, then have the computer present specific feedback to that problem. CourseWriter II had some really nice capabilities. Central to these were the answer analysis alternatives. For each question, the author specified the answers that were correct and the feedback that the student would receive if they answered the question correctly. Similarly, the author could specify specific wrong answers and the feedback that the students would encounter if they had given that answer. Finally, a special set of routines handled the unanticipated answers: those that did not match any of the identified correct or wrong answers. The author could specify different actions for the first, second, etc., unidentified answer(s). These actions were usually used to direct the student towards the correct answer.

While we developed a lot of CAI courseware on the IBM 1500 at the University of Alberta, there are two courses that were remarkable, or ones that I remember especially well. The first of these was a 30-hour cardiology course, "CARDI," that presented real multimedia. For example, students could use the light pen to select a target on a graphic of a torso, and the computer would play the sounds that would be picked up by a stethoscope placed on the torso of a real patient who evidenced the disease under study. For realism the audio was provided through a headset that looked and felt like the headset on a stethoscope. The computer could also position a filmstrip to a specific location to display pictures or X-ray images under either student or instructor control. Dr. Dick Rossall, the cardiologist who designed the CARDI program, was really enthralled with the capabilities of the computer. He often commented in his public presentations that using the computer allowed him to give his students experiences that they would never be able to see if they spent every day of their medical education on a cardiology ward. The students liked the course — even though it was "being taught by a computer," and consistently rated it as their second favorite course – immediately behind "patient rounds."

The second memorable course was an introductory statistics course, "STAT1," developed by Drs. Steve Hunka, Tom Maguire, and Gene Romaniuk. STAT1 taught basic statistical concepts from descriptive statistics through Analysis of Variance and contained approximately 60 hours of instruction. Student comments on this course included how "patient" the computer was, and how it allowed them to go at their own speed. The authors of this course even began streaming students in different sections of the course — those who understood calculus could follow one instructional stream, while those who had no calculus could follow another stream. The introductory graduate statistics course that used this course went from being thought of as the "screening course" for M.Ed. students, to one where "everyone passed." At first people suggested that the tests had been made less rigorous once CAI was used. When the instructors/developers, all educational measurement specialists, demonstrated that the exams were being developed from the same database of questions that had been used before STAT1 was used, this criticism quickly disappeared.

Working with people who had produced such high quality computer assisted instruction and having access to these courses gave graduate students an experience that was without equal. Each of us found exciting areas for research, from studying Aptitude Treatment Interaction to developing systems to help instructors improve their instruction.

The CourseWriter II language provided something that was relatively unheard of at that time: performance recordings. Each time the student entered an answer a 300-character performance record was generated to magnetic tape. This record contained a dump of every piece of information that pertained to that student at that time, including the answer, the latency from the time the question was asked until the student responded, the precise response, including backspaces and corrections, the contents of all system variables, counters and switches, etc. The trouble was that while we had all this information, there was no way to tie it back to the contents of the screen, to combine it with other students' responses to the same question, etc.

Gene Romaniuk and I decided to do something with this data. We wrote a set of routines that essentially processed the CourseWriter code to regenerate the contents of the screen each time a question was asked. We then sorted the student responses according to the order questions appeared in the "normal" prosecution of a course, and then merged either the individual or grouped student responses into a printed report.

The individual student analysis allowed us to retrace a student's progress through a course, in order to explain to them where they had gone wrong. This was very annoying to a number of students who came to us to complain that the computer had screwed up, and that they had indeed given the correct answers, only to be shown keystroke by keystroke, with time to the nearest tenth of a second exactly what they had done and what the computer had done.

By far the most interesting results, though, were those that allowed us to look at the merged student responses. For each question we could see how many students got the correct answer on the first, second, etc., pass, what wrong answers were given and, very importantly, what unidentified responses the students made. Analysis of this latter information revealed a number of places where a student had given a correct answer — just not one that the author had identified beforehand as a correct answer. Similarly, some of the unidentified answers clearly pointed to an incorrect perception of the topic that had been created by the instruction. It was a very humbling process for course developers to realize that students had, for example, been progressing reasonably well through the material, when, suddenly, a large group of them started to founder. A review of the instruction usually revealed that the instruction had fallen apart, moved too quickly, or even given an incorrect impression.

We published our work at a couple of local or national conferences (Romaniuk & Montgomerie, 1976; Montgomerie & Romaniuk, 1976) but we saw this as essentially a rather complex data processing task. At the time we didn't see any major research contribution from this work. In hindsight, it is obvious that this work was relatively unique, and provided an avenue for investigation that was not being pursed by other CAI researchers and, to date, is still not pursued as assiduously as it should be.

Around this time, the National Research Council of Canada began work on the development of a National Authoring Language (NATAL-74). Steve Hunka's group, which at that time included a really exciting group of faculty and graduate students, contracted to write the specification document for the kinds of ancillary processes that should be provided for such a system (Hunka *et al.*, 1978). Romaniuk and I took on the writing of the specifications for collecting and student processing the performance recordings. This was the final work we did in the area of performance recordings. IBM withdrew support for the IBM 1500 in 1980 and the efforts of the people in DERS became redirected towards finding a replacement and porting courses to the new system.

The Dark Days — Stand Alone Microcomputers

In 1977 Apple produced the Apple II computer — the first consumer-oriented microcomputer. The microcomputer introduced a new age in the use of computers in education. For those of us working in the area of CAI, this ushered in a whole new era. Terminals that were connected to the IBM 1500 had to be located within a very short distance of the central computer, and were connected to it by a couple of 1 inch thick cables. With the microcomputer, we could have a computer (hence CAI) anywhere there was power. Many of the researchers in the area immediately saw the microcomputer as the next best thing in computing — and it was. I spent about four months converting existing programs to run on microcomputers.

So why do I call it the "Dark Days"? At the time, the microcomputers came with one language: BASIC. Originally being a scientific programmer, well versed in FORTRAN, I had no trouble using BASIC. Quickly though, we realized that the programs that had been built in CourseWriter II couldn't easily be converted to BASIC. In CourseWriter II we had functions that performed answer analysis, such as looking for keywords in a string, or evaluated an answer as equivalent to a keyed answer even if there were a few spelling mistakes. Such things didn't exist in BASIC. So we had a new delivery mechanism, but no appropriate language to use on it. BASIC was really good at evaluating numerical answers, and many people began writing programs with less complex answer analysis, using multiple choice answers, or numerical answers. In hindsight, this is probably one of the major reasons that CAI became seen as nothing but drill and practice.

A second problem with microcomputers in the late 1970s was that they didn't communicate with each other very well. With mainframe computers and terminals, we were working on, essentially, a single computer. If we updated a piece of courseware because we had found an error, the correction was immediately available to all the students in the course. If we were working with a class at another university, we could send a copy of the corrected course to that university and know that all the students there immediately received the corrected version. Systems analysts were paid a lot of money to make sure that changes to courseware went smoothly and that updates to courses were made appropriately. Similarly, since students were all working on a single computer, if we wanted to collect performance data, all the data was collected in a single place and again, professional systems people made sure data were collected correctly and prepared in a way they could be analyzed.

With microcomputers, each person was responsible for their own computer. We shared programs on floppy disks or consumer-grade cassette tapes. We could never be sure that the students were working on the latest version of a course. Similarly, if we wanted to analyze performance data, we had to trust a student to find the correct file on a disk, copy this to a cassette or floppy disk, and return it to us. Needless to say, those of us who relied on centralized services for the kind of research we wanted to do found a whole new set of problems in the era of the stand-alone microcomputer. I became somewhat disenchanted with the area of instructional computing and once again shifted my research — this time to the use of database systems in educational administration.

Communications and Distance Education

I completed my PhD in Educational Administration in 1981 and immediately took a position helping design and implement an extended campus M.Ed. in Educational Administration at the University of Alberta. I transferred from being a full time programmer analyst to a soft tenured assistant professor. This, of course, was accompanied by a rather significant reduction in salary — I had purchased my last Porsche!

The concept of an extended campus program was that we would extend the campus to meet the student needs. Central to this approach was the silver bird model of distance education. The instructors got on a plane and flew to the location where a cohort of students met in order to deliver face2face instruction. Each of these cohorts met in a community that was served by a community college, and we arranged to use their facilities. We placed sets of textbooks and reference books within the community college libraries for the use of the students. I had designed a system a few years earlier that allowed a user to construct an ERIC search interactively, and then submit this for batch processing. We placed a TI700 terminal in each of the communities for use of the students for the duration of their program, and then taught them how to use email and perform ERIC searches. While the Internet wasn't generally available in rural Alberta at this time, a packet switched network did exist and we connected back to the main campus computing network via the packet switched network. Students would email requests for ERIC articles and microfiche to a graduate assistant who was hired to facilitate these requests, and to otherwise act as the hands and feet of the extended campus students on the campus. Over the duration of the program, the program increased the use of communications technology to use the Internet, but never included technologies like audio or video conferencing.

The extended campus program ran for over ten years and was extremely successful. We estimate that the approximate completion level for those in the extended campus M.Ed. was similar or even higher than for the traditional on-campus M.Ed. We certainly met the expectation of the students — a number of graduates have moved into senior administrative posts. I am constantly surprised when students from the program, now superintendents or assistant superintendents of schools, contact me about the use of technology within their jurisdiction. They often report that they are seen as very technologically proficient by their staffs — because of the skills (however minimal) they learned in the extended campus program.

Time Out of Time — Seconded to the Office of the Vice President (Research)

The end of the 1980s and beginning of the 1990s was a very interesting time. The Internet was beginning to make its presence felt on the campus. A major reorganization of computing on campus was undertaken, with a major commitment to the client-server model. The president of the university personally allocated funding to install a fiber optic backbone to every building on the main campus of the University. The fact that previous planners had installed a tunnel system that connected every major building on campus made this implementation rather easier than some might think. This new network would use the Internet Protocol (IP), and every unit on campus was urged to convert their local area networks to the IP protocol and to connect to this campus backbone. In 1993 I was seconded one-third time for one year to the Office of the Vice-President (Research) to help develop a plan to convince the deans and department chairs that they should take advantage of this network to change the way they did administration, teaching, and research. We were successful. By the end of the year, every faculty but one had committed to converting to the IP protocol and using the new network.

In the early 1990s, the Alberta Government had provided funding for a supercomputer that was seriously under-used. In 1993, a joint committee of university and industry was put together to find a way to encourage joint use of this facility. As the "computer guy" in the VP (Research) office, I was asked to represent the University on this committee. This committee became the Western Universities Research Consortium (WURC), and I became a member of the Board. One of the first things we realized was that we had a supercomputer located in one city in the province, prospective users throughout the province, and essentially no way for remote users to communicate with this computer. We had to build a network. Coincidentally, the Government of Canada had created the Canadian Network for the Advancement of Research, Industry, and Education (CANARIE) to promote the use of next generation networking across the country. CANARIE created CA*Net, a national network that was connected to the international IP Research network (e.g., Internet 2 in the US). CANARIE encouraged the creation of, and helped fund, provincial networks to connect to this national network. WURC saw this as an excellent opportunity to develop the network to provide access to the super computer, and became the regional network for the western provinces. WURC became WURCnet (to reflect that networking had become much more important than access to the supercomputer) and eventually Netera Inc. Netera became very active as a fair agent acting to bring university and industry researchers together on very large, multi-institutional projects in areas related to broadband networking and, when requested, acts as a project manager for large projects releasing the researchers to do research rather than administration. After my period in the VP (Research) office ended, I was asked to continue as the University's representative on the Board and I am still on the board. My role has changed from being the designated member representing the University of Alberta to the elected chair of the User Advisory Committee (UAC). An unexpected benefit of working with Netera has been that I meet with researchers from a broad range of industrial and educational agencies on a regular basis, we end up talking about common interests, and end up collaborating on cross disciplinary and inter-institutional research projects that require substantially greater financing than is usually available in faculties of education.

Meanwhile, Back in the Faculty of Education

In 1994 the faculty was reorganized, and one of the major changes was that all the academics that were interested in the use of technology in education were brought together as the Instructional Technology group within the Department of Educational Psychology. This resulted in the creation of a critical mass of instructional technology faculty and graduate students in a single unite, the first time this had been done since the IBM 1500 was decommissioned in 1980.

As a group of instructional technology professors, we decided to practice what we preached, and not only make our courses about the use of technology, but to infuse the use of technology throughout our courses. Since a number of us were involved in some way with the STAT1 course, and were aware of how effective it had been, we decided that it would be an interesting project, both for us and for students, to redesign the STAT1 course for use on a stand-alone microcomputer, in the process, updating it to incorporate the latest multimedia capabilities. A number of us had used *Authorware* and it's predecessor, *Course of Action*, and were comfortable that this program had the capabilities we needed to redesign the course. I took on the job of principal investigator and project manager. I worked with a group of professional programmers and media designers to develop a consistent interface for presenting a course-length CAI program. Using different groups of students over a period of approximately four years we redeveloped the STAT1 course into a stand-alone course called *Understanding Statistics*.

I am sure you are asking: "Why would you develop a stand-alone course for a microcomputer when you criticized them a few pages earlier?" That is a good question. I agreed to take on this task only if we could use the Internet to provide centralized performance recording. Authorware has the ability to link to other programs to extend the capabilities of the language. A programmer, Alan Davis, a graduate student, Gary Duguay, and I designed and implemented a system that: (1) collected student performance data and passed it back to a central host, (2) allowed a student to restart their instruction from any Windows or Macintosh microcomputer that was connected to the Internet, even without the course code being present on that computer, and (3) automatically checked for, and, if it was necessary, updated a course segment from a central host each time a student logged on. Since we had a naïve belief that we might be able to market this course, we also implemented a management system that allowed us to issue both institutional and individual licenses, and to deny updates to those who had not updated their subscription. We were successful in developing all the features we had set out to achieve in early 1997. Gary Duguay was beginning to convert all the code from Perl (an interpreted language that left our code susceptible to hacking) to a language that had better security when he suddenly passed away. This effectively stalled further work on the development of the centralized support system.

While we were working on redeveloping Understanding Statistics, we were also very interested in a new thing called the World Wide Web, and its promise for instruction. Dwayne Harapnuik, one of my grad students, and I undertook to develop a graduate-level Web-based course called *The Internet: Communicating, Accessing, and Providing Information*. We began development in May 1995, offered the first face2face session in September 1995, and offered it as a fully Web-based course for the first time in May 1996. In 1996 the N.A Web Developers association named this course the Best Academic Web Site. Student reviews of the course were also very positive, and, though it was an optional course, enrollment averaged over 100 students per term. Most of the students were from off campus and students enrolled in the course from throughout Canada and the US as well as from many different countries. This was quite unexpected, as the University of Alberta is not a distance education institution. The Department of Educational Psychology was charged with offering a course in educational technology to all undergraduate students enrolled in the Faculty of Education. Enrollment in this course is approximately 800 students per year. A colleague, Mike Carbonaro, and I, along with Joanne Davies, a PhD student, decided to convert this course to a Web-based learning course using active learning principles under a constructivist philosophy. While the instruction was Web-based, every student was assigned to an actual laboratory section in a real laboratory with a real laboratory assistant. The course assignments could be completed in the lab, and the lab assistants would help students if they couldn't follow the Web-based instruction. The first offering of this course *Technology Tools for Teaching and Learning* was in September 1997. We were very pleased with the overall achievement of the students in this course but student response to the course was mixed. While we received a number of unsolicited comments from students who loved the way the course was offered, we also received complaints from a number of students who were extremely unhappy with the method of instruction. To try to understand why we were receiving extremely different responses to the course, another PhD student, Patricia Medici, interviewed and observed 116 students of the 700 students enrolled in the course between September 1998 and June1999. She found that the majority of students interviewed liked the course and spoke positively about the self-directed, active learning experience. One younger student who was quite adept at using computers before entering the course summarized the experience: *"I think this course is fun. It's a breeze. The [Web] site is cool. I am pretty comfortable with all software. The TAs are great. I can do all these things – no problems."* A mature, single parent identified a specific benefit: *"I like this course. I don't need to be on campus; I can be at home with my two year old boy and work on the modules at the same time. It saves me time and money – I don't need to find a baby-sitter."*

About 30% of the students who were interviewed found difficulty with the course. The students' reaction varied a great deal. Some reactions were very apathetic, some were very positive, and others were very negative. Responses tended to fall into a number of major categories. Some of the respondents indicated that they were overwhelmed by the course content. A young male student exemplified this: *"It's so overwhelming... I have to learn [how to use] the Web site and there are so many new words, computer terminology... Searching the Internet is so frustrating... I never get the things I need... I never choose the right words."* Some had problems with the method of communication, i.e., typing rather than talking. A young female student said *"I express myself better talking than writing.... In a distance situation I prefer talking on the phone. It saves time. In this course I have to write emails when I have problems... I have to wait for answers that usually don't help much."* Some doubted their own ability to contribute to a class online discussion. One young female student typified this with: *"I have difficulty expressing myself. I don't have much knowledge about computers... I don't know how to give smart or relevant contribution to the Web-Board. So, I don't use it...I don't go there...It doesn't help me... I don't waste my time reading it."* The most commonly identified issue, though, was concerned with the self-paced, active learning orientation of the course. Although students had access to both a face2face lecture and a Web page that explained active learning in detail, some students could not internalize this knowledge. One older male stated: *"I need to be taught. After I can do things [by] myself. I don't like classes [where] I never see the instructor. The TAs don't know everything. I just can't stand it. It is not my style… I am too old to change now."* Another showed frustration and lack of understanding: *"In the email the instructor told me I must be responsible for my own learning, but what does it mean? I am a responsible person.* A young female student stated: *"I don't understand active learning. I am going to teach in a traditional way. I am in elementary. I don't even need this."* A young male student added: *"I am not an independent type of person. I need help to learn."*

On the other hand, some of the students had more positive reaction and they were very optimistic about active learning. A young female student said: *" I always have been very independent since school. I take this course from home…I don't think I learned how to be independent. It is just the way I am. I don't know if am practicing active learning in this course, but at least I am trying."*

It must be stressed that the student achievement in this class was outstanding. While some had real problems with the way the subject matter was presented, even though they may have expressed frustration, overall and individually they achieved much more than we would have expected from a face2face class. Essentially what we learned is that those students who are predisposed to be active learners are quite robust in a passive learning (lecture) mode. They may or may not pay any attention to what is being "fed" to them, but their natural way of learning allows them to transcend the classroom situation and learn on their own. On the other hand, those students who have become passive learners and who, for some reason either can't or won't develop good active learning skills have nothing to fall back on when we take away the lectures. In many cases, particularly since the topic area (instructional technology) was already overwhelming to some students, trying to help them learn how to learn in this different paradigm was beyond them. While we subscribed to the basic principles of adult learning, many of these students didn't.

This made me seriously consider whether creating courses that require all students to be active learners are appropriate for use with a wide range of students who may not be ready for active learning without extensive preparation. Active learning just isn't appropriate for some students.

Videoconferencing and Teaching

In the late eighties I was asked to participate in a program to deliver instruction using point-to-point videoconferencing systems in a traditional office environment. I met with the prospective participants a couple of times via videoconference and realized that I really liked the possibilities, but while a traditional videoconference system worked really well for seminar-type classes with small groups at each location, there were some areas that needed improvement for larger group instruction, particularly where more than two locations needed to be connected (multipoint). The cost of connecting locations for videoconferencing using POTS (Plain Old Telephone Service) was also something that seemed a major barrier for educational users. Over the years, I observed a number of uses of videoconferencing equipment in education and kept thinking that this was a really powerful medium, but systems needed to be designed specifically for use in teaching and learning, and the connectivity costs had to be reduced.

In 1994 the province of Alberta's two major research universities, the University of Alberta (in Edmonton) and the University of Calgary (in Calgary), realized that, in a tightening economy, it was going to become increasingly impossible to hire professors in every specialty at each university. One solution was to hire a specialist at one university and have that person teach classes at both. This was not an unreasonable idea, except that the two cities are 180 miles apart. The search began for a technological solution that would allow professors and students to interact in a "traditional lecture format" without requiring the professors to change, substantially, the way they taught (Franklin & Peat, 2001).

The president of the University set up a small committee to look at alternatives. After a review of available technologies and a tour of a number of sites where different types of "smart classrooms" were installed, we recommended that a pair of classrooms could be set up to meet our needs, and using existing technology. At the same time, the Western Universities Research Consortium (WURCNet) set up Wnet, a high speed Internet research network in Alberta which was associated with CA*Net, the national high speed Internet research backbone in Canada operated by CANARIE Inc. Wnet was operated over an experimental ATM network that allowed very high speed data communications between the two university campuses. A classroom at each campus was designed and implemented providing two-way, broadcast quality digital video. Classroom capabilities included different views of the class at each location (e.g., instructor podium, full class, each individual seat). A visualizer and computer workstation linked to a scan converter allowed still images to be presented to students at both locations and each student seat had a "Question" button with queuing control by the instructor. Signals were encoded as Motion JPEG (MJPEG) and transmitted over Wnet. In 1998 the video codecs were converted to MPEG-2.

Bringing It All Together: Developing Specifications for a Distance Education System

In 1998 Mike Davenport, the Superintendent of Schools in the Fort Vermilion School Division (FVSD) in the very north-eastern corner of Alberta, and a close personal friend posed a challenge to Graham Fletcher, another friend and the president of an Internet Service Provider and myself. He wanted us to design a 21st Century distance education system that would provide students in remote, rural classrooms with as good education as they would receive taking the same courses in a classroom in a large urban school division. FVSD had been delivering high school courses via audio graphics since 1991. Both teachers and students were quite unhappy with this technology for a number of reasons. Some of the main complaints were that students could not see the teacher or other students, the teacher could not see the students, and the audiographics were limited. Teachers complained that students could mute the audio convener in a room, and the teacher was not aware of what might be happening in that room. Teachers, parents, and students had all been pressuring the division to provide a better way to deliver learning to these students.

We decided to start from the position that cost was no concern. We'd develop a system that gave the best possible services to the students, then find out whether it was possible to build it. Finally, if it looked possible, we'd find out what we had to modify to make it happen.

We posed three theoretical questions.

1. What kind of teaching and learning do we want to facilitate?
2. What kinds of technological capabilities should we provide to the teachers and the students?
3. How will we provide communications between the schools?

In looking at the kinds of teaching and learning we wanted to facilitate, we quickly realized that there was a real split among the teachers — many were traditionalists, seeing their job as information providers. Others took the position that the students needed to develop their own reality, and that teachers were only facilitators to help them construct that reality. Many other points of view were evident within the jurisdiction. While we tended towards the philosophical position that students are active partners in the learning process and both students and teachers should be able to interact with each other and with information and instructional material in many different ways, we realized that many people would demand that teacher-centered instruction be supported. We decided that we would support multiple methods of teaching and learning including both synchronous and asynchronous learning opportunities. We wanted to implement technology that made teachers' jobs easier, allowing them to interact with students in a familiar manner, but also provide facilities that allow them to investigate new ways of teaching and learning. To support this last goal, we decided that we needed to provide professional development.

After an examination of a number of distance education systems, we decided that we should design our own system based upon the idea that no single technology was "THE" appropriate technology for distance education, but that providing teachers and students with a number of different capabilities would allow each to use the most appropriate technology for their particular task. We decided that we needed to build a set of classrooms, which we call Virtual Presence Learning Facilities (VPLEs). Each high school would have one VPLE. The main use of the VPLE would be to support synchronous learning between the schools, but every synchronous course would be recorded so students could access their class later for review (or in case they missed the class). Each VPLE included the ability to:

- simultaneously connect to up to seven other VPLEs;

- act as either the originator of a lesson, or the recipient of a lesson;

- provide the teachers and students with three common communications channels: (1) a broadcast quality audio and video image of the presenter (the teacher or other person designated by the teacher), (or presenter) on one large screen; (2) a broadcast quality audio and video image of a collage of all the students in the class on a second screen; and (3) a data stream, containing digital data for ancillary equipment (such as shared whiteboards, visualizers, etc.);

- interface all the signals so that students and teachers would all appear to be within a single facility;

- share a common electronic whiteboard;

- display three dimensional objects as well as two dimensional pictures and text;

- allow students to indicate that they would like to ask a question;

- allow students to indicate that they are lost, and that the teacher needs to review a point;

- give the teacher control over the whole network via a simple GUI interface;

- allow the teacher to designate a particular student to be the "presenter," moving their image to the presenter screen, while the teacher's image takes the place of that student's image within the student collage;

- give students access to a complete lecture after class;

- provide common asynchronous tools for the teacher to allow the development of support facilities (reading lists, course outlines, submission of assignments, posting of grades, etc.);

- use laptop and desktop computers within their classes;

- allow students to work in small groups, where the groups must also not be within one location; and

- allow students to access appropriate materials (data banks, simulations, software, etc.) from the Internet.

We knew that we also wanted to provide students and teachers with authenticated access to their lessons and other materials from their home computers.

When we started this project, FVSD was using POTS for communications between schools. We were familiar with how well an IP-based network and planned to build this network ourselves. During the specification/design stage, the Alberta government announced the intention to build the Alberta SuperNet (http://www.albertasupernet.ca), which would provide "equal access for equal cost to the highest quality high-speed broadband access to the Internet to every hospital, school, library, and government facility in the province within three years" (Alberta Innovation and Science, November 2, 2000). The Government requested that we delay implementation of our network until the Alberta Supernet was built.

The Rural Advanced Community of Learners

The Rural Advanced Community of Learners (RACOL) is the implementation of the specifications that we developed. RACOL has set out to create an environment that puts students and teachers who are located at great distances from each other together in a common, real time environment that also provides quality, asynchronous support. One major change between the specifications and the implementation was that the visualizer display was routed to the presenter display rather than through the data display. At the time we built the system, the cost of connecting the visualizer to the data stream was too high to justify the small increase in usability.

Synchronous Delivery

One classroom in each of six high schools in FVSD, one seminar room at the FVSD central office, and one seminar room at the University of Alberta were converted to Virtual Presence Learning Environments (VPLEs) by equipping them with a SMART Board electronic whiteboard, an ELMO visualizer, laptop connections, and four ViaVideo equipped personal computers. Figure 1 provides photos of a VPLE, while Figure 2 shows an annotated diagram of one of the VPLEs.

Figure 1: "As built" views of a virtual presence learning environment.

One of the specifications for synchronous delivery was that all student locations should be visible to each other and to the teacher. At the time the project was designed, no commercial Multipoint Control Unit (MCU) for MPEG-2 equipment existed so we commissioned the design, development and implementation of an MPEG-2 MCU. The SMART Board computers at each location are connected over with a computer running application sharing software (e.g., Microsoft NetMeeting) program via Alberta Supernet. This allows the presentations or notations on any of the SMART Boards to immediately be reflected on each of the other SMART Boards.

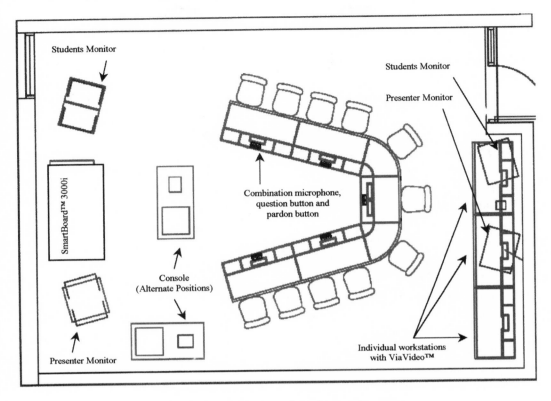

Figure 2. Virtual presence learning environment.

Video cameras are located at the rear and front of each classroom. Each of these camera signals is encoded separately using Amnis MPEG-2 codecs. The codecs are connected to the central MCU via the Alberta Supernet. The rear camera records the "presenter image" or the person presenting to the class (if there is someone presenting in that classroom), while the front camera captures student images." In almost all cases the teacher is the presenter, but the teacher does have the ability to designate any student as the "presenter." This displays that student's image on the "presenter" screen while the teacher's image takes the students place on the split "student" screen. Two monitors at the front of the classroom respectively show the image of the current presenter and a split-screen collage of the students at all locations. These monitors are replicated at the rear of each classroom so that if someone is presenting from that room they can see the monitors without having to turn around.

Students share a table that contains a microphone and two buttons: a question button and an "I'm lost" button. When a student asks a question by pressing the question button, the student's location is placed in a queue on a touch panel at the instructor's location. The instructor can elect when to take a question and in what order the questions should be taken. When an instructor acknowledges a question request, the local student camera focuses on the student asking the question, the student's microphone becomes active, and the student's image become larger in the student monitor. Once the student asks the question and the instructor cancels the question indicator, the local camera returns to a full room view and that student's microphone becomes inactive. When a student presses the "I'm lost" button an accumulator that is displayed on the instructor's touch panel is incremented. No indication is given of where the lost student(s) is/are located. This is an attempt to replicate the sense that an instructor in a face2face situation can gain from looking around the room and seeing how many puzzled looks there are. If the "I'm lost" accumulator begins to mount, the instructor should take the queue to go back and explain a concept again. A single touch resets the "I'm lost" accumulator to zero.

AsynchronousDelivery

We needed to record three concurrent streams (the "presenter" stream, the collage of the "student" stream, and the SMART Board or display stream), then stream them back to students at a later time. Also, these three streams needed to be delivered at either of two speeds: one "high speed" stream for use within the school system, and a second for access by students from home who may have 56K Modem access only. After significant investigation, it was decided that we would have to develop this application (see Montgomerie, Davis, & Boora, 2004, for a complete description). Figure 3 shows an example of the interface that allows students to select and play the different video streams. Note that the stream is date/time stamped and includes the ability for students to bookmark locations in the video for future review.

Network

RACOL has been implemented over the Alberta Supernet. Alberta Learning provides each school with a free 10 megabit connection, and upgrade to 100 megabit or higher is available at costs that are similar to those charged in a large urban centre. The Alberta Supernet provides Quality of Service, so synchronous protocols such as those used in RACOL receive priority.

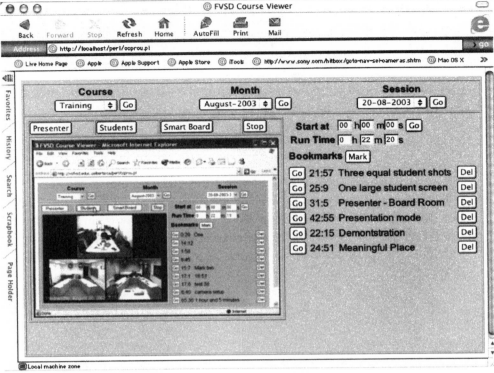

Figure 3: Asynchronous access to a class.

Distance Learning in the Future — Better than Face2Face?

At the very beginning of this chapter I talked about Arcadia Darrel's transcriber. Are we there yet? We certainly have computer programs that you can talk to and to some extent they spell and punctuate correctly. But I recently bought a PDA that is also a cell phone. It is advertised as a mobile office. I can talk to it and it transfers that verbal information to someone else, but I can't verbally enter the telephone number and tell the PDA to dial it. The PDA can't take dictation and convert that to text even though it contains both a microphone and a fairly advanced computer and these capabilities have been available on laptop/desktop computers for years. I really want a nice little hand held device that responds to both my verbal commands and acts as my personal secretary. Somehow, the PDA folks haven't got it quite right yet.

When we talk about people learning to use computers, we usually label one of the higher stages "integration." This is when the student has learned how to use a number of individual programs, and finally comes to realize that there is data, and there are tools that operate on data. Once the student knows what operation needs to be performed, and how the data is formatted, that student can choose the appropriate tool to transform the data in any way they want. What I want in a PDA is a fully integrated office system.

I think we are at a similar stage in the use of technology in distance education. There are a number of different instructional models and a number of different technologies that are currently being used quite successfully in distance learning. Each instructional model and each technology works for some students, and fails for others. Similarly, each instructional model and each technology has proponents and detractors. Naturally, as academics, we have extremely specialized areas of research. I believe we are at a nexus in distant learning. Each of us needs to back up a little and look at the audience that needs to learn, the subject matter and level that are being taught and see which distance education technologies can be combined to give the students the best experience that is possible. RACOL is a first attempt to try integrating different kinds of distance education technologies and different teaching and learning models into a single system. We believe that we may be offering education that is better than most face2face instruction — but then, most face2face instruction still consists of a teacher, a blackboard, and an overhead projector. I long to see the day when people point at the RACOL classrooms and describe them in the same kind of terms that we technology types currently describe the chalk and slate classroom of yesteryear.

References

Alberta Innovation and Science (2000, November 2). SUPERNET to connect communities to the 21st century at warp speed). Retrieved September 2, 2002, from the World Wide Web: http://www.gov.ab.ca/acn/200011/9894.html

Apple Computer Inc. (1977). *Suggested Retail Price List April 1977*. Retrieved October 9, 2003: http://apple2history.org/museum/computers_apple1/price1977.html

Asimov, I. (1953). *Second foundation*. Garden City, NY: Doubleday.

Franklin S., & Peat M. (2001). Managing change: The use of mixed delivery modes to increase learning opportunities. *Australian Journal of Educational Technology, 17*(1), pp. 37-49.

Hicks, S., & Hunka, S. (1972). *The teacher and the computer*. Philadelphia: Saunders.

Hunka, S. M., Hunka, J., Kearsley, G., Maguire, T., Margolus, N., McGinnis, N., Montgomerie, T. C., & Romaniuk, G. (1978). *Preliminary specifications for an instructional support system for NATAL-74* (Contract No. OSU77-00260, The National Research Council of Canada). Edmonton, AB: Division of Educational Research Services, University of Alberta.

Kubrick, S. (1968). *2001 A space odyssey* [motion picture]. Hollywood, CA: Warner Bros.

Montgomerie, T.C., Davis, A.R., & Boora, N. (2004). Automatic recording and streaming of synchronous distance education classes. In *Proceedings: PTC2004: New times – New strategies: ICT rising from the ashes*. [CD-ROM]. Honolulu, HI: Pacific Telecommunications Council.

Montgomerie, T.C., & Romaniuk, E.W. (1976). Interactive programs: A simple way to allow naive users to manipulate extensive databases. *Proceedings of the University of Alberta* users applications symposium (pp. 121-144). Edmonton: University of Alberta.

Romaniuk, E.W., & Montgomerie, T.C. (1976). After implementing your course – What's next? *Proceedings of the second Canadian Symposium on Instructional Technology* (pp 377-396). Quebec City: National Research Council.

Chapter 17

Experiencing the Online Revolution

James L. Morrison

James L. Morrison, Professor of Educational Leadership Emeritus at the University of North Carolina at Chapel Hill, has founded and served as editor of three periodicals, "On the Horizon" (http://www.emeraldinsight.com/oth.htm), a futures journal for higher education; "The Technology Source" (http://ts.mivu.org), an e-journal designed to assist educators as they face the challenge of integrating information technology tools into teaching and into managing educational organization; and "Innovate" (http://fgse.nova.edu/innovate), an e-journal that focuses on the creative use of information technology to enhance active learning methods irrespective of sector (K-12, colleges and universities, corporate universities). He has published over 230 articles, book chapters, books, and monographs on environmental scanning and forecasting, planning, management, and using technology in educational organizations. In 1999 he received the Distinguished Scholar Award from the American Educational Research Association's Special Interest Group on Strategic Change.

In a comprehensive book entitled *The Diffusion of Innovations*, Everett Rogers (1995) characterizes people who adopt innovations as being in one of five categories: innovators, early adopters, early majority, late majority, and laggards. I am an early adopter. In this chapter, I describe how I became an early user of Information Technology (IT) tools in my work as a professor and the lessons that I have learned over the years. I conclude with brief comments on the major forces impacting education and the changes that will mark colleges and universities in the future.

Early Efforts: My First Use of Technology in the Classroom

I began my professorial career in 1969, but it was an Army Reserve assignment that first introduced me to personal computers in the mid-1980s. I was tasked to prepare a preliminary report for a general officer steering committee at the Pentagon, and I was told to use a Compaq "luggable" so that my unit would have an electronic copy of the document. I quickly saw the advantages of using a computer to write and modify manuscripts. When my duty ended, I purchased a personal computer, which I used mostly for clerical tasks. I enjoyed the fact that I was no longer dependent upon a secretary who worked for six other professors to type and retype manuscripts and letters.

It was several years before I began to integrate technology into my courses, and I was one of the first in my school to do so — albeit in an elementary manner. I used Microsoft PowerPoint to present introductory lessons and Word to conduct interactive group process sessions. For example, in an educational management course that I team-taught in 1989, I used the Nominal Group Technique (Morrison, 1998) to focus discussion on the topics for which I was responsible. I first asked a topic question (e.g., What potential developments on the horizon could affect the future of education?) and then requested that students compose responses on paper. After 5 to 10 minutes, I began a round robin, where each student in turn suggested one answer to the question. I typed these comments on my laptop and displayed them on a large screen via a projector. I asked students to think about each nominated response from their colleagues: Did it bring to mind a point that they had not previously considered?

When responses to the question were exhausted, we began our discussion of each response. Did everyone understand what was meant by the comment? Did everyone agree that it was an appropriate response to the question? This discussion resulted in a collaborative effort to refine and edit student answers. By using Word and a projector, we found such editing relatively easy, particularly when contrasted with the use of flip charts and magic markers. I printed the results of the discussion after each class and distributed them at the beginning of the next class meeting. Employing PowerPoint and Word jazzed up my classes, and I viewed the use of these tools as state-of-the-art instructional technique. I received outstanding student evaluations for the course.

The very questions that I asked my students were the crux of my own research. I was a futurist who focused on identifying signals of change in the macroenvironment and deriving their implications for education. In 1992, I founded a professional publication titled *On the Horizon* (http://www.emeraldinsight.com/oth.htm) to explore important trends (e.g., the globalization of the economy, the impact of telecommunications on this economy, the growth of the Internet, and the development of new pedagogical technologies) and their implications for educational leaders who were guiding their schools into the future. It became clear to me that to be successful in the Information Age, college graduates needed to do more than master the content in their chosen fields; they also needed to be technologically literate. The growing use of technology tools to enhance productivity in professional workplaces, the boom in online education initiatives, and an expanded emphasis on *evolving competencies* (rather than static knowledge) demanded that students — particularly those preparing to become educational leaders — develop and continually update a new set of computer skills.

One day it struck me that although my classroom use of PowerPoint and Word was a good example, my efforts were only minimally enhancing the ability of my students to use technology themselves. These people were preparing for careers as educational leaders, primarily in public schools. It was vital that they have not only a conceptual understanding of technology use in education, but also the practical ability to demonstrate its advantages and facilitate the integration of technology in the curriculums of their organizations.

The Transition: Redesigning One Course to Enhance Technology Competencies

I slowly began the transition from my exclusive use of technology in the classroom to my students' use of technology when I began to team teach the course with David Thomas. In the fall 1991 offering, we included this objective: "Use technology as an aid to your work as a manager." Professor Thomas agreed to handle the majority of topics in the course (e.g., site-based management, staffing, budgeting, special populations) and to teach students how to write decision memos and book reviews. My responsibility was to teach the strategic management portion of the course, which included the major project; I also assumed responsibility for technology integration. Professor Thomas and I both reviewed students' work and mutually determined grades.

For my portion of the course, I had students read a strategic management text (that I was writing with two colleagues) as a guide for their course projects. The assignment was either to work with practicing school administrators to develop a strategic plan for the institution, or to simulate being on a team charged with planning a new school in the local county. I set up a class listserv to facilitate communication and required that the projects be turned in on disk and presented in class using PowerPoint at the conclusion of the semester. (The written project and presentation constituted 35% of the semester grade, decision memos constituted 40%, and class participation constituted 25%.)

I specified that PowerPoint be used in the project presentations for three reasons. First, the university had a site license for Microsoft Office, thereby making the software a relatively inexpensive purchase. Second, Microsoft's productivity tools were supported by the university's Office of Instructional Technology, which periodically scheduled training programs; this meant that students could get help if they needed it. Third, our lab had only Macs at the time, but many students had PCs at home; Office allowed students to transfer data files from Macs to PCs and vice-versa with ease.

I also required that students join three mailing lists where the main topic of discussion was the future of education. We started the semester with an environmental scanning assignment in which students sought articles or listserv postings that described signals of change in the external environment. Students were required to abstract two such articles or postings, add a section titled "implications for public education," and post their drafts to the class listserv. In class, I showed students how to download postings from email, take out the paragraph markings at the end of each line, format their manuscripts, and place the files in a folder on their hard drives (or, if they were in the computer lab, on a floppy disk). These manuscripts were to be used as part of the external analysis portion of their projects.

Because written communication skills are important tools for educational leaders, I projected one draft abstract from each student on screen and focused class discussion on how it could be better written. I assigned the second draft abstract from each student to a classmate, who had to write a critique of it. In order to reduce anxiety, I did not grade either the draft abstracts or the critiques.

At the beginning of the semester, no student had an email address or had ever subscribed to a listserv, and only one student had ever used a presentation software program; by the end of the course, students were competent in the use of these technologies. Although their course projects were good in many respects, Professor Thomas and I felt that the quality of their writing could be improved. We offered students the option to revise their written projects and decision memos, with the possibility of receiving a higher grade. The university's graduate school handbook specified that a grade of P (pass) be given to work normally expected of graduate students, an L (low pass) to substandard work, and an H (high pass) to exemplary work. Professor Thomas and I awarded Ps to all but a few of the papers initially submitted. Every student who received a P completed at least one revision of his or her work, a process that greatly improved the written documents, the student's knowledge, and, in some but not all cases, the student's final grade.

Student Complaints and a Second Attempt

Professor Thomas and I thought that the course was highly successful. Unfortunately, the students' perspective was quite different, and they gave the course a mean rating below the school of education average. Chief among their complaints was that the emphasis on technology and on learning to use technology took away time that should have been devoted to lessons on school management.

I was dumbfounded, but after some thought, I came to two conclusions: (1) I had not sufficiently "sold" my rationale — that written and oral communication skills and the use of technological productivity tools were so important that they would be factored into student grades; and (2) I had not compensated for the fact that these added requirements increased the class workload substantially. Students had not expected the class to consume so much of their time and energy; they found learning to use email, listservs, Internet search engines, and presentation software a burden.

I relied on this analysis when charged with taking sole responsibility for another class entitled "The Social Context of Educational Leadership." This course was originally designed with specific content and taught via lectures and discussion. I made sure that my version was congruent with the objectives expressed in the university bulletin, but I redesigned the course to focus on career challenges the students were likely to face in the Information Age and the competencies they would need to navigate these challenges successfully. In a world where the professional knowledge base was changing rapidly, it was clear that these prospective administrators needed to be able to access, analyze, and communicate information with both traditional methods and information technology tools. The question then became: What kind of learning experience do the students need to develop these skills?

I used an active-learning simulation approach, whereby students were to act as a task force that informed the U.S. Department of Education of the major issues challenging public education. The task force consisted of several teams assigned to prepare and present issue-analysis papers. To complete this assignment, the students — all of whom were experienced public school teachers — first had to identify the issues through an environmental scanning exercise and then develop issue-analysis papers. To access and communicate this information, they had to learn to use such tools as Internet search engines, a Web page editor, file transfer protocol (FTP), and presentation software.

I made a detailed syllabus (available only through the Web) to structure this enterprise, and I helped students learn how to use information technology tools and improve their papers and presentations. In essence, scanning and issue analysis — plus the resulting papers and presentations — constituted the content of the course. I acted as a mentor, facilitator, and guide. The only content I provided was several papers on anticipatory management that I made available on the Web, via the syllabus.

In terms of outcomes, the course was successful. Students developed their own Web pages, each of which included a resume, an environmental scanning abstract, an issue-analysis paper, and PowerPoint presentation slides. These products reflected competencies that few of the students had prior to the course. Moreover, their abstracts and papers were quite good, especially after several revisions. These materials were published online and became useful to the broader educational community (I have received notes from many authors who have cited material from student papers).

But this does not mean that the students were happy campers. In fact, they were dissatisfied with their experience. When I asked students on their comprehensive examination to explain the anomaly of successful learning outcomes and relatively low course ratings, I received a number of explanations. I was told that:

- I provided little content in the course.
- My critiques of their writing and presentations were too severe, and their extra revision efforts did not necessarily lead to higher grades; indeed, my critical attention was perceived to be a threat to their grade point averages.
- My emphasis on communication skills was out of balance with the title of the course. (A sample comment: "This course should be retitled 'Technology and Journalism.'")
- Learning to use technology tools was not worth the time and effort expended, especially given their heavy schedules (16 semester hours) and the different skills they perceived as important to their future roles as assistant principals.

In addition, several students pointed out that the course required skills and behaviors quite different from those encouraged in other classes: Students typically worked alone, but in my course they were required to work as part of a team; students were accustomed to learning and recalling concepts presented by their professors, but in my course almost all of their time was spent applying knowledge and skills; students usually turned in their work for evaluation at the end of the semester, but in my course they received steady feedback on their work throughout the semester, which required continuous revision; students were comfortable completing their assignments using the library and basic word processing, but in my course they had to work with multimedia materials, the Internet, email, and the Web, as well as the library. In other words, this course demanded a shift in their approach to learning and performing—a shift that made them uncomfortable.

Some students were so uncomfortable that they complained to an incoming dean that the course had no content (I gave only one lecture, and that at the beginning of the semester). The dean's response was to order my program chair to remove me from teaching the course and assign me other duties. When I asked her about this decision, she told me that "students expect faculty members to provide knowledge—to lecture. If you won't lecture, you cannot teach required courses, only seminars." My resolution was to buy out my teaching time; in my last 2.5 years on the active faculty, I taught only one full course, which was, ironically, the social context class because no other professor was available to teach it that particular semester. I also was assigned to teach a half-course once a year on using technology in education — a class in which I was not expected to lecture — and to assume other additional duties and committee assignments.

Underlying Issues and Professional Costs

I have related these experiences to illustrate the disjuncture involved when a social institution is undergoing a paradigm shift (Mack, 2003). I changed my role as teacher from actor to director and demanded a corresponding transition in student behavior that countered prevailing norms. Several of my colleagues were upset because I had deviated from a paradigm that regarded educational administration/leadership as a field of defined knowledge that is taught to students, usually sequentially. My constructivist approach focused on process, not defined knowledge. In essence, the course consisted of students' scanning abstracts, collaboratively writing issue-analysis papers, and presenting those papers. Students chose their own topics; my role was to help them learn how to use listservs and search engines, to explore the issues they identified as most critical to the future of education, and to provide a professional critique of how they argued these issues to the world at large. Therefore, student papers—not my lectures—constituted the "content" of the course.

Ironically, the way in which I taught was consistent with the Secretary's Commission on Achieving Necessary Skills (SCANS) report (1992) for classroom reforms, a report that was required reading in other educational leadership courses. In essence, the report advocated moving from a passive to a participative classroom environment as described in Table 1.

Table 1: The Conventional Classroom Compared with the SCANS Classroom	
From the conventional classroom	To the SCANs classroom
Teacher knows answer.	More than one solution may be viable and teacher may not have it in advance.
Students routinely work alone.	Students routinely work with teachers, peers, and community members.
Teacher plans all activities.	Students and teachers plan and negotiate activities.
Teacher makes all assessments.	Students routinely assess themselves.
Information is organized, evaluated, interpreted, and communicated to students by teacher.	Information is acquired, evaluated, organized, interpreted, and communicated by students to appropriate audiences.
Organizing system of the classroom is simple; one teacher teaches 30 students.	Organizing systems are complex: teacher and students both reach out beyond school for additional information.
Reading, writing, and math are treated as separate disciplines; listening and speaking often are missing from curriculum.	Disciplines needed for problem solving are integrated; listening and speaking are fundamental parts of learning.
Thinking is usually theoretical and "academic."	Thinking involves problem solving, reasoning, and decision making.
Students are expected to conform to teacher's behavioral expectations; integrity and honesty are monitored by teacher; student self-esteem is often poor.	Students are expected to be responsible, sociable, self-managing, and resourceful; integrity and honesty are monitored within the social context of the classroom; students' self-esteem in high because they are in charge of their own learning.

Source: The Secretary's Commission on Achieving Necessary Skills (1992, April), Exhibit 4, pp. 10-11.

Joel Barker (1993) argues that our paradigms powerfully distort and even blind us to self-evident truths until we experience the moment of insight which enables us to "see the world anew." Immersing people who have not had that insight in paradigmatic change produces cognitive dissonance. Although my students experienced the SCANS reading regimen, they had a difficult time when placed outside of their conventional classroom comfort zone.

From my perspective, requiring that students learn to apply information technology tools to complete course requirements was an opportunity to prepare them for the future world of work. No doubt it would have been easier for them to adjust to these requirements had they been adept at using the basic tools before they enrolled in the course. The students' unfamiliarity with these tools, the fact that in the early to mid-nineties email programs and HTML translation programs were not intuitive, and the fact that anti-virus programs did not handle computer viruses easily or effectively served to increase student frustration. All in all, the combination of my conducting the course in a different way and the students' discomfort with the technology available in those days entailed significant changes for all of us.

Moreover, these students were adult learners — practicing teachers who already had experience in the field and who had opinions about what skills they needed to be successful administrators. Technological proficiency rated low on their lists. Ed Neal, the director of faculty development at my university's center for teaching and learning, put the problem this way: "Learning to use electronic technology might . . . seem pointless, since [the students] have typically worked in public school environments that have little technology available. The promise that these tools will eventually be as common as the telephone is insufficient to convince them that they should spend time learning them now." The gap between my definition of a successful course and that of my students arose, Neal surmised, from a mismatch between my goals and expectations for students and their own goals and expectations (personal communication, May 22, 1998).

While the technology component obviously unsettled the students, their complaints also pointed to two separate, underlying issues: grade inflation and the concept of writing as a process. In the school of education at my university, H became the common grade — in part, I suspect, because of the importance of student evaluations in tenure and merit decisions. Indeed, some of my colleagues routinely gave all students a "high pass" (H) and announced that they would do so near the beginning of the semester; their rationale was that this approach removed the tension of grades and allowed them to focus on learning. I did not adopt this view, but followed the grading standard specified in the graduate school bulletin. In a course that already asked students to think, work, and participate differently, my adherence to strict grade standards violated the student norm that if you worked hard, you deserved an H.

The same might be said of my emphasis on writing as a process. Many students were accustomed to spending all semester gearing up for a single paper or project that would be handed in on the last day of class and comprised a substantial portion of their final grade. Some professors might provide a few written comments or suggestions for revision, but by that time the course was over and the assignment was completed. I stressed the value of multiple drafts, peer and instructor feedback, and improved writing skills as a worthwhile goal in and of itself (rather than as a guarantee of a better grade). All of the technological tools that I employed and that I asked students to master facilitated this approach, but students generally overlooked the underlying pedagogy. Students were also slow to link constructive criticism with their attractiveness as job candidates. I pushed them to write better papers and publish their final projects on the Web not to increase their stress levels, but to give students an opportunity to contribute to the broader scope of knowledge. Ideally these students would market themselves by applying their coursework to their careers rather than just to their degrees.

The technological components that I mention above (computer projection equipment, presentation and Web page software, listservs, and so on) are basic ones—very useful but also somewhat rudimentary in terms of the more recent advances in educational technology. At that point, I had not stepped very far out on the technology/constructivist learning limb, but my "unorthodox" teaching methods nonetheless had professional costs: After a 30-year career as a professor, I essentially was relieved of my teaching duties and assigned to various committees and projects in which I had little interest.

I made the best of the situation, however, by pouring my energy into *On the Horizon* and into the development of a new peer-reviewed electronic journal focused on the potential of technology to enhance and improve education. With a former student (James Ptazynski), I founded *The Technology Source* (http://ts.mivu.org) in1997, and today it remains a valuable and trusted resource for educators worldwide. As editor, I enjoy publicizing the newest and most exciting trends in the field: the proliferation of academic e-journals that use information technology tools to enhance professional communication; the movement for open, electronic archives of scholarly research; the impact of blogs on social and political policy; advances in publishing made possible by rich site summary . . . the list of innovations (in terms of both new technologies and new applications of older ones) is too great to exhaust.

Course Adjustments and Positive Feedback (At Last)

Rogers (1995) describes early adopters as opinion leaders. This was not true in my case. In my enthusiasm to apply a constructivist perspective to teaching, incorporate requirements to use IT tools, focus on writing and presentation skills, and maintain the university grading standard, I violated faculty and student norms. Rather than "showing the way," I suffered criticism from both faculty members and students. My colleagues felt that I was not providing content, and although they did not seem to mind my emphasis on writing and presentation, they themselves did not incorporate their evaluation of these skills when assigning grades. Students felt that I overemphasized the need to learn IT tools and to increase writing and speaking competency to the exclusion of content. My behavior did little to affect these norms.

I took all criticism seriously, however, and modified my approach over time in an attempt to make it more acceptable to everyone involved. Initially, for example, I critiqued student papers using the "track changes" feature of Microsoft Word and then returned the annotated papers to students via email. Later I modified this procedure to require a face-to-face session in which I reviewed my critique with each student. I also changed the course schedule to allot much more time to student presentations and related discussion and to require one less rewrite of the major paper. In the last class I taught, I provided only formative evaluations as we proceeded through the semester; students did not know their course grades until they received them from the registrar. In that class, my student evaluations were above the school mean.

Some one to three years after my students had completed the social context course, they took comprehensive exams and had the option of responding to the following prompts: (1) "Comment on the anomaly of the course producing successful outcomes but generally receiving low ratings"; (2) "What are the implications of the social context course (content as well as instructional process) for you in your role as an educational leader?" Notably, many students gave positive responses, among them the following:

- "I acquired greater detail and synthesis of information because I was responsible for myself and to my team members as we worked together to construct the issue analysis paper. This was an important experience because in most positions of leadership, the leader will be required to work in an effective, collegial manner with faculty and staff colleagues."
- "Although the class was a painful experience for many, it was a fruitful one with boundless new opportunities within our grasp after the completion of the expectations and course requirements. . . .We as educators are human and react just as the students we taught. We want to be spoon fed. We want to be lectured to. We want bold print and make sure that important things are repeated three times. Why do we desire this format? It is what we know. It is what we are used to. Those are the very reasons you should not change a thing! It was a painful GOOD learning experience for us."
- "This course changed my paradigm of learning. I now realize the power of knowing how to learn. I was always good at memorizing facts, but now I

understand the importance of doing research to find facts, thinking critically about them, and then integrating them into concepts. The course also taught me how to use technology to do better research, write, and then present information."

- "As a course designed more for skills development than transference of information, it has provided me with the primary and most essential tools for dealing with change: The capability to recognize it, make sense of it, and communicate what I see on the horizon of the educational landscape."

Finally, at a program lunch to which I was invited after my retirement, I sat next to a newly appointed professor. Responding to my comment that I had experienced criticism during my final years at the university, she said that the word on me was that I was "ahead of my time."

Final Thoughts: The Future of Education

I believe that we are in a period of transition in higher education, one driven by the combined forces of demographics, globalization, economic restructuring, and information technology; I am confident that these forces will lead us to adopt new concepts of educational markets, organizational structures, how we teach, and what we teach (Morrison, 2003). Globalization requires that employees become adept at working with people from diverse cultures, and that they become proficient in the effective use of IT tools. Globalization also spurs economic restructuring, which increases the need for workers to be productive and to the demand for retraining by workers who are "downsized." Consequently, we are experiencing a large growth in the number of people who need higher education, and, since we do not have sufficient space on existing campuses to accommodate the demand, we are seeing an exponential increase in online courses and programs that do not require classrooms.

In the not too distant future, colleges and universities will expand their markets to include all people who have Internet access. We will see an increase in virtual universities. Residential campuses will offer predominantly hybrid courses. Substantial online instructional capability will be a standard feature of practically all institutions. Moreover, institutions will predominantly use competency-based exams (rather than credit-hour accomplishment) to award degrees and will guarantee that individuals who receive those degrees are indeed qualified to perform at the implied level.

As changing demographics and technology alter the context of higher education, the mindset of faculty members will need to change as well.

Specifically, instead of viewing themselves primarily as content providers in their teaching role, professors will see themselves as designers of learning experiences for an increasingly diverse student population. Students, viewed today as sponges whose task is to soak up knowledge from their professors (Spector, 2002), will become junior colleagues who acquire knowledge while working through project-based courses. Faculty members will no longer work in isolation, but will serve on teams of instructional designers, media support staff, and assessment specialists. These teams will prepare courses that can be taught online or as hybrid courses in campus classrooms. Classes will be conducted largely by junior professors, instructors, or (in universities) by graduate assistants who will mentor students as they progress through virtual courses.

At the same time that information technology is revolutionizing the world of teachers and students, it is also changing the context of scholarship. Specifically, the movement spearheaded by MIT to put faculty scholarship online, in conjunction with the efforts of the Scholarly Publishing and Academic Resources Coalition (SPAR) and the free online scholarship movement, will establish the acceptability of peer-reviewed online scholarship in terms of merit, tenure, and promotion activities.

The higher education landscape will look quite different in 2020 than it does today. There will still be many "bricks-and-mortar" residential campuses, particularly for the young, but their classes will be hybridized (i.e., a combination of online and in-class instruction). Lectures will no longer be the predominant mode of instruction; rather, group and individual project-based learning will be the norm. The focus of education will be to produce graduates who can use a variety of information technology tools and techniques to access, evaluate, analyze, and communicate information and who can work effectively in teams with people from different ethnic groups to address a wide range of real-world issues and choices, too complex to be solved by tidy textbook answers.

The world is evolving, and our teaching and learning paradigms must evolve with it. The goal is not to replace the instructor with a computer, but to use technology in appropriate ways to support and enhance learning, to prepare students for a workplace that increasingly values technical skills, and to create new ways of discovering and applying knowledge. The road to that end may be bumpy, but I see the sun rising ahead on a promising educational future. This is a journey worth taking.

References

Barker, J.A. (1993). *Paradigms: The business of discovering the future*. London: HarperBusiness Books.

Mack, T. (2003, Spring). An interview with a futurist. *Futures Research Quarterly*, *19*(1), pp. 61-69. Retrieved January 8, 2004, from http://horizon.unc.edu/conferences/dead_files/interview.asp

Morrison, J.L. (1998, June). The nominal group process as an instructional tool. *The Technology Source*. Retrieved January 8, 2004, from http://ts.mivu.org/default.asp?show=article&id=466

Morrison, J.L. (2003). US higher education in transition. *On the Horizon, 11*(1), pp. 6-10. Retrieved January 8, 2004, from http://horizon.unc.edu/courses/papers/InTransition.asp

Rogers, E. (1995). *The diffusion of innovations (4th ed.)*. New York: The Free Press.

Spector, M. (2002, September 27), "Look at me!": A teaching primer. *The Chronicle of Higher Education*. Retrieved January 8, 2004, from http://chronicle.com/weekly/v49/i05/05b01501.htm [Access restricted to subscribers.]

The Secretary's Commission on Achieving Necessary Skills. (1992, April). *Learning a living: A blueprint for high performance*. Washington, U.S. Department of Labor.

Chapter 18

Big Skies and Lone Eagles:
Lending Wings to Others, Online — A Rural Perspective

Frank Odasz

Frank Odasz has been a carpenter, oil field roughneck, dude ranch manager, college professor, and now a "Lone Eagle," an independent instructional entrepreneur. In 1982, Frank attended the University of Wyoming to learn the benefits computers and telecommunications could bring to citizens. As one of the earliest pioneers with both online learning and community networking, he founded the Big Sky Telegraph network, 1988-1998, one of the first online systems to offer online courses. He was also a cofounder of the Consortium for School Networking (CoSN) and has taught at Western Montana College and the University of Colorado.

Prelude

If asked to condense to a single sound bite the most important lesson I've learned about successful online interaction I'd have to say that it is all about trust. One begins with a simple game of catch. I trust that if I send you a message you'll respond back and you trust I'll do likewise. That if I support you with fair and honest communications, you'll return this same level of support back to me.

With this trust relationship as the foundational conduit for the transfer of knowledge, the most scalable packaging of knowledge is the mastery learning format of self-directed modules or lessons providing optimal convenience for an unlimited number of learners. If properly structured, this leaves precious interaction time reserved for general encouragement and specific questions to sustain the essential motivation and self-confidence.

As self-confidence with online learning builds, the door opens for more advanced tools and pedagogies, ultimately resulting in a motivated, self-directed Internet learner fully aware of one's own potential as dramatically enhanced by the historically unprecedented power of the Internet and related technologies. Human potential has never had such powerful enablers as we find at our fingertips today, but the art of developing social acceptance and best practices for leveraging these tools is still in its infancy.

The global impact one creative individual can make applying these new capabilities is unlimited. The potential impact of empowering the majority of the world's population with such abilities is literally the task at hand.

In 1983, as the visions for the Big Sky Telegraph project first began to form — from my rural perspective — the challenge was to create opportunities for participatory action research to learn how quickly rural citizens, and educators in particular, could embrace the full dimension of the unlimited potential for online learning, teaching, and purposeful collaboration to effect positive community and global change.

20 Years and a Million Miles

During the past 20 years since I first came online, I've traveled over a million miles presenting on online learning and the potential for community networking. This year I've presented keynotes for the Jamaican and Australian Governments and visited remote Aboriginal communities slated to receive broadband. Seven weeks were spent in Alaskan Native village schools who received their first satellite Internet systems five years ago. Major challenges still exist and it appears the devil is in the details and that good intentions alone won't deliver the hoped-for benefits. To my chagrin the rural economic decline has accelerated despite local access to the Internet as an educational and economic tool.

In short, the vision I'd hoped the world would embrace two decades ago is still largely missing; that by combining caring and connectivity with common sense we'll all have access to all our knowledge. Yet there are signs that awareness is indeed growing that there is indeed something more to being online than solo surfing and simple email.

The Big Picture

In our world today, half the population lives in dire poverty and has yet to make their first phone call. In the next few decades, over 15,000 cultures and most of the planet's population will receive high speed Internet due to advances in satellite and wireless technologies. For the first time in human history we have the tools to literally change the world though low-cost ubiquitous online education. But, before I attempt to detail the possibilities of the near future, I've a story to tell about my quest to earn my own wings of freedom and to learn how best to lend these wings to others. It bears reasons for the telling.

A Sense of Community
Born in 1952 in Cody, Wyoming, the close knit community ties of the 50's made a deep impression regarding my sense of belonging. Suddenly having to move away at age seven, my growing up was a long wait seeking to return to this lost sense of community. For the decade of the sixties I lived in what was to become Silicon Valley, the bay area south of San Francisco, California.

Upon graduating in 1974 from University of California, Davis, with a BA in Psychology, I had the choice of becoming a computer programmer or moving back to Wyoming to work as a roughneck on oil rigs. The starting wages were the same for both jobs. My perception of computers after learning about punch cards and the Fortran programming language was that there is nothing more lifeless than sitting at a computer all day long. My choice was easy, I headed home to the Rocky Mountains, soon to be spending the nights working outdoors at 40 below zero — and I was wildly happy to be there.

A Vision for the Ultimate Freedom
When I read Alvin Toffler's book *Future Shock* it shared the vision that someday, personal computers would be small enough and cheap enough we each could afford one, and that someday, telecommunications would allow us to live and work anywhere we pleased. I immediately made the decision to watch for the emergence of these opportunities for extreme freedom! It could be a potential solution for my long-term repatriation to Cody, Wyoming. All I had to do was wait for these promises to become reality. Over much of the next decade (1974-1982) I worked as an oilfield roughneck, carpenter/painter, and enjoyed three years as a dude ranch manager — waiting.

Finally, finally, in 1982, IBM announced their first personal computer and the Apple IIe enhanced version had just come out. Modems had just been dramatically upgraded from 300 to 1200 baud. Online communications using microcomputers was opening doors to unknown possibilities. It was time to pursue Toffler's vision, urged on by the 1981 recession and being once again unemployed. In 1982, I enrolled at the University of Wyoming as one of the first four students for a new masters program in Instructional Technology.

Two years later, in 1984, with my new masters degree in hand, I was caretaking a ranch near Walden, Colorado, teaching "Microcomputers in Agriculture" for Colorado Mountain College while looking for fulltime work to leverage my new degree. At that time microcomputers were still so new that most people were frightened of them and there was little demand for expertise in instructional technology.

I was online via $18/hr toll lines at 2400 baud with a bulletin board system called "The Little Red Electronic Schoolhouse" run by a retired army colonel, David R. Hughes (see Appendix). Tentatively, I called Dave from my isolated ranch house hoping to learn more. Two hours later, I pried the phone from my ear having received my first passionate tutorial from the Cursor Cowboy. Here was a man with a vision! This would become a weekly ritual for the next ten years.

The Bull Colonel Online Mentoring Model

In addition to providing my first online learning experience, Dave provided me with an unfailing mentoring model. His bull colonel tenacity was not about to let me fail and I learned to implicitly trust in his ongoing support. Today, when I mentor educators in my online graduate courses my role is based on the mastery learning guaranteed level of support I learned from Dave Hughes. Failure is not an option!

One Up Dialogs

In person, we'd often both be talking at once, each interrupting the other frequently without either of us taking offense and I imagined we looked like two buffalos clawing the ground and huffing. Our ideas would build upon one another in rapid-fire fashion, each idea suggesting the next logical possibility. It was exciting to be inventing, discovering, and exploring all at once — the potential future of the world.

We began imagining what the high end educational applications of microcomputer telecommunications might be. We'd each try to top the other's imaginings by going one better as an exercise to develop a vision for the best possible working model to try out in an actual project. Eventually we evolved the idea of creating the Big Sky Telegraph to connect the 100 one-room schools across Montana. But it was to be four years before we'd finally win the funding.

Becoming an Assistant Professor

A one-inch ad from Western Montana College, a hundred-year-old teachers' college in Dillon, Montana was run once in the Chronicle of Higher Education. Frustrated from years of underemployment, I bought a pinstripe suit, shaved my beard and drove 1000 miles to put in a face-to-face appearance and was soon hired as their first Microcomputer Applications instructor. Upon arrival they ushered me down a narrow stairway to an unfinished basement room with cement walls and ceiling. Twenty-five boxed Apple IIes received through a grant sat unopened. The future of the world was before me.

High Tech- High Touch

Microcomputers were not considered important or even desirable by the administration and faculty, but as we opened the doors to the public many older returning students hoping to gain new employment skills signed up for my microcomputer applications classes. White footprints were common in the computer lab as workers from the nearby talc plant became regular students.

It was not uncommon for some female students to be near tears in apprehension before we'd even turned the computers on. Fearing their inadequacy to learn computers, many students soon taught me that emotional encouragement was essential to being an effective microcomputer applications instructor. John Naisbett's book *Megatrends* stated that high touch is needed to balance high tech if people are to accept the technologies. This has since proved to be all too true, amplified by the foreign nature of the online medium.

Big Sky Telegraph (BST)

This name was intended in invoke an image of an expansive imagination, unlimited possibilities, and of an old-timey non-threatening communications technology metaphor.

In 1987, I won a small grant for $37,000 from the M.J. Murdoch Foundation, to engage Dave Hughes' expertise in creating one of the first Internet hosts running on a microcomputer to offer online courses. The new 386 computer was just fast enough to run SCO Unix and the Big Sky Telegraph went online, January 1, 1988. Without compensation for my time, throughout the next year the BST offered free 2400 baud modems to a pilot group of two dozen one-room school teachers along with an online course with ten one-hour mastery learning lessons titled "Microcomputer Telecommunications Basics." As most educators and rural citizens had no idea of the "online" possibilities, our challenge was to bring to them their first experiences of online learning, *one at a time.*

Social Engineering to Create the Greatest
Potential Impacts for Online Learning

Given the unique ubiquitous nature of online learning and teaching, the challenge of how to motivate engagement with the best and broadest educational applications the medium allows suggested that designing a scalable train-the-trainers model with social recognition incentives might be profoundly powerful.

With this goal specifically in mind, the social role of Big Sky *Telegrapher* was created and those completing the online course "Microcomputer Telecommunications Basics" would be authorized to teach the lessons to others, ideally for a fee. Though many teachers were quite proud of having completed the online course very few took advantage of their potential to train others, online. Perhaps the transition from mentee to mentor was too big a conceptual leap. Still, the potential was there for scalable use of high quality online lessons mentored by an unlimited number of people encouraging and supporting the online learning of anyone, anywhere, anytime. It was the right idea, but not the right time for the idea to catch fire in the popular imagination. In contrast, our peer circuit riders providing face-to-face training proved to be appropriate for the time.

As educators completed the online course they received an embroidered patch (see Figure 1) and diploma signifying that they were among "the first educational pioneers to blaze the trail on the electronic frontier that others might follow." As the years went by we trained over 900 educators in 19 states, and Finland. Our 700 collected lesson plans eventually (in 1995) became one of the very first educational resources to be posted by the U.S. Department of Education on their new Website.

Figure 1. Big Sky Telegraph patch.

In 1989, US West granted $280,000 for an expansion of Big Sky Telegraph to 100 one-room schools. With the additional technical expertise of David Hughes Jr. (Dave's son), we began creating the first of 29 local dial-up community bulletin boards using an elegant cost-effective Fidonet system which collected emails bound for distant systems and the Internet for automated exchange during the low-cost nightly phone rates. As a representative application Junior High School students in Montana and Wyoming rural schools used these systems to learn Chaos Theory Mathematics online — direct from Dr. George Johnston of the MIT Plasma Fusion Lab.

We'd created affordable local community networks (bulletin board systems) with an economical option for global email allowing rural educators, students, and citizens opportunities for their first global collaborations. Our greatest challenge was sharing the vision for how these tools could be used to generate collaborative capacity. But the technologies changed faster than we could thoroughly demonstrate their capabilities and engage citizens in understanding their full potential.

Several BBSCON conferences were held during the late 1980's and early 1990's bringing together hundreds of electronic bulletin board systems (BBS) operators from all over the country. After the World Wide Web hit, these became ISPCON conferences (for Internet Service Providers) and somehow the emphasis for building collaborative capacity disappeared and was replaced by the goals of profit from selling Internet access.

Native American Share-art
In 1989, Dave and I held a workshop on the Crow Reservation for Native American artists from five Montana reservations. They learned to use computers to create original artwork in the NAPLPS format for sale online using the shareware model — thus creating share-art that while shareable online, was intended to be paid for if anyone were to keep or use the artwork. A photograph of the artists appeared in a congressional report on the future potential of the online world. The NAPLPS format turned out to soon be preempted by other formats, but the idea of digital art as a culturally reinforcing economic activity would survive.

The Telecom Trappers Rendezvous
The era of the first white trappers lasted only twenty years before the settlers followed them and ended their era. Dave and I decided to hold a special conference in Cody, Wyoming to recognize the passing nature of the era of the early online pioneers. Our goal for the rendezvous was to acknowledge and celebrate our awareness of the brief nature of the era of the first explorations on this new frontier, knowing that the pristine online landscapes would soon

change forever as the dust clouds of the advancing settlers were already on the horizon.

Twenty-five persons attended, coming from both coasts and we sat in a Rocky Mountain meadow of wildflowers on a spring day with a microcomputer at the end of a couple hundred feet of extension cords to view some of the first Native American digital Share-art in history and to talk about themes such as "with power comes responsibility" and how online communication was unlocking profound potential for global education, community empowerment, cultural sovereignty, and more, much more.

It was this visioning that was special to our group and we intuitively knew the future would be limited only by our imaginations. This was to prove all too true in the coming years. Our key concern and topic for discussion was the question of whether our vision would become widespread or somehow be lost. As we spoke of the potential for a true electronic democracy, there was another online project gearing up in California, called America Online.

The Reach for the Sky Project

In 1993, a grant was written and promptly won $880,000 for the Reach for the Sky project. The Annenberg Science and Math Initiative and U.S. West co-funded a three-year project to create three online classes for 20 master science and math teachers to receive online via their new laptops with the intent they would use these classes to mentor science and math educators across a five-state region. My chosen role was creating and teaching the online courses. The Reach for the Sky Lessons are still quite viable and are available online at http://www.learner.org/courses/rfts.

Within the first few weeks of the first online course it became clear that despite each of the teachers being a master teacher, their readiness to embrace the online learning mode differed wildly. We quickly adjusted to an individualized learning format as a few were already way out ahead, and a few just couldn't seem to get their minds around the simplest concepts of online interaction. Concrete linear "left brain" thinkers seemed to have a much harder time than spatial "right brain" thinkers particularly with global concepts.

National and Global Impacts of Big Sky Telegraph (BST)

Over time it became clearer that the biggest impacts of the BST project were not on those who participated directly, but were on those in other states and countries who read the colorful stories written by Dave Hughes on the pioneering teachers in remote one-room schools sharing curriculum online and beginning to communicate with educators globally. Many people became inspired that "if they can do it in rural Montana, why can't we do this in our state?" Larger than life stories created major motivation for grassroots champions in other states to imagine what's possible and to generate dozens of projects that ultimately went beyond the scope and scale of the Big Sky Telegraph.

As there were few rural online learning projects during the late 1980s and early 1990's, I enjoyed being a frequent presenter at national educational technology and community networking conferences. Online learning and collaboration naturally supported building both virtual and geographical communities. Some weeks I'd fly coast to coast twice. From 1988 to 1998 I averaged roughly 50,000 miles a year.[1]

The Community Networking Movement

Participating in online discussions on electronic democracy in 1987 was very exciting as national experts articulately built upon each others' ideas to create exciting new possibilities which evolved daily. In 1994, I was asked to serve as Senior Advisor for Community Networking for the newly formed Morino Institute (http://www.morino.org) lead by Mario Morino. Partnering with Apple computer, the Morino Institute co-hosted two national community networking conferences titled "The Ties That Bind." One was held in Cupertino in 1994. The following year another as held in Taos, New Mexico, home of the La Plaza Telecommunity.

National Public Telecomputing Network
In 1986, I met Tom Grundner, who created an online community network called the St. Joe's Silicon Hospital, which evolved into the Cleveland Freenet. Eventually over 120 Freenets were created in the U.S. and Canada and the National Public Telecomputing Network (NPTN) was formed. These text-only bulletin boards were the first to offer free Internet access with intuitive recognition of the importance of ubiquitous Internet access.

In retrospect there really wasn't much you could do with the Internet at that time other than email. However, information retrieval systems were rapidly

---

[1] I still get email from graduate students in other countries studying the Big Sky Telegraph.

evolving with systems like Gopher, Veronica, and others. To the best of my knowledge, the Big Sky Telegraph was the only educational community network/freenet offering online instruction and as such was something of an anomaly. We were grateful to be generously included despite our educational emphasis. At that time the two worlds of online learning and community networking were quite separate.

It was becoming clear that indeed the potential for community benefits from online knowledge sharing was also limited only by our imaginations and surely everyone would soon see the wonderful possibilities. It seemed obvious that a community networking movement had begun and that the ascent would be rapid. But, what happened next was unexpected. The Web happened.

The Graphical WWW Preempts the Community Networking Movement
In 1994, the World Wide Web appeared and suddenly the power and purity of text-only communications was viewed by most as inadequate and suddenly obsolete. The reading and writing medium emphasis was displaced with a point-and-click graphical emphasis and entertainment displaced purposeful collaboration, much to the chagrin of the early pioneers who understood the power of online written interaction.

Originally, the Big Sky Telegraph offered dial-up Internet access for only $10/month, but now local Internet services were becoming available. They were certainly more affordable than long distance calls to BST, offering unlimited local access for a flat fee. This new option caused people to leave the collaborative Big Sky Telegraph to become solo-basement browsers. When the IRS announced that institutions of higher education could no longer charge for providing dial-up Internet access, the economic sustainability of the Big Sky Telegraph disappeared and US West ended their funding support.

The NPTN Freenets rapidly lost their paid clients and their sustainability eventually disappeared along with the visions for online community-building and the power of collaboration for building collaborative capacity. It would be another decade before the vision for purposeful collaboration would again begin to regain prominence.

Instead of the community networking movement growing to match the potential of the new technologies, the passionate vision almost flickered out. The Association for Community Networking (http://www.afcn.org) was formed in 1995 by a small cadre of dedicated community-builders, destined to be keepers of the flame for the next eight years without significant support or funding.

Up to the current day, hundreds of community networking projects were created by grassroots champions with a vision for what could be, and all but a precious few failed to find sustained funding support. A vast boneyard of failed projects marks the brief history of the community networking movement. Yet these were not failures as much as they were the evolutionary first steps forward demonstrating to the world fundamentally powerful new ways of building local and global collaborative capacity.

After 1994, as the bell curve of the community networking movement took a nosedive, the community technology center movement was on the upswing. While non-technology oriented foundations found the concepts of online interaction and community networking daunting, the tangibility of a community technology center won approval and computer labs sprung up in housing projects and communities nationally. A national Community Technology Center (CTC) organization was formed (http://www.ctcnet.org) and after ten years of operation has over 1200 CTC's as members and holds an annual conference.

But, most CTC's do not emphasize teaching online collaboration and online learning skills or prepare citizens for online participation in community networks to build collaborative capacity. Most centers have only a vague idea of what curriculum will be most empowering. As an initial practical strategy they tend to focus on teaching employability skills often limited to word processing and computer basics.

My own experience suggests that community technology centers need to prioritize teaching self-directed Internet learning skills and online collaboration skills, ideally generating local community networks as the hub for local online capacity building, focusing on collaborative local problem-solving. Short learning modules should be sequenced in a progression of empowering capabilities with certification for specific skills achieved. Civic participation and mentoring others would be inherent as part of the essential skill-building activities. My challenge was emerging as to how best to articulate the full vision for an ideal empowerment curriculum.

Lone Eagle Consulting: Attaining the Ultimate Freedom

After a full ten years of teaching rural teachers online through the Big Sky Telegraph, Western Montana College told me if I didn't win another grant soon, they'd discontinue my position. My last grant didn't come through so after 1.4 million dollars of funding and ten years of championing the cause of online learning and community networking, they showed me the door and pulled the plug on the Big Sky Telegraph (January 1, 1988 to January 1, 1998). The only tenure I was awarded was a ten-year certificate as I held only a masters degree. I left to seek a higher education.

It was actually something of a mutual decision. If they didn't wish to back my online support of rural educators, the college was no longer where I needed to be. I'd become weary of the grant-writing carousel, the passive institutional resistance to innovation, and believed it would be more important to model how one can become independent of grant-writing and institutions.

Fifteen years after I'd returned to earn my degree to fulfill Alvin Toffler's promise of independence, I left Western to found Lone Eagle Consulting. A $500 office visit to a lawyer secured the creation of an S-corporation. A visit to an accountant secured the payroll and financial expertise for payroll deductions for the corporation's president and sole employee. As a fledgling Lone Eagle about to spread my wings for the first time, my opportunity was now to demonstrate how to win and sustain the ultimate freedom as online learner, teacher, and instructional entrepreneur. I've never looked back.

Lone Eagle Consulting's mission is to provide the very best fast track online Internet training possible for rural, remote, and indigenous learners (http://lone-eagles.com):

"The greatest freedom one can give to another is how to become a self-sufficient learner and earner, via the Internet. This site is dedicated to those who lend their wings to others."

My first contract was with the Agency for International Development to create a cross-cultural self-directed online learning Internet guide intended for use in Jamaica. I'd also received an invitation to provide the first Internet workshops for 11 Alaskan Native villages that were soon to receive satellite Internet systems. I began adapting this resource guide for use by Alaskan Natives and Native Americans. Materials created for these projects include:

Common Ground: A Cross-Cultural Self-Directed Learner's Internet Guide
http://lone-eagles.com/guide.htm
Created for USAID, AT&T, and the ERIC clearinghouse.
An instructional brokerage resource with emphasis on pointing to the best
online tutorials and educational resources on the Internet for self-directed
learning. This is the text for the online course "Making the Best Use of
Internet for K-12 Instruction" (http://lone-eagles.com/asdn1.htm)

Echoes in the Electronic Wind — A Native American Cross-cultural Internet Guide
http://lone-eagles.com/nativeguide.htm
A hands-on self-directed learner's Internet skills training guide with over 20
pages of Native American and Alaskan Native Web sites. Available in printed
form; 177 pages.

*Realizing Cultural and Community Sustainability Through Internet Innovations
in Alaskan Native Villages*
http://lone-eagles.com/village-sustainability.htm
A detailed review of strategies for cultural sovereignty to produce measurable
outcomes. Many grant templates and online self-directed resources are
included.

Indigenous Internet Empowerment Resources
http://lone-eagles.com/alaskan-resources.htm
The master listing of Lone Eagle's Indigenous empowerment resources.

Sharing the Vision with Alaskan Bush Villages
During 1998-2000, the first Internet satellite systems were installed in the 11
bush villages of the Yukon-Koyukuk School District (YKSD). Three one-day
Internet workshops were held in these 11 bush villages over a two-year period
(see Figure 2).

My first workshop was in Nulato, 250 miles west of Fairbanks on the Yukon
River. The small eight-seat Cessna plane had duct tape holding the windows
and seats together. I'd been advised to dress for subzero temperatures in order
to survive any unscheduled landings. I was led to the school library and shown
where I could roll out my sleeping bag between the bookcases. Looking out the
window, the snow was blowing sideways and I could see the wide white
expanse of the frozen Yukon river. Just outside the window was an iron post
where the Internet satellite dish was supposed to have been installed prior to
my arrival. I had just begun to learn about organizational capacity issues in
bush villages. I was keenly aware I was experiencing one of the last days ever

that this village would be as it always had been — without Internet — without a direct conduit to the world's knowledge base.

Figure 2. Internet in the Alaska bush.

That night I thought hard about my past ten years of teaching rural teachers online and was full of eager anticipation for the wonderful empowering capabilities I had the opportunity to impart to the bush teachers the next day. I was fully prepared to lend my wings to the village teachers and was eager to do so. I'd come prepared with Internet sites on CD-ROMs, and with dozens of Web sites captured on my laptop using an offline browser. I had a digital camera, a digital art tablet, and a MIDI musical keyboard. The next day I taught both teachers and students how to create Web pages, to browse and search, to create digital art, and to manipulate digital photos. My first challenge was to create motivation for future learning and to begin to help overcome their adversity to technology.

After leaving, and once the Internet satellite dish had finally been installed, the teachers were invited to join my online class to continue their learning and in particular to become comfortable with learning and communicating online. The results were significant but not nearly as exciting as I'd hoped for.

Inconsistent local technical support, weak district support for learning technologies, and other factors combined to create few incentives for ongoing learning and most of the busy teachers exercised their option to maintain their status quo by doing as little as possible. There were cultural tensions resisting the continual pressure of the dominant white culture, of which technology was initially perceived to represent. Over time, the technology would take on a Native voice as the benefits of family communications between villages was embraced using Hotmail. I returned for one-day workshops twice more over the next two years and found that due to a 49% annual turnover in teachers and administrators, I had to begin anew each time.

There were of course many significant successes, such as the innovative principal in Koyukuk who helped his students post community Web pages and Athabascan language Web pages on the school Web site (http://kyu.yksd.com). And the teacher in Allakaket who modified my Rural Ecommerce lessons to help her sixteen teenage students in becoming the first Athabascan youth to ever complete online Ecommerce lessons. But, she's gone now. Cultural shifts take time and there were also political limitations which prohibited wireless home access for Ecommerce using E-rate funded Internet dedicated for school use, only.

Making the Best Use of the Internet for K-12 Instruction
In 1998, Lone Eagle Consulting created two online courses for Alaska Pacific University. The first course "Making the Best Use of Internet for K-12 Instruction" proved to be very effective by providing immediate practical benefits and motivation for bush educators. With effusive emotional support teachers became self-directed learners able to find and utilize vast archives of educational resources as well as creating their own Web-based project-based learning units. Seeing the explosive motivation of these teachers has clearly and powerfully validated the value of online learning and friendly online mentoring in my own experience. Expectations increase with experience.

This course integrates standard K-12 education with the development of self-directed Internet learning as basic skills, project-based learning in a service learning context to generate meaningful content for local community networks, and relating ecommerce and entrepreneurship to youth retention and relevancy to elementary education.

The course and resulting first Web-based curriculum created by participants are at http://lone-eagles.com/teachercreated.htm

The Invisibility of a Few Key Rural Inevitable Truths

The significance of the fact that rural citizens typically isolated from information resources and learning opportunities could suddenly have unlimited learning opportunities was unprecedented in its implications. What would it take for rural citizens to see their dramatically enhanced potential? If "We are what we know," then the opportunities for human potential development in rural areas has suddenly increased many orders of magnitude — IF people can understand and embrace their new opportunities.

A fact of rural reality is too often we don't know what need to know unless someone makes a point of telling us directly. For example, there is an invisible relocation drama taking place in rural America where those who resist or are denied learning how to use information technology to be able to live and work in rural areas are being forced to relocate to the cities to find work. Conversely, those in the cities who do learn these skills find themselves able to relocate to sublime rural areas often buying the homes of displaced rural workers. The Internet can be an ongoing solution to staying current on knowing what we didn't know we needed to know IF we are able to connect with the right relationships and expertise.

Another major invisible issue related to rural relocation is that generational turnover requiring decades may prove necessary before a new generation of rural leaders emerges who are willing to allow necessary change to occur. Rural citizens may eventually understand and regret what they could have done today UNLESS a dramatic surge in self-awareness and proactive leadership takes place soon. The downside risk is displacement of a majority of rural citizens and the pain that goes with losing one's cherished rural lifestyle.

While state governments talk about E-government and using Internet for Ecommerce to adjust to a changing economy, the real innovation is taking place at the citizen level in lieu of any real governmental leadership. The top-down governments and telecommunications corporations need to learn from the bottom-up innovators about the dynamics of adapting to a changing world.

As the pace of technological advancement intensifies, there is a corresponding increase in the rate of change in the global economy and societies. The pressure is on to learn how E-governments can learn to adjust more quickly. At the same time those creative individuals who have learned how to upgrade themselves are quietly setting an example for the attitudes, skills, and behaviors required for successful adaptation and harmonic survival.

While it is becoming widely accepted that something has to change and that education, learning something new, is necessary, no one has yet owned the responsibility, not local or state government, or K-12 schools, or higher education institutions. This is ultimately everyone's responsibility. New forms of community learning are badly needed.

Synergies Between the Online Learning and
Community Networking Movements

Language has inherent limitations as words are but block sculptures of reality. Often the terms we use can be unwittingly self-limiting. For example, the terms "online learning" and "community networking." In my mind the two mean the same thing: "knowledge sharing to build individual and community capacity using the best technology tools." Over the last 20 years I've had a foot in both camps and have seen a steady merging of both movements.

Simply stated, this synergy is tantamount to defining e-life recognizing that there are progressive stages based on the truism "expectations increase with experience." Inherent in this progression is the potential for an ideal curriculum begging to be validated and widely taught.

As one learns to use search engines well one develops self-directed learning skills able to teach oneself on any topic as necessary. Collaborative problem-solving taught through project-based learning activities builds knowledge worker skills. As favorite sites on topics of interest are cut and pasted and posted as community resources a civic contribution is realized. Such action reveals a potential social role as mentor and local expert. In addition to creating free community resources and peer mentoring, service learning activities lead toward potentially offering knowledge-based services on a for-profit basis. In a knowledge and service economy instructional entrepreneurship emerges as a way to simultaneously create both social and economic value.

Ultimately, as both social and economic value are created, there is a maturing of self-esteem, self-confidence, self-worth, personal identity, and defining a contributing role within the community. As such meaning and identity are developed the awareness grows for potential impacts well beyond the community — limited only by one's imagination. The highest stages attainable through e-learning are marked by taking action regarding e-democracy and transnational activism — *through leadership teaching others.*

This broader perception of e-learning grows in significance when one realizes the potential of the Internet for creating "The New Gold Rush: Mining Raw Human Potential Using Web Tools" (http://lone-eagles.com/mining.htm) and is fundamental in "The War Against Ignorance" (http://lone-eagles.com/hope.htm).

The past history of rural life is marked by severely limited access to information and learning — fundamentally "doing without." But, the future of rural life has more to do with managing and balancing information overload through mutual collaboration to sustain communities while sculpting a lifestyle; literally *making a life while making a living.*

The Milkstool Theory and Implications

The milk-stool theory says that communities stand on the four legs of government, business, education, and health care. Each of these now begins with an "E" — representing the best uses of information technology. If we add to this the inevitable emergence of best practices for e-citizenship and e-community, the issue become defining the best replicable process and exactly what this all means. Does this mean simply we all learn how to browse the Web and use email, or is there more?

We dream that information and communications technologies (ICT's) will be well used, but the devil is in the details. How well we use ICT's depends on the quality of the education we each receive.

E-government, e-business, e-education, and e-health all require citizens to be able to access essential information and to become self-directed Internet learners able to collaborate effectively both online and offline. E-citizenship, e-communities, and e-democracy require an informed and participatory populace. Our shared challenge is to harness the inherent human potential of each of us. What's the best a rural community can do for itself morphing into a vital learning community? This has become the big question. The future of America's rural communities hangs in the balance.

The Clarity of Common Sense

The common view of rural communities is: "We've yet to see a rural community benefit significantly from use of the Internet." There's an important missing link here between the glowing promises of the telecommunications companies and the government that broadband is essential and indisputably beneficial, and the opposite perception of rural citizens based on their very practical experience that there are no proven benefits.

An Inevitable Reality for Communities Hoping to Be Competitive

As broadband becomes increasingly commonplace, communities are beginning to understand that they will compete on the demonstrated talents of an inspired and motivated citizenry. Visible demonstrations of advanced telecommunications and technology applications are a selling point for communities seeking to showcase their ability to learn, innovate, and grow.

An Issue of National Competitiveness
The vigor of our communities, our nation, and all other nations, will depend on creating motivated lifelong learners, proactive citizens who are value-driven, innovative entrepreneurs, skilled collaborators, and citizens who are both consumers and producers —both learners and teachers, all the time.

Those communities first to show true widespread participation in realizing tangible benefits may well enjoy a cottage industry for decades to come teaching other communities how to replicate their success, online. It is just a matter of who and when.

Struggling to Share the Vision
If you were to ask Montanans the definitions of ignorance and apathy, you might well hear: "I don't know and I don't care." While they'd be correct in this instance, you might get the same answer if you asked about the Internet, ecommerce or online collaborative capacity-building. Can the significant cultural shift take place while there's still time?

Community success stories giving tangible examples are needed to change attitudes about what's possible regarding online learning, successful online collaboration, and ecommerce. (Two Years of Successes in Montpelier, Idaho http://lone-eagles.com/montpelier-story.htm)

Citizenship, Community-building, and
Entrepreneurship in the Knowledge Age
Needed is a specific curriculum for educators and those who work with youth which presents a hands-on review of Internet resources and curriculum templates integrating K-12 curriculum with online collaboration and the essential skills related to growing successful citizens in the "knowledge age." Emphasis is needed on developing both local, and global, citizenship concepts, skills, and practices.

Success creating knowledge workers prepared for work in a global knowledge economy requires a K-12 emphasis on developing the social value and self-worth of students and requires they become skilled at creating and maintaining meaningful relationships both offline and online.

There is an immediate need to bridge the gap between K-12 education and the ability to use the Internet for economic development. The accelerating pace of change requires that students learn how to think innovatively and to maintain awareness of successful innovations related to emerging vocational and entrepreneurial opportunities in their communities. A service learning project creating local Web-based content for their communities showcasing local and regional E-commerce and entrepreneurial Internet innovations would be an example of the trend necessary for students to become involved with their communities' economic development and sustainability issues.

Teaching Students Global Citizenship
in the Knowledge Age: Hands-on
Many realistic student-driven community activities can be presented for students to initiate community interaction. Examples include gathering content for local Web display to raise community awareness about the genuine opportunities the Internet represents, as detailed in the Bootstrap Academy (http://lone-eagles.com/academy.htm).

Citizenship education needs to include values development in the form of character education and service learning. A knowledge society and an electronic democracy require educated citizens with skills in both offline, and online, articulation, and collaboration. Internet skills for self-directed learning and Web self-publishing are required for competent citizens in a knowledge society. Character Education Web Tour (http://lone-eagles.com/chared.htm).

There are many models for using project-based learning methodologies to stimulate student creation of Web-based content to benefit the local community which could be consolidated into a course for educators. As awareness grows through the use of existing curricular models, educators will learn to use existing templates to begin to create their own innovative curriculum. Students will also learn to use templates to create instructional experiences for both other students and adults in the local community.

Here are a few project examples related to community content created by students:
- The Global Schoolhouse, http://www.gsh.org, is a projects directory where teachers can post multi-classroom collaborative projects to find international partners. Collaborative tools and pedagogies are listed as well.
- The International Cyberfair competition, http://www.gsh.org, has elementary students create Web pages celebrating eight categories of local achievement.

- At Thinkquest, http://www.thinkquest.org/library, students internationally have created over 5,000 instructional Web sites to help others learn online.
- At Camp Internet, http://www.campinternet.net, are family learning expeditions to engage families with learning together how to use the Internet for learning.
- 4-H youth Tech Teams train rural adults in Internet skills. http://www.4-h.org (Click on technology.)
- Webquest curriculum templates are available for both teachers and students to learn to create online project-based learning units, often based on real-world problem-solving. http://webquest.sdsu.edu/
- Integrating all the above innovations is discussed at http://lone-eagles.com/capacity.htm

Project-based learning curriculum directories and resources can be found at http://lone-eagles.com/projects_tour.htm and http://lone-eagles.com/pbl.htm.

Entrepreneurship sites and cooperatives for youth and women are listed along with Ecommerce Start-up training resources and sites offering free Ecommerce Web sites at http://lone-eagles.com/entrelinks.htm.

For Mentoring Models, Guides, and Resources, see http://lone-eagles.com/mentor.htm.

Changing Perceptions for Online Learning After 20 years and a Million Miles: What's the Same and What's Different

The original essays and vision of the Big Sky Telegraph are as relevant to the modern day as they were in the late 1980's. The technologies are a thousand times more powerful, but somehow the ability to imagine what's possible has stalled. Tired of corporate hype and overwhelmed with too much useless information, many have turned away from believing in the power of thoughtful online learning and interaction.

In 1988, my license plate read "Online" and at that time "online" meant bibliographic searches by a university librarian. Over the years the popular perception of the word "online" kept changing, soon it suggested use of electronic bulletin board systems, then it was the World Wide Web as an esoteric activity and the arena of billionaire geniuses from Silicon Valley, then it was mainstream AOL chat and shopping, and after the stock bust it was the tired activity of the failed dreams of dot.com businesses. Today "Online" represents a rather confused mix of spam, scams, hoaxes, pornography, lurking pedophiles, malicious viruses, pop-up ads, and hyped promises of valueless corporations vying for control over the world view of hapless consumers.

Bringing Back the Vision

Many teachers still view online learning as direct competition with traditional classroom learning, and as a potential threat to their jobs. On the brighter side, as more teachers get hands-on experience with online learning they realize their challenge is really how to bring the best of both mediums to their students such that they can use the Internet for self-directed Internet learning as well as purposeful collaboration and self-expression.

Traditionally, online degrees were considered inferior, but this attitude is also changing. The validity of quality online learning and the integrity of using the Internet wisely are growing. Today one U.S. worker out of ten engages in telework, able to live and work anywhere, anytime. Companies are beginning to recognize their most talented workers are increasingly demanding the flexibility that comes with telework. Truly skilled knowledge workers have no limits on the specific information and assistance of peers worldwide they can call to their fingertips at a moment's notice.

We're Limited Only by Our Imaginations

Recently, I received an online tutorial, "live" using voice over the Internet, remote application-sharing, co-browsing, and two-way PC-based video conferencing in preparation for a project training disabled workers in rural ecommerce and telework skills over the next five years. I've developed a rural ecommerce non-credit online class offered for rural citizens to learn *what's working online for others like them*, as their first online learning experience.

I'm in touch with helping planners regarding Jamaican and Australian indigenous training projects by articulating the new role of education and Internet as related to rural workforce development, and all the while mentoring teachers and citizens in online classes taught through three universities; Alaska Pacific University, Seattle Pacific University, and Idaho State University. I'm also advising government leaders for the States of Idaho and Montana on e-learning and community networking while continuing model work with Montpelier, Idaho aimed at producing the first rural community success story in Idaho (E-commerce curriculum and success stories: http://lone-eagles.com/connect-idaho.htm).

Once an isolated rural citizen struggling for manual labor employment, I've expanded my creative capacity a hundred fold by learning to develop my own self-directed Internet learning and teaching skills. And my impact on others to date can be counted in the thousands, and will soon grow exponentially once again.

Constructivism "Yagga Yagga" Style

The essence of constructivism to build one's own knowledge is "learning by doing." The literacy levels worldwide are an issue. Recently I was in the Aboriginal community of Yagga Yagga in Western Australia showing an Aboriginal woman how to use a digital camera to become instantly a digital author and storyteller. The Sony CD-550 camera records audio with photographs and can save video on the 3-inch CD, ready to pop into a computer and play. Then she learned to use a digital art tablet and within minutes was smiling broadly as she swirled together one of the first examples of digital Aboriginal artwork.

With the obvious motivation from these first experiences comes the question of what the best ongoing training program might look like. While reading and writing might be an initial barrier, email using voice files and digital storytelling and art could allow language-based Internet interaction at many levels, seeding the confidence and motivation for further learning as a fun social culturally-relevant activity rather than a Victorian colonializing regime; empowering rather than dominating.

Recommended reading is "Authenticating Rural Broadband Benefits — A Reality Check" (http://lone-eagles.com/wings.htm) written for the Australian government regarding their national plan to deploy broadband to rural and remote areas. The Lone Eagle keynote for a national broadband conference, Oct. 6, 2003, focused on the advice to avoid the U.S. dilemma of a "lose-lose" situation where government and telecommunications corporations have failed to communicate to citizens the benefits of broadband and as a result have a severely weakened business case. And on the other hand citizens are not benefiting from existing broadband as intended and are not creating a vibrant market for additional broadband deployment. This situation can and must be reversed!

As I finish this writing I'm bringing online an open source content management system with the technical assistance of David Hughes Jr. at http://lone-eagles.oldcolo.com, which will integrate online learning and community networking with advanced broadband distance learning technologies and unique social engineering methodologies. In conclusion; this is where the real story will begin.

You're invited to continue to follow the adventure and to join in directly at http://lone-eagles.com/new.htm

Appendix

My Work with Distance Learning, 1980-2004

David R. Hughes

From the time I started using the earliest personal computers — Radio Shack Model I — with the first text processor for such a computer, Electric Pencil, in 1977, and then with a 300 Baud Acoustic Cat Novation Modem in 1979, running the simplest terminal programs and Xmodem invented to support a new medium called a 'Bulletin Board' by Ward Christiansen about the time when the earliest commercial, online dialup Service emerged — The Source, which predated Compuserve, America Online, much less the Internet — it was clear to me that this medium could and should be used for Education. K-99.

Having, as a West Point graduate (1950) taught English at the Military Academy in the late 50's. And then, as a senior advisor to the then Secretary of Defense Robert McNamara in 1966, I saw the 'miniaturization' of technology and global, affordable telecommunications coming. So I was fully ready in 1977, after having retired in 1973 from 27 years active military service, for the first microcomputers which emerged from Apple and Radio Shack. They were tools for general and universal 'communications.'

I have been working in advanced Telecommunications the 30 years since then. And implicit in all that work, is teaching and learning, online. Above all, I understood by 1979 that the two basic subjects which were declining in mastery by American school children — written English and Math — could be taught via such instruments. And I saw by closely observing one of my own children who had mild dyslexia, that English could not only be taught, but in my opinion better, more comprehensively and faster via personal computers and modem communications. And as a lifelong writer and poet, I saw that 'back space and blot out' would be a revolution in the reading and writing of text.

I also was aware that it would be rural schools which would be left behind, not because personal/classroom computers would be unaffordable — but that the government regulated costs of rural voice telephone communications used for modem connection could make 'online' instruction prohibitively expensive.

So I set about exploring this medium, connecting with every public-access online service in the US, and several in foreign countries (Japan and England especially) spending freely for the connectivity until I understood just how revolutionary it was, and why and how, students from a young age should be exposed and tutored in its use. As a quite successful writer, I was paid liberally for my short pieces I wrote from the Korean War battlefield. My literary genes descended from 13 generations of Welsh preachers from that land that so celebrates language, story telling, the bardic tradition, and the mysteries of poetry. I even began to see and feel subtle characteristics in both online and onscreen text that went beyond Gutenberg and the printed page.

In fact, while still on the Source, and later on CompuServe, I began to experiment with modes of written expression that took account of the number of characters across the computer screen — 80 — and the number of lines per screen — 25 — and the phenomenon of 'scrolling' text, and the effect on 'meaning' of the motion of letters or punctuation on the screen, as they moved. Today I write almost entirely for screens. Rarely for paper.

Over time I developed a wholly new literary form which I called 'Word Dance' that recognized that words in the form of light, on a computer screen had the added — to words on fixed surfaces, property of Time. I — and anyone else could — using the computer processor with appropriate software, present text anywhere on the screen — not, ala traditional upper left to lower right while the eyes moved over the text — cause it to move, blink, change slowly — giving it 'meaning' more akin to variations in voice — a kind of visual speech, even to the point of holding the eye fixed on the center of the screen while the text came at one in a digital stream. Only text.

And I concluded the most 'natural' and effective form of writing in the constrained, but dynamic space online was poetry — not prose. And began to write pieces, such as 'The Dance of the Red Leds' which could not be reduced to paper, or read aloud, but could only exist on dynamic computer screens. I observed that the only place this was done in our culture was in Television advertising — dynamic words. Visual speech. But very costly to produce on specialized machines. Not for Everybody — yet.

Now all of this would have just been academic and arcane research, and the experiments of an artist, except I was aware that youngsters growing up looking at text and blinking numbers on LCDs on their watches, their school and home computer screen, ATM machines — dynamic digital displays. That they were going to use 'language' differently from their parents who grew up watching television, or their grandparents who grew up reading text on paper. That if children were to be taught properly in school how to deal with language in the future via computer networks — which everyone would eventually have — they needed to be taught differently from the emerging trend in some colleges and even schools in just putting lessons on computer screens which were indistinguishable from the same text in a book or on paper.

So, by 1980 I had developed formal courses which could only be delivered online, and interactively with the students. I called the form 'Electronic English.' And it was aimed far more at the teachers, than the K-12 students, for I saw that they, even when they were quite computer literate, and getting used to online forms, knew little of how different this form really was. Which courses not only delved into the subtleties some of the subjects above raise but also how the style of email, mail lists, interactive group real-time or computer conferencing 'chats' differed as much from text papers, as delivered speech differed from paper. It would be a major third form of human discourse.

In the fall of 1981 I was asked by local Colorado Technical College — if I would teach for them. I agreed. Using the Source as the link between remote and local classroom students, most but not all adult, I taught the first formal credit college course of Electronic English in July, 1981. Two 'students' were as far away as Australia and Alaska (the past Lt Governor Red Boucher, who paid by credit card from Anchorage). One of them who took the course was Frank Odasz, from Western Montana College. He had found me via my own Old Colorado City Electronic Cottage Bulletin-Board, and its 'Lil Red Electronic Schoolhouse' section. I had said to him, he should not attempt to teach online courses until he at least had taken my course himself, and knew what it means to be an online student. He did well, and went on to create Big Sky Telegraph.

These efforts were covered widely by the print press and media, starting with technical magazines, then newspapers, and finally by educational journals. I was asked to speak in many venues throughout the 80s. This evolved to courses I then fashioned and taught for Pikes Peak Community College specifically for teachers. I used my own servers by this time, and more advanced software optimized for the purpose.

I was approached by Physicist Dr. George Johnston, MIT in 1990 who stated that MIT was concerned about the state of math and science education in the nations schools. That MIT professors had been visiting Boston Schools to help teachers, but that was very local, and costly in time. Could I help using distance learning techniques? (The Internet had not arrived yet nationally.) I said yes, and very quickly, with my setting up the networks, which included Fidonet links in Montana and Wyoming, UUCP between Unix systems in larger cities, Dr. Johnston taught the first credit high school courses in the Math and

Physics of Chaos to a virtual classroom of 40 students, who were in one small school in northern Montana, the High School in Cody, Wyoming, Air Academy High School in Colorado Springs, as well as two Junior High schools whose students were in AP classes. That was September 1990. In several cases the math teachers who did not know the subject of Chaos (which did not exist when they got their degree, or in their refresher training) took the course alongside, collaboratively, with their own students. It worked. And one young woman in Cody, Wyoming whose high school could not even offer her AP Calculus, took the course, and with Dr. Johnston's help matriculated at MIT.

In 1991 I was asked to submit papers for a study about 'NREN' — National Research and Educational Network — for Senator Al Gore's Staff by the Congressional Office of Technology Assessment on K-12 online education. I did that and was told later that it was the first appearance in Washington of a case for extending the emerging 'Internet' to K-12 distance learning. A paper from that, called "Appropriate and Distributed Networks: A Model for K-12 Educational Telecommunications" was circulated widely in Washington, including being requested by the staff of Congressman Edwin Markey of Massachusetts, who was increasingly interested in the use of networks for education.

About this time also, 1992, I retained the programming expertise of Russians in Moscow, to create a program called 'Troika' which carried out my Word Dance ideas in an OSI protocol called NAPLPS, which, not so incidentally could permit the easy composition on any personal computer, without broadband, in all foreign language fonts, from Cyrillic and Arabic, to Chinese and Norweigan. It was no longer needed after the World Wide Web came on the scene. But it incorporated many language-teaching techniques.

By this time, in 1994, while 'online learning' was beginning to appear more generally, I was researching alternative ways to get broadband to rural communities and schools — which were falling far behind the Internet extension to urban schools. Broadband was needed for the transmission of graphics and multimedia sufficient enough to support online instruction in any subject. The Fidonet, and Ufgate technologies, based on UUCP protocols of 'Store and Forward' technologies were not enough, in the always-on and long time connected era of TCP/IP and the Internet. The cost over rural telephone lines would be prohibitive. So I was a very early investigator and user of Wireless, including the new unlicensed wireless that has evolved into Wi-Fi connectivity in urban areas.

In 1995, I was approached by the Networking Division of the National Science Foundation, some of whose Project Officers were deeply interested in using advanced Internet in ways beyond what the NSF Educational Division was, and I was asked to accept a grant of $350,000 to experiment with Wireless for Education. I agreed, but only for education in rural and remote areas. So, from 1995 to 1998, as Principal Investigator, I extended wireless Internet links to Schools in such places as the poor, Hispanic San Luis Valley of Colorado (see http://wireless.oldcolo.com/course/reports.htm).

And I retained the services as a CO-PI of Dr. Johnston, MIT who then taught an accredited course in Math and Science to teachers in both rural schools and urban schools linked by wireless broadband — so I could evaluate the adequacy of the tools needed to really support bandwidth-demanding online math and science by extending, wirelessly, the closest fat pipe from a commercial ISP. In the San Luis Valley, I was able to make a 30 mile, zero operating cost link from the small San Luis School, to Alamosa for the $1,000 cost of two digital radios. US West wanted $2,000 a month for the same distance, by tariffed T-1. US West was not pleased by my legal bypass of their rural wire-monopoly networks.

From the work I did in Lewistown, Montana in 1997 supporting the teaching of Field Science by wirelessly connected data loggers by 7th Grade Science Class students and teachers to field data site miles out of town, the NSF showed a different interest. Finding the wireless technology I developed of direct benefit to university level environmental and biological field scientists, they asked me to accept a three year, $1.2 million grant to 'Model' Wireless for fields science projects in Alaska, Puerto Rico, Wisconsin, and Virginia. This took most of my efforts from 1998 to 2002, so I did not pursue online formal teaching in the US after that. However, I successfully asked research scientists to incorporate bright science-oriented students from linkable local schools as 'remote lab assistant' in their field work. That begins to open up connectivity between universities and K-12 school kids and their teachers, letting exceptional students advance more rapidly than the resources of the school can support.

Currently I have been taking all I have learned, and applying it to formal school level Distance Education in more remote areas — rural Wales, and very remote Nepal. I trekked up in October 2003, on the route to Mt. Everest to 12,000 foot Namche, Nepal donating and installing for the very isolated Sherpa people in Namche, and the very poor school in Thame, wireless Internet connectivity through a satellite IP link. It includes Voice over the Internet SIP technology.

In February, 2004, Sherpa Mingma of Pittsburgh, PA began teaching, by natural voice over the Internet into a speaker VOIP phone in the Sherpa classroom, oral English, and then written English, which the Nepalese teachers cannot teach properly locally. And finally teach them computer science and the Internet on their linked computers (see http://www.linkingeverest.com/gallery/index.php)

Chapter 19

Who's Afraid of Distance Ed?

Jason Ohler

Jason Ohler is the President's Professor, Educational Technology and Distance Learning, at the University of Alaska and recipient of a Distinguished Career Citation by the Alaska State Legislature. From 1985-2003, he was the Director of the Educational Technology Program, University of Alaska Southeast. He has spent twenty years developing innovative programs in e-learning as well as on-site programs to help teachers use technology "effectively, creatively and wisely." He received his PhD from Simon Fraser University.

"In order to be a good teacher you've got to be a good student."
Then What? Everyone's Guide to Living, Learning, and Having Fun in the Digital Age.
Brinton Books, 2001

One of the greatest challenges for each of us during this time of rapid change is maintaining a set of core beliefs while being flexible enough to consider new viewpoints. If we grip our core beliefs too tightly, we become extremists; too lightly, and we become politicians. Now and again an issue emerges in higher education that taxes the ability of academics to deal with this challenge. Distance education is one such issue.

My twenty years in distance education began in the Neolithic period of e-learning, circa 1984. By the time the Internet had been "invented" by Al Gore and others in the early 1990s, I had already served over 1000 online students using BITNET and our university's proprietary system. Even though I was director of a program whose mission was to explore and facilitate technology in the classroom, it became clear that technology's role was to expand learning to points beyond it. I spent much of the 1980's and early 1990's helping K-12 and higher education teachers overcome barriers of time and geography in reaching students by honing their online skills (for details of my work, see http://www.jasonohler.com).

The Mosaic browser provided the first glimpse of a platform from which to offer entire programs. By the mid-1990s, Mosaic had become Netscape, which was powerful enough to use to offer portions of our educational technology endorsement and master's degree online. By 2000, my programs were entirely online. Most of my research efforts during this time were directed at understanding not just the pedagogy, but the psychology and anthropology of online communities.

As I moved into the world of distance education I became a reluctant focal point for change at my institution. What seemed to me to be challenging and fun was viewed by many as a threat to much of what was good about higher education. Debates about distance education were often "religious" in nature in that people came to them with their belief systems firmly in place — both for and against it — and were rather impervious to considerations of change.

I have observed three basic approaches by higher education to addressing distance education: (1) avoidance, the time-honored approach of ignoring what confounds or scares us, (2) pursuit of rational balance, which is only available to the emotionally secure, and (3) psychological implosion, caused by the need to control a situation that is outside the realm of one's experience. Rather than see the world of distance education as an opportunity to enter a new realm of academic experience, its detractors often prefer to view it in black and white terms and then adopt a hard-line attitude that emphasizes its weaknesses.

While the educator in me has been attracted to distance education's contribution to teaching and learning for some time, the anthropologist in me has been equally fascinated by the cultural flashpoint it has created. While there is plenty to study about the irrational exuberance distance education sometimes attracts, I am much more interested in the other end of the spectrum: fear and disdain. That is the topic of this chapter.

Please note that much has been written about a number of valid issues that compel people to become frustrated or concerned with distance education, such as copyright ownership of materials, faculty incentive, the cost and trouble of adapting to new media, and so on. But I am more interested in the more emotional reasons that I have heard over the years. These are explored below.

1. I receive SPAM about getting a degree online, therefore all online education is suspect.

I am one of the few people I know who has not turned off SPAM, largely because I find it so interesting. Among the countless ads for Viagra and home refinancing, I get an occasional ad for how to get a degree over the Internet. This raises the specter of "credit mills" or "degree mills" — institutions that sell credits over the Internet the way some companies try to sell trinkets and miracle weight loss plans. While my unofficial research suggests that the overwhelming majority of online institutions strive for quality and integrity (and don't use SPAM to get audience attention), the very existence of shady cyber-entrepreneurs provides an example of how the Internet equalizes in a disturbing way — Harvard and Joe's College of Knowledge have equal reach; students morph into shoppers and consumers, and are left to fend for themselves. Simultaneously, virtual arms of perfectly legitimate brick-and-mortar institutions find themselves competing in a market place in ways often foreign to them that potentially diminish quality and integrity, which I will explore next.

2. Distance education is a buyer's rather than a seller's market, which means that universities will lower their standards to attract customers.

Competition for most universities no longer consists only of brick-based institutions at other distant locations; it consists of click-based online portals available from the comfort of home, a fact that is especially appreciated by returning or mature students. As of the creation of the World Wide Web, students have had the ability to "shop and compare" for their learning and otherwise treat education as a marketplace with far greater ease than ever before. Academics, often used to being free of marketplace constraints and demands (one of the ivory tower's most endearing qualities), view the advent of the educational marketplace suspiciously, fearing that it cheapens an institution's academic integrity.

Their fear is well intentioned, stemming from a belief that an institution's move toward marketability will cause that institution to lower its standards just to increase enrollment. Taken to an extreme, if the student is now a customer — and if the customer is supposedly always right — can students demand an A when they don't deserve it?

The answer is: obviously not. There are many professional models in existence for this. We do not pay doctors or lawyers to lie to us; we shouldn't pay teachers or researchers to do so either.

Yet, distance education has given rise to new kinds of students who are demanding the same customer service they ask of doctors, lawyers, and the other professionals in their lives. Traditional academics on the other side of the podium can find this unfamiliar, threatening, and impertinent. Successful distance educators have learned how to live in two worlds, in which they view students as both customers deserving first rate service, as well as learners who should be challenged to work hard and produce quality work. Traditional academics venturing into distance education tend to resolve this duality of purpose internally by simply continuing to teach the same way they always have, regardless of audience or medium. The hope is to preserve the quality implicit in the traditional approach to education by not changing, the topic of the next point.

3. I taught a distance education class once and my students hated it. Therefore, distance education is no good.

There are perfectly legitimate reasons why a distance education class fails, such as a lack of coordination or technical support. But failure also occurs because a teacher drones into a TV camera or audio conference microphone for hours while students' minds wander elsewhere, often into a game of solitaire on their computers.

There are two points that are often overlooked in such cases. First, materials and teaching styles need to be adapted to the media of distance education in order to be successful. Professional development is required to facilitate this, a fact which traditional teachers and/or institutions can be unprepared to consider, psychologically and financially. Second, droning on from behind a podium doesn't work in a classroom either, a fact that is even more painful when projected through a medium. This leads to the next consideration.

4. Students need to spend the same amount of time listening to an instructor at a distance as they would if they were onsite.

The implicit issue here is "contact hours" or "seat time" — the amount of time students spend in a classroom in the presence of a teacher. For many years, this has been one primary measure of the quality of the education. The hope with this approach is that there is a correlation between time in class and student success.

Many in distance education began to question this correlation, primarily for financial as well as technical reasons. That is, in the early days of digital age distance education — circa 1985 — it was simply too difficult or expensive to duplicate the classroom experience, especially when using TV or audio conferencing, the predominant technologies of the day.

However, what emerged from the search for alternative forms of delivery was the realization that student competency, and not seat time, should be the goal of any academic enterprise. Thus, distance educators, as well as others interested in the effective integration of technology in education, assumed a leadership role in the expansion of pedagogy to include peer coaching, cooperative learning, extended discussion using messaging systems, and other creative means that emphasized 'the guide on the side rather than the sage on the stage.'

The result is that distance education has completely redefined education in pedagogical terms and has influenced on-site pedagogy in important ways. Distance education now goes by many names, including "distributed learning," "blended learning," and just plain "learning." Whatever its name, it mixes media, on-site and on-line experiences, and pedagogies. Of course, valuing these contributions of distance education would require academia to value advances in pedagogy, the topic of the next point.

5. Real academics advance content area knowledge; advancing pedagogy is for wimps.

Academia does not traditionally consider teaching or pedagogical research with the same esteem that it considers subject area research. It's that old saying: 'those who can, do research; those who can't, take teaching seriously.'

The result is that there is little incentive for academics to explore pedagogy as a field of research or even personal interest. Because of this, "the system" is stacked against teachers who want to explore innovative uses of technology and teaching techniques, cornerstones of the distance delivery revolution. In addition, research institutions are often held in higher regard than teaching institutions; salaries at the two different types of institutions usually reflect this disparity.

The irony here, if not irresponsibility, is that we have created a nation of educators at the higher education level who view teaching as a second-rate endeavor! Related to this is the fact that those entering academia primarily to conduct research but are also required to teach can be ineffective in the classroom. Clearly, equating the importance of teaching or pedagogical research with conducting more traditional kinds of research would go a long way to encouraging the innovative development of distance education. But doing so would expose the fact that effective teaching is not an area of great interest to some academics, especially given that it might detract from the time spent on content area exploration. In the case of online learning, it further exposes professors to unprecedented public scrutiny, the topic of the next point.

6. Academics fear a risk of exposure going online.

When professors are confined to the classroom, they enjoy a certain degree of anonymity. The door closes and a fairly private world is created that the teacher controls. Once teachers take their classes online, their visibility is dramatically increased. Unless password protected, teachers' materials, reading choices, syllabi, viewpoints, and other aspects of their professional life are open to public scrutiny. For those not used to it, this can be very unsettling.

A companion issue, copyright, simply exacerbates this. For teachers who feel their materials belong to the world, the Internet has become a long awaited vehicle. For those who do not, it threatens to eliminate academic selfhood.

But a primary fear of teachers considering teaching at a distance is the change in teaching style, addressed next.

7. The need for detailed advanced planning can kill spontaneity and the fun of teaching.

I first heard the term "doorknob" lesson planning as a student teacher: you decide what you are going to teach as you turn the doorknob to enter your classroom. While this is not advisable for any teacher, regardless of the medium or teaching venue, it is clearly impossible in distance education.

Because teaching at a distance often requires packaging course materials prior to delivery, it requires a great deal of forethought, long range planning, resource gathering, and assembly well in advance of the first class. A simple syllabus will not suffice; handouts, Web sources, reading materials, and activities all require a degree of detailed planning not always found in on-site education. Distance education is, in many ways, the antithesis of the spontaneity that professors enjoy. Because of this, it can feel like an assault on academic freedom.

In addition to this, some teachers believe that having fun is inversely proportional to the amount of technology required to facilitate the learning experience. That is, the on-site classroom was one of the few refuges left in which unmediated interaction was the predominant form of interaction. Interestingly enough, those of us in distance education continue to hear about how the technology increases the level of personal interaction.

Final Thoughts

My favorite theology teacher used to say, "We are drops of reason in oceans of emotions." This has certainly been true of my experience with distance education over the past twenty years. It is as though distance education has provided a stage for higher education to act out its greatest hopes and fears about living in the Digital Age. We 'strut and fret our hour upon the stage,' while in the meantime the worlds of onsite and distance learning merge. In fact, a decade or two hence there will be far more similarities than differences between onsite and online education; they will require similar technologies, pedagogies, and planning processes.

But in the meantime, we are left to navigate the transition period as we move from centralized to distributed education, a dynamic that few have been prepared for and even fewer embrace. We are essentially asking university professors to seek their comfort zone within a system developed in the middle ages while embracing the discomfort of living during a time of deep and rapid evolution. It is up to each institution to decide the presence it wishes distance education to have and then support faculty who are willing to rise to the challenge with whatever resources, training, or therapy they require.

Chapter 20

No Significant Differences Revisited: A Historical Perspective on the Research Informing Contemporary Online Learning

Thomas C. Reeves

Since receiving his PhD at Syracuse University in 1979, Professor Reeves has developed and evaluated numerous interactive learning programs for education and training. In addition to more than 100 presentations and workshops in the USA, he has been an invited speaker in other countries including Australia, Brazil, Bulgaria, Canada, China, England, Finland, Malaysia, the Netherlands, New Zealand, Peru, Portugal, Russia, Singapore, South Africa, Sweden, Switzerland, and Taiwan. He is a former Fulbright Lecturer, and a former editor of the "Journal of Interactive Learning Research." His research interests include: evaluation of instructional technology for education and training, mental models and interactive multimedia, multimedia user interface issues, and instructional technology in developing countries. Professor Reeves is a co-founder of the Learning and Performance Support Lab at the University of Georgia.

Introduction

In an important historical text, *The Evolution of American Educational Technology*, Saettler (1990) concluded that "no particular event or date marks the beginning of a modern science and technology of instruction" (p. 53). However, most North American authorities trace the roots of contemporary online learning environments to the correspondence schools that began to appear in the late 1800s at institutions such as the University of Chicago (Bunker, 2003; Pittman, 2003). In many ways, today's high tech online learning environments are worlds apart from distance education via print and mail. But with respect to the research applied to these instructional media, there has been little change (Noble, 2001). As with seemingly every other educational technology (Cuban, 1986; Saettler, 1990), the most common approach to conducting research with online learning and earlier forms of distance and flexible learning has been to compare the technological approach with traditional classroom delivery approaches.

The dominance of media comparison studies is hardly surprising given that it appears to be basic human nature to compare anything new with what came before it, i.e., the old. In addition to appealing to common sense, the comparative method is the research and evaluation strategy most frequently recommended in the professional literature. Experimental (or more realistically, quasi-experimental) methods have long been heralded as the "gold standard" of educational research and evaluation methods. For example, Suchman (1967) praised experimental comparisons as a basis for evaluation, concluding that: "the logic of this design is foolproof. Ideally, there is no element of fallibility. Whatever differences are observed between the experimental and control groups, once the above conditions are satisfied, must be attributed to the program being evaluated" (pp. 95-96). More recently, Mantyla (2000) advised that "an evaluation can first and foremost determine whether the distance learning version worked as effectively as, or better than, the standard instructional approach — teaching students face to face" (p. 262).

Despite their popularity, there are significant weaknesses in the application of experimental comparisons to educational technologies, including online learning environments. First, the strict control of treatment and control variables, as required by experimental methodologies, is impractical in most online learning systems contexts. For example, the same online resources available to online students are often available to face-to-face learners as well. In addition, decades of implementation studies clearly indicate that there are substantive differences between the designs of innovative learning environments and products and their actual implementation. This is especially evident within the context of online learning where the variance in hardware features, connectivity speed, time-on-task, motivation, and many other factors is quite high. Second, the tests used to measure educational outcomes in experimental studies are rarely reliable and valid. And even when they possess some modicum of reliability, the tests do not assess the most important outcomes of online learning environments. Third, the experimental approach is limited to supporting or failing to support pre-stated hypotheses; it cannot discover unexpected effects of an online learning environment. Fourth, randomized experiments are extremely difficult to conduct in most educational contexts and may be unethical in some online situations.

As a result of these weaknesses, researchers operating within the experimental model frequently fall back upon designs that can be most easily managed, focus on variables that are easiest to measure, apply statistical methods without meeting the assumptions underlying their use, and draw conclusions that have little or no practical application (Schwab, 1970). It should surprise no one that their application has largely yielded a legacy of "no significant differences."

In light of this lamentable situation, this chapter has two major purposes. First, it reviews the history and current status of the "no significant differences" phenomenon, especially with respect to online learning. Second, and most importantly, it concludes with recommendations for a robust "design" or "development" research agenda that has the potential to enhance the future effectiveness of online learning.

On a personal note, I have been promoting alternative research and evaluation methods in educational technology for at least two decades (Reeves, 1986, 1993, 2000; Reeves & Hedberg, 2003; Reeves & Lent, 1984). I first came to understand the limitations of traditional media comparison studies in several graduate courses taught by Professor Richard E. Clark, one of my professors in the doctoral program at Syracuse University in the late 1970s. Despite the criticisms offered by Clark (1983) and others, comparative media studies proliferated throughout the 1980s, 1990s, and into the 21st century as new interactive multimedia systems and eventually online learning environments were developed. During a recent stint as Editor of the *Journal of Interactive Learning Research* (http://www.aace.org/pubs/jilr/), I was appalled by the number of submissions reporting quasi-experimental comparisons of online learning with classroom instruction, most often reporting "no significant differences." Sometimes I fear that I am becoming one of those cranky old folks harping on one issue who are inevitably found in every field. But on the other hand, given that this chapter will appear in a book meant to interpret the history of online learning, it seems worthwhile making yet another plea for better research methods.

The "No Significant Differences" Phenomenon

As noted above, educational researchers have conducted media comparison studies from the earliest days of the introduction of technology into education. For example, Saettler (1990) found evidence of comparisons of educational films with classroom instruction being conducted in the 1920s. Comparative research designs were applied to every new educational technology as it was developed, including programmed instruction, instructional television, and more recently computer-based instruction. However, for decades the results of such media comparison research studies have usually been "no significant differences" (Clark, 1983; Lumsdaine, 1963; Mielke, 1968; Schramm, 1977).

Turning to online learning, Pittman (2003) noted that "the usual trend in distance education has been to use new technologies to make independent study more closely resemble the conventional classroom" (p. 31). Given this trend, it was inevitable that experimental research and evaluation methods would be applied to test the assumptions underlying the introduction of technology into distance education. Indeed, the proliferation of online technologies in distance and flexible learning contexts brought forth a whole new wave of comparison studies (e.g., Cheng, Lehman, & Armstrong, 1991; Collins, 2000; MacDonald & Bartlett, 2000; Souder, 1993).

Recently, Bernard *et al.* (2003) reported a large-scale meta-analysis of 157 empirical comparisons of distance education courses with face-to-face instruction courses published between 1985 and 2003. Although they found over 1,000 such comparisons in the research literature, the majority of the studies did not meet their criteria for inclusion in the meta-analysis. Earlier reviews have found that such media comparison studies are often flawed by problems such as specification error, lack of linkage to theoretical foundations, inadequate literature reviews, poor treatment implementation, major measurement flaws, inconsequential learning outcomes for research participants, inadequate sample sizes, inaccurate statistical analyses, and meaningless discussions of results (Reeves, 1993). Bernard *et al.* (2003) report a very small, but statistically "significant positive mean effect size for interactive distance education over traditional classroom instruction on student achievement" as well as a small, but statistically significant, "negative effect for retention rate" (p. 2). Their analysis is still underway, but preliminary results indicate that that synchronous communication and two-way audio and video are among the conditions that contribute to effective online learning. Unfortunately, the findings from this important meta-analysis and other research syntheses fall far short with regard to specifying design guidelines for online learning.

Some authorities have proffered a curious interpretation of the lack of robust findings in favor of technological advances in distance and flexible learning. Whereas many educational technologists have lamented the lack of significant educational achievement differences found between technological innovations and traditional instructional methods, some in the distance education world appear to regard such results as a point of pride. A popular Website called the "No Significant Differences Phenomenon" (http://teleeducation.nb.ca/ nosignificantdifference) lists hundreds of studies that have shown no significant differences in academic achievement between distance education instruction (including online learning) and traditional face-to-face instruction. The creator of this site, Russell (1999) maintains that this research record "proves" that distance education instructional designs are just as effective as traditional classroom instructional methods. As noted in Long (1994), this type of interpretation encourages researchers like Cheng, Lehman, and Armstrong (1991) to issue statements such as: "Most research evaluating the outcomes of distance learning in higher education and business has shown consistent positive results. No differences, in terms of achievement, between traditional instructional methods and distance learning have been indicated" (p. 52). It is not clear to me how "positive results" are derived from the consistent failure to find any differences.

A Call for Design Research

Fortunately, there are better ways to do research to advance the state-of-the-art of online learning. To provide design guidelines for developing and implementing effective online teaching and learning environments, there is an urgent need for what has been labeled design research (Bannan-Ritland, 2003; Design-Based Research Collective, 2003; Kelly, 2003), or alternatively, development research (van den Akker, 1999). In contrast to media comparison studies, design/development research:

- focuses on broad-based, complex problems critical to education;
- involves intensive collaboration among researchers and practitioners;
- integrates known and hypothetical design principles with technological affordances to render plausible solutions to these complex problems;
- conducts rigorous and reflective inquiry to test and refine innovative learning environments as well as to reveal new design principles;
- requires long-term engagement that allows for continual refinement of protocols and questions; and
- maintains a commitment to theory construction and explanation while solving real-world problems.

Design/development research is not just for educational technologists, instructional designers, computer scientists, and others engaged in the development of online learning. Faculty from all disciplines can use this approach to engage in the "scholarship of teaching" intended to optimize the roles of human teachers and online technologies in higher education (Shulman, 2001). Not enough is known about the demands of online teaching on instructors and learners, nor do we completely understand the most effective alignments of educational objectives, content, subject matter expertise, instructional methods, technological affordances, and assessment strategies for online learning. Despite a rosy future for online learning predicted by Duderstadt, Atkins, and Van Houweling (2002), Pittinsky (2003) and others, our current state of knowledge in this area is woefully inadequate, and research findings are often contradictory. We must encourage active participation in design research focused on online learning across the entire academic spectrum.

What questions should be pursued to advance the state-of-the-art of online learning? Since 1990, the Campus Computing Project (Green, 2001) has conducted an annual survey of more than 600 colleges and universities in the United States concerning the role of information technology in teaching, learning, and scholarship. According to the summary of the 2001 survey results, respondents across all sectors of higher education identified "assisting faculty integrate technology into instruction" as the single most important IT issue confronting their campuses "over the next two or three years." A recent survey of college administrators (Allen & Seaman, 2003) indicates that a majority of administrators at institutes of higher education "say online learning is just as good as traditional, face-to-face classroom instruction," and "nearly three out of four academic leaders say learning online may be better within three years." However, professors and their students seem much less certain of this brave new world of online learning (Cuban, 2001; Hara & Kling, 1999; Noble, 2001; Reeves, 2002, 2003).

Faculty members around the globe are under increasing pressure to design online courses in ways that help students to achieve higher order outcomes such as thinking like experts and developing robust mental models of complex processes. But most of them are unable to accomplish this without substantial instructional design support. Instead of long term support, the best most of them get is a workshop or two on their institution's particular course management system. Although the technological features of Blackboard, WebCT, and other course management systems can support the engagement of students in solving complex problems or undertaking authentic tasks, few instructors capitalize on these affordances in their use of the tools.

To realize the fullest potential for online learning, our methods of research and development must be fundamentally changed, but additional changes are needed. First, we must shift from a position that views learning theory as something that stands apart from and above instructional practice to one that recognizes that learning theory is collaboratively shaped by educational researchers and practitioners in context. Educational technology is a design field, and thus, our paramount goal of research should be solving teaching, learning, and performance problems, and deriving design principles that can inform future decisions. Our goal should not be to develop esoteric theoretical knowledge that we expect practitioners to apply. This has not worked since the dawn of educational technology, and it won't work in the future.

In addition, the reward structure for scholarship must change in higher education. Educational researchers should be rewarded for participation in long-term design research projects rather than for the number of refereed journal articles they publish. In addition, faculty in all disciplines should be provided time for participation in this type of formative research, reflection, and continuous professional development with respect to online learning.

Finally, additional financial support is needed for long-term design/development research initiatives. In the USA, private funding agencies such as the Alfred P. Sloan Foundation (http://www.sloan.org/main.shtml) and the Spencer Foundation (http://www.spencer.org/) as well as the National Science Foundation (http://www.nsf.gov) have funded a large number of projects designed to advance the prospects for online learning in higher education and other contexts. Unfortunately, few of these initiatives have been sufficiently integrated with long-term design/development research agendas.

Will the problems with online learning research described above ever subside? During the few next years, I'll be reviewing papers submitted for presentation at conferences such as ED-MEDIA (http://www.aace.org/conf/edmedia/) and refereeing submissions to publications such as the *Educational Technology Research and Development* journal (http://www.aect.org/). I won't be surprised if among these submissions are reports of studies comparing online learning with classroom learning. But I also wish that there will be more and more reports of successful design/development research initiatives. I can only hope.

References

Allen, I.E., & Seaman, J. (2003). *Sizing the opportunity: The quality and extent of online education in the United States, 2002 and 2003*. Needham, MA: The Sloan Consortium. Accessed online on December 12, 2003 at: http://www.aln.org/resources/sizing_opportunity.pdf

Bannan-Ritland, B. (2003). The role of design in research: The integrative learning design framework. *Educational Researcher, 32*(1), pp. 21-24.

Bernard, R.M., Lou, Y., Abrami, P.C., Wozney, L., Borokhovski, E., Wallet, P. A., Wade, A., & Fiset, M. (2003, April). *How does distance education compare to classroom instruction? A meta-analysis of the empirical literature*. Paper presented at the Annual Meeting of the American Educational Research Association, Chicago, IL. Accessed online on November 3, 2003 at: http://doe.concordia.ca/cslp/

Bunker, E.L. (2003). The history of distance education through the eyes of the International Council for Distance Education. In M. G. Moore & W. G. Anderson (Eds.), *Handbook of distance education* (pp. 49-66). Mahwah, NJ: Lawrence Erlbaum Associates.

Clark, R.E. (1983). Reconsidering research on learning with media. *Review of Educational Research, 53*(4), pp. 445-459.

Cheng, H-C., Lehman, J., & Armstrong, P. (1991). Comparison of performance and attitude in traditional and computer conference classes. *The American Journal of Distance Education, 5*(3), pp. 51-64.

Collins, M. (2000). Comparing Web, correspondence, and lecture versions of a second-year non-major biology course. *British Journal of Educational Technology, 31*(1), pp. 21-27.

Cuban, L. (1986). *Teachers and machines: The classroom use of technology since 1920.* New York: Teachers College Press.

Cuban, L. (2001). *Oversold and underused: Computers in the classroom.* Cambridge, MA: Harvard University Press.

Design-Based Research Collective. (2003). Design-based research: An emerging paradigm for educational inquiry. *Educational Researcher, 32*(1), pp. 5-8.

Duderstadt, J.J., Atkins, D.E., & Van Houweling, D. (2002) *Higher education in the digital age: Technology issues and strategies for American colleges and universities.* Westport, CT: American Council on Education and Praeger.

Green, K. (2001). *Campus computing report 2001. Encino, CA: The Campus Computing Project.* Accessed online on December 9, 2003 at: http://www.campuscomputing.net/

Hara, N., & Kling, R. (1999). Students' frustrations with a Web-based distance education course. *First Monday, 4*(12). Accessed online on December 12, 2003 at: http://www.firstmonday.dk/issues/issue4_12/hara/

Kelly, A. E. (2003). Research as design. *Educational Researcher, 32*(1), pp. 3-4.

Long, M. (1994). A study of the academic results of on-campus and off-campus students: Comparative performance within four Australian tertiary institutions.

A report produced for the Australian Higher Education Council. Accessed online on December 10, 2003 at: http://www.dest.gov.au/nbeet/publications/pdf/94_31.pdf

Lumsdaine, A.A. (1963). Instruments and media of instruction. In N. Gage (Ed.), *Handbook of research on teaching.* Chicago: Rand McNally.

MacDonald, M., & Bartlett, J.E. (2000). Comparison of Web-based and traditional delivery methods in a business communications unit. *Delta Pi Epsilon Journal, 42*(2), pp. 90-100.

Mantyla, K. (Ed.). (2000). *The 2000/2001 ASTD distance learning yearbook.* New York: McGraw-Hill.

Mielke, K.W. (1968). Questioning the questions of ETV research. *Educational Broadcasting, 2,* pp. 6-15.

Moore, M.G., & Anderson, W.G. (Eds.). (2003). *Handbook of distance education.* Mahwah, NJ: Lawrence Erlbaum Associates.

Noble, D.F. (2001). *Digital diploma mills: The automation of higher education.* New York: Monthly Review Press.

Pittinsky, M.S.(Ed.). (2003) *The wired tower: Perspectives on the impact of the Internet on higher education.* Upper Saddle River, NJ: Prentice Hall.

Pittman, V.V. (2003). Correspondence study in the American university: A second historiographic study. In M.G. Moore & W.G. Anderson (Eds.), *Handbook of distance education* (pp. 21-35). Mahwah, NJ: Lawrence Erlbaum Associates.

Reeves, T.C. (1986). Research and evaluation models for the study of interactive video. *Journal of Computer-Based Instruction, 13,* pp. 102-106.

Reeves, T.C. (1993). Pseudoscience in computer-based instruction: The case of learner control research. *Journal of Computer-Based Instruction, 20*(2), pp. 39-46.

Reeves, T.C. (2000). Socially responsible educational technology research. *Educational Technology, 40*(6), pp. 19-28.

Reeves, T.C. (2002). Distance education and the professorate: The issue of productivity. In C. Vrasidas & G. V. Glass (Eds.), *Distance education and distributed learning* (135-156). Greenwich, CT: Information Age Publishing.

Reeves, T.C. (2003). Storm clouds on the digital education horizon. *Journal of Computing in Higher Education, 15*(1), pp. 3-26.

Reeves, T.C., & Hedberg, J.G. (2003). *Interactive learning systems evaluation.* Englewood Cliffs, NJ: Educational Technology Publications.

Reeves, T.C., & Lent, R.M. (1984). Levels of evaluation for computer-based instruction. In D. F. Walker & R. D. Hess (Eds.), *Instructional software: Principles and perspectives for design and use* (pp. 188-203). Belmont, CA: Wadsworth.

Russell, T.L. (1999). *The no significant difference phenomenon.* Montgomery, AL: International Distance Education Certification Center.

Saettler, P. (1990). *The evolution of American educational technology.* Englewood, CO: Libraries Unlimited.

Schramm, W. (1977). *Big media, little media.* Beverly Hills, CA: Sage Publications.

Schwab, J.J. (1970). *The practical: A language for curriculum.* Washington, DC: National Education Association, Center for the Study of Instruction.

Shulman, L. (2001), Inventing the future. In P. Hutchings (Ed.), *Opening lines: Approaches to the scholarship of teaching and learning.* Menlo Park, CA: Carnegie Publications.

Souder, W.E. (1993). The effectiveness of traditional vs. satellite delivery in three management of technology master's degree programs. *The American Journal of Distance Education, 7*(1), pp. 37-53.

Suchman, E.A. (1967). *Evaluative research: Principles and practice in public service and social action programs.* New York: Russell Sage Foundation.

van den Akker, J. (1999). Principles and methods of development research. In J. van den Akker, N. Nieveen, R. M. Branch, K. L. Gustafson, & T. Plomp (Eds.), *Design methodology and developmental research in education and training* (pp. 1-14). The Netherlands: Kluwer Academic Publishers.

Chapter 21

Building Communities of Learners Online

Margaret Riel

Margaret Riel is a Senior Researcher at SRI, International, and Visiting Professor in the Pepperdine University online Master in Educational Technology program. Her interest in online teaching and learning arises from decades of research and development in the area of communication technology and education with a focus on collaborative learning. She received her PhD from UC, Irvine.

My experiences in network education began in the early 80's at the University of California, San Diego where I created a "mental gym" with Apple II computers to help elementary school "learning disabled" children. With the help of Jim Levin, I started as many others have, with a computer pals project. We connected students in California with students in Alaska, using accounts on the Source,[1] an early network provider. The logistics of matching students in classes of different sizes, the unpredictable rates of exchange and possibility of disconnect were so great, and the educational benefit of friendly letters so minimal that we gave up on this approach. Personal communication did not stretch students' capabilities and most letters, even from very distant places, carried very similar content. The few messages containing insightful views, cultural contrasts, or valuable learning content were narrowly directed to a single student (Levin *et al.*, 1984; Riel & Levin, 1992).

Network education, we believed, should be linked to the classroom curriculum, involve students in sharing their diverse experiences, and engage students in writing, editing, and reflection. Given the large differences in curriculum in different countries, variations in school schedules, and the difficulties of matching students, we shifted to models of cross-classroom collaboration and group-to-group communication.

Jim Levin, Marcia Buruta, and I created a student newswire service —"The Computer Chronicles" — to which students could contribute and retrieve

---

[1] In these early years, network providers multiplied but communication was fragmented. To communicate, people had to have accounts on the same service. Those involved in early networking, used the reverse side of business cards to list user names for each of the many service accounts, for example, The Source, CompuServe, McGraw Hill Information exchange (MIX), FREdmail, and AT&Tmail.

stories (Riel, 1985). This made it possible for a classroom to publish a school newspaper with international stories written by student reporters from around the world. It also provided for a very different kind of school writing — students had authentic audiences and a communicative purpose for their writing.

In 1985-87, with funding from an Apple Computer grant, and the additional help of Moshe Cohen from Israel and Naomi Miyake from Japan, we linked schools in six locations to create the "InterCultural Learning Network." This "design experiment" explored how computer networking could create distributed learning contexts for elementary and secondary students and their teachers (Riel, 1987).[2] The communication systems we used were difficult, expensive, and incredibly slow. However, we suspected that the technology would develop much faster than our ideas and plans for using it.

Early research on this writing and editing process demonstrated strong student gains on holistic scoring of writing and on standardized tests of reading and writing as a result of cross-classroom collaboration (Cohen & Riel, 1989; Riel, 1990). This model seemed to be an effective way to develop literacy skills in the context of social science in elementary and secondary students. We also found that this cross-classroom communication provided teachers with a rich network of professional peers for thinking about different instructional practices and educational theories often in relationship to the use of technology.

A critical observation from this early research was that the learning outcomes of project work were strongest for the students in the classroom that created or sponsored the project. Possible reasons included higher motivation derived from a sense of ownership, closer alignment of project work with local classroom curriculum, and the expertise of their teacher on the selected topic. These same conditions did not often exist in participating classrooms. We also noted that the success of a project did not require the participation of all students. One or two quality responses from each of the sites were sufficient to create a meaningful, rich learning environment.

---

[2] ICLN was the incentive for Al Rogers to create FREdmail, a network of computer nodes, that made it possible for more teachers to work with peers in distant locations. Modeled on FidoNET developed among some universities, FREdmail nodes called only the nodes nearest to them, in the evening when the rates were very low and exchanged messages directly between computers using acoustic couplers attached to the phone. While it took as long as two days for email to pass through all computer nodes from California to the most distant locations in Australia, it was relatively inexpensive and for teachers who had a FREdmail node in their local calling area, it was free.

Learning Community Approach: Learning Circles

By the late 80's early 90's many network learning efforts included large conferencing models, project based activities with scientists, telementoring, and electronic field trips (see Riel & Harasim, 1994, for a review). In 1987, building on my experiences from the InterCultural Learning Nework, I developed the "Learning Circles" model of cross-classroom-collaboration for the AT&T Learning Network. Learning Circles[3] created an open structure for extending rather than replacing existing curriculum with online learning. The Learning Circle model capitalized on the vast expertise of classroom teachers and the resources of learners in different regions.

Learning Circles grouped 6-10 classes located throughout the world to work on theme-linked projects sponsored by the schools. Each teacher and class sponsored one circle project ideally linked with local curriculum. The sponsored project was the central focus as students requested, collected, organized, edited, and published the work of their distant peers. Their participation in projects sponsored by other classes took place concurrently with small groups of students working on each project. This structure helped teachers maximize the time students spent on curriculum-linked work. Projects often engaged students in real problems located in their community, focused on multi-disciplinary themes, and engaged students in cross-age learning. The Learning Circle cooperatively published the project work and these publications were used to assess the quality of learning (Riel, 1992).

Research on Learning Circles indicated that it was an effective learning environment for students. Student outcomes were easiest to document in the areas of reading and writing because these are measured on yearly standardized tests. In two small-scale studies, students who participated in Learning Circles showed gains of one to two years in standardized test scores (Riel, 1994). In response to surveys over the years, teachers consistently ranked "learned more about themselves" higher than "learned more about others" as one of the most valuable learning outcomes of the exchange. Perhaps this was because many teachers joined the network with the goal of providing more global connections for students they perceived to be isolated by remote regions or by social situations. These teachers and their students were surprised by the high interest expressed by distant students in their lives. Students on rural farms, in remote villages of Alaska, in special educational contexts, in home schools, lockup

---

[3] For more information on Learning Circles, which are currently offered by a number of institutions worldwide, see http://www.iearn.org/circles

programs, and mobile schools were expected to be experts on activities or cultural practices that made up the tacit unexamined aspects of their lives. To respond to questions, students invited the elders, visited museums, or used community resources to describe their lives. Explaining their culture, region, or social circumstances to others led them to them to see themselves through the imagined lens of distant students, and created a new self-awareness.

In addition, connecting teachers from distant locations was a promising strategy for professional development. Learning Circle teachers reported professional and personal growth that paralleled that of the students: "There is a certain pride and dignity when you know that your work is being read by a great number of highly skilled educators" (Sherwood, 1990). In Learning Circle evaluations teachers consistently rated their own learning higher (4.5 on a 5-point scale) than they did their student learning (3.8). Using teacher feedback over many years, I reported four ways in which teachers benefited from their participation in Learning Circles (Riel 1990). First, they acquired new content knowledge by learning from students and teachers at a distance. Second, they benefited from a diffusion of instructional practices as they discussed ways of designing projects. Third, many reported increased professional stature or recognition as a leader in education because of their ability to integrate world-wide learning resources mediated by technology into their teaching. And finally, the development of worldwide personal and professional networks provided for many teachers a "community of practice" (Lave & Wegner, 1991) that was not available in typically isolated classrooms.

Observation After Two Decades of Organizing Learning Circles

Students need a personal connection with each other before they are able to teach and learn online. In Learning Circles, students begin by sharing information and sending artifacts (pictures, sports cards, school emblems, stickers, postcards) about themselves, their school, and their community. All of the introductory activities helped students answer a very basic question: How are these people similar and different from us? When students did form a strong personal connection to Circle partners, teachers reported an increased attention of their students to global affairs related to their partner sites. For example, when students worked with peers from Japan or Israel they became more attentive to news and events in these countries because these events affected their circle partners. Students also provide their unique view on events, such as the tidal wave created in a swimming pool during an earthquake in California.

However, working with students at a distance does not always motivate students to learn. Groups have their own chemistry. I have never been able to organize groups where all of them are successful. Over the years, my colleagues and I have figured out many of the factors that appear to contribute to success:

- Circle size that balances diversity with intimacy (about 6-10 classes in different locations)
- Range in age and skills between 1-3 years or 1-3 grade levels
- Ready access to computer and communication technology
- Class experience in collaborative project work
- Students who are engaged learners in their classrooms
- Teachers who understand the reciprocal commitment involved in online project work
- An experienced teacher and class to facilitate the circle

We tried to match groups to achieve the best possible balance of these factors. Learning Circles have an experience facilitator, a mix of new and experienced teachers, and the best possible match of schools that we form for the set of participating schools.

But no matter how I have tried to perfect the matching process, I found similar results. About one-third of the circles produced incredibly engaging learning contexts and a wealth of examples of highly effective network learning. Another third of the circles managed to complete their work or most of it with only sparks of, rather than, sustained engagement. The last third of the circles either failed to get started, or started but didn't finish. If I focused on the participation within the circle, I find the same rule of thirds. Is there something about the way that school is organized that produces this distribution? Are there ways we could use technology to redesign learning contexts to address the needs of all students? My experience with learning and Learning Circles at the university level suggests that it might be possible to do this. But it would take a reacculturation process that placed a higher value on collaborative learning (Bruffee, 1993).

Learning Communities, Distance Education, and University Teaching

The work I have presented to this point describes educational experiments in the K-12 setting. Online learning and distance education within the university also advanced in the early 80's. But there was a strong distinction between those who saw it as a new medium of distance learning information delivery (Keegan, 1980; Sewart, Keegan, & Holmberg, 1983) and those who viewed it as a way to reshape the social dimensions of learning (Dede, 1996; Harasim, 1993; Jacobson & Levin, 1995; Pea, 1993).

College and university administrators who struggled with a lack of "expert" teachers particularly in science, math, and foreign languages and worried about the costs of small courses saw in computer networking a new and inexpensive medium to transmit information from expert to multiple learners — even when those learners were in different locations. The educators who had, in the past, designed correspondence courses and televised courses now began to include computing networking in their educational plans and together these approaches were called "distance education." Keegan (1980) in the first issue of *Distance Education* described this new approach as "involving a physical separation of teacher and student" as well as "the absence of the learning group throughout the length of the learning process." Students were taught as individuals, and not in groups.

Distributed Learning in Network Communities

Independent of efforts to use networks to transfer knowledge from expert to learners, other educators viewed computer networking as a way to link people with distributed expertise in community-based learning. These online "learning communities" represent a different pedagogical approach than the approach of distance education. Based on a socio-cultural perspective on intellectual dialogue and collaborative activity, the role of the learner was significantly changed from isolated individuals to collaborating partners. A second, equally important goal was to provide a community for educators to work with their peers developing professional expertise.

Communities of Learners in Networked University Education

After several decades of development and research in online education in elementary and secondary schools, I have more recently joined university colleagues, specifically the Graduate School of Education and Psychology at Pepperdine University where I teach in a Master in Arts in Educational Technology program. This program deviates from distance education approaches by creating a highly collaborative context and aiming at transformational learning rather than information transfer. This model of online education is community-based in three overlapping and important ways:

collaborative learning in the context of a student cadre, theoretical learning through community experiences, and transformational learning in one's community of practice.

(1) Collaborative Learning in the Context of a Student Cadre

The students experience the program as member of a learning cadre — a group of twenty to twenty-five students who take all of their courses together. The cadre includes students from diverse locations (Japan, Italy, Alaska, Hawaii, and across the U. S) different backgrounds, and work experiences. To build a strong learning community, the students come together in person at the beginning, at the midpoint, and at the end of the program. This combination of in-person and online interaction helps create a strong community of learners.

Cadres have an intellectual advisor, a "cadre-madre" or "cadre-padre," who supervises their action research and their general progress through the program. This advisor role combines instructing and supporting students as they engage in original research. During the first face-to-face session, students master the technology communication and Web design tools needed to work together in an online context. They also learn about the resources of the group because distributive expertise is an important part of the social capital for learning. After this initial time together, they continue to interact through a series of organized online activities that make up the coursework of the program. The combination of creative, narrative, and analytical modes of thinking seems to support deep understanding while building very strong inter-student relationships. Their work together in a learning community provides them with access to variations in practice, and thus to discussions and work groups aimed at improving practice. The experience in a cadre provides an environment to experiment with methods of group leadership and to provide experiences in leadership as service to the collective.

The student cadre works as a team to develop possible solutions to the set of educational problems they have identified. They learn from and teach each other how to use the tools that mediate solutions to these problems. There are no courses centered on a specific form of technology or computer application. Technology is viewed as a form of social mediation: as shared minds made visible. The reason to have students take more responsibility for learning today's technology in a community context is to help them define technology learning as a fluid, ongoing process. By making them responsible for directing their own learning and supporting the learning of their cadre members, they develop transportable practices that are available when they leave the program.

Learning circles are used to create smaller grouping of five to six students to work more intensely on each other's action research. While all students design their own research, students in the learning circle are educational consultants whose task is to improve the quality of the work of the other members in the circle.

(2) Theoretical Learning Through Community Experiences

Like most graduate programs, Pepperdine students are expected to develop an understanding of the work of scholars who have wrestled with issues of learning, teaching, and technology. Current theories place a strong emphasis on the historical, social, and interactive context of learning and development, the role of distributed expertise, and the effect of dynamic scaffolding of learning. All knowledge has historical and cultural roots (Vygotsky, 1978) and is socially constructed (Mehan, 1983). Technology serves to mediate between past and future ideas by embedding shared knowledge in tools — tools that help us construct new knowledge. Learning happens between and among people, and insights are constructed from the ideas of others which gain value when they are shared.

Our online methods of instruction are not used to transmit knowledge, as is common in distance education. Instead we place students in contexts where they participate in knowledge-building community dialogues, sharing their evolving understandings. Their dialogue and projects rely on the distributed expertise within the group, and on intellectual scaffolding and dynamic support from their professors. Students build and use multimedia representations, models, personal narratives, and visual metaphors to illustrate their understanding and to engage others in building knowledge. Theoretical knowledge serves as a tool that students use in activities that are located in their workplace communities of practice. As student read work related to their research topic, they are encouraged to see the authors they read as members of an intellectual community — researchers who care about similar topics, or activists who have struggled to similar problems in other contexts. And to see this as a community that they can join by contributing their findings from action research. The Pepperdine program helps students to understand, both theoretically and practically, the social construction of situations and their own identity in communities of practice.

(3) Transformational Learning in One's Community of Practice

The process of learning involves action, reaction, analysis, and reflection. This statement, which is consistent with the ideas of (Piaget, 1952), defines the process of action research. Comparative research shows that the students who engaged in this process of inquiry to solve math problems embedded in video stories developed complex problem solving skills (Cognition & Technology Group, 1992) which is essential to developing adaptive expertise. Adaptive expertise (Hatano,1990) is the ability to apply prior knowledge in creative ways to build new knowledge. Students need to learn to go beyond the information given, to apply what they learn in new contexts (Bruner, 1973). To integrate technology, students need to engage in a process of inquiry and experimentation to think about teaching and learning in progressively more expert ways (Bereiter & Scardamalia, 1993).

The Pepperdine application procedure requires students to identify a problem in their field of practice. The collective set of issues or problems students bring to the program help the faculty shape the curriculum to address these workplace problems. This means that the content of graduate courses changes in response to the unique configuration of each cadre's needs and interests. The overarching goal of the program is for each student to understand their role in a primary community of practice, and then develop new strategies for how they might serve this community in effective ways. Each student brings a personal, local version of technology in education as practiced in his or her workplace. Students come to the program from primary and secondary higher educational communities as well as social, organization, and corporate communities. The work experiences they share in the ongoing discourse of the program's yearlong action research project and companion courses offer a view of the variations and the commonalities in problems, issues, objects, histories, and goals. The elementary school computer lab teacher and the aerospace information technology worker share common frustrations at the consequences of working on the peripheries of their organizations. The high school English teacher and the university media specialist share their common concerns about information literacy and acceptable use policies for student Internet use. The role of each of these students in their communities of practice is the basic unit of design of each learning experience.

The cadre-madre or cadre-padre helps the students frame good research questions and collect evidence which will help them think more deeply about the problems in their workplace and progress towards framing increasingly better solutions. The action taken might be to listen, perform, connect, build, design, write, or interact in some way that effects a change in a social context. The evidence collected helps them analyze the reactions. Reflection on previous action-reaction cycles helps them to plan the next cycle of action (Mills, 2003). The process is cyclic because contexts shift — people and technology evolve. What works well at one time can almost always be improved in the next cycle. Students engage in a number of action research cycles with the support of the cadre and under the direction of their cadre advisor and course professors. The goal is transformative, making the process of the research the central focus. The faculty seeks to develop in students a habit of inquiry and a deep understanding of social context and social change dynamics. Often students experience a transformation of their identity within their community of practice. They come to see their role as one of leadership through service to the community, which in turn changes the dynamics of the communities.

Concluding Observations

While technology does not directly address the problems of personalizing learning, it can increase the number of people that are engaged in the teaching and learning process. Network education can makes teaching and learning a more public, distributed, community activity. But technology can also be used to depersonalize education, creating just-in-time training machines that do little to engage students in creative formation of interesting problems and their emergent solutions. As technology becomes more portable and communication more pervasive, how we structure education will depend more on the social networks we create than on the forms of technology that supports them.

References

Bereiter, C., & Scardamalia, M. (1993). *Surpassing ourselves: An inquiry into the nature and implications of expertise.* Chicago, IL: Open Court.

Bruffee, K. A. (1993). *Collaborative learning: Higher education, interdependence, and the authority of knowledge.* Baltimore: Johns Hopkins University Press.

Bruner, J. (1973). *Going beyond the information given.* New York: Norton.

Cognition & Technology Group at Vanderbilt. (1992). The Jasper series as an example of anchored instruction: Theory, program description, and assessment data. *Educational Psychologist, 27*(3), pp. 291-315.

Cohen, M., & Riel, M. (1989). The effect of distant audiences on students' writing. *American Educational Research Journal, 26*, pp. 143-159.

Dede, C. (1996). Emerging technologies and distributed learning. *American Journal of Distance Education, 10*(2), pp. 4-36.

Harasim, L. (1993). *Global networks: Computers and communication.* Cambridge, MA: MIT Press.

Hatano, G. (1990). The nature of everyday science: A brief introduction. *British Journal of Developmental Psychology, 8*, pp. 245- 250.

Jacobson, M. J., & Levin, J. A. (1995). Conceptual frameworks for network learning environments: Constructing personal and shared knowledge spaces. *International Journal of Educational Telecommunications, 1*(4), pp. 367-388.

Keegan D., (1980). On defining distance education. *Distance Education, 1*(1), pp. 13-36.

Lave, J. & Wenger, E. (1991). *Situated learning: Legitimate peripheral participation.* New York: Cambridge University Press.

Levin, J. A., Riel, M., Rowe, R. D., & Boruta, M. J. (1984). Muktuk meets jacuzzi: Computer networks and elementary school writers. In S. W. Freedman (Ed.), *The acquisition of written language.* Hillsdale, NJ: Ablex.

Mehan, H. (1983). Social constructivism in psychology and sociology. *Sociologie et Societes, XIV*(2), pp. 77-96.

Mills, G. (2003). *Action research: A guide for the teacher researcher* (2nd ed.). Upper Saddle River, NJ: Prentice Hall.

Pea, R. (1993). Practices of distributed intelligence and designs for education. In G. Salomon (Ed.), *Distributed cognitions: Psychological and educational considerations* (pp. 47-87). Cambridge, UK: Cambridge University Press.

Piaget, J.-P. (1952). *The origins of intelligence in children.* New York: International Universities Press.

Riel, M., (1985). The Computer Chronicles newswire: A functional learning environment for acquiring literacy skills. *Journal of Educational Computing Research, 1*, pp. 317-337.

Riel, M. (1987). The InterCultural Learning Network. *The Computing Teacher, 14*, pp. 27-30.

Riel, M. (1990). Telecommunications: A tool for reconnecting kids with society. *Interactive Learning Environments, 1*, pp. 255-263

Riel, M. (1992). A functional analysis of educational telecomputing: A case study of learning circles. *Interactive Learning Environments, 2*, pp. 15-30.

Riel, M. (1993, Fall), The SCANS Report & the AT&T Learning Network: Preparing students for their future. *Telecommunications in Education News, 5*, pp. 10-16.

Riel, M. (1994). Educational change in a technology-rich environment. *Journal of Research on Computers in Education, 26*(4), pp. 452-474.

Riel, M., & Harasim, L. (1994). Research perspectives on network learning. *The International Journal of Machine-Mediated Learning, 4*(2&3), pp. 91-114.

Sewart, D., Keegan, D., & Holmberg, B. (1983) *Distance education: International perspectives*. London: Croom Helm.

Sherwood, L. (1990). Personal communication via email; elementary school teacher in Hilton, New York.

Vygotsky, L. S. (1978). *Mind in society: The development of higher psychological processes*. M. Cole., B. John-Steiner, S. Scribner, & E. Souberman (Eds. and Trans.). Cambridge, MA: Harvard University Press.

Chapter 22

Online Learning: Are We on the Right Track(s)?

Alexander J. Romiszowski

Alexander J. Romiszowski is Research Professor and Technical Director, Training Systems Institute, Syracuse University. He has worked as consultant to many private and public organizations, including United Nations' projects in Spain, Italy, Hungary, and Brazil. Before coming to Syracuse, he taught instructional technology at universities in England, Brazil, and Canada. He received his PhD from Loughborough University.

Factors Affecting the Development of Online Learning

Technological Synergy: Four Converging Trends

Within the last two decades, the synergetic fusion of telecommunications technologies with computing technologies has accelerated the rate of change of many services and functions of modern society. Castells (2000) presents a very detailed analysis of these trends. One of the services affected is education. Castells does not devote a whole section to this area of change, as he does to most other areas, such as the world political order, business organization, employment, communication and the way people live. The education trends have to be teased out by reading across many chapters and even "between the lines." However, other authors, for example Tiffin and Rajasingham (2003), have presented detailed accounts of the probable trends in education as we progress towards a "networked society." As the costs of transport increase and at the same time telecommunications costs decrease, it makes ever less economic sense to bring students together in places called schools or colleges for the purpose of education. The alternative of distributing education via networks is becoming economically very much more attractive. The current trend toward online learning is in large part fueled by such economic considerations.

A second area of technological synergy is the current "hypermedia/multimedia revolution." In education, the term "multimedia" has been used for generations to describe teaching methods and learning experiences that utilize all the senses of a learner and not just one. Multimedia learning environments, using combinations of simple media like books, photographs, and audio/video tapes, have been used in education for over 50 years, accompanying the invention and maturation of the photo, audio, and video technologies. The principal innovation in the last few years is that all forms of information, whether visual, graphic, moving, or auditory, are now stored digitally and can therefore be conveniently accessed and mixed for alternative presentations under computer control.

A third area of technological synergy is occurring through the fusion of computer and telecommunications technologies. The full automation of the telecommunications system and its increased power for data transmission, as it progresses to fiber optics, satellite, and other wireless distribution technologies, is rapidly creating a worldwide broadband communication network that is coming to rival face-to-face communication in terms of effectiveness as well as cost. Thus, the Internet was born.

These three areas of technological synergy are themselves synergistically integrating. The multimedia/hypermedia revolution integrated with the telecommunications revolution enables the dreams of a "world library, democratically open to all" to become a reality. The knowledge-base available to an individual is no longer restricted to what can be stored in one computer or one local area network, but is rapidly becoming a "seamless" integration of all forms of information, distributed in a vast number of digital libraries. Thus, the World Wide Web has been born.

One more essential element to be integrated into the communication and education systems of the future is the network of "end-users." The self-driven learner, while searching the world's hypermedia libraries for information, also must be able to interact with other persons who have similar interests but maybe contrasting points of view, or who have teaching skills that will support the learner by means of personalized tutorials. This fourth element of technological synergy — the integration of the new electronic technologies with the practical realities of human communication and instruction — can best be achieved by the systematic application of the disciplines of instructional design and development.

The State of Health of Online Learning
The current interest and increased activity in distance education (DE) is largely driven by increased availability and decreasing costs of the new technological infrastructures that make it possible to offer e-learning on both a national and international scale. This technological revolution has created the pressures for change that now exist in many countries. However, there is also the added factor introduced by Web-based e-learning: the globalization of access to courses for students from any country. As an example of the current trends, one may refer to the case of the University of South Queensland (USQ), in Australia, a dual-mode university where about one quarter of all students are

campus-based and three quarters are distance-learners. In 2003, almost one quarter of all students (about 4500 in all) were overseas students, studying at a distance from a total of 78 different countries (Taylor, 2003). This trend, replicated in several other Australian universities, has elevated Higher Education (HE) to the level of one of Australia's most important exports — accounting for more export income than, for example, agriculture.

If education is exported, then it is also being imported. By whom? Currently, there is growing interest and discussion of the place of HE in the international trade scenario. The UN's International Trade Organization is debating and proposing international legislation that may regulate the import and export of HE courses and diplomas. Some countries are in favor and others against the UN's proposals. It is significant to note that of the 4500 overseas distance-learners at USQ, almost 4000 are from just two countries — Malaysia (2327) and Singapore (1598). Both these countries have public policies that encourage and promote the import of HE opportunities, both through joint ventures with national HE institutions and as direct offshore initiatives by foreign institutions. This is in stark contrast to the policies of some other countries, including for example Brazil (Litto, 2002), that have restrictive policies designed to keep foreign HE institutions out. This does not mean, however, that countries have no regulatory policies to assure the quality of the imported courses. The case of Malaysia shows a government preoccupation with evaluation and quality assurance, implemented in a manner that does not impede or slow down the provision of new HE opportunities from overseas sources (HjNawawi, Asmuni, & Romiszowski, 2003).

In addition to international trade and competition in HE, the e-learning phenomenon has instigated new forms and dimensions of in-country collaboration and competition. Many countries are in the process of forming consortia of universities in order to collaborate, rather than compete, in the area of e-learning provision. But in parallel, especially from the private sectors of HE, there has been an increasing amount of inter-institutional competition for the same student populations. This has inevitably led to the relative success of some initiatives, for example, the University of Phoenix in the USA, and the relative failure of others, which include the projects of such prestigious institutions as Columbia University, New York University, and even the thwarted attempt of Britain's Open University to install itself in the USA's HE market (Romiszowski, 2003).

Do the success stories of certain pioneering institutions necessarily reflect the overall picture of e-learning and its acceptance as a major educational innovation? Or does the increasing number of cases of failure indicate that e-learning, like so many other promising educational innovations in the past, shall have a short and meteoric rise in popularity, followed by rejection and retraction? Also, what are the factors that lead some e-learning projects to be successful and others to fail? And are these factors the same in the contexts of formal education and corporate training? Some of these issues are explored in an article that I recently wrote for *Educational Technology* Magazine (Romiszowski, 2004).

Is E-Learning Following the Same Route as E-Commerce?
What are the philosophies, theories, and other forces that are fueling the current interest and activity in network-based distance education? To what extent are schools and other organizations that opt for online learning acting on the basis of a systemic analysis of their needs and problems and a research-based selection of appropriate solutions? Or, alternatively, to what extent are they just following fashion or seeking to save costs?

In the USA, for example, the universities have over recent years invested very heavily in a variety of e-learning projects. One indicator of this growth is the number of US higher education institutions that offer distance learning courses and programs. In 1993 this was below 100, by 1996 it had grown to over 700, and by 1999 was in the region of 1500, according to the figures published from 1996 to 2000 in Peterson's annual Distance Learning Catalog. However, more recently, we have seen an increasing number of projects slowing down and many cases of universities pulling out altogether from the e-learning race. An article in the New York Times (Hafner, 2002) documents some of the indicators of this retraction. New York University recently closed its Internet-based learning venture, NYU Online. The University of Maryland University College closed its separate, profit-based, e-learning institution, absorbing the existing online courses into the regular program of the college. Temple University's "Virtual Temple" closed in the summer of 2002. Hafner also documents a similar retraction in venture-capital financing for new online courses and virtual universities: "In 2000, approximately $482 million in venture capital was spent on companies building online tools and technologies aimed at the higher education market — in 2002 (till May 2002) that amount had dropped to $17 million." Extrapolating from these figures, venture-capital investment during the whole of 2002 would be about 10% of the 2000 figure.

On the other hand, the meteoric growth in the use of online learning in the corporate training field seems to be continuing unabated. The overall figures on use and predictions made by such future-forecasting organizations as IDC seem to indicate continued growth of e-learning in this sector. However, the overall figures may obscure certain more detailed aspects of this trend. In general, the available figures do not distinguish between the use of electronic communication technologies for the convenient distribution of individualized learning packages and just plain reference materials (as were previously available in CD-ROM or other distributable storage media), from the conduct of full courses that require considerable amounts of interaction with distant tutors, and between the participants themselves (which are characteristics of the bulk of the online courses in the higher education sector).

It is therefore unclear to what extent the growth of e-learning merely represents the transfer of previously used methodologies and materials to a more convenient distribution and delivery medium, rather than real innovation in the manner in which training is planned and conducted in the business sector. Further analysis of the trends in the corporate education sector is necessary in order to unravel what is really happening, what is working, and what is not. This may reveal that, in some respects, corporate training and higher education may face some similar problems in getting a return on their investment in online learning.

Major Obstacles to Growth of Online Learning

The "Macro" Level: System Effectiveness and Efficiency

The previous section suggests that, already in the first decade of the "e-learning revolution," we are witnessing some signals of retraction. Like "The Rise and Fall of the Roman Empire," we may soon be writing the definitive history of the rise and fall of e-learning. We should not be surprised. The histories of the rise and fall of educational television, of programmed instruction, and of several other promising new applications of technology to education have already been written. And all these retrospective accounts point out that the "fall" was due NOT to inherent weaknesses or inadequacies in the technologies, but rather to the errors made by people and institutions in the process of attempting to implement the innovations. But that sad story has an optimistic side to it. If the causes of failure have more to do with the actions of people and organizations rather than with inherent limitations of the technologies and tools, then these failures are avoidable. People and at least some organizations (the "learning" organizations) have an in-built ability to learn from experience. Let us hope it is not too late for the e-learning movement/industry to start learning from experience and so turn around the downward trend that seems to be developing.

But, is there really a downward trend in the e-learning world? It depends on where you look and what set of figures you study. In the University sector, in the USA, the "boom" of a few years ago has slowed down considerably. Many of the most ambitious projects of for-profit online universities been closed (see the discussion in the previous section). The not-for-profit initiatives, that are a part of the activities of nearly all US universities today, are also confronting unexpected problems, such as dropping student enrollments and even "strikes" by the faculty. One contributing factor, which we shall discuss later in this chapter, is that faculty have discovered that in order to provide a satisfactory learning experience, full of interaction, group activity, and personal attention to individual students, the teachers have to work much more than they are accustomed to in the face-to-face course context. So, either the teachers fail to give the amount of attention that students expect (which leads to reduced enrollments in future online courses), or they "work their tail off" for a semester or two and then decide to opt out, refusing to teach any more online courses — unless teaching workloads are reduced or salaries increased.

In contrast to these troubles facing the higher education sector, e-learning continues to expand in the training sector, with strong support from many corporate learning programs. In the USA, for example, Home Depot is in the middle of a program to install computer kiosks in its stores to allow training of its 300,000 employees. Black & Decker University has similar programs in place with favorable results; an official from the company said that "each hour of e-learning is replacing three to four hours in the classroom." Other companies, such as McDonald's, as well as various federal agencies and the U.S. armed forces, also have invested significantly in e-learning programs. However, a closer analysis of these programs reveals that they are generally focused on training of basic procedural skills and the e-learning models they employ are largely the self-instructional tutorial approaches that have been successfully automated for decades. They succeed despite the lack of effective conversational activities because they do not require these activities for their success. Unlike the formal educational sector, a major part of the e-learning "boom" in the business world is the transfer of well-tried CBT (Computer Based Training) materials to the online delivery platform.

The "Micro" Level: Sustainability

An extensive and detailed account of two years of e-learning in a university context is presented in a report on a study performed at Syracuse University (Doughty, Spector, & Yonai, 2003). This study focuses on the factors that impact the cost-effectiveness and sustainability of online university courses. This study, which is part of an ongoing program of research funded by the

Andrew Mellon Foundation, is investigating the real benefits — and the costs — of online learning in USA university contexts. The results of this study show quite clearly that both students and teachers actually spend significantly more time in online versions of a course as compared to the conventional face-to-face versions of the same course. The percentage increase in student workload is not enormous and may indeed be sustainable over time, given the other possible benefits of online study. But the teacher workload is reported to be more than double across whole semesters and programs. This raises the question of whether online learning, as a regular and mainstream course delivery alternative, is in fact sustainable over the longer term. Will students regularly devote extra time in order to participate in online collaborative learning activities. Will teachers devote the very significant extra time required for the teaching of online courses, on a regular basis, without due recognition and extra compensation?

The "Mellon Study," as it is colloquially named, reports on research performed in a university context in the USA. It is a worth considering the extent to which e-learning in corporate contexts, or in other countries, is following a similar course. In the present author's view, the detailed results may vary somewhat in different countries or cultures — people in different contexts may have different expectations, motivations, and reactions in relation to the detailed aspects of an innovation such as e-learning. These differences must be identified and measured, or at least estimated, if a project is to have a good chance of long-term success.

Key Theoretical and Research Issues

"Presential" vs. "Distance" Learning: What Really Is New?
In this section, I introduce the term "presential learning" as a more meaningful alternative to the much-used "face-to-face instruction." Also, I have used the word "learning" and not other possible words, such as "courses" or "education," to emphasize that the planning decisions on whether it may be best to use "presential" methods or distance learning methods are more appropriately taken at the "micro" level of planning the learning activities within courses, rather than at the "macro" level of deciding whether a given course should be offered at a distance or in a classroom. Nevertheless, it is true that, quite often in practice, a "macro" decision is taken to set up a whole new course as a distance-learning course. Or even, a new institution, such as the UK's Open University, is founded to operate exclusively as a distance-learning provider.

These "macro" decisions are typically based on political or macro-economic considerations, stimulated by some large-scale inadequacy of educational provision that was previously provided by the "conventional" system. But what exactly do we understand by "conventional" systems of education and training? A primary or secondary school student attends classes in a conventional school for between four and six hours per day, depending on the country and the school system. A proportion of these are hours devoted to subjects, such as physical education, that do not normally expect students to do any homework activities. But the core subjects such as mathematics, sciences, social sciences, and languages do generally expect further out-of-school learning activities to be completed. Typically, a secondary school student may be expected to do between two and three hours per day of extra study, either individually or in project groups. Therefore, the "conventional" secondary school curriculum is approximately two thirds "presential" and one third "non-presential." If we take a more "micro" view and focus on specific disciplines such as mathematics or science, the ratio of presential to non-presential learning activities probably approaches 50/50.

If we now consider the typical "conventional" university course, the proportion of presential activities falls much lower. In the case of my own Syracuse University, there is a formal policy governing this issue. As in most USA universities, courses and their subject matter components are measured in terms of "credits." In the "conventional" manner of measuring student workload, one credit represents one hour of classroom activities per week for one semester. A typical "three credit" course, therefore, represents three hours of presential learning activities per week. But the University considers a full work-load to be four such courses. This is because it is formally recognized that a three-credit course does not represent three hours, but more like TEN to TWELVE hours of study per week — three hours of classroom learning plus up to SEVEN to NINE hours of individual or small-group study. Thus, four such courses represent a theoretical workload of 40 to 48 hours per week. Therefore, up to 75% of a "conventional" university-level course may in fact be non-presential.

In the large non-presential part of any course, participants study various instructional materials, make use of reference materials, execute various practical learning tasks and projects and, possibly, meet in small groups for collaborative learning activities with their colleagues. The difference between many presential courses and equivalent distance-learning courses boils down to a change in the media: instead of using the school library or books from the bookshop, students access the Internet; instead of setting up group meetings with other colleagues at mutually convenient times, they interact online in "chat" rooms or, more frequently and even more conveniently, by means of email, listserv, or other asynchronous means of communication. But the objectives of these activities and the learning processes involved have changed very little. Only the media have changed.

It may be interesting, in this context, to mention my own experience as a student of physics and engineering at the University of Oxford in the late 1950's and early 1960's. At that time, the great traditional European universities, including among them Oxford, Cambridge, and Durham in England, still practiced the "tutorial system" of teaching. The tutorial system was the "conventional" methodology in all universities before the advent of the industrial revolution and the resultant tendencies towards "massification" of educational provision.

In the tutorial system, each student is allocated to a personal tutor. Typically, students have one meeting per week, of about one or two hours' duration, with their tutors. This was the only obligatory presential component of the course. Attendance at classes and lectures — there were many alternatives on the schedule — was NOT obligatory. In fact, in many cases, one's personal tutor would advise one not to attend certain classes — "that professor just verbalizes excerpts from his book: buy the book — he writes much better than he speaks." In my personal case, I sometimes went months without attending a single class. In my estimate, my whole university course became about 5% face-to-face (this including the time spent with my personal tutor and the classes I did attend) and as much as 95% non-presential (including a large amount of practical laboratory and workshop activities that were obligatory and rigidly scheduled, but did not involve any face-to-face contact with teaching staff).

Is this situation an exaggeration? Are the ideas here presented strange or irrelevant? I do not think so. In my personal view, university-level courses with a non-presential portion of less than, say, 75% are examples of poor instructional design, incapable of preparing the participants for today's professional world, where the ability to learn on your own throughout the rest of your working life is one of the most important survival skills that may guarantee "employability."

So in conclusion, we hear a lot spoken about "new educational paradigms, facilitated (or even introduced) by the new information and communication technologies (ICT)." But in reality, pedagogically speaking, very little real innovation is taking place. Many of the things that tend to be seen as innovations are not really all that new. It is probably fair to say that the new information and communication technologies do not really offer any revolutionary new pedagogical innovations, but rather that they facilitate the re-discovery and cost-effective implementation of good teaching-learning methodologies that were known for eons, but largely ignored as impractical, or even forcibly abandoned (for practical and cost reasons) with the advent of mass education as part of the industrial revolution. The theory and research agenda for the "online learning revolution" should therefore be an "evolution" of what is already known and has already been researched, seeking to identify how the new tools offered to education by technological progress in other spheres may be employed to further the goals of education as defined from study of the human and social sciences. An example of part of such an agenda is presented below.

Online Learning: The "Gap" Between Theory and Reality
During the period of just over a decade (1985-1996) that I spent full-time at Syracuse University in the USA, one of my principal areas of research was on the methods, media, and tools for online learning that might best promote and support the development of critical thinking skills. The rationale for this research agenda ran as follows:

(1) We are on the verge of a new form of society — a "Knowledge Society" — in which it becomes ever more important for all citizens to have the capacity to become "knowledge workers" — to have the skills of using existing knowledge in order to create new knowledge that may be applied to newly emerging problems and opportunities.

(2) These "knowledge work" skills are dependent on the development of the basic general skills of analysis, synthesis, and evaluation or in other words, "critical thinking skills."

(3) Existing research on learning and instruction strongly suggests that such critical thinking skills are best developed through methods that involve "conversation" about complex problems and issues — this conversation may be between a student and a "mentor" (e.g., as in the "Socratic Dialogue" advocated by Plato), or between groups of interested students engaged in organized discussion that is focused on creative problem-solving, including such well known methods as case-studies, simulation-games, and brainstorming sessions.

(4) The one-on-one Socratic Tutorials and the organized small-group discussion methodologies all have one common characteristic — a small number of students working at the same time together with an exceptionally knowledgeable and pedagogically well prepared teacher/facilitator — a "rare and costly breed." In other words, these

methodologies are effective, but not cost-effective, and, due to their cost, they are under-utilized in reality.

(5) The world is therefore faced with a paradox. Faced by the challenge to constantly innovate in order to keep up with technological change, globalization and the realities of ever more limited resources for the education of ever larger student populations, we shall face another challenge — how to provide the students with the forms of learning experiences that are appropriate for the development of their critical thinking skills.

(6) Given this paradoxical trend in educational practice, towards "providing less and less of what the students need more and more," I set up a research agenda that explored how to multiply the provision of effective group conversations without multiplying the costs.

One essential aspect of this agenda was the investigation of technological solutions that might provide students with the essential deep conversational experience without any increase (indeed with a decrease) of involvement of the teacher in the process. Quite simply, the teacher cannot "converse" with thousands (even dozens) of students at one time in an educationally effective manner — and we do not have the resources to employ the thousands of gifted teachers that are necessary in order to replicate small-group discussion activities for all students with adequate frequency. Therefore, we should research how to automate some of the functions of the skilled and gifted group discussion (or "conversation") facilitator. See Boyd (2004) for a review of conversation theory.

Please note that this issue is very different from the automation of the functions of a skilled content presenter and instructor/tutor. This was to a great degree achieved in the 1960-70's — through audiovisual media technologies as regards content presentation and by programmed instruction as regards tutoring. These methodologies are still today the basis of much the pedagogical practice built into CBT (Computer Based Training) modules, whether presented by CD-ROM or online as a part of an e-learning system. However, such automation of direct instruction, though effective and economically important in relation to the teaching of basic procedural skills, does not serve so well for the development of creative problem-solving and critical-thinking skills.

Our research therefore focused on ways in which small-group problem-solving activities could be in some way "multiplied" through the use of technology. We focused specifically on the Case-Study method and turned to online group learning environments as the way to implement such exercises. This is not the place to present the details of our research and transform this editorial into a scientific paper. Details of the studies, illustrating the evolution of our thinking and the practical methods we employed may be found elsewhere (e.g., Chang, 1994; Romiszowski, 1990, 1994; Romiszowski & Chang, 1992; Romiszowski & Villaba, 2000).

It is sufficient to say here that our researches demonstrated that it was possible to achieve similar, or indeed superior, learning results (in terms of critical-thinking skills development) from online study and discussion of case material (like for example the Harvard Business Cases), as was typically achieved in small-group class sessions led by skilled and experienced facilitators. Furthermore, the online case discussions were so instrumented as to function effectively with minimal involvement of teachers or facilitators. This instrumentation was based on the adaptation of a methodology named Structural Communication (SC) that was initially proposed in the UK in the 1960's as an alternative to the then-popular programmed instruction methodologies, but designed for subject matter and learning situations that demanded critical analysis and discussion of alternatives as opposed to giving correct responses to predetermined, well structured problems (for a full description and some examples, see: Egan, 1976; Hodgson, 1972; Hodgson & Dill, 1971; Slee & Pusch, 1997).

In summary, our research showed that it is possible to multiply and extend the opportunities to incorporate effective group learning activities without the parallel multiplication and extension of the workload of the available teacher/facilitators. This is the key to the solution of the paradoxical situation outlined above. However, it seems that the "key has been lost"! The research being performed at Syracuse University was not the only agenda that was exploring the issues of using new technologies for the improvement of "higher order learning," such as, for example, critical-thinking skills. Many research groups were exploring the potential of, for example, hypertext technologies for the promotion of non-linear and structural thinking. Dozens (if not hundreds) of conferences were held and many papers and whole books were written, all devoted to sharing the results of such research (e.g., Jonassen & Mandl, 1990; McAleese, 1989).

We are now over a decade further down the line. Where are the practical implementations of all this research? A look at the leading commercially available e-learning environments shows that the principal collaborative learning tools we use are the (asynchronous) discussion forum and the (synchronous) chat room. It is, I think, very fair and accurate to say that these two group discussion tools show little if any influence of the several decades of research devoted to effective group collaboration. They are the products of Information Technology, rather than "Knowledge" Technology — and are certainly not good examples of "Educational" Technology. Let us analyze this aspect in some more detail.

ICT and Education: Theoretical and Philosophical Aspects

Is the Medium Really the Message?

Moore (1993) presents an optimistic perspective on the contribution of online technologies to the effectiveness of distance education. Moore, as well as other educational theoreticians, has for many years promoted the concept of "transactional distance," that is, the psychological distance that may exist between student and teacher (or indeed between students), which may not necessarily be related to physical or geographical distance. The argument is that a well-designed and implemented distance-delivered course may, in reality, appear to the participants to be less "distant" than some conventional campus-based courses that cram hundreds of students into lecture halls and offer little or no chance for questions or other interactions. The closing of transactional distance depends on creating and exploiting opportunities for more frequent and richer interaction. Moore illustrates how the new tools for teleconferencing — both synchronous and asynchronous — offer the opportunities for both increasing and enriching interactivity in distance-learning systems. However, the existence of such opportunities does not mean that they will be effectively exploited. What are the design principles that will lead from opportunities to results?

Some authors, for example Guimarães (2002), argue that the new information and communication technologies, when freely available, create a new form of "educational ecosystem" that influences in very fundamental ways the behavior of the creatures that inhabit it — in the case of schools, the students, and the teachers. Thus, the mere existence of a new technological communication infrastructure may significantly transform the nature of education in ways that we may not even have predicted in advance. This line of argument is in line with the theories of Marshall McLuhan, whose observation of such sociological impacts of media on man and society led him to coin the phrase "the medium is the message." But we must be careful not to carry such arguments too far and assume that the media themselves, without attention to the content and the design of the messages they carry, can be relied upon to cause real improvements in education. We should seek to find ways to integrate the opportunities offered by the new media with the needs and capabilities of the "clients" of our educational systems — the students. Once more, we are faced with a design problem that is only in part technological.

Other authors, for example Chadwick (2002), argue that maybe we expect too much from media. Chadwick advocates caution in our reliance on computers to resolve all the problems we encounter in our education systems. Despite decades of research on artificial intelligence, computers are just machines with little of the analytical and critical capacities that are exercised by competent teachers as they help students to overcome their learning difficulties. Chadwick is not alone in arguing that the instructional power of the computer is limited and unlikely to increase significantly. But what about Moore's viewpoint that a major contribution is not so much through student-computer interaction, but through the computer (network) acting as a medium by which interaction may occur between people? This systems view is developed more fully in Moore and Kearsley (1996).

Implications for the Design of Online Learning Environments
Teaching via the Web is an opportunity to create activities that may facilitate learning directed towards the individual objectives of each student. Although the Web (as the physical medium through which the educational message is communicated) favors interactivity, in order for this to occur in a meaningful and useful manner from the viewpoint of the expected learning results, it is necessary to do a lot of basic planning. The Web has emerged as a powerful interactive medium, excellent for the exchange of information. It has stimulated reflection on the need for new educational paradigms. But of itself, the Web is not a quality teaching-learning system. This has to be created, and in this process of creation of quality learning environments one has to consider the older, well-established principles and also the latest discoveries in learning psychology, as well as developments in the new information and communication technologies.

When designing learning activities for the Web, we should try to exploit in an effective and efficient manner the potential of the medium to promote learning activities that are appropriate for the "realities" that we face. These "realities" include the characteristics of the "end-users" — the students whom we wish to teach — who have changed little over the centuries in terms of their basic characteristics of thinking and learning skills, or in their preferred study styles. They also include the characteristics of the "content" — the subject matter to be communicated and learned. This may largely be "new" in the sense that it deals with recent discoveries or current events, but at the same time it is "old" in terms of the types of communication and comprehension challenges that it presents both to teachers/communicators and to students. Therefore, the modern practice of online distance education (e-learning) should be based on teaching-learning principles that in large part were established and experimentally tested in the past. The new technologies bring new ideas and new possibilities, but these do not invalidate the older, well-established teaching-learning principles.

There is, of course, a growing "new" literature base on the design of online learning environments. Unfortunately, as yet, there are more papers published that promote certain philosophies, general models, or specific procedures, than research studies or case reports that document what works and what does not. However, the philosophical and theoretical arguments are an important starting point for practical application and subsequent action research. Many recent authors on the philosophical bases of online learning (e.g., Inamorato, 2002) present arguments for "why" and "how" to implement e-learning that are derived from constructivist approaches to the design of adult teaching-learning processes. Inamorato bases her arguments on research and theory drawn from andragogy and from the work of adult educators such as Paulo Freire. She also identifies some problems that, in practice, impede the adoption of constructivist approaches, especially in the context of online courses for adult learners, suggesting that there is a critical "gap" between philosophy and theory on the one hand, and effective/efficient implementation and management of online learning environments, on the other.

Among the smaller body of papers that report findings, Lewis (2001, 2002) presents some interesting research results on the use of alternative learning activities in an online course for university students. She compares the performance of students on the final exam on different sections of the course. Some of the sections were studied by means of activities based strictly, in an objectivist manner, on the questions used in the final exam and other sections were studied by means of discussions in an electronic forum, a supposedly constructivist learning model. The results of this research are interesting in that they do not show an absolute superiority for either the constructivist or the objectivist lesson designs, but point towards another factor that possibly led one group to achieve greater success than the other: the manner and the intensity of participation in the collaborative online learning activities. So we come up with the (not so surprising) conclusion that how the learners choose to interact with the systems, activities, and materials we provide for them is probably just as important as the specific educational philosophies or learning theories that the design of our activities and materials reflect.

Such results help to demonstrate the complexity of the teaching-learning process and identify some important aspects of the instructional design of online learning environments. Space precludes a more in-depth analysis of the design issues involved. I have elsewhere published a review of some of the relevant literature and a proposed general model (Romiszowski, 2004). This review demonstrates that the existing literature on what works in online learning and what does not is a somewhat confused jumble of different perspectives that have not yet been organized into a general, systemic, view. One example of the confusion that reigns is presented in the next section.

Instructional Design vs. Graphic Design vs. Web Design

Educational projects that employ learning on the Web are developed by a multidisciplinary team that includes professionals, with different training backgrounds and experience, who must all collaborate in an effective and efficient manner for the success of the project. In addition to instructional designers, who have the role of planning of the teaching-learning process on the basis of proven psychological and pedagogical principles, the team may contain other categories of "designers." One of these categories is the graphic designer, a professional whose training and experience is in areas such as communication and art. More recently, a third type of designer has also appeared — the "Web Designer," whose training and experience is most typically acquired in the areas of computer science and programming.

It so happens that, in practice (and increasingly so), it is getting more difficult to distinguish these three types of "designer." In many teams, for both practical and financial reasons, one person may assume more than one role. That is natural and unavoidable, although a bit "dangerous" if the individuals concerned are not adequately trained and prepared to execute all of their roles. But, in many cases, the terminology used to describe the jobs of these professionals helps to create greater confusion as the managers and project leaders of the teams do not respect, recognize, or even understand the profound differences that exist between these three functions, the different areas of theory and practice that each are based upon, and the distinct and important contributions that each can make to the overall success of the project.

It is important that we clearly distinguish the functions of the instructional designer, the Web designer, and the graphic designer. The latter two are more concerned with the development of an overall plan, or design, that has been previously conceived by the creative (but theory-based) work of the instructional designer. In the online learning context, the Web and graphic

designers use a variety of communication and information TECHNIQUES —
they are TECHNICIANS in the true sense of the term. The prior creative
design of a theory-and-research-based solution is the role of instructional
designers and represents an instructional TECHNOLOGY. It is important,
however, not just to distinguish these roles and understand the different areas
of expertise they represent, but also to harmonize these three forms of
different, but equally important, professional contribution to the design and
execution of effective and efficient online distance education projects.

Design and Development vs. Implementation and Management
Some years ago, I had the pleasure and good fortune to be a member of the
dissertation committee of a doctoral study on the "Relational Aspects of
Educational Technology." The doctoral candidate, Joseph Kessels, now a
professor in the Department of Educational Technology of the University of
Twente, in Holland, presented a study that showed very forcefully, through
many longitudinal case studies in a variety of contexts (each one involving data
collection during many years) that educational technology projects are
successes or failures more as a result of the quality of their implementation
than the elegance of their design or the soundness of their theoretical bases. In
other words, a project based on a "mediocre" design, but well implemented
and managed, has a greater chance of success than the best (instructional,
graphical, and Web) designed project in the world that then suffers from
mediocre implementation and management (Kessels, 1993; Kessels & Plomp,
1997). This research emphasizes the importance of giving much greater
attention than is commonly given to the stages of project implementation and
management.

A full treatment of these aspects, specifically in the context of online learning,
and what factors to consider in order not to overlook them, may be found in
Khan (2003) and Romiszowski (2004). In conclusion, therefore, we may make
some important observations. First, it is quite sobering to reflect on the history
of many promising innovations in the field of instructional technology that
have been rejected or mis-applied. One such example is the previously
mentioned Structural Communication (SC) methodology that has been
subjected to detailed study in many research projects over several decades and
has, specifically, been demonstrated to be an excellent manner of implementing
some forms of collaborative learning (e.g., the case study method) in online
learning environments. Yet despite all this research and many publications,
none of the developers and vendors of the leading commercially available
Learning Management Systems (LMS) seem to have made any effort to
implement the tools that would enable the pedagogue to implement such

learning activities and exercises in online courses. We have a long way to go before the reality of e-learning matches up to its theoretical potential.

Thus in conclusion, much is written and said about technology being the "source of the tools that enable the pedagogue to create an appropriate learning environment and implement an appropriate instructional design." However, it seems that the everyday reality is often one of the pedagogue being a slave of the tools that happen to be available. Let us continue in the next section with some provocative comments on one recently emerging "tools" development.

Emerging Trends and Their Impact on Online Learning

Learning Objects and SCORM — Progress or Pipe Dreams?
Before coming to the main point I wish to make in this section, I would like to recount some personal recollections from the past. The project that I joined in São Paulo, Brazil, in 1973, was a part of Brazil's UNDP program that was being executed by the International Labor Office (ILO). This was one of many UNDP supported projects throughout the world that were designing, developing, and implementing education and training systems. In the process, most of these projects would generate new learning materials. It was realized that in many cases the projects in one country would be developing almost the same curricula and courses as other projects in other countries. Therefore, throughout much of the 1970's it was standard practice for all projects that developed any educational or training materials to send a copy to the ILO headquarters in Geneva, where a samples-library was maintained. New projects could benefit by selecting and re-utilizing, or re-purposing existing relevant materials, rather than "re-inventing the wheel" every time.

 In just a few years, the samples-library grew in size so that it filled several large rooms in the ILO building. All projects dutifully sent in copies of the learning materials that were developed locally. But it was found that very few of the projects made any use of the library. There were several reasons for this. They included the following:
— The process of searching through the growing store of samples was inconvenient and time consuming. The materials were mainly print-based, with some audio-visual and video packages as well. They were bulky.
— They had to be read or viewed in order to judge their relevance and quality. So, either all possibly relevant materials had to be copied and shipped out to the new project, or the project staff had to spend considerable time in Geneva browsing through the samples collection.
— There was the question of possible language differences, requiring translation

of the materials. Sometimes, there were (real or hypothetical) regional /cultural differences that may require "localization" of materials.

— The materials were not designed and developed according to a standard design model, so different modules selected from different samples would be quite different in presentation style and instructional design.

— The materials designers were not always competent instructional designers, so the quality of the materials was variable. And the personnel of the new projects also were not always competent to judge the quality of the materials, so there was no guarantee that "good" materials would be selected and "poor" materials rejected.

— The overarching reason, however, was that most projects had some internal or local contextual factors at play that reinforced the local generation of new materials rather than the reutilization of existing materials.

The end result was that, one fine day, just a few years after the start of the UNDP samples-library project, all the materials stored at the ILO office in Geneva were removed and burned. It is worth reflecting on this 1974 case from the perspective of the year 2004. Many recent information technology developments could go a long way towards overcoming some of the problems and issues listed above. Electronic storage could eliminate the physical volume of the collection and also make it available on an "any time/anywhere" basis. Indexing standards and "metadata," such as implemented in SCORM protocols for "learning objects," could help to reduce the time spent in searching the collection and selecting relevant items. There is some progress in the area of automatic translation, but this technology is still rather primitive.

To move on to the "soft" technologies, the use of a uniform set of instructional design standards and methodologies may ensure both compatibility of presentation style and pedagogical quality — provided, of course, that the people applying the standard procedures in specific contexts are skilled in the application of the methodologies. But it is about at this point in the list that the contribution of information technology stops. It is most unlikely that all personnel in all projects will ever be fully skilled and competent in the application of the new technological tools. Mistakes will continue to be made — that is a characteristic of human beings. Also, the existence of new technologies does not ensure that they will be applied — experience shows that personal and organizational attitudes, cultures, or politics do not change just because it is technologically possible, or convenient, for them to change.

Standards for the design of online learning environments are being developed and published, or example by IBSTPI (Richey *et al.*, 2001). But such standards

are often ignored and the imposition of standards is often strongly resisted. Some of the issues that are typically raised and common arguments for the non-re-utilization of previously developed materials include:
— do we wish to encourage a uniform approach to instruction?
— and if so, who is to say which possible approach should be the standard approach?
— what is/are the approach(es) that we should adopt for open and distance learning systems?
But really, all this questioning and discussing is often just a smokescreen to conceal the fact that the people employed on innovation projects just want to "do their own thing."

We are now witnessing the creation of many consortia that seek to collaborate on the design, development, and implementation of learning objects. Projects abound that seek to create banks of reusable mini-modules, appropriately tagged for identification purposes, by means of so-called "meta-data." Unfortunately, the meta data standards by themselves are insufficient to guarantee that all manner of human beings who may wish to make use of the learning objects will in fact be skilled in the use of the systems to select appropriate and reject inappropriate materials. The tools do little to address the pedagogical issues involved in evaluating and selecting learning materials. Also, the tools do nothing to overcome the cultural and organizational resistance that may appear to the very concept of inter-institutional collaboration and materials reutilization. So a host of questions remain to be answered. How should such consortia organize their work so as to ensure a return on the invested effort and resources? Will the promised "learning object economy" ever become reality?

What About the Rest of the Distance Education System?
In addition to the planning and implementation of the distance-teaching process, it is also necessary to give attention to a series of other sub-systems: preparation of evaluation instruments, production of copies of all learning materials, setting up of Websites on the Internet, development of interactive software, control of the logistics of instructional materials and media distribution, ensuring the correct functioning and regular maintenance of all communication media and, finally, the management of this bunch of interdependent activities. All this is included in the original concept of an "Educational Technology" — this implies a much broader-based concept than just the use of computers or television in the teaching process. Let us remember that the original dictionary meaning of the word "technology" is "the application of scientific knowledge to the solution of practical problems."

One should remember that educational technology, in this sense, has a history of research and development that is much older than computers and other such recently invented "technologies."

The message is quite clear. If technology is to "serve the needs of humans" then technological innovations must be developed as "human-machine systems" rather than merely as new "machines." In the specific context of education, the technological trends, described above, make it possible to invent new methods and tools for education at a distance — new "machines." However, if the use of these tools is to result in effective education, then attention must be given to the broader issues of designing and developing effective and efficient systems that apply the new technologies to support the preferred learning styles and exploit the existing learning skills of the students, and also takes into consideration all the broader contextual factors that may influence the adoption/rejection of the innovation and the effectiveness/ efficiency with which it is implemented and used.

A true educational technology, based on the original meaning of "technology," must be based on a sound scientific knowledge base. Hence, the importance of theory and research as a basic foundation and a systems approach as the methodology for the design, development, implementation, and management of online learning systems.

Changes in Perspectives and Paradigms: The Pendulum Swings

The constraints on the size and scope of this chapter preclude the inclusion of a complete and systematic analysis of the trends and probable future of online learning in all its variations and in all contexts where it is practiced. Hopefully, the sum total of the chapters will give such an integrated, yet multifaceted, view of the field. Many longer works have analyzed the field, either from the point of view of theory and research, or from the vantage point of pragmatism and practicality. An example of the former is Romiszowski and Mason (2004), included in AECT's *Handbook of Research on Educational and Communications Technologies* edited by Jonassen (2004). A modest example of the latter is my recent review of trade and practitioner literature regarding the success or failure of e-learning (Romiszowski, 2004). The thoughts and suggestions presented in this concluding section are based largely on these two works.

Some Theory/Research Based Changes in Perspective

From Place-Based to Mobile Learning
The move from home, office or campus based e-learning environments, to the possibility of more mobile access to education, is now occurring at a speed that was difficult to predict just a year or two ago. With the rise in use of mobile telephones, and their convergence with PDAs (personal digital assistants) and similar devices, new possibilities are opened for the intersection of communication and education. In addition to the range of technological issues, there are many interesting social issues that present opportunities for research and the development of new ways of education. There may also be some unexpected side-effects if the students are truly able to study anywhere, anytime, and both receive and provide information and interaction wherever they may be, thus "intertwingling" educational and social communications inextricably.

From Formal Courses to Informal Learning and Discussion Environments
Communities of practice may be formally constituted, but there is increasing scope, with the widespread adoption of flexible approaches to continuing professional education. There is much supporting evidence for more informal approaches, generated from the needs of practitioners. Many issues around the nature and extent of such vicarious learning would seem to be ripe for research over the coming years.

From Structured Learning Activities to Informal Unstructured Learning (and Back)?
Asynchronous discussions and individual messaging are an important component of most models of online courses (Mason, 1998). In order to encourage the implementation of discussion within taught courses, it has been found to be important for course designers to structure the online environment. This involves devising stimulating individual and group activities, providing small-group discussion areas, and supporting students through facilitative rather than instructive moderating (Salmon, 2000). However, this need for structure may seem to be at odds with the opportunities introduced above for informal learning, with potentially much less structured development. Here is a classic case of perspectives and paradigms swinging like a pendulum to and fro between structure and "de-structure," yet to find the ideal point of equilibrium — if indeed there is such a point.

From Offline to Online Assessment of Online Learning — in Search Of New Approaches
Much of the assessment of e-learning, up to recent times, used essentially offline methods, usually with little variation from classroom-based practice.

Many current forms of online assessment are also based on what we have used in the classroom for decades, including quizzes and submission of essays. There has been relatively little attempt to explore new forms of assessment that might be made possible by online interaction, especially among groups of learners. The assessment procedures currently used in tertiary education are particularly ill suited to the digital age in which the ways people use information are more important than simply rote learning and regurgitation of facts.

From Adapting the Learner to the Technology to Vice-Versa: Learning Styles
For learners who come to e-learning from a cultural tradition that is based around a teacher-centered approach, autonomous group collaboration and discussion may not work well. It is suggested that e-learning facilitates different learning styles, but research is needed into the practical application of different learning styles in the design and development of e-learning. Related questions include whether, or to what extent, different types of learners need to belong to a community in order to maximize the chances of success in both the development of the learning community and the meeting of individuals' learning needs.

From the "Online Classroom" to "Something Entirely Different"
Much of online learning to date has been grounded in replication of what can be done offline, in face-to-face encounters or by other technologies such as the telephone. However, just as the ways in which telephone use changed after it became widespread within the population, and in some unexpected ways, so we should expect that the use of online learning will change. What Mason (1998) terms 'pedagogical evolution' refers not to a notion of teaching getting better, or the invention of new and different methods, but working with the technology (itself a moving target) and with course participants to arrive at new perspectives on how learning is best encouraged and supported in the online environment. Whether such new perspectives can be achieved is, to some degree, an assumption, and itself needs testing.

Some Pragmatism/Practicality Based Changes in Perspective

The following additional trends were identified in a recent search of the trade and practitioner literature that I undertook to write a paper (Romiszowski, 2004) on the factors that are seen to lead to success or failure of e-learning. It is interesting to mention that a search of the standard research literature sources, such as the ERIC database, yielded just a handful of relevant papers, while a general search of the WWW, using Yahoo and other search engines, uncovered many hundreds of relevant publications in the non-academic press. Some of the trends uncovered in the analysis of this body of literature are presented below. The comments and criticisms are my own.

From "Presential" to Online, and Now Back to "Blended"
Through the later 1990's, various (e-learning) industry reports painted a picture of a massive swing to Web-based training, especially in the area of end-user computer skills training. Not only was the face-to-face classroom replaced by individualized, technology-based self-instruction, but the Web, as a delivery medium, was seen to dominate, representing a much higher proportion of all such training than CD-ROM, video, and print-based materials combined. Towards the end of the 1990's, these reports claimed that over 70% of all computer skills related training in Fortune 500 companies was delivered via the Web.

However, my review of the last two or three years of trade and practitioner literature related to e-learning paints a somewhat different picture. One of the latest "waves" that is reflected in this literature is the return of classroom based instruction for at least part of the training process. The new fashionable technical jargon is "Blended Learning" and the battle-cry voiced in many articles is "Blended is Better!" This "new wave" should be no news whatever to the instructional design profession, who would (or should) have been preaching all along that a one-size-fits-all approach to training and education just does not work. However, the danger of this new wave, or backward swing of the pendulum from "only online" to "blended is better" is that it seems to be occurring at a "macro" level, substituting whole online courses for "blended" courses, somewhat like a blender mixes up several ingredients to make a cocktail, when in reality, the ingredients have separate and precise roles to play at separate and precise points in the overall program. There is a lack of a systems approach, applied at the "micro" level of instructional design.

From CAI to CMC — and Now Where?
In the formal education sector, under the influence of constructivist philosophies of education and some hard research on the value and effectiveness of collaborative learning, the pendulum has swung from the intensive use of self-instructional materials and a variety of computer assisted instruction (CAI) methodologies, towards the intensive use of online discussion and collaborative learning activities. This is all very well, in theory, but once more, there are associated dangers if the pendulum swings too far.

One danger is that, once more, the swing occurs at a "macro" total-course level, forgetting to apply a "micro-level" systemic approach to the revision of course components as they are transformed from "presential" to online formats. This is illustrated by the previously discussed Lewis (2002) study which investigated the effects of the observed mass-migration in many universities from more conventional course activities to blanket use of online discussion forums as the principal learning activity.

Another danger, illustrated by the previously discussed "Mellon Study" (Doughty, Spector, & Yonai, 2003) is that however appropriate, well intentioned and well designed the swing from didactic instructional models towards collaborative learning models, the end product may not be economically sustainable, on a large scale, in real-life contexts unless serious changes occur in the organization, management, and funding of education as a whole. There is need to dampen the unrestricted and unrealistic swings of the pendulum and seek sustainable ways of achieving the goals expressed in the new philosophies and theories of education, as well as satisfying society's needs for more and better development of higher order thinking skills at all levels of education.

From "CompuServe" to the WWW — and Now to the Educational Utility?
This final section highlights one further trend that seems to be particularly dangerous and particularly unlikely to be sustainable over the long term. I am referring to the sustainability of the Internet, and specifically the World Wide Web, as a principal medium for both the storage/dissemination of information and for the maintenance of communication between the members of professional and (especially) learning communities. Not so many years ago the leading online services providers, such as CompuServe, charged subscribers by the amount of use made of the system — by the minute of connection or the bits of information consumed. Then along came the Internet , which expanded from its military and then academic roots to become everybody's medium of online communication. The Internet user cost is generally independent of the amount of usage made. And then the WWW made possible the vision of "all the world's libraries interlinked and open to all." This is all well and good, but many potential dangers may undermine the long-term sustainability of this new infrastructure.

Some of these dangers are external, such as the proliferation of computer virus attacks that use the Internet to spread and wreak havoc. Others are the internal attacks, such as the growing waves of spam that are cluttering up the system and disrupting much of the other purposeful uses of the Net. But, most dangerous of all in my opinion — because it is seen as one of the major benefits of the WWW — is the free and unbridled publication of just about anything by millions upon millions of authors. This information-garbage will, sooner or later, destroy much of the benefit that the Internet can offer.

There are ways to combat this danger. A viable solution was proposed as long ago as 1986, somewhat accidentally, for it was prepared in the CompuServe era and before the Internet and the WWW had become public property. Dennis Gooler, in his book *The Education Utility: The Power to Revitalize Education and Society* (Gooler, 1986), proposed a model for the regulation and control of education and information networks that may well be the basis for future approaches to the beneficial control of the Internet and WWW environments, upon which we have come to depend so much. And which could so easily be disrupted, not so much by the ill-intentioned actions of external terrorists, as by the well-intentioned, but ill planned and totally unmanaged actions of its main users and beneficiaries. It may be a good idea to search Amazon and other sources on the Web and get a copy of this book before it goes completely out of print, or becomes an expensive cult and collector's item on eBay.

References

Boyd, G. (2004). Conversation theory, In D.H. Jonassen (Ed.), *Handbook of research on educational communications and technology* (2nd ed.) (a Project of AECT). Mahwah, NJ: Lawrence Erlbaum Associates.

Castells, M. (2000). *The rise of the network society* (2nd ed.). Oxford, UK: Blackwell Publishers

Chadwick, C. (2002, Sept./Oct.). Why computers are failing in the education of our children. *Educational Technology, 42(5).*

Chang, E. (1994). *Investigation of constructivist principles applied to collaborative study of business cases in computer-mediated communications.* Doctoral thesis. Syracuse, NY: Syracuse University School of Education.

Doughty, P.L., Spector, J.M., & Yonai, B.A. (2003). Time, efficacy and cost considerations of e-collaboration in online university courses. *Brazilian Review of Open and Distance Learning, 2*(1). Available online at www.abed.org.br

Egan, K. (1976). *Structural communication.* Belmont, CA: Fearon Publishers.

Gooler, D.D. (Ed.).(1986). *The Education utility: The power to revitalize education and society.* Englewood Cliffs, NJ: Educational Technology Publications.

Guimarães, A.S. (2002). Novo ecossistema cognitivo: Pensamentos sobre tecnologias de informação e comunicação e a metamorfose do aprender (The new cognitive ecosystem: reflections on information and communication technologies and the metamorphosis of learning). *Brazilian Review of Open and Distance Learning, 1*(1). Available online at www.abed.org.br

Hafner, K. (2002, May 2). Lessons learned at Dot-Com U. *New York Times.*

HjNawawi, M., Asmuni, A., & Romiszowski, A.J. (2003). Distance education public policy and practice in the higher education: The case of Malaysia. *Brazilian Review of Open and Distance Learning, 2(2).* Available online at www.abed.org.br

Hodgson, A.M. (1972). Structural learning in social settings: Some notes on work in progress. *Programmed Learning and Educational Technology, 9*(2), pp.79-86.

Hodgson, A.M., & Dill, W.R. (1971, Jan./Feb.). Programmed case: Reprise of the missfired missive. *Harvard Business Review*, pp. 140-145.

Inamorato, A. (2002). Web-based adults' courses: searching for the right pedagogy. *Brazilian Review of Open and Distance Learning, 1(*1). Available online at www.abed.org.br

Jonassen, D.H. (2004). *Handbook of research on educational communications and technology.* Second Edition. Mahwah, NJ: Lawrence Erlbaum Associates.

Jonassen, D.H., & Mandl, H. (1990). *Designing hypermedia for learning.* Berlin/New York: Springer-Verlag.

Kessels, J.W.M. (1993). *Towards design standards for curriculum consistency in corporate education.* Doctoral dissertation. Enschede, NL: University of Twente.

Kessels, J.W.M., & Plomp, T. (1997), The importance of relational aspects in the systems approach. In C.R. Dills & A.J. Romiszowski (Eds.), *Instructional development paradigms.* Englewood Cliffs, NJ: Educational Technology Publications.

Khan, B.H. (2003). *E-learning strategies.* Beijing, China: Beijing Normal University Press.

Lewis, B. (2002). The effectiveness of discussion forums in online learning. *Brazilian Review of Open and Distance Learning, 1(1)*. Available online at www.abed.org.br

Lewis, B. (2001). *Learning effectiveness: Efficacy of quizzes vs. discussions in on-line learning*. Doctoral Dissertation, Syracuse University School of Education.

Litto, F. (2002, January). The hybridization of distance learning in brazil: An approach imposed by culture. *International Review of Research in Open and Distance Learning*. Available online at www.irrodl.org

Mason, R. (1998). Models of online courses. *ALN Magazine, 2(2)*. Available online at www.aln.org/alnweb/magazine/vol2_issue2/Masonfinal.htm

McAleese, R. (1989). *Hypertext: Theory into practice*. Norwood, NJ: Ablex.

Moore, M.G. (1993). Theory of transactional distance. In D. Keegan (Ed.), *Theoretical principles of distance education* (pp. 22-38). London: Routledge.

Moore, M.G., & Kearsley, G. (1996). *Distance education: A systems view*. Belmont, CA: Wadsworth.

Richey, R., Fields, D., Foxon, M., Roberts, R.C., Spannaus, T., & Spector, J.M. (2001). *Instructional design competencies: The standards* (3rd ed). Syracuse University, NY: ERIC Educational Resources Information Clearinghouse on Information Technology.

Romiszowski, A.J. (1990, Jan./Mar.). Computer-mediated communication and hypertext: The instructional use of two converging technologies. *Interactive Learning International, 6(5)*.

Romiszowski, A.J. (1994). *The development of critical thinking skills through online electronic discussion in virtual groups*. Proceedings of the 17th International School Psychology Colloquium, Campinas, Brazil, International School Psychology Association.

Romiszowski, A.J. (2003). The future of e-learning as an educational innovation: Factors influencing project success and failure. *Brazilian Review of Open and Distance Learning, 2(2)*. Available online at www.abed.org.br

Romiszowski, A.J. (2004, Jan./Feb.). How's the e-learning baby? Factors leading to success or failure of an educational technology innovation. *Educational Technology, 44*(1), pp. 5-27.

Romiszowski, A.J., & Chang, E. (1992). Hypertext's contribution to computer mediated communication: In search of an instructional model. In M. Giardina (Ed.), *Interactive multimedia learning environments: Human factors and technical considerations on design issues.* Berlin: Springer-Verlag.

Romiszowski, A.J., & Mason, R. (2004). Computer-mediated communication. In D.H. Jonassen (Ed.), *Handbook of research on educational communications and technology* (2nd ed.). Mahwah, NJ: Lawrence Erlbaum Associates.

Romiszowski, A.J., & Villaba, C. (2000). *Structural communication and Web based instruction.* Proceedings of the ED-MEDIA2000 International Conference, Montreal.

Salmon, G. (2000). *E-moderating: The key to teaching and learning online.* London: Kogan Page.

Slee, E.J., & Pusch, R.S. (1997). Structural communication: A tactical paradigm for implementing principles from constructivism and cognitive theory. In C.R. Dills & A.J. Romiszowski (Eds.), *Instructional development paradigms.* Englewood Cliffs, NJ: Educational Technology Publications.

Taylor, J. (2003). *Fifth generation distance education: Managing on the edge of chaos.* Keynote presentation and workshop at the 2003 ABED International Conference on Distance Education, Porto Alegre, Brazil. Brazilian Association for Distance Education/Associação Brasileira de Educação a Distância (ABED)

Tiffin, J., & Rajasingham, L. (2003). *The global virtual university.* London, UK: Routledge-Falmer.

Chapter 23

Online Learning and Knowledge Building Environments

Marlene Scardamalia

Marlene Scardamalia is the Presidents' Chair in Education & Knowledge Technologies at OISE/University of Toronto and the Director of the Institute for Knowledge Innovation and Technology, a worldwide network of innovators working to advance the frontiers of knowledge building in various sectors. She is the inventor of CSILE (Computer Supported Intentional Learning Environments), which was the first networked knowledge building environment for education. Her work has led to several honors and awards, including a fellowship at the Center for Advanced Study in the Behavioral Sciences, election to the U. S. National Academy of Education, and an Ontario Psychological Foundation Contribution to Knowledge award. Dr. Scardamalia was the K-12 theme leader for Canada's TeleLearning Network of Centres of Excellence, 1996-2002.

New knowledge media provide new opportunities and means for addressing fundamental problems in education. But there are now so many designs for online learning that choosing between them is difficult. Advancing the state of the art will require greater clarity regarding different possibilities and the ways in which designs reflect different underlying theoretical frameworks and research bases. This chapter highlights a particular form of online environment, a knowledge building environment (KBE), and contrasts it with online environments designed more specifically for course delivery and distance learning. Although a KBE can be used for these purposes, its distinctive strengths emerge in contexts — educational and other — where the emphasis is on knowledge creation and sustained idea improvement.

Socio-Cognitive Dynamics of Knowledge Building

In his book *The Mind's New Science,* Howard Gardner elaborated the role of cognitive science in uncovering what goes on in minds and between people as they solve problems. Through studying expert and novice problem solvers in action, cognitive scientists have uncovered the cognitive activity that underlies expert problem solving. Carl Bereiter and I focused our early studies in this field on novices who were on a trajectory to become experts, as opposed to novices who evolve into experienced non-experts (Bereiter & Scardamalia, 1993). Results from this work, from the broader base of cognitive, socio-cultural, and constructivist theorists, from the history of science, self-organizing systems, and memetics (the evolution of ideas), have made it possible to identify the socio-cognitive dynamics of knowledge building. Salient features include:

Knowledge Processes
- direct engagement with problems of understanding
- work with emergent rather than fixed goals
- evolution of goals toward higher-level formulations of problems
- self-organization around promising new directions rather than mandated work on other-directed and scripted activities
- work at the edge of competence
- self-monitoring and self-correction, without undue dependence on external evaluation
- engagement with knowledge intensive processes that lead deeper and deeper into the field of inquiry
- productive use of idea diversity
- risk taking
- responsibility for high level socio-cognitive activities such as setting and refining goals, providing resources, and identifying different perspectives

Cultures of Innovation
Cultures of innovation enable the processes listed above and encourage collective responsibility for knowledge creation. They additionally support the discourses and reflective processes required for continual idea improvement, ensuring that innovation becomes the cultural norm.

There are parallels in the processes of knowledge creation across disciplines and cultures, and a developmental trajectory that extends from early, playful work with ideas to the sustained, disciplined creativity of mature knowledge workers. By taking advantage of these parallels and continuities we can identify generic systems for the design of KBEs. Before elaborating these we take a closer look at online learning.

Online Learning, Distance Education, and the Internet

To this point, online learning seems to have been less driven by theory than by cleverness in converting traditional learning forms into e-learning parallels. The following table itemizes some of these parallels:

Traditional Technologies	Online Technologies
mentoring	telementoring
discussion	threaded discourse, bulletin boards, chat
lectures	broadcast media, online lectures
conferences	teleconferencing, telepresence, streaming video
courses	courseware
research projects	computer-mediated projects
consultation (office hours)	email

The first exposure most educators have to computer networks is through distance media such as email, computer conferences, Website visits, teleconferences, and courseware. Online learning environments are now so inextricably related to the use of the Internet that many educators have never experienced the potential of a local-community network or intranet. And many fail to see its value for students who meet face-to-face.

There is less skepticism regarding the value of intranets in business contexts where there are real costs, and loss of productivity associated with covering old ground over-and-over. Under these conditions the value of local-area networks to support organizational memory is obvious. Education, in contrast, has been built around tasks and activities designed to cover old ground. Creating an organizational memory under these conditions could, arguably, result in little more than a record of naïve understandings. But even in organizations where the value of organizational memory is evident, a gap typically exists between "knowledgeware" and "courseware." The former is used to support the knowledge productivity of the organization, the latter for online learning. The result is separation of e-learning from the ongoing creative work of the organization. A KBE aims to integrate the ongoing creative work of the organization with learning.

Theoretically it should be possible to get from distance learning to knowledge building. However, designs have not advanced in this direction. Courseware, for instance, has come to include administrative systems that facilitate the creation of course lists, presentation of course outlines, and compilation and reporting of grades. Users become increasingly dependent on these adjunct facilities to run their courses. This fine-tuning of environments for specific educational activities leads to the need for different online environments for different purposes. KBEs, in contrast, aim to make explicit and support interactions that lead to knowledge advances across a broad array of contexts.

Knowledge Building Environments (KBEs): Interactions Within and Across Communities, Intranets, and the Internet

Carl Bereiter and I introduced the concept of "knowledge building" into the educational literature in the 1980's to bridge the gap between innovation as carried on in the larger knowledge society and similar work that can be carried on in education. Knowledge building is activity focused on the generation of new knowledge and the continual improvement of ideas. Knowledge builders do more than learn — they produce ideas that have a life beyond their own minds, beyond personal notebooks, and beyond short-lived discussions. Knowledge building requires that ideas be revisited, revised, linked to other ideas, raised to higher status, reframed in light of new findings, and evolve into new forms. The overarching goal is to transform education by shifting emphasis from staying abreast of information to contributing to the development of new cultural artifacts; from individual learning and achievement to the building of knowledge that has social value; from focus on tasks and activities to a focus on continually improving ideas; from a focus on set course outlines to systems of emergence and self organization; and from a predominantly facilitator-directed discourse to distributed knowledge building discourses (Bereiter, 2002; Scardamalia, 2002).

The Power of a Local Area Network
Our design of online environments started in 1983 before the World Wide Web. Computer Supported Intentional Learning Environments (CSILE) made use of a local-area network to create a multimedia community knowledge space. From the first use to this day we have experienced enormous potential in the use of this community space for transforming the intellectual life of classrooms and courses.

Advantages of Long-Term Organizational Memory
CSILE was not management, planning, or productivity software retooled for educational use; it was technology specifically designed to support knowledge creation. With traditional educational media, ideas are recorded in course papers; blackboards and walls serve as display spaces, with items posted there for approximately 2-6 weeks. E-learning spaces often mirror these qualities. For example, if we consider courseware environments such as WebCT, it supports threaded discussions, with ideas recorded in notes that are not revised after they are saved. The time during which those ideas are actively reviewed and worked on is limited to the duration of the discussion. Course papers are typically submitted online as end-of-course contributions. KBEs, in contrast, provide

long-term organizational memory, and supports for continually improving ideas in both local- and wide-area networks. There are many opportunities for ideas to come to life after periods of inactivity, through multi-faceted searches and reconstructions of knowledge spaces designed to keep ideas from being encapsulated in discussion threads or other bounded contexts.

Supports for Interactions Within and Between Communities
KBEs place a high priority on interactions between people and ideas, enabling a flow of information within and between organizations, disciplines, sectors, cultures, and ages, and encouraging participants to work continuously at the cutting edge of their understanding and the field. Consistent with this goal is the need for integrated Intranet/Internet protocols.

The Evolution of a Knowledge Building Environment

Growing numbers of online environments are described as KBEs in the literature on Computer Supported Collaborative Learning. This review focuses on the evolution of CSILE, the founding KBE, which is now in second-generation form as Knowledge Forum®. Knowledge Forum, in turn, supports the *Knowledge Society Network*, a cross-age, cross-discipline, cross-sector, cross-culture community of knowledge building communities. CSILE was first prototyped in 1983, in a university course of over 300 undergraduate psychology students. By 1986 a fully-functioning networked version was in daily use in an elementary school, thanks to Bob McLean who created a network database that had the capabilities of a conferencing system (it allowed comments on other people's entries, for instance, and display of the identities of contributors) but it had the cumulative properties of a database. The second-generation environment, Knowledge Forum, published by Learning in Motion (http://www.knowledgeforum.com), offers both browser and client versions, with the Internet enabling Knowledge Forum's distinctive supports for advanced knowledge processes to operate in both local- and wide-area contexts. The ease with which it has been possible to integrate local and global initiatives supports the theoretical framework from which designs were derived.

The Knowledge Society Network
This network supports work in education (grade 1 to graduate), health care, community, and business contexts, in the Americas, Asia, and Europe. Nurturing a knowledge-building culture within the local community remains a vital and challenging part of this work. The Knowledge Society Network is an example of a knowledge network as defined by Stein, Stren, Fitzgibbon, and MacLean (2001). Knowledge networks:

- produce new knowledge through transdisciplinary research on problems as they are experienced across international boundaries in different contexts;
- produce 'operational' knowledge, acquired through context-bound interactions among multiple sectors of expertise; and
- disseminate knowledge by blurring the boundaries between participants and researchers, thereby ensuring that 'global' knowledge is introduced locally and that 'local' knowledge shapes and, at times, redefines global knowledge. (p. 4)

There are striking differences between what typically goes on in classrooms and courses and what goes on when experts are at work on knowledge problems. In the former the focus is on tasks and activities generated by teachers and facilitators; in the latter the focus is on problems of understanding growing out of previous problem solving efforts. Online environments for knowledge creation require rendering hidden dynamics of knowledge building transparent and embedding them in enabling environments that reflect knowledge work as it goes on in knowledge-creating organizations. If we accept this analysis of the challenge underlying the design of KBEs, then an environment that is only effective in educational contexts is not a KBE. This design framework, along with our understanding of the dynamics of knowledge building presented above, has informed the design of CSILE/Knowledge Forum, as elaborated below. For a more detailed account see Scardamalia (2004).

CSILE/Knowledge Forum is built around a multimedia community knowledge space that provides supports for the creation of notes and for displaying, linking, and reconstructing ideas to produce increasingly high level, coherent, and novel accounts. Shared, user-configured design spaces allow users to deal with idea diversity while going beyond given contributions. In addition to providing organizational memory, the evolution of ideas is evident in the citations, references, and build-ons that accompany the rising status of ideas that have undergone review and achieved broader usefulness. Opportunism in idea advancement is supported by multi-faceted search, notification, and other supports for linking people and their ideas. A customizable environment enables within- and between-community explorations that extend and provide continuity in knowledge work.

Through these and other means it is possible to view ideas from multiple perspectives, and for teams to form and dissolve, with members working individually or through group authored notes and views. Multimedia, multiple-literacy supports provide a way in for all participants to a common discourse, and flexible build-on structures provide an alternative to downward branching threaded discourse. Idea connectedness is further facilitated through annotation, citation, and reference links, and advanced knowledge processes are supported through scaffolds and supports for elaborating problems of understanding. "Rise-above" notes and views help users synthesize ideas, create historical accounts and archives, and reduce redundancy. Idea improvement is further reflected in publication and high-order conceptual frameworks.

Research tools work in the background of Knowledge Forum to automatically record activity patterns, which can then be fed back into the work as it proceeds, rather than waiting until the end of a unit of work to provide feedback, when it is too late to make adjustments. Across many contexts, the use of CSILE/Knowledge Forum has led to advances in textual, graphical, and computer literacy, as well as to depth of inquiry, collaboration, and a host of mature knowledge processes (Scardamalia, Bereiter, & Lamon, 1994; Scardamalia, 2002).

New Developments and New Design Challenges

Anytime, anywhere, anyone access to technology has become the mantra of online education, with newer mobile technologies such as Personal Digital Assistants (PDAs) promising to bring this goal ever closer. From the point of view of knowledge building, the goal is not ubiquitous computing but rather pervasive knowledge building. Just as the Internet can support quite varied forms of online work, ranging from courseware to knowledge networks, mobile technology can be used in quite varied ways. For example, PDAs can support personal work and customized assignments, creating a sense of individual ownership. But from the perspective of knowledge building theory, mobile devices have greater educational potential as intermediaries between individual minds and minds in society. This design challenge is evident in research by Nirula, Woodruff, Scardamalia, and MacDonald (2003), and Teplovs, McLean, and Scardamalia (1999). Mobile devices are used to beam ideas to community spaces and to download Knowledge Forum's community spaces to mobile devices for offline work, and later updating the community space. Pervasive knowledge building places the design challenge at the intersection of socio-cognitive and technological innovations. As important as technology is, it alone cannot do the job. If socio-cognitive and technological innovations are not in synchrony — if there is no interest, no time, no use — then anytime, anywhere, anyone access makes little difference.

As the design of educational technology becomes a theory-driven science, and as digital technologies become embedded in the normal workings of society, we should see a shift from current popular and divisive questions such as "Is online or face-to-face education better?" to questions that are concerned with realizing the full potential of new knowledge media: "How can we maximize the affordances of traditional and new knowledge media to improve education?" In the course of answering the latter question designers will take advantage of the full range of local- and wide-area-network possibilities for transforming education. At that point online learning as a specialty sub-field will likely disappear and education will move a step further toward a progressive design science that channels the potential of new media into increasingly effective theories and designs.

References

Bereiter, C. (2002). *Education and mind in the knowledge age.* Mahwah, NJ: Lawrence Erlbaum Associates.

Bereiter, C., & Scardamalia, M. (1993). *Surpassing ourselves: An inquiry into the nature and implications of expertise.* Chicago: Open Court.

Gardner, H. (1985). *The mind's new science: A history of the cognitive revolution.* New York: Basic Books Inc.

Nirula, L., Woodruff, E., Scardamalia, M., & MacDonald, P. (2003). Handhelds in a grade two classroom: Innovations to support knowledge-building and epistemic agency. In K. T. Lee & K. Mitchell (Eds.), *Proceedings of the International Conference on Computers in Education 2003.* Hong Kong: ICCE.

Scardamalia, M. (2002). Collective cognitive responsibility for the advancement of knowledge. In B. Smith (Ed.), *Liberal education in a knowledge society* (pp. 67-98). Chicago: Open Court.

Scardamalia, M. (2004). CSILE/Knowledge Forum®. In *Education and technology: An encyclopedia.* Santa Barbara: ABC-CLIO.

Scardamalia, M., & Bereiter, C. (2003). Knowledge building. In *Encyclopedia of education* (2nd ed., pp. 1370-1373). New York: Macmillan Reference, USA.

Scardamalia, M., Bereiter, C., & Lamon, M. (1994). The CSILE project: Trying to bring the classroom into world 3. In K. McGilly (Ed.), *Classroom lessons: Integrating cognitive theory & classroom practice* (pp. 201-228). Cambridge, MA: MIT Press.

Scardamalia, M., Bereiter, C., McLean, R.S., Swallow, J., & Woodruff, E. (1989). Computer supported intentional learning environments. *Journal of Educational Computing Research, 5*, 51-68.

Stein, H.G., Stren, R., Fitzgibbon, J., & MacLean, M. (2001). *Networks of knowledge: Collaborative innovation in international learning.* Toronto: University of Toronto Press.

Teplovs, C., McLean, R., & Scardamalia, M. (1999, June). *A Model for distributed knowledge networks.* Poster presented at the National Educational Computing Conference, NECC-99, Atlantic City, NJ.

Chapter 24

Learning Without Boundaries:
Prospects and Perspectives for Online Learning

Robert J. Seidel

Dr. Robert J. Seidel is Research Chief Emeritus at the Army Research Institute. He attained his PhD in Experimental Psychology from the University of Pennsylvania and was a NIH Special Postdoctoral Fellow at Stanford University. He has taught full-time at Denison University, and part-time at George Washington University, the University of Maryland, and Trinity College in Connecticut. He has a varied and rich experience base spanning over 36 years of research, development, and management in the areas of experimental design, individualized instruction, computer-administered instruction, technology transfer, distance learning, and evaluation.

From my education at the University of Pennsylvania graduate school in psychology, I developed a healthy skepticism for the theories of learning and theoretical developments in general in psychology. Perhaps it was because there was no messiah at the University of Pennsylvania, but we were trained with a critical eye towards systems and methodology in the field of experimental psychology. Indeed, it was probably because of the rigor of our training that the first paper I attempted was entitled "Carry Your Theories and Paradigms Lightly." While the paper per se was never published in its original format, the ideas have been incorporated in all of my talks and writings over the years.

Early on, I was impressed in particular with the way learning theorists such as Hull and other behaviorists attempted to generate a theory of learning to cover all species and all forms of learning when the paradigms that they were using were limited to runways or t-mazes, the students of which were rats. My mentor, Dr. William A. Shaw, reinforced my skepticism; and we collaborated on some rather unique learning experiments with hooded rats. It was our position that in order to determine how this species might be able to learn, we needed to provide the paradigms within which they could express the limits of their abilities. To support this position, we used the paradigm consisting of a circular tabletop, upon which we placed five objects from a pool of 30 objects. The experimental conditions ranged from combinations of constant spatial relations or identical five objects trial to trial, to various combinations of one object constant, just spatial relations constant, or nothing constant trial to trial. Food was placed behind one object on the tabletop each trial. The fascinating result for us was the fact that in two conditions these animals showed the capability for abstract reasoning, heretofore unheard-of with this species. The group that had only spatial relations constant learned that food was in a sense "over there" in relation to the other objects. Perhaps even more fascinating was the fact that the control group, with nothing constant except the fact that food existed on the table, learned over time to approach a given object only once until they found food. The only analysis that made any sense to explain these data was an informational analysis (Shaw & Seidel, 1969).

When I switched my career towards studying how humans learned in complex environments, I carried this perspective with me. Therefore, whenever I approached an innovation in the field of psychology, I was probably as quick to look for the limitations of the innovation as well as appreciating its value in solving problems. When I first started working in the field of technology for instruction, I was so taken with the possibilities for creating reliable, competent instruction that I saw the use of computers as the way of ridding all instruction of poor teachers. After all, I also had a great skepticism about the competence of teachers. Gradually, my arrogance gave way to maturity; and I was able to see technology-augmented instruction and even broader, technology-supported education, as integral components for vastly improving the education and training systems.

Total Systems Projects

While at HumRRO (The Human Resources Research Organization), over 35 years ago, my staff and I initiated *the single largest total systems* R&D program in computer-based training for the Army. Our concerns were how to develop, and/or assemble the necessary components of a total computer-based training system (hardware, software, courseware, and instructional decision model, or pedagogy) in order to provide and maintain optimal online learning conditions for the student. We set about to put together instructional decision models which would consider the subject matter structure, the nature of the individual student characteristics, and the information to be presented as components of our total system. Unfortunately, the hardware and software technologies which we were using were not up to the task of providing the artificial intelligence required to accomplish our goals. Nevertheless a number of significant outcomes did occur. For example, my staff devised a very superior time-sharing system, using 110k bytes, to monitor and provide for interactive learning across 10 terminals! The added capability was provided, again the first of its kind, to allow the separation, physically and logically, of instructional content from the logic of the pedagogy by which it was organized. This approach was subsequently used by a very large civilian supported effort called TICCIT and then subsequently Micro-TICCIT. The latter project was supported by the National Science Foundation and produced materials commercially that were used in public education from varying classes and disciplines, such as English, language arts, biology, and mathematics.

Our staff therefore produced a very profound example of technology transfer from the military to the civilian community. Also, during the time frame of this R&D project, called Project IMPACT, a number of technical reports, publications, and presentations at national conferences (Seidel & the IMPACT Staff, 1969, 1970; Stelzer & Garneau,1972) communicated not only the uniqueness of the approach, but as well spawned other computer related, call them online related, projects at HumRRO. We experimented with the inclusion of early graphics tablets as a natural interface for writing COBOL programs in our R&D efforts in problem solving. Dr. Ron Swallow, biophysicist and electrical engineer, invented a cost-effective, 3D color and surface graphics system in 1972, far in advance of others working in that area (Swallow, 1974). This attracted support from IBM among others, who saw the potential of such a system for simulations in training.

We also used that total system as a research environment experimenting with variables thought to be important in the development of instructional models, for maximizing learning in a problem solving situation. The uniqueness of our approach was that we were not concentrating, as many academic research programs were at the time, on instruction consisting of about half an hour to one hour's worth of learning. We developed a course in COBOL with 16 hour's worth of self-contained, online instruction. In our paradigm we both duplicated and expanded the concept of learner by treatment interaction to include learner by treatment by task interaction. We found that high performing learners in one part of the COBOL course were not the same as the high performing learners in the second half of the course (Seidel et al., 1978). We also showed the value of using confidence measures as well as the accuracy of student answers, and developed a model for predicting learning in this problem solving environment.

One of the most significant related total system efforts occurred when we developed for the Postal Service an online training system for postal letter sorter operators. In this instance, we literally bent metal to build computer terminals and incorporated a scaled down version of the above noted innovative technology, the CHARGE System, (Swallow, 1977). The Postal RFP called for a representation of 5000 pieces of mail, whereas with Dr.

Swallow's invention, we could literally simulate an infinite number of types of envelopes and handwriting. Moreover, we were able to mimic the movement of mail from right to left in front of the operator in the same manner as in the operational environment.

We evaluated this online system with our prototype; and it was used in the Cleveland Post Office until it just wore out. We showed through our analysis of error data that the Postal Service could save $270,000 in one year at one site if it adopted our system. It therefore could save millions of dollars if they were to adopt our system in large cities around the country. Unfortunately, the internal political warfare between factions in the Postal Service prevented this from happening. This bittersweet experience reinforced one of the most important lessons that seems to be repeated again and again throughout the attempts to institutionalize online learning/training. Quite simply, the organizational as well as individual stakeholders must be part of any project, from start to finish, if the goal is to implement and institutionalize the results of research and development.

Evaluation of Technology Innovation

As a result of this insight, at HumRRO we shifted our interests to emphasize evaluation of technological innovations, from the narrow project focus to the broader program level.

We took on a role of observers and synthesizers regarding developments and projections of new generations of educational technology, studying the barriers and needs in education/training to be addressed in order for implementation of innovations to occur. We organized symposia for the National Science Foundation to document these factors.

In one symposium, "Computers and Communications," technologists, educational researchers, and government personnel were assembled to synthesize technological developments and to forecast the educational implications of technology including the issues surrounding economic, regulatory, institutional, and instructional needs as well as requirements for future R&D. Many technological predictions by the participants concerning lower costs for increasingly greater speed and power of computers did happen with the development of micro-microchip technology. One prediction, significant for the field of training, was that interactive videodisc instruction would make the next important contribution, and this was borne out. But the educational predictions did not occur as predicted. There were competing predictions made by the experts concerning the shape of the development and use of computers in education during the following 10 years from 1975 to 1985. For example, Don Bitzer predicted the development of a large centralized computer system connected to one million terminals providing cost-effective instruction for the educational masses. At the other extreme was the prediction by Seymour Papert, predicting entire educational reform through the use of high-powered, locally controlled, interactive computers in order to facilitate learning by doing.

As indicated at the time, "Both of the above approaches are examples of valid educational uses of computers. The important point is that they reflect different educational purposes. Unfortunately for the conference, these issues were never explicitly addressed. The result was that many participants argued at length at cross purposes" (Seidel, pp. xvii-xix of the Preface in Seidel & Rubin, 1977). Neither prediction exactly came to fruition. However, approximations to the technological capabilities have appeared with the resources provided for mass access via the Internet to materials and experts on a worldwide basis, and to highly interactive, flexible, local, personal computing because of the incredible advances in microchip technology. But the wholesale revolution in education has not taken place as either of these projections imply. It needs to be emphasized that the cross purposes and lack of explicit uniting of stakeholders with purposes for the use of online learning has been a continuing stumbling block to widespread educational implementation of online learning (Seidel, 1992).

In 1980 with support from the National Science Foundation, HumRRO convened a national conference on Computer Literacy composed of educational technology experts. The purposes of the conference were to provide a means for discussion and movement towards greater consensus on the needs in goals nationally for computer literacy and to discuss the research, implications, and methods for infusing computer related objectives and activities into curricula at various age levels, to identify the issues and the barriers in developing national goals to achieve computer literacy, and generally to plan the directions and national goals for computer literacy for a five-year period. The resultant published volume presaged the transformation of our society into a postindustrial or information society (Seidel, Anderson, & Hunter, 1983). It also highlighted, therefore, the need for transforming our educational institutions, including teacher training and K through college into computer literate systems.

By 1983, our staff reviewed two decades of CAI projects, and found that there were a number of positive accomplishments made in the field of online learning in education. As noted, there were significant achievements in prototype development, conceptual demonstrations, major implementations, dissemination, authoring, and innovative learning environments (Kearsley, Hunter, & Seidel, 1983). It is also true that as Becker's surveys showed, the number of computers available in schools continued to increase over the past 20 years (Becker, 1991, 2000). The problem is that in education not that many computers have found their way into students' hands for a variety of uses in the classroom. In his 1991 study for example, Becker found "... the number of students in one school who can simultaneously use computers remain small compared to the number of students who can be simultaneously served by teachers, blackboards, books, worksheets, manipulative materials, or even film and video projectors" (p. 389). Moreover, Becker noted in his 2000 report that larger numbers of computers have become available, yet usage by teachers in U.S. schools is still quite limited. Computers in schools "...number over 10 million..." yet "the most common frequent uses are in computer and business classes" (p. 2).

Subsequently, at the Army Research Institute, our efforts on evaluation for online learning continued. In examining the early artificial intelligence instructional systems, we pointed out the need for employing theoretically and empirically based, separate instructional modules, in order to determine the contribution of various student and subject matter variables to online learning (Park, Perez, & Seidel, 1987). We developed an approach to aid developers of online instruction in the evaluation and selection of authoring systems (Seidel & Park, 1993).

With all of these rewarding experiences, the recurrent most important lesson which I learned during my 40 years of research and development concerning the use of computers for online instruction has been that overwhelming advances in technology have continued to push the technical boundaries far beyond the users' ability and/or motivation in the field of education and training to determine how best to exploit those advances. Time and again, those of us who were joining in the effort to push the fields of training and education into new areas found some willing listeners and participants. Yet, there always seemed to be a widespread, vested interest in retaining the old way of doing things. As a result of the latter, my interests shifted from research and development and the study of new learning principles, to the fascinating complexities regarding individual and organizational users of technology. These were synthesized in a recent chapter speaking to the issues regarding the management of implementing successfully education and training technology (Seidel & Cox, 2003).

Models for Evaluating Technology

Along the way, a couple of models were developed to describe these complexities and to suggest ways that the users, which we preferred to call "stakeholders," might become partners in the implementation of change. The first thing that my colleagues and I emphasized in developing one model (see Figure 1) was the fact that the introduction of the computer in and of itself does not constitute a uniform treatment in education. Secondly, evaluating the effects of the use of computer technology requires a much larger unit of time and is normally thought of as foreign to experiments; e.g., a school year. Thirdly, it was clear to us that the environmental variables play a significant role concerning the effectiveness or not of computer use. These variables must include the classroom, the school, the school system, and the surrounding community. All these entities (as well as the student) are stakeholders. The model attempts to measure the impact of technology on instruction or education in general and one must measure the process of implementation as it is affected by how it affects the stakeholders.

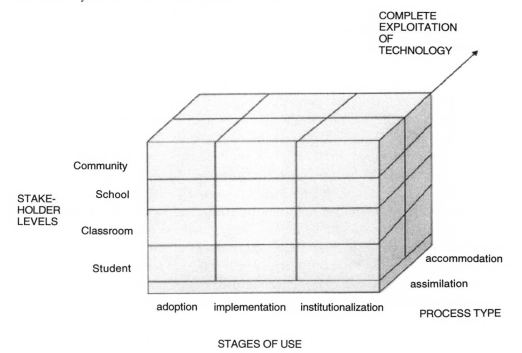

Figure 1. A model for technology evaluation (from Seidel & Perez, 1994).

In this model in order to effect the institutionalization of the technological innovation, we proposed that three stages of use needed to be addressed while including all stakeholders as partners in this effort. The first stage of use we call adoption, where there is a single initial use of the technology within an administrative unit (e.g., one course within a department). In the next stage, where the innovation is used beyond the initial adoption such as across the board in an entire school system, we call implementation. Finally, the ultimate goal is to institutionalize the innovation, which means that it has become an integral part of the entire education or training system.

In order to accomplish this, the model proposes that there are two processes which must be considered: assimilation and accommodation. By assimilation, we mean the user gets to incorporate words or the innovation into the existing education or training environment such as by employing the computer to accomplish record-keeping or other very familiar tasks and a quicker, better, or cheaper, or some combination thereof, capacity. Only after this has happened is the user more likely to be open to accommodate the education or training environment to exploit the capabilities of the new technology. This would allow for development of collaborative work among students from local area networks to perform simulation tasks otherwise not able to be performed, and have the computer serve as a true partner in exploration of solutions to all manner of problems (Seidel & Perez, 1994). *When one considers research in such a context there is a requirement for the linking all the dimensions of research, management of instruction and training, and the operational education/training system itself.*

The implementation of a pilot program exemplifying the point cited above was accomplished with the establishment of The Training Technologies Field Activities program (TTFA). A partnership was created between the research arm of the Army working closely with the policy headquarters, Training and Doctrine Command (TRADOC), and the pilot schools, which were the training sites for the new program. Products were developed by this approach, including a computer managed instruction product, a procurement techniques for a particular schools use, and a technology transfer model to apply to all Army schools following the pilot efforts. There was some success, however severe budget cuts undermined the required infrastructure to support continuing the TTFA work. Nevertheless, the program itself did provide support for the partnership, stakeholders model (Seidel & Perez, 1994).

Clearly, from my experience, the stakeholders must be convinced that the proposed technology would provide a value added capability, or possibly a cost-effective capacity, for their education or training system.

Cost-Benefits of Technology

In the military, it was not difficult to provide cost and safety justifications for using simulations and simulators instead of expensive operational equipment. Therefore, technical training in the military became a welcome test-bed for new technologies. A prime example of this in the Army was the development and use of helicopter simulators at Ft. Rucker (e.g., Caro & Easley, 1966a, 1966b). Use of the technologies for knowledge and skills based training in general, however, did not proceed apace until budget reductions with accompanying loss of key instructional personnel demanded more cost-efficient ways of training. Questions arose concerning how we could train personnel without having them leave their jobs. Could we keep people productive on the job while simultaneously offering them training on site? Answers to these questions resulted in providing training from an instructor at a distance. It was easy to demonstrate the cost savings from less travel and fewer instructors, while accomplishing the same objectives (e.g., Wisher, Curnow, & Seidel, 2001; Wisher & Priest, 1998). In the first study, for example, the National Guard customarily required students taking an administrative, clerical course to transport themselves to a central location and to be housed at local facilities for number of days. In one instance, by allowing these trainees to stay at home and use auditory teletraining, the National Guard saved on the order of $30,000. Moreover, the distance learning group performed as well or better than the on-site group.

Such conclusions, combined with reduction in force in the military, led the U.S. Army in 1998 to establish a vast, multi-billion dollar, organized program to provide training on demand at the duty station, rather than forcing trainees to travel and needing to provide housing and other logistics support for the training (The Total Army Distance Learning Program is described at its Web-site: www.tadlp.monroe.army.mil). So the irony is that reform in training is taking place, not because of the promise of greater cognitive and skill achievement (which many of us old futurists contended), but because of the necessity of reducing costs. Providing training on demand can accomplish this. Computers in education can be an extremely cost-efficient way of providing instruction to K-12 poor children who otherwise would not receive quality education. The literature is replete with instances of the value of drill and practice and other CAI techniques, which provide such a function. In one study, sponsored by the National Science Foundation, in which I was principal investigator, I developed a cost-productivity-gain index based upon a very simple finding that it costs so much money per day in public education per student. We were able to show that through the use of the computer-augmented instruction, absenteeism in those pilot schools dropped significantly. This was accompanied by increases in achievement. The school system thereby gained more value for the dollars expended on the children's public education. I should add that we made a strong recommendation that in order for the gains to be maintained or increased, the superintendent would have to appoint a full-time coordinator out of his office to oversee the implementation and integration of computing technology into the educational system. Although he nodded in complete agreement and turned to his assistant requesting money be set aside for this, it did not happen (Seidel, 1978). Today, the selling points to school systems to incorporate online learning have capitalized on the fact that expert personnel in various fields can be made available as resources for the learner. With the increase in the number of computers available in K-12, and with the development of the Internet, resources have become almost limitless for the learner.

In general, the education field, while providing all sorts of interesting and unique ways that people might learn through the use of technology, has also seen a growth in distance education as a way of further accomplishing cost avoidance. Costs of education have gone up tremendously in recent years. It is not unusual to see annual costs per student at private universities to be $40,000, or more; and, for example, for middle-class students to attain a degree at college or university, the computer and distance education have become a cost-effective means to achieve this goal. The university has benefited by not having to hire as many new, full-time faculty in order to accomplish their goal of providing education for all those deserving students.

A Model for Distance Learning

Distance learning, distance education, e-learning, and online learning — I see these as a natural progression of a continuing search for the realization of technology integrated with instruction. Many of the old problems do not go away, however; they simply get represented in a new venue. The quality of courseware design, the evaluation of resources available on the Internet, and validation procedures continue to represent serious challenges for the would-be user of online learning. And as with all other innovations in strategies for learning, the user must not be taken in by commercial claims that online learning is a single solution for all education or training problems.

A few years ago while I was consulting with NATO on the implementation of distance learning, we developed a framework for characterizing learning systems (see Figure 2).

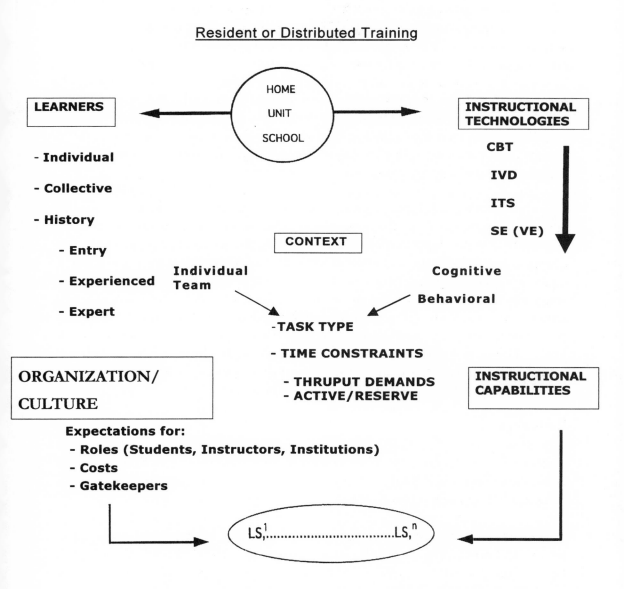

Figure 2. Toward a comprehensive and responsive training/learning system (from Seidel & Chatelier, 1994).

The framework takes into account tasks to be learned, their context (group or individual, equipment based or not, etc.), the organization culture, the number of learners per unit time, deadlines for training or education to be completed, the various technologies available (from programmed texts, computers, networked systems, to virtual reality, etc.). Finally, the location(s) is/are recommended for completing portions of some, or all, of the learning tasks. These locations may be at home, the job site, or a classroom environment. The point that I emphasize is that each case demands careful attention to the variables involved prior to making the decision that we would use distance learning (online learning) and/or other strategies as part of the overall learning system for a particular task. Online or distance learning is shown as one component of a strategy within a learning system.

The view here is that online learning will take its rightful place in the future of education and training as one component, albeit a most significant one, in a revolutionized conception of the fields of education and training. There is no question that it has been a catalyst along with the computer for a shift in the educational and training focus towards student centered learning. If there is a single caveat, it is that with the increasing, and sometimes overwhelming, amount of information being made available online at an almost exponential rate, it becomes even more important to have an effective evaluation system in place. This is absolutely necessary if we are to help the learner sift through the available resources, separating the vital from the vacuous information, and thereby create a viable system of learning without boundaries.

References

Becker, H.J. (1991, January). How computers are used in United States schools: Basic data from the 1989 IEA computers in education survey. *Journal of Educational Computing Research, 7(4)*.

Becker, H. J. (2000, July). Findings from the teaching, learning, and computing survey: Is Larry Cuban right? Proceedings, January 2000 School Technology Leadership Conference of the Council of Chief State School Officers, Washington D.C.

Caro, P. W., & Isley, R. N. (1966, April). Changes in flight trainee performance following synthetic helicopter flight training. Paper for Southeastern Psychological Association meeting, New Orleans, Louisiana. *HumRRO Professional Paper 1-66*, AD-630 484 ED-015 422, Alexandria, VA.

Caro, P.W., & Isley, R.N. (1966, November). Helicopter trainee performance following synthetic flight training. *Journal of the American Helicopter Society, 11*(3); HumRRO professional paper 7-66, AD-646 157.

Kearsley, G., Hunter, B., & Seidel, R.J. (1983, February). Two decades of CBI research: What have we learned?, *HumRRO Professional Paper 3-83*, Alexandria, VA.

Park, O., Perez, R.S., & Seidel, R.J. (1987). ICAI: Old wine in new bottles, or Is it a new vintage? In G. Kearsley (Ed..), *Artificial intelligence and education*. Reading, MA: Addison-Wesley.

Park, O. & Seidel, R.J. (1989). A multi-disciplinary model for development of intelligent computer-assisted instruction. *Educational Technology Research and Development, 37*, pp. 72-80.

Seidel, R.J. (1978, August). D.C. Secondary School Project for Adopting Computer-aided Instruction, Final Report to National Science Foundation.

Seidel, R.J. (1992). It's 1992, Have you found your computer yet? *T.H.E. Journal.*

Seidel, R.J. (1997). Lessons learned or lessons not yet learned (but often revisited) about the design, application, and management of learning technologies. In R.J. Seidel & P.R.Chatelier (Eds.*), Learning without boundaries: Technology to support distance/distributed learning*. New York: Plenum Press.

Seidel, R.J., Anderson, R., & Hunter, B. (1983). *Computer literacy: Issues and directions for 1985*. New York: Academic Press.

Seidel, R.J., & Chatelier, P.R. (1994). Overview Chapter. In R.J. Seidel & P.R. Chatelier (Eds.), *Learning without boundaries: Technology to support distance/distributed learning*. New York: Plenum Press.

Seidel, R.J., & Cox, K.E. (2003). Management issues in implementing education and training technology. In H.F. O'Neil & R.S. Perez (Eds.), *Technology applications in education: A learning view*. Mahwah NJ: Lawrence Erlbaum Associates.

Seidel, R.J., & the IMPACT Staff (1969, March). *Project IMPACT: Computer administered instruction: Concepts and initial development.* HumRRO Technical Report 69-3, AD-685 457.

Seidel, R. J., & the IMPACT Staff (1970, December). *Project IMPACT: Computer administered instruction: Description of the hardware/software subsystem.* Project IMPACT Staff, HumRRO Technical Report 70-22. AD-721 159   ED-047 528.

Seidel, ·R.J., & Park, O.K. (1993). An evaluation of CBT authoring systems: Need a data base. In R.J. Seidel & P. R. Chatelier (Eds.), *Advanced technologies in training design.* New York: Plenum Press.

Seidel, R.J., & Perez, R. (1994). An evaluation model for investigating the impact of innovative educational technology. In E.L. Baker & H.F. O'Neil (Eds.), *Technology assessment.* Hillsdale, NJ: Lawrence Erlbaum Associates.

Seidel, R.J., & Rubin, M., (1977). *Computers and communications: Implications for education.* New York: Academic Press.

Seidel, R.J., Wagner, H., Rosenblatt, R.D., Hillelsohn, M.J., & Stelzer, J. (1978). Learner control of instructional sequencing within an adaptive tutorial CAI environment. *Instructional Science, 7,* pp. 37-80.

Shaw, W.A., & Seidel R.J. (1969), Informational context as a determinant Of what can be learned. *Acta Psychologica, 31,* pp. 232-260.

Stelzer, J., & Garneau, J. (1972, August). *Project IMPACT: Software documentation : Overview of the computer administered instruction subsystem,* HumRRO Technical Report 72-21. AD-751 776   ED-067 883.

Swallow, R.J. (1974, December). *CHARGE, Interactive graphics system terminal: Theory of operation.* HumRRO Technical Report 74-26.

Swallow, R.J. (1977). Charge and its potential in CAI. In R.J. Seidel & M. Rubin (Eds.), *Computers and communications: Implications for education.* New York: Academic Press.

Wisher, R.A., Curnow, C.K., & Seidel, R.J. (2001). Knowledge retention as a latent outcome measure in distance learning. *The American Journal of Distance Education, 15(3),* pp. 20-35.

Wisher, R.A., & Priest, A. (1998). Audio teletraining for unit clerks: A cost-effectiveness analysis. *The American Journal of Distance Education, 12(1),* pp. 38-51.

Chapter 25

Diffusing E-Learning:
Myths, Questions, and Experiences

Lorraine Sherry

Lorraine Sherry, PhD, is a Senior Research Associate with RMC Research Corporation in Denver. Her primary responsibility has been to lead RMC Research's Technology Team in evaluating a number of Technology Innovation Challenge Grants (TICG) and Preparing Tomorrow's Teachers to use Technology (PT3) Catalyst and Implementation grants. She has done extensive research on online discourse and technology teacher leadership.

The Myths

Those of us who are familiar with Eastern mythology will recognize the fabled "Wish-Fulfilling Cow"— a mythological beast that grants humanity all of its sustenance and desires. On the other hand, those who are familiar with Western fables will recognize "Pandora's Box"— a box that was thought to be full of wondrous gifts, but that actually contained a swarm of flies, mosquitoes, and other noxious insects. How shall we approach online learning? What questions should we be asking as we approach the cow or attempt to open the box? Can these questions be answered? As an evaluator of Technology Innovation Challenge Grants (TICG) and Preparing Tomorrow's Teachers to Use Technology (PT3) grants, my questions generally revolve around progress toward meeting objectives and measuring outcomes, exploring mediating factors that facilitate or hinder the growth of online learning, discovering emerging trends, and creating models that can be "bootstrapped" from collected data. Another important outcome is lessons learned; that is, the answer to the question, "If you had it to do over again, what would you change?"

I think the first step is to dispel some of the myths by introducing a touch of reality. All proposals start with a collage of facts and myths: rosy predictions of how shifting from bricks to clicks will transform learning, whether by students, teacher candidates, or teacher practitioners. Unfounded, untested hypotheses or propositions, which I call "myths," arise when there are insufficient data to provide a basis for informed decision making. Only through an array of mixed methods including surveys; in-depth interviews and focus groups; observations; and a thorough analysis of teacher-created and student-created products, artifacts, and shared documents, can we begin to acquire the sobering touch of reality that can dispel the initial myths and expectations and help us to develop recommendations. Those recommendations can then guide the decision makers to implement the types of midcourse corrections that are required to keep a project on track.

I will touch on some of those myths and my own experiences in this chapter. I will also focus primarily on the process of diffusing online learning and professional development programs for teachers and teacher educators within schools and universities, and within programs that are embedded in local, state, and national organizations, rather than on the process of designing, developing, implementing, delivering, and evaluating online learning per se.

My First Online Course

My very first online learning experience was at the University of South Florida (USF) when I was a Master's degree candidate and graduate assistant. The telecommunications course, appropriately offered via telecommunications, using the Florida Internet Resources Network (FIRN) system and the university server, was made up of ten highly structured modules with some broad expectations of content-related online interactions, either with the professor of record, or with a cadre of students who had already taken the course and served as mentors in return for free email and server space. Those were the days of the command line interface (i.e., pre-Mosaic, pre-Netscape, pre-Internet Explorer). Fortunately, the professor decided to offer a blended course — a very new idea in 1990 — with all participants meeting face to face for the first and last class sessions. The rationale was not "We will offer online courses to save money," but rather, "Let's explore new modes of distance and distributed learning and see what we can learn from them." Students came from all over Florida, some driving for a day and a half to meet in Tampa and associate faces with the names that they would later see on the class discussion lists.

Things went well for the first two weeks after the initial meeting, while the course still focused on technology basics, such as "how to use email," "how to use gopher," "how to use Archie and Veronica," "how to ftp a document," and the like. However, when the class activities turned to treasure hunts, Internet research, and creating lessons and classroom activities that used the Internet, my fellow students were overwhelmed by the amount of time, effort, and good humor that was required for effective searching and the creation of a modicum of scholarly work. We continually ran into carrier drops, the "World Wide Wait," difficulties navigating back to some reasonable starting point in a hypertext document, the primitive types of keyword searching that could be done at the time, a plethora of UNIX commands, acronyms to be memorized, and an unimaginable amount of disorganized content of often dubious veracity. Clearly, the myth that answers *to any ill-defined problem can be found on the Internet* was dispelled very quickly. Online discussions were limited to the "request-respond" interaction: someone posted a question and all participants were expected to post an answer. Often, answers involved more venting and socializing than course-related content. The "request-respond-reply" interaction (Sherry, 2000; Sherry, Tavalin, & Billig, 2000) was nonexistent.

As the course became more problematic, one of my fellow graduate assistants came up with a bright idea: "Why not have a virtual student lounge? We can set up an additional discussion list where students can post informal messages that are not related to the course content, but which will enable them to do more sharing with their classmates, who may, in turn, be able to help them with their problems." This novel idea was approved by the department, and it succeeded in motivating students to mentor one another as they attempted to find operational solutions for their problems. Moreover, it built a group memory or longitudinal continuity (Crook, 1994a, 1994b), an online community of practice with its own peculiar culture and norms (Lave & Wenger, 1991), and personal, supportive relationships between list participants; that is, the "glue" that was needed to hold the class together (Herrmann, 1995). In the virtual student lounge, request-respond-reply interactions became the norm rather than the exception. Thus, the myth that *all interactions are expected to be either administrative in nature or content-related* was dispelled by the introduction of collegial and supportive interactions into a structured course. The course proceeded well from that point onward. In addition, visiting the virtual student lounge built comfort, confidence, and competence among the students who used the lounge to discuss ideas, problems, and solutions.

One example stands out in my mind. About halfway through the course, a classmate posted a question to the lounge:

> This week's assignment is about creating a lesson that uses the Internet. All the lessons and activities I see on the Internet, and which the rest of the class are discussing, are targeted to middle and high school students. Where can I find some lessons for kindergarteners?

One response was: "I don't think there are any. There's your niche. How can you take what you do every day with the children and see how telecommunications can expand or enhance it?" By the time the course was over, my colleague had created a Halloween lesson titled "Monsters, Monsters, Monsters" for her class. A more polished version, located at http://www.2cyberlinks.com/monster.html, went on to win several awards and was used subsequently by hundreds of youngsters throughout the United States.

When I taught my first blended course at the University of Colorado at Denver (UCD) in 1999, I used the same technique, and I found that the virtual student lounge concept worked just as well as it had nearly a decade ago. It afforded students a way to overcome the isolation and anonymity often associated with online courses. At about the same time, I used my USF classmate's question as the starting point for creating the Teachers' Internet Use Guide (http://www.rmcdenver.com/useguide) for RMC Research Corporation. This modular, online professional development product walks teachers through a four-step process of designing, developing, implementing, and assessing a standards-based lesson that uses the Internet (Hoffman, Sherry, Lurie, & McDaniel, 2001). Currently, the guide has about 900 mirror links from teachers, educators, and professional organizations; a steadily growing bank of teacher-created lessons; and hundreds of annotated URLs with lessons, activities, and resources that can assist teachers as they begin to infuse the Internet into their classrooms.

The UCD Internet Task Force

As I entered the doctoral program at UCD in fall 1994, just as Netscape Version 1 was released, an ad hoc group of students and recent graduates, together with our academic advisor, Brent Wilson, founded the UCD Internet Task Force. Having already encountered obstacles with infusing telecommunications and online learning into post-secondary course work, we set out to create a networked learner support environment for both the Information and Learning Technologies (ILT) Master's degree program and the Instructional Technology (IT) thread of the doctoral program. The task force had three broad objectives: to support the School of Education in its move to join the emerging Internet culture through a variety of online and offline tools, support, training, and policy initiatives; to develop ways that the Internet could be used as a knowledge-building tool within graduate classes and seminars; and to reflect on and conduct research on users' needs, support tools, adoption processes, cultural change, and collaborative learning communities. I felt that stage models of adoption (Dwyer, Ringstaff, & Sandholtz, 1991; Hall & Hord, 1987) were informative but limited. Thus, I based my own theoretical foundation on Rogers' (1995) *Diffusion of Innovations*, thinking that Rogers had identified all of the variables, including the five perceived attributes of innovations, which moderated technology diffusion within an organization.

That was another myth that needed to be dispelled. In fact, Rogers stated:

> *One problem with measuring the five attributes of innovations is that they*
> *may not in all cases be the five most important perceived characteristics for a*
> *particular set of respondents. The solution, of course, is to elicit the main*
> *attributes of innovations from the respondents as a prior step to measuring*
> *these attributes as predictors of the rate of adoption. (p. 209)*

In spring 1995, several of our members carried out a short research project
(Ryder & Wilson, 1996; Sherry & the Internet Task Force, 1996; Wilson, Ryder,
McCahan, & Sherry, 1996) that involved several activities: a literature review of
factors that were critical to a user's choice to join the Internet community; and
a user survey of faculty and students in the IT department to determine their
levels of use, objectives for use, and obstacles faced in the use of the Internet
as well as their preferred performance and training supports. To explore some
of these issues in greater depth, some of us interviewed a group of students in
the IT seminar who were exploring the Internet, developing home pages,
conducting online searches, uploading and downloading files, and participating
electively in discussion lists. We followed up the group interview with a short
email questionnaire in fall 1995 and collected responses from seven of the
original thirteen interviewees. Finally, we interviewed three faculty members to
determine their role in setting a tone for the department's local culture.

Five mediating factors emerged from the collected data:
- *Clear benefit and value.* There needs to be some compelling need for a
  student to engage in the discomfort attending the learning of new
  technologies.
- *Developing self-efficacy.* Lack of self-efficacy is common when a person
  both believes in the value or necessity of learning and using some
  new technology and simultaneously feels incompetent or unable to
  learn how to use it.
- *Cultural/personal compatibility.* Technology occasionally conflicts with
  people's learning styles, self-concepts, and lifestyles.
- *Proper scaffolding.* People need a scaffold or support structure as they
  engage in complex performances outside their normal repertoire of
  skills.
- *Finding a voice and having something to say.* Here, users are more
  concerned with the content of their messages and products rather
  than with the technology. This is especially important when dealing

with a textbased interface where no social or nonverbal cues are available.

The first four factors were identified in prior research (Bandura, 1982; Collins, Brown, & Newman, 1989; Hodas, 1993; Rogers, 1995), but the fifth factor surprised us until we read Berge's (1997) article on computer conferencing and the online classroom. I felt that this was the factor that contributed to the success of the USF virtual student lounge.

Our task force continued its investigations over the next two years:

- presenting our research (Sherry & Myers, 1996; Sherry, Wilson, & Ryder, 1995; Wilson *et al.*, 1997);
- conducting a developmental research study (Sherry & Myers, 1998) on the process of collaboratively designing a mediated learning environment;
- collaborating with Dan Surry of the University of South Alabama in several AECT panels on technology adoption and diffusion for the next three years;
- repeating the user survey in 1997; and
- following up with more interviews, focus groups, and analysis of electronic portfolios and other online artifacts created by UCD graduate students.

This ongoing research built the foundation for my dissertation, and my publications and presentations became the core of my electronic portfolio — the first electronic portfolio to be defended in the UCD School of Education. All of this work blended seamlessly with my ever-growing list of program evaluations at RMC Research.

The Boulder Valley Internet Project

Shortly after joining RMC Research, my first assignment was to evaluate the Boulder Valley Internet Project (BVIP) (Lawyer-Brook & Sherry, 1997; Sherry, 1997; Sherry, Lawyer-Brook, & Black, 1997), sponsored jointly by the National Science Foundation and the University of Colorado at Boulder. The project focused on the integration of telecommunications throughout the Boulder Valley School District (BVSD) and emphasized inquiry-based and problem-based learning. Because the BVSD was a complex system, my team used multiple qualitative and quantitative measures in order to produce converging lines of inquiry. I looked at technology adoption from the viewpoint of the user, as well as the complex needs of the organization and identified three distinct strands or clusters of internal factors that directly impacted Internet use in the teacher-trainees' classrooms: *technological factors, individual factors,* and *organizational factors.* However, in the in-depth interviews, focus groups, and case studies conducted with the teacher-trainees, a fourth thread emerged: *instructional factors* (Lawyer-Brook & Sherry, 1997; Sherry, 1997; Sherry, Lawyer-Brook, & Black, 1997). The affordances of the Internet as an instructional tool; that is, its opportunities for action (Allen & Otto, 1996; Norman, 1993), were unclear. I observed examples of incompatibility with teachers' needs and wants, diminution of observable benefits, and lack of relative advantage as compared with traditional classroom practices, especially for those teachers who had given up searching the Web for resources after finding no information that they could actually incorporate into their curriculum.

Throughout the evaluation, I also found that there were major differences between Rogers' (1995) theory and the reality of the BVIP, and that diffusing the Internet throughout a large school district could not be fully described by the Rogers model. The BVSD was a decentralized institution, characterized by site-based management. The evolution of the Internet was exponential, and the professional development content shortly became outdated. The use of a peer trainer-of-trainers model limited diffusion horizontally to teachers, media specialists, and technology coordinators, and the use of the Internet to support personal productivity and instruction did not diffuse vertically to the administration or the policy-making bodies. External factors, such as a clash of vision between the school board and the teachers, exacerbated the situation. Clearly, the myth that *diffusion of the Internet throughout an organization may be explained by internal factors alone* needed to be dispelled. In the case of the BVSD, external factors played an important role in the diffusion process.

Regarding internal factors and organizational learning, what I observed was similar to Schein's (1996a) lack of alignment of subcultures within a learning organization, where the visions of *the corporate folk* were not aligned with those of *the ordinary folk* nor with *the techie folk,* which often led to rejection of the innovation rather than renewal, reaffirmation, or reinvention (Hodas, 1993). Throughout the evaluation, I found myself addressing many of Rogers' (1995) concerns and reflecting on his findings as I collected data from surveys, interviews, focus groups, a work group, examination of system logs and artifacts, observations, and an embedded case study. The situation in the BVIP was aptly described by Zaltman, Duncan, and Holbek, 1973 (cited in Rogers, 1995):

*Low centralization, high complexity, and low formalization facilitate
initiation in the innovation process, but these structural characteristics make it
difficult for an organization to implement an innovation. (p. 381)*

Another lesson I learned from this project echoed Elmore's (1996) findings: If
individual teachers considered the innovation to be a tool that made their work
easier and more efficient, then they were likely to adopt it. However, if
adoption of the innovation meant that they had to change the cores of their
instructional processes—especially without an observable incentive structure to
reward their efforts—then in all likelihood, the innovation would not be
adopted. Thus, the myth of *if you build it, they will come* was summarily dispelled.

We did find some pockets of excellence, though. Students' growing interest in
cyberspace was one factor that persuaded some teachers to take the time to
learn how to use the Internet and access the district's telecommunications
system. As one teacher commented, "The students are pushing the
technology." In several elementary school classrooms, the technology resource
person reported that student engaged learning was enhanced by immediate
access to the Internet and exchange of information with other learners, by
communication on a high level through online discussions, and through global
collaboration with colleagues. Moreover, with the Internet, distant resources
became local for the students. Real time collaboration made learning more
relevant, and the students were highly motivated and enthusiastic to learn.

We conducted some observations at one of the high schools, at which a teacher
had assembled a multi-age group of students who were dissatisfied with the
traditional form of science instruction, but who were basically interested in
science as a field of study. Since the high school shared a campus with the
local elementary school, the teacher gathered students from 4th through 12th
grades and created a multidisciplinary, project-based science course
encompassing such diverse subjects as oceanography and astronomy. Using
problem-based learning techniques, she allowed her students to generate their
own questions and take ownership of their research projects. A typical
question was, "What happens as you go deeper and deeper into the ocean?"
Students researched the problem on the Internet and produced several good
projects and products, some of which were exhibited at the Denver Natural
History Museum. They also built a class home page that was linked to the
Jason Project, with which they had collaborated. The students worked in teams
and developed good negotiating and communication skills. Most of all, they
were energized by the online learning process and were proud of their
accomplishments.

An interesting finding from the BVIP was that there is a particular stage in a teacher's professional growth at which the innovation decision takes place. Revisiting the data from the project, I developed a new model that integrated the adoption process with the learning process. As teachers learned about new technologies, specifically email and the Web via the trainer-of-trainers program, and as they began to use these new resources in their classrooms, they moved through four stages of change in a more or less sequential process: learning from their peers; experimenting and adopting; co-learning and co-exploring with their students; and finally, reflecting and either rejecting the adoption decision or reconfirming it and continuing the cycle to become the next round of peer trainers. The success of this "Learning/Adoption Trajectory" process hinged on communicating a shared vision among all members of the educational system, including teachers, administrators, parents, the community, and the policy-making bodies, and on gaining principals' support for student use of the Internet.

My model was a bit different from Rogers' (1995) model of the innovation decision process, in which the decision occurs prior to the implementation phase and the confirmation occurs after the implementation phase. Although the four stages of *teacher as learner, teacher as adopter, teacher as co-learner,* and *teacher as reaffirmer/rejecter* were clearly evident, additional research was necessary to establish the reliability of this model. That research was subsequently performed during The Web Project.

The Web Project

Conceptualized as a project to "Create a Web of Evidence" and to improve student learning through the use of multimedia and telecommunications, The Web Project was one of the 19 Technology Challenge Innovation Grant winners from the first competition in 1995. Over its five years of funding, The Web Project created a set of strategies that impacted teachers' instructional practices and students' learning processes and gave a new meaning to the term "learning community." Based in Vermont, The Web Project established a system that linked ten participating schools and districts and multiple statewide, cooperating initiatives in online discussions of student work. Art and music students posted works in progress — traditional art, digital art, and MIDI compositions — and received constructive feedback from teachers, community practitioners, mentors, artists in residence, musicians at distant sites, and other students. Middle school students from three schools across the state of Vermont conducted book discussions, facilitated by staff from the Vermont Center for the Book and their teachers. Teachers, in turn, discussed challenges;

conducted action research, and shared results; and co-developed rubrics to assess process, progress, and outcomes. As a result, The Web Project contributed substantially to knowledge of effective practice for conducting online dialogue and design conversations, and went on to win national recognition for its innovative activities, which are still being sustained.

In contrast with the USF telecommunications course, which was originally based on the myth of *standardizing student learning rather than faculty practice*, The Web Project supported individualized student learning. The philosophy of The Web Project foreshadowed an important finding from Twigg's (2001) *Innovations in Online Learning* report and provided

> *. . . appropriate human interaction with experienced online instructors providing thoughtful remarks and monitoring class-wide conversations in ways that foster student-to-student interaction and reinforce student responsibility for their own learning. (p. 2)*

An important feature of The Web Project was the creation of two guides for teachers, students, and mentors, which were used throughout the program. The first was "A Guide to Online Critique" (Tavalin, 1998), which set forth a set of agreements about how online critique should function: describe in detail what you are trying to do; request feedback, but be open to more than what is asked for; give specific and detailed comments that are based on helping a person reach his/her intent; and communicate using a cycle of request-respond-reply. The second was "A Guide to Online Discussion" (Tavalin & Boke, 1998), which identified lessons learned from previous online experiences and set forth five guidelines for successful dialogue about current events or assigned readings:

1. Follow the conferencing structure.
2. Stick to the discussion topic.
3. Respond to each other's postings.
4. Ask for what you need.
5. Know in advance that the discussion may nonetheless appear disjointed.

The request-respond-reply cycle was emphasized. The guide also contained standards and a simple 3-point scale for assessing student performance in reading comprehension, informed decision making, responding to text, and use of evidence and data to support decisions and stands taken by students throughout the online discussions.

Through effective professional development, clear guidance, strong visionary leadership by the project director and her cadre of experts, strong project support, stress on meeting state and national standards for student achievement, opportunities to disseminate information within the project and at national professional conferences, and relatively plentiful resources, The Web Project produced outcomes in several major areas:

- creation of student products, some of them exemplary, including musical compositions played by the National Symphony Orchestra;
- student and teacher acquisition of technology skills;
- student acquisition of content area knowledge in the areas of music and art;
- student motivation to learn;
- creation of a new paradigm for learning communities that linked teachers, mentors, students, and outside experts in an online network of co-learners and co-explorers that pre-dated Carroll's (2000) vision for the Preparing Tomorrow's Teachers to Use Technology (PT3) initiative;
- advancement of knowledge about online conversation;
- changes in teacher practice; and
- validation of some theories and advancement of other theories about technology innovation adoption and diffusion.

Specifically, the Learning/Adoption Trajectory process, first developed through research with the BVIP, was validated, expanded, and refined (Sherry, 1998). Data for the 1998-99 academic year were gathered from:

- interviews, focus groups, and classroom observations that took place during site visits to participating schools;
- surveys of students, teachers, and administrators;
- participants at project retreats during summer 1999; and
- an analysis of artifacts, such as teacher and student publications and project publications and CDs, threaded discussions, and student projects, posted on The Web Exchange, the project's Web site.

A cross-case analysis was performed between participating sites to identify general trends, and the data were analyzed to ascertain the early impact of the project as a whole on student performance.

When our team compared the trends from the cross case analysis of The Web Project with the original model of the Learning/Adoption Trajectory, it became clear that participants in The Web Project had progressed beyond the teacher as co-learner and teacher as reaffirmer/rejecter stages. The traditional role of the teacher was being restructured. Professional networks of participating teachers were expanding, and teachers were sharing their ideas online, beyond the bounds of their schools and districts. Teachers were creating and sharing standards and rubrics rather than simply following them. At some cooperating schools, teachers began to institute trainer-of-trainers programs at the schools or among their online learning networks, using students and peers as assistants and co-trainers. At one school, the role of a teacher was restructured so that she could serve as a mentor for other teachers across the entire project.

Thus, in contrast with findings from earlier instructional technology projects, a fifth stage must be added to the model as it applied to The Web Project: Teacher as leader (Sherry, Billig, Tavalin, & Gibson, 2000). In this stage, experienced teachers expand their roles to become action researchers who carefully observe their practice, collect data, share the improvements in their own practice with their peers, and teach new members of the learning community. Their skills become portable. It is at this point that the system really began to build capacity. Moreover, this is the stage at which the local community expanded beyond its initial bounds to encompass a wider community, linked through an electronic learning network to the environment in which it was situated.

While their students used feedback from the mentors and experts in the online community to revise, refine, and republish their works, participating teachers mentored one another and worked through common problems using their online network. Their learning process was similar to Schein's (1996b) view: as members of a learning organization, they began to unfreeze their perceptions as their experiences with telecommunications failed to match their preconceived notions; went through a change and refocusing process; and then a few of them refroze their concepts to match their current experiences. In contrast, the project as a whole never became caught up in the refreezing process. Instead, the project director, and most of the teachers, mentors, and students all became quite good at soliciting feedback and using it for continuous learning and improvement. Two of the participating teachers reflected:

> *There were many pages of discussions when a mentor crossed the line of personal well being for the student and the teacher. Some of these discussion threads reached beyond the objectivity of the project and exchanged personal feelings, opinions, and experiences. I feel that clarifying the places and positions that we*

come from and discussing these online can support another way of opening our minds and expanding our life experiences, while we maintain our friendship.

Networking among teachers builds bonds, shares resources, and helps us to utilize materials. Keeping connected online lets us know that there are others going through the same process. It opened avenues of teachers learning with students. There was a positive impact on the student to know that the teachers were learning too.

A key new technology strategy that emerged from The Web Project was to keep a central focus on online professional and learner-centered exchanges that examined student work and products (Sherry, Billig, Tavalin, & Gibson, 2000). The give and take interactions among students, teachers, and professionals helped all participants understand their own thinking strategies and the contexts of others. As the extension of the original model indicates, the use of telecommunications can evolve to expand the professional networks of teachers and experts. This includes involving them in collaborative professional development planning with technology professionals, as well as building the skills, knowledge, and in-depth understanding of the content and pedagogy required for effective teaching and learning, both online and in the traditional classroom. This was the strategy that led us to build on the work of The Web Project and initiate the Teacher Education (TEN) PT3 grant project in 2000.

As with many of the original hypotheses that are formed through scientific research, data collection and hypothesis testing allows researchers to dispel old myths or theories and either refine old models or build new models. Concurrently, Hagenson (2000) validated the five-step Learning/Adoption Trajectory model with College of Education faculty members in her thesis at Oklahoma State University. Thus, the new model was generalizable to university faculty members as well as teacher practitioners. Discussing the fifth and last stage, she reported:

This stage consists of all the other stages put together providing an overall learning of technology. Faculty have mastered technology usage in and out of the classroom. To increase IT knowledge faculty must have outside collaboration and support increasing role changes (ex., Leader instead of co-learner), peer coaching, and outside support. Faculty must have the knowledge and time to disseminate data through workshops to their peers (teaching others about the information they have learned about using technology in the classroom). Faculty who reported to be in this state may enjoy using technology and may use it without the help from anyone or without incentives from anyone. (pp. 58–59)

The TEN PT3 Grant

The Teacher Education Network (TEN) is a Preparing Tomorrow's Teachers to Use Technology Catalyst grant awarded in 2000. During its existence, TEN fulfilled a critical need for bridges among national-level agencies with complementary missions on topics of teacher preparation and development. It also successfully implemented a model for creating and sharing flexible electronic tools to support the work of educators engaged in preservice teacher education reform. While the affordances of the developed toolsets were direct extensions of TEN's goals for supporting educational change, the implementation of the toolsets was tailored to solidify and advance the agenda of each participating institutional partner. According to the TEN project director:

> *I believe in data-driven change. We start with data on needs and demands. Next, we need to measure the needs and gaps in existing programs and have our partner organizations set their priorities by consensus. Then we need to respond quickly to those priority needs. That's how the work of TEN was designed. There are now tools that can help these organizations keep up with their change work. The surveys help them identify their needs and demands for change, and the portals point them to examples of best practice.*

The tools and expertise that TEN provided were tailored to supporting partner activities that, in turn, supported attainment of TEN's goals. The toolset, developed by TEN partner National Institute for Community Innovations (NICI) included:

- online survey tools to assess user knowledge and organizational preparedness for using online resources for ongoing professional development;
- the Personal Learning Planner (PLP) (Havelock, Gibson, & Sherry, 2003; Sherry, Havelock, & Gibson, 2003), an online environment for mentoring, collaboration, and publication of individual or group e-portfolios that could be used within educational programs as well as by professional institutions to foster professional growth and development;

- a set of virtual campuses "owned" by participating professional organizations that supported online collaboration and resource sharing; and

- a set of portals located at http://edreform.net, each owned by a professional organization or a nationally recognized IT expert, which provided customized, metatagged, and often refereed, online resources from a national clearinghouse to members, teacher educators, and teacher practitioners that were aligned with their field of interest, such as urban preservice education, technology infusion, technology applications for learning, or digital equity.

Each portal was developed through a partnership with a professional association or network of experts capable of pointing educators to best practices in a given reform dimension. For each portal, TEN enlisted one or more nationally recognized experts to coordinate efforts to identify, annotate, and catalog exemplary Web-based information. By spring 2003, each portal had a lead person who was hired to serve as the "first source" channel. Concurrently, usability testing was performed on the interface of the Urban Teacher Education Portal, "owned" by the Urban Network to Improve Teacher Education (UNITE). User ratings generally exceeded a value of 4 on a scale of 1 = "low" to 5 = "high" (Conceição, Sherry, & Gibson, 2003; Conceição, Sherry, Gibson, & Amenta-Shin, 2003). Although use of the www.edreform.net portals was slow at first, the number of online resources reached Rogers' (1995) critical mass of online resources and users by July 2003, and the usage statistics showed exponential growth throughout the rest of the summer (Sherry, 2003a). By now, I was reconsidering the myth of *if you build it, they will come,* and I found that truly, "they did come."

The Virtual Campuses, which were designed to foster collegial interaction among teams of professionals in between face-to-face meetings, institutes, and planning sessions, were more problematic. Although they provided server space for shared documents and resources and supported threaded discussions among communities of teacher educators, they were underutilized (Sherry, Cronjé, Rauscher, & Obermeyer, 2003). My personal explanation for this phenomenon was that the developers of the Virtual Campuses had built a resource for adult learners that was similar to The Web Project's collaborative learning environment, which was used so successfully by students, but they assumed that *adult learners would function cognitively like students,* which was another myth. As Hartley (1999) pointed out in the online discussion about effective pedagogies for managing collaborative learning in online learning environments:

Some students and teachers need to learn how to collaborate, which is a big shift in thinking from teacher based to student based. (p. 8)

Interviews with teacher educators who used the UNITE and Great Cities Universities Virtual Campuses revealed that:

- the members of these organizations felt that the campuses were only useful as placeholders for their content;
- their use for organizational learning was a low priority compared with teaching, getting tenure, or fostering university-school partnerships;
- there were too many other distractions that required their attention at work when using the threaded discussions for professional development and shared learning;
- the virtual campus was a complex environment compared with telephone calls and email; and
- the social interactions and brainstorming afforded by small face-to-face meetings could not be matched within an online environment.

Although the project directors seeded the online conversations, provided rapid feedback, attempted to foster interactions that respected and valued differing perspectives, provided automatic email notification to all subscribed members when a new discussion thread message was posted, and provided guidelines for discussions about goal-related activities to be accomplished between face-to-face meetings, there were no incentives and no pressure for busy teacher educators to participate in the discussions.

I saw the same phenomenon in the free online professional development courses addressing assistive technology and barrier-free Web design that were provided by the GENASYS PT3 Catalyst grant for members of other PT3 grants, and in the fee-based courses provided by the University of Southern Maine's Virtual Assistive Technology University (VATU) for aspiring special education teachers. The content was high quality, the course instructors were nationally recognized experts in their field, and their online discussion moderation skills were excellent, but the online discussions were sporadic at best. Even when student assessment depended on participation in the VATU courses, the myth that *a collaborative spirit could be infused into an online learning environment if the students felt pressured to participate* was dispelled. It was certainly dispelled for teacher educators when no pressure was present, despite the exemplary online content and the collegial support of the moderator and the other participants.

The Personal Learning Planner (PLP), an outgrowth of The Web Project and an innovative program at Montpelier High School that placed individual educational plans for every student at the center of its long term strategic plan, met with a good deal more success than the Virtual Campuses. Based on an electronically-supported action planning framework and linking to a portal with customized Web-based resources, the PLP is part collaboration tool and part e-portfolio builder, with an emphasis on the online dialogue and design conversations between learners and the people advising them. The learner is situated in an institutionally-specific context of explicit standards and goals built into the PLP by each implementing program. It contains a portfolio space for both working and showcasing collections of work. It also supports online mentoring, advising, and an improvement process for artifacts intended to be incorporated into e-portfolios. The flexibility of this Web-based learning environment supports an adopting school, district, or institution with both generic multimedia tools and a customized application for considering and evaluating student works-in-progress.

Results of pilot testing and field testing indicated that innovative education systems — networks of learners, mentors, and evaluators within and across institutions, as well as students in both K-12 and postsecondary programs — were able to create and productively develop and use standards-based performance reviews in this new online environment. Within school and university programs, the PLP was viewed as a useful tool for developing e-portfolios that could be used by students to demonstrate mastery of competencies required for credentialing, as a collection of products and artifacts that could be presented when applying for a teaching job, and as a means of providing data for National Council for Accreditation of Teacher Education (NCATE) re-accreditation. In New Hampshire, a faculty member at New England College used the PLP in the context of a course on technology and education, and creation of a PLP-based portfolio was offered as an optional honors assignment. In Iowa, one teacher educator used the PLP with over 300 teachers to support a class on e-portfolios and the action research cycle of 146 learning teams. A UNITE member at the University of Wisconsin at Milwaukee reported that she used the PLP in all of her instructional technology courses.

Based on the success of The Web Project with students engaging in design conversations with teachers, mentors, and other students, and continuously refining and revising their work based on feedback received from peers and experts, I expected that *the success of the PLP with adult learners would be matched with the success of The Web Project with K–12 students*. Moreover, with the current emphasis on standards and assessment, I expected that *educational programs would wholeheartedly adopt the PLP because it was standards-based and provided an excellent vehicle for assessing the student learning process as well as students' products and learning outcomes.* These were two myths I created. However, introducing the PLP into a higher education system proved more difficult than expected.

Deeper investigations at the University of Tennessee and the University of Colorado at Denver (Sherry, 2003a), using multiple methods of data collection, provided insights into knotty implementation issues that surfaced during the pilot phase. Prominent among these was an issue identified by Rogers (1995) and validated in my work with the UCD Internet Task Force: the cultural/personal compatibility of an innovation with the norms or status quo of the organization into which it is introduced. The embedded structure of the PLP contains a way of thinking about assessment, mastery, and the learner's role in the learning process that resonated to different degrees with different implementing programs. For example, while many faculty members at the University of Tennessee saw the PLP as a vehicle for showcasing completed work rather than as a communication and collaboration tool for developing work, the local program administrator saw the PLP as providing the ability to more closely track and advise students over the course of a multi-year program involving various classes and instructors.

Similarly, at UCD, participants in the Educational Leadership and Innovation (EDLI) doctoral program felt that their program as a whole already encouraged the process of getting feedback for revision, and the group was especially receptive to the aspect of the PLP that facilitated dialogue and design conversations between the learner and the program committee or advisors. The tight connection of the PLP to a predetermined set of standards or guidelines, however, presented an epistemological quandary when it was implemented in a loosely structured doctoral program that focused on candidates developing their own goals and showing progress toward meeting those goals in unique, creative ways, rather than documenting achievement of a fixed set of standards. One of the program administrators reported that it was not the cultural issue that presented implementation challenges for the PLP; rather, it was a deeper concern about the nature of emerging knowledge and personal creativity that doctoral candidates were expected to exhibit:

> *How should we — or should we — codify student performance? That limits their possibilities. So those who see a reason to work with rubrics do meet and work on them, but it's only those who agree with the idea of using rubrics. Others think that by specifying outcomes, you limit the ability of students to*

> *explore their universe of possibilities. It has to do with the nature of knowing,*
> *the nature of a doctoral program, and the whole belief system about setting*
> *standards.*

Thus, different programs' and institutions' pilot engagements with the PLP were influenced by the aspects of their existing culture and norms that had parallels in the PLP's design for learning and assessment. Where learners were already accustomed to monitoring their own progress and considering the relation of their work to standards and program requirements, PLP implementations gathered momentum more quickly. Where the PLP was seen as a vehicle for tracking the learning process rather than for collecting finished products, programs adopted and used it more quickly.

Throughout the three years of TEN's implementation, the project's activities were based on a data-driven approach to change that it characterized as "responsive dissemination" (Gibson & Knapp, 2002). This change model builds on self-assessment, professional development, and technical assistance, all supported by the integrated toolset. One of the project leaders described the model:

> *Instead of me inventing something and disseminating it to you, you are the*
> *user, and through your actions in the world, information comes to you online*
> *that helps you with your actions in the world. It's like Activity Theory: it*
> *puts the focus on the actions of the learner. The learner conducts searches,*
> *creates documents, and builds channels for information to flow through. These*
> *are all different ways of interacting with the world. These actions should*
> *trigger a responsive information system to meet the needs of the learner and*
> *make available whatever resources are necessary.*

In contrast to the one-way channels of traditional dissemination, responsive dissemination seeks continuous improvement and responsiveness to the needs of potential audiences by bringing data from those audiences into the ongoing development and refinement of the materials to be disseminated, in a spiral process. The responsive dissemination model embedded both scalability and sustainability into each aspect of TEN's work. It began with TEN leadership's inquiry into the nature and needs of this audience. Central to this work was engaging the leadership of national organizations and educational programs in exploring how technology could help and support their work and their own mission. The set of interoperable tools emerged and morphed to address the evolving interests and priorities of those organizations and programs. Interview data from a range of sites, including national networks, colleges of teacher education, professional organizations, local educational agencies, and

K–12 institutions suggest that responsive dissemination strongly supports long-term sustainability of newly-adopted innovative practices. Awareness and use of these tools is reaching new audiences, while repeat and expanded uses of the toolsets by existing audiences suggests the durability of the tools as sustained and integrated components of educational programs. TEN's partner organizations, such as the 31 universities in UNITE and the 19 universities in Great Cities Universities, are now appropriating these tools as focal points for future proposals and projects.

One of TEN's initial goals was to create online graduate programs in urban teacher preparation for preservice students and non-licensed or under-prepared practicing educators nationally. Spearheaded by TEN partner UNITE, the objective was to develop an online master's degree program that better prepared teachers to work in urban environments. However, during Year Two of the TEN project, UNITE's members decided that developing an entire master's program in urban teacher education should be a long-term goal, while UNITE focused in the near term on developing, reviewing, and disseminating exemplary curricular materials and information on effective strategies for transforming teacher preparation, recruitment, induction, and retention via TEN's Urban Teacher Education portal. UNITE also instituted a process for nominating, reviewing, and organizing these resources within its portal, and a librarian set about cataloguing the resources and incorporating them into the http://edreform.net clearinghouse's database.

Great Cities Universities

In a concurrent activity, TEN partner Great Cities Universities/Urban Educator Corps (GCU) was actively engaged in developing a Virtual Curriculum of its own for urban teacher preparation. The UNITE and GCU activities were closely related, but they were not meant to be identical. Thus, in Year Three of the TEN PT3 grant, there was close collaboration on ideas and activities between TEN and GCU, both of which had a common goal in creating an online program for urban teacher education. As part of its own PT3 Catalyst grant activities, GCU designed, developed, and pilot tested five online drop-in modules that could be assembled or integrated into courses at each university, within each teacher preparation program's local context. Throughout the following year, these modules were well received and institutionalized within each development team's teacher education program as modules, courses, or enrichment activities for field placement (Sherry, 2003b).

GCU also conducted a Rubric Retreat in fall 2003, assisted by members of UNITE and the International Society for Technology in Education (ISTE). The purpose was to facilitate development of a GCU rubric of comprehensive reform for the preparation of teachers in urban settings. The proposed rubric was intended to serve as the mutually agreed upon assessment tool to begin the work of identifying and addressing gaps in the various university-school partnership teams' community plans. Rich conversations on the GCU Virtual Campus took place around topics of:

- engaging university presidents and the broader university leadership;
- developing and sustaining inclusive partnerships in which all stakeholders are represented;
- creating a pipeline of teacher recruitment, training, induction, retention, and professional development; and
- clarifying what technology infusion means, such as the difference between programs that use technology to deliver a virtual curriculum and teachers who use technology to enhance teaching and learning.

The natural clustering of messages around these four themes matched the structure of the self-selected teams that then proceeded to create four rubrics on leadership, partnerships, preservice teacher education, and technology infusion. The rubrics had three purposes: first, to help the individual partnership teams identify gaps in their community plans, which would then allow the GCU leadership to provide technical assistance to address those gaps; second, to identify potential areas in which additional virtual curriculum modules or courses could be designed and developed; and third, to provide a theoretical framework for the surveys that would eventually form the front end user self-assessment surveys for the various www.edreform.net portals. The first survey, which matched the technology infusion rubric and addressed digital equity as well as some of the National Educational Technology Standards for Teachers (ISTE/NETS), was incorporated into GCU's Preservice Technology Infusion Portal in spring 2003.

The myth that *the instructional design process follows a logical progression of analysis, design, development, implementation, and evaluation,* was dispelled within a few months. The process of developing virtual curriculum modules, which addressed specific, critical needs in urban teacher preparation that were addressed by the GCU Steering Committee, was logical. So was the collaborative development of rubrics that were intended to identify actual needs in existing programs and individual users' knowledge and skills, which could then be addressed by providing exemplary online resources through the various portals or the virtual curriculum modules. However, the process of creating an online survey that would actually be used for self-assessment was anything but straightforward. The software architecture was in place to build the surveys (Kurowski, Knapp, McLaughlin, & Gibson, 2003), but the surveys themselves were underutilized because many of the partnership teams already had self-assessment procedures in place, and they did not match the rubrics that were used to develop the GCU portal survey. Interviews and open-ended survey questions elicited some striking comments from GCU members regarding the rubrics and the survey, for example:

> *There's lack of consensus about our priorities across the GCU. Some people want to drive their own ideas.*

> *It's hard to help people that are so diverse, all over the place with technology. So I listen to the people who have real solutions.*

Finally, the use of the online survey was postponed, and the Steering Committee proposed that site visits take place in Year Three to further the work of self-assessment and technical assistance. Clearly, building a set of virtual curriculum modules was not the crux of the problem; it was the lack of common norms, contexts, policies, and priorities across the 19 participating universities that made the work of building a virtual curriculum and infusing technology into existing programs difficult. For example, a university that created and implemented a virtual curriculum module in WebCT could not share that module with another university that used Blackboard or some proprietary courseware or enterprise system, without converting the entire module to HTML and either burning it onto a CD-ROM or DVD, or uploading it to the GCU Virtual Campus. Moreover, when dealing with a national organization, policy issues came into play that were nonexistent at the institutional or state level, such as setting the per-credit-hour cost of tuition for a course or dealing with teacher credentialing and certification requirements (Sherry, 2003b). These are issues that GCU is still struggling with, and will continue to address as the idea of designing and developing a virtual curriculum for urban educators begins to mature.

Two insightful comments from project leaders and GCU Steering Committee members exemplify some of the lessons learned during this complex process:

> *You have to be flexible and not be bent out of shape. You have to remain open to understand that the things you planned evolve as they are implemented, and what you get may not be what you originally intended.*

It's very easy for a group of people to design a new theory-based model that's intended to improve practice, but it's very hard to make the structure of that model clear and to make the implementation process of that model clear and concrete.

Final Comments

My perspectives about educational technology, instructional design, and online learning and professional development have slowly evolved over the past fifteen years since I initially entered the field and have seen a number of myths dispelled as the technology evolved concurrently. At the beginning, the issues were all about getting the technology to work, designing an interface that was both functional and user-friendly, and persuading users that the new, online system was better than the status quo. Now, I see that the issues are not technological, but organizational in nature. They have to do with deep-rooted social and cultural issues, as well as epistemological issues that are far more difficult to deal with. Moreover, moving from the individual institution such as USF or the BVIP, to a statewide network such as The Web Project, and finally, to national organizations of national partners such as the TEN and GCU projects, reveals increasingly complex and knotty policy issues that must be addressed. Research done in conjunction with the TEN (Gibson & Knapp, 2002) project indicated that convergence of resources at the highest organizational level within a system, mutual benefit to users on each side of a system boundary, such as an individual institution and a national organization, and clear communication across subsystem boundaries are all crucial for the institutionalization and sustainability of a project.

Although the technologies and e-learning systems produced by each of these projects fostered system-wide communication and provided mutual benefit for individual users, educational programs, and national organizations, it was convergence of resources that presented the biggest problem. It all has to do with generalizability and scalability. Will pockets of excellence that emphasize inquiry-based learning, such as I found within Boulder Valley's BVIP, generalize to a standards-based educational program found in Texas or California schools? Can the types of online student learning and design conversations found in The Web Project generalize to adult learners at a university or within a professional development community? Can curriculum modules or full courses that have been institutionalized within a university in Ohio, Virginia, or Indiana be shared among a national network of universities that is scattered across the country but connected through common discourse and shared document channels and supported by a responsive dissemination network? These are the real theoretical and research issues that have yet to be explored.

References

Allen, B.S., & Otto, R.G. (1996). Media as lived environments: The ecological psychology of educational technology. In D. H. Jonassen (Ed.), *Handbook of research for educational communications and technology* (pp. 199–225). New York: Simon & Schuster Macmillan.

Bandura, A. (1982). Self-efficacy mechanism in human agency. *American Psychologist, 37(2)*, pp. 122–147.

Berge, Z. (1997). Computer conferencing and the online classroom. *International Journal of Educational Telecommunications, 3(1)*, pp. 3–21.

Carroll, T. (2000, February). *If we didn't have the schools we have today, would we create the schools we have today?* Keynote speech presented at the annual meeting of the Society for Information Technology and Teacher Education, San Diego, CA.

Collins, A., Brown, J.S., & Newman, S.E. (1989). Cognitive apprenticeship: Teaching the crafts of reading, writing, and mathematics. In L. B. Resnick (Ed.), *Knowing, learning, and instruction: Essays in honor of Robert Glaser* (pp. 453–494). Hillsdale, NJ: Lawrence Erlbaum Associates.

Conceição, S., Sherry, L., & Gibson, D. (2003). *Using developmental research to design, develop, and evaluate an urban education portal.* Manuscript in review.

Conceição, S., Sherry, L., Gibson, D., & Amenta-Shin, G. (2003, June). *Managing digital resources for an urban education portal.* Paper presented at Ed-Media, Honolulu, HI.

Crook, C. (1994a). *Computers and the collaborative experience of learning.* London: Routledge.

Crook, C. (1994b). Computer networking and collaborative learning within a departmentally focused undergraduate course. In H.C. Foot, C.J. Howe, A. Anderson, A.K. Tolmie, & D.A. Warden (Eds.), *Group and interactive learning.* Southampton, United Kingdom: Computational Mechanics Publications.

Dwyer, D.C., Ringstaff, C., & Sandholtz, J.H. (1991). Changes in teachers' beliefs and practices in technology-rich classrooms. *Educational Leadership, 48*(8), pp. 45–52.

Elmore, R.F. (1996). Getting to scale with good educational practice. *Harvard Educational Review, 66*(1), pp. 1–26.

Gibson, D., & Knapp, M. (2002). *Measuring your needs and finding resources to match: An XML-based responsive dissemination system.* Paper presented at E-Learn 2002, Montreal, Canada.

Hagenson, L.C. (2000). *The integration of technology into teaching by university College of Education faculty.* Unpublished dissertation, Oklahoma State University.

Hall, G.E., & Hord, S.M. (1987). *Change in schools: Facilitating the process.* Albany, NY: State University of New York Press.

Hartley, J. R. (1999). *Effective pedagogies for managing collaborative learning in online learning environments.* Retrieved April 16, 1999, online from http://ifets.gmd.de/periodical/vol_2_99/formal_discussion_0399.html

Havelock, B., Gibson, D., & Sherry, L. (2003). *The Personal Learning Planner: A learner-centered e-learning management system.* Brief paper presented at E-Learn 2003, Phoenix, AZ.

Herrmann, F. (1995). *Listserver communication: The discourse of community-building.* Proceedings of the CSCL'95 Conference. Indianapolis [Online]. Retrieved February 20, 1996, from http://www-cscl95.indiana.edu/cscl95/herrmann.html

Hodas, S. (1993, September). Technology refusal and the organizational culture of schools. *Education Policy Analysis Archives* [Online serial], *1*(10). Retrieved April 1, 1996, from http://olam.edu.asu.edu/epaa.v1n10.html

Hoffman, D., Sherry, L., Lurie, J., & McDaniel, J. (2001). The teachers' Internet user guide: Web-based training for educators. In B. Khan (Ed.), *Web-based training* (pp. 485–490). Englewood Cliffs, NJ: Educational Technology Publications.

Kurowski, B., Knapp, M., McLaughlin, R., & Gibson, D. (2003). *An application of the semantic Web for school improvement.* Unpublished manuscript, National

Institute for Community Innovations (NICI). Available from dgibson@vermontinstitutes.org

Lave, J., & Wenger, E. (1991). *Situated learning: Legitimate peripheral participation.* New York: Cambridge University Press.

Lawyer-Brook, D., & Sherry, L. (1997). *Boulder Valley Internet Project: Final report.* Denver, Colorado: RMC Research Corporation.

Norman, D.A. (1993). *Things that make us smart.* Reading, MA: Addison-Wesley.

Rogers, E.M. (1995). *Diffusion of innovations* (4th ed.). New York: The Free Press.

Ryder, M., & Wilson, B. (1996, February). *Affordances and constraints of the Internet for learning and instruction.* Paper presented at the annual meeting of the Association for Educational Communications and Technology, Indianapolis, IN.

Schein, E.H. (1996a). *Three cultures of management: The key to organizational learning in the 21st Century.* Unpublished manuscript.

Schein, E.H. (1996b). *Organizational learning: What is new?* Unpublished manuscript.

Sherry, L. (1997, September). The Boulder Valley Internet project: Lessons learned. *T.H.E. Journal,* pp. 68–72.

Sherry, L. (1998). An integrated technology adoption and diffusion model. *International Journal of Educational Telecommunications, 4*(2/3), pp.113–145. Retrieved online December 23, 2003, from http://carbon.cudenver.edu/~lsherry/pubs/aect98.html

Sherry, L. (2000). The nature and purpose of online conversations: A brief synthesis of current research. *International Journal of Educational Telecommunications, 6*(1), pp.19-52. Retrieved online December 23, 2003, from http://www.rmcdenver.com/TEN/dialogue.htm

Sherry, L. (2003a). *Teacher Education Network (TEN): Year 3 Evaluation.* Denver, CO: RMC Research Corporation.

Sherry, L. (2003b). *Great Cities Universities (GCU): Year 2 Evaluation.* Denver, CO: RMC Research Corporation.

Sherry, L., & Myers, K.M. (1996, June). *Developmental research on collaborative design.* In proceedings of the 43rd Annual Meeting of the Society for Technical Communication.

Sherry, L., & Myers, K.M. (1998). The dynamics of collaborative design. *IEEE Transactions on Professional Communication, 41*(2), pp. 123–139. Retrieved online December 23, 2003, from http://carbon.cudenver.edu/~lsherry/pubs/ieee.html

Sherry, L., & the Internet Task Force. (1996, October). Supporting a networked community of learners. *Tech Trends, 41*(5), pp. 28–32. Retrieved online December 23, 2003, from http://carbon.cudenver.edu/~lsherry/pubs/TECH_TRENDS.html

Sherry, L., Billig, S., Tavalin, F., & Gibson, D. (2000). New insights on technology adoption in schools. *T.H.E. Journal, 27*(7), pp. 43–46. Retrieved online December 23, 2003, from http://www.thejournal.com/magazine/vault/A2640.cfm

Sherry, L., Cronjé, J., Rauscher, W., & Obermeyer, G. (2003, June). *Online conversations: Two cases that break the mold.* Paper presented at Ed-Media, Honolulu, HI.

Sherry, L., Havelock, B., & Gibson, D. (2003). *The personal and professional learning planner: An online environment for mentoring, collaboration, and publication.* Manuscript in review.

Sherry, L., Lawyer-Brook, D., & Black, L. (1997). Evaluation of the Boulder Valley Internet Project: A theory-based approach to evaluation design. *Journal of Interactive Learning Research, 8*(2), pp. 199–233.

Sherry, L., Tavalin, F., & Billig, S.H. (2000). Good online conversation: Building on research to inform practice. *Journal of Interactive Learning Research, 11*(1), pp. 85–127. Retrieved online December 23, 2003, from http://www.rmcdenver.com/TEN/JILR.htm

Sherry, L., Wilson, B., & Ryder, M. (1995, June). *IT Connections: An instructional technology resource on the World Wide Web.* Steamboat Springs, CO: Technology in Education (TIE).

Tavalin, F. (1998). *A guide to online critique.* Montpelier, VT: The Web Project. Available: The Web Project, 58 Barre Street, Montpelier VT 05602.

Tavalin, F., & Boke, N. (1998). *A guide to online discussion.* Montpelier, VT: The Web Project. Available: The Web Project, 58 Barre Street, Montpelier VT 05602.

Twigg, C. (2001*). Innovations in online learning: Moving beyond no significant difference.* The Pew Learning and Technology Program. Retrieved March 18, 2003, from http://www.center.rpi.edu/PewSym/mono4.html

Wilson, B., Jenlink, P., Surry, D., Sherry, L., Lowry, M., & Myers, K. (1997, February). The Boulder Internet Project. *Adoption of technology and systemic change: Multidisciplinary perspectives.* Panel presentation at AECT In-CITE'97 Conference, Albuquerque, NM.

Wilson, B., Ryder, M., McCahan, J., & Sherry, L. (1996). Cultural assimilation of the Internet: A case study. In M. Simonson (Ed.), *Proceedings of selected research and development presentations.* Washington, DC: Association for Educational Communications and Technology. Retrieved online December 23, 2003, from http://carbon.cudenver.edu/~bwilson/cultass.html

Zaltman, G., Duncan, R., & Holbek, J. (1973). *Innovations and organizations.* New York: John Wiley and Sons.

Chapter 26

Learning Through Online Collaboration

Robert Tinker

Robert Tinker has, for thirty years, pioneered innovative approaches to education that exploit the power of technology such as probes and collaborative networking. He founded the nonprofit Concord Consortium in 1994 to concentrate on research and development of educational technologies. Prior to that, he was one of the principals of the Technical Education Research Center. He earned his PhD in physics from MIT in 1970.

Introduction

I welcome this chance to shed the academic third person and narrow focus on results. It is important to review the history of educational computing to capture the best developments, to avoid the pitfalls, and to take a longer perspective that allows us to look forward with greater confidence. Perhaps the sweep of history, which is so difficult to piece together from the academic literature, popular journals, or education books, will reveal itself more coherently in a personal narrative.

Since this is not to be an academic paper, it is important to start by revealing my background, biases, and guides. By reading Martin Gardner, I fell in love with numbers and logic as a kid and so, in 1957, jumped at the chance to program an IBM 650 to generate prime numbers. I then wrote an Algol-like compiler and was so hooked on the technology that I dropped it cold out of fear that it would interfere with my academic work. I had so thoroughly left computers behind that it was only in 1972 when I was safely ensconced in the Amherst College physics department that I saw the first example of an educational application of computers that appealed to me: a planetary motion simulation that Al Bork demonstrated in Chicago using his remote time-share computer in Irvine. I loved the fact that I could explore the effect on planet orbits of different force laws and starting conditions. This was a perfect example of a computer model that could be treated as an experiment that simulated a real system that would not fit in the lab.

With the advent of the first microcomputers in 1974, I let myself resume my love affair with computers because they could be used in a science instrumentation course I was teaching. The idea that a digital computer might actually help with scientific measurements — which are inherently analog —

402

was a revelation that I was handed by Greg Edwards, a program officer at the NSF. I clearly remember concluding in 1976 while driving on I-91 to my classes at Springfield Technical Community College, that I could contribute to society through the intersection of science, education, and technology. That led me to a long string of developments in connecting sensors to microcomputers for instructional labs, now known as "probeware" and an important tool for science teaching and learning. But that is a different story.

Network Science

Greg Edwards, the first futurist I ever met, also predicted in 1975 that networking would be one of the most important applications of computers, a nugget of wisdom that I was unable to appreciate at the time. This observation did, however, inspire my team at Amherst and Hampshire Colleges in 1978 to develop NOS, a networked version of the CP/M operating system that worked across multiple S-100 computers to share disks and printers. About this time, inspired by Seymour Papert and Logo, we also built the first affordable high-resolution graphics cards (480x640 pixels of up to four bits each) and shared access to them over the network. With the help of TERC founder Arthur Nelson, we even formed Cambridge Development Labs to market this advanced hardware and software.

This was the wrong direction, because others would build more robust and affordable hardware and software. Being first is not always good business. More importantly, the significance of educational networking is not the minor cost savings, but the ability to communicate and collaborate. This requires long-distance networking that had to wait for widespread access to low-cost modems and email. The situation changed by the early 1980's, when the first commercial dial-up email services became available.

The Kids Network

As a consequence of President Reagan's attack on federal support for education, TERC[1] was without funding in 1982 except for a life-saving grant from the Carnegie Corporation that allowed us to analyze the educational applications of networking. We identified collaborative knowledge construction as the key added capacity of networking and our analysis gave us confidence to imagine building student collaboration into a curriculum. When the NSF

---

[1] Known at that time as the Technical Education Research Centers, a nonprofit R&D group. See http://terc.edu

recovered from Reagan, its first initiative in 1985 was to call for publisher-researcher partnerships that would develop bold but sustainable new approaches to elementary science. While we would have preferred to start in more advanced grades, we partnered with Monica Bradsher at the National Geographic Society (NGS) to propose Kidnet, a set of grade 4-6 science curriculum units that relied on student peer collaboration. This was a risky proposal that was roundly rejected at the preliminary stage.

To make a stronger case for the final proposal, Jan Mokros and June Foster at TERC and Priscilla Laws at Dickenson College created, administered, and evaluated a trial unit that was taught in nine schools nationwide in 1986. At that time, Easterners were complaining about dying forests and the Reagan administration was denying that there was a connection between this and acid rain from Midwestern coal-fired power plants. We decided that we could engage students in this debate by having students collect data on the geographic distribution of the pH of rain. An understanding of chemistry, acids and bases, and meteorology would be needed to make sense of the data, giving need-driven reasons to study of these topics.

The results exceeded our wildest expectations. The teachers and students in the trial implementation loved it. The idea of sharing data with kids in Harlem, Kansas, San Francisco, and elsewhere was thrilling. During the test, acid rain was all over the newspapers and enterprising teachers assigned students to bring in related articles, adding to the students' sense of importance. The excitement of actually relating to an adult concern of national interest unleashed a level of seriousness and dedication that surprised every teacher. Teachers appreciated that the activities were connected to quality science content that students learned more willingly and thoroughly than ever before. Our group also learned that teachers needed strategies for dealing with the combined data. In the trial, each school received pH values from the eight other schools, but none of the teachers knew how to analyze these data. One had the kids simply memorize all the pH values!

The proposal passed peer review with flying colors and by early 1987 the Kidnet project was underway, initially under the direction of June Foster and then, for most of the project, Candace Julyan. To gain additional classroom experience, the project revised the Acid Rain unit and tested it again in a number of classrooms, but only using telecommunications to share pH data, not for messaging. The students spontaneously started communicating through postcards to other participating classes. In this way, the students taught us something we should have known: that creating a community was an important part of the collaborative learning process, and that we should have used our technology to foster community building. The desire to create an effective electronic community, and the difficulty teachers had with the combination of new technology and new pedagogy, led to the creation of an introductory unit, called Hello! This unit helped create the trust and understanding needed in an online learning community while introducing the Kidnet approach and technology in the context of some very simple science — the pets that students own. We initially saw Hello! as a waste of valuable instructional time, but came to realize that it was essential to create a functioning online community. This need to invest in community building has been recognized independently by many other groups as essential to realizing the educational benefit of online collaboration.

One of the important lessons of Kidnet is that the quality and extent of the curriculum materials were essential to its success. Teachers crave high-quality curriculum packages that address significant topics and they want substantial curriculum units, not single activities or some software package that they have to integrate into their lessons. Teachers were not attracted to the materials because of the technology, but they were willing to put up with the additional logistical problems the technology created, because they recognized the educational value of the integrated curriculum–technology package. Educational needs must drive the technology, not the other way around.

The project went to great lengths to simplify implementation by providing detailed instructions and day-by-day lesson plans that even included sample classroom discussions. The project ensured that the software was powerful, attractive, and intuitive. Project staff, under the direction of Cecilia Lenk and Stephen Bannasch, created an integrated, award-winning application that included an email editor, automatic dial-up, email packing and unpacking of data, a grapher, and simple GIS (Geographical Information System) functions that featured data display on a zoom-able map. A heroic effort was required to make this functionality run on a 128K Apple IIgs connected to an email system through a 1,200-baud modem.

The Kidnet project eventually developed a dozen units like Acid Rain, each running six to eight weeks in a typical elementary classroom. The units were published by the NGS and implemented in tens of thousands of classrooms. Over one million students used the material, making it by far the largest network-based educational curricula. The project could be flourishing now, but the Internet made the technology obsolete and the project was dropped by the

NGS.[2] The kind of broad adoption Kidnet enjoyed is not possible with materials that are generated quickly and cheaply, demonstrating once again that significant advances in education require large-scale, sustained funding. Technology does not provide a way around this fundamental fact, it just adds to the cost. One of the reasons that there is no comparable technology-enhanced curriculum at present is that there is no comparable sustained, large-scale funding available. Kidnet proves that exciting technology-enhanced curricula are feasible.

The Global Lab

Kidnet inspired a wide range of subsequent projects that engaged students in the scientific process through gathering, sharing, and analyzing data (Feldman, Konold, & Coulter, 2000). In addition to fostering Kidnet-like projects (Barstow, Tinker, & Doubler, 1996; Cohen, 1997; Tinker & Kapisovsky, 1991, 1992), we wanted to explore a more sophisticated approach that was closer to scientific research. In Kidnet, the question, method, and data analysis were spelled out in detail except in one draft unit that tested well but was too different from the other units to fit into the Kidnet series. We decided to expand on this initial success and build curricula that would lead to student-designed collaborative experiments. In 1990, this gave birth to the Global Lab project at TERC and, later, at The Concord Consortium (Berenfeld, 1994).

Each of the Global Lab's participating classes establishes a study site, which it characterizes and describes to other participating classes. Over the course of a year, all the classes use inexpensive instruments to study the soil, water, and air at their sites. Sharing their observations with students at other sites enriches this experience and helps give students ideas for their studies. As students gain familiarity with their sites, their sites' ecology, and the instrumentation, they naturally begin to ask questions. These questions are shaped into research projects that are written up and shared with peers through the network. We found that student critiques could be quite harsh and inappropriate, so we needed to prepare the way with online discussions about trust, goals, and helpful criticism. After a round of criticism, the classes undertake their research and eventually publish their findings online.

This process closely follows the scientific process and gives students unique insights about the social norms of scientific communities. The network

---

[2] Revised, Web-based versions are now available from TERC for grades 2-8. See http://LL.terc.edu

community of participating students provides peer review and a knowledgeable audience for research findings. Instead of memorizing "the scientific method" (a fiction) or reading about how science is done (boring), students experience scientific research and learn that they, too, can be scientists. Networking is not the project's focus, but without networking the project's high quality of learning would not be possible.

One of the challenges of the project was providing affordable general-purpose instrumentation and apparatus that students could use to get reliable and comparable results. We created a range of innovative equipment, drawn from our probeware experience and the advice of experts in low-cost apparatus, especially Jorge Trench, John King, and Forest Mims.

The NSF funded the Global Lab project for almost a decade under the leadership of Boris Berenfeld, Stephen Bannasch, and me. During that time, students did many exciting and inspiring studies. The following quotes from teachers participating in the project give a sense of its impact:

> *Science isn't good for anybody if it's out of a book. I want my kids to know that science is applicable to their lives. This is the first time they will be involved with real science.*
> *The Global Lab Project has had an immense impact on science instruction at our school. In large measure, the goals of this project have become the goals of our science department. ... In essence, we want our science students to "be scientists." By actively living this role, students develop an understanding and appreciation of science that includes and transcends the facts and concepts emphasized in traditional secondary science courses.*

The Kidnet-Global Lab strand has inspired many projects that engage students in genuine science (Cohen, 1997; Feldman *et al.*, 2000; Tinker, 2003), but neither has survived. Kendall-Hunt publishes the Global Lab but it has not caught on for a number of reasons. The material has proven to require unusual teachers who are willing to take risk and who understand science research from personal experience. In addition, the equipment, while inexpensive by professional standards, is out of reach of most school budgets and requires patience and ingenuity to use. But most importantly, the project requires extensive and expert facilitation of the student online collaborations. If this is omitted, the benefits of collaboration are lost; if it is supplied, it pushes the total costs beyond what schools are prepared to pay. In this age of standards, tests, and budget squeezes, there is little room for an open-ended curriculum with such exciting but unquantifiable goals.

Online Courses

In 1994, we launched the nonprofit Concord Consortium and turned our Global Lab experience in facilitating online collaboration to online courses for teachers. While the Web was still in its infancy, it was clear from reviewing prior successes with online courses (Harasim, 1990; Romiszowski & de Haas, 1991) that the Web was just the technology needed. Thus began a strand of research to exploit online courses for teachers, students, and online course facilitators.

INTEC

The International Netcourse Teacher Enhancement Collaborative (INTEC) was a project at the Concord Consortium that started in 1996 to study the efficacy of online teacher professional development to help teachers achieve difficult learning objectives. The goal of the NSF-funded project was to change the instructional style of secondary math and science teachers so that they were comfortable using inquiry as their primary teaching strategy. Inquiry-based learning is central to the new science standards but very difficult for teachers to implement, in part because few teachers have ever been taught this way in teacher training programs or had any other opportunity to practice inquiry-based learning.

The INTEC project, under the direction of Ray Rose and George Collison, was a yearlong graduate level course requiring about five hours of concentrated time each week. It started by having the participants learn through inquiry and then reflect on their experiences. The reflection, which is a central part of the learning process, took place in local study groups and in threaded discussion groups on the Web, guided by a trained facilitator. It thus used a "blended" approach, mostly online but partly face-to-face. We selected this design because we were unsure that a totally online course would be effective. The course had a complex design that involved strands of content specific to mathematics, biology, chemistry, and physics that were addressed in the context of educational issues such as assessment, student groups, misconceptions, and standards. Participants had a "home" group, but often joined a discipline group with participants from other groups. The course was rigorously scheduled so that all participants were ready to think together about the same activity at the same time. When teachers are motivated to keep up with this schedule, the experience is transformative. Teachers begin to use more inquiry and, sometimes, to influence their peers to do the same.

The "blended" nature of INTEC was double-edged. Many teachers reported that the face-to-face conversations were the most valuable part of the course. In many cases, the local study groups involved spirited conversations between teachers in different disciplines in the same school who had never talked about educational issues. On the other hand, these conversations seldom carried over to the online groups and actually subtracted from their value. This made it very difficult to capture what was learned in the study groups and to share it with others. In a blended model, there must be different learning goals for the online and face-to-face groups so they do not compete.

INTEC was designed to reach over 800 teachers in groups of twenty. To scale up to meet this goal, we had to learn how to train effective facilitators for the all-important online discussions. Initially we did the training face-to-face, but we later developed an effective online course for the facilitators. Effective facilitation is central to the success of online collaboration and, although it requires many of the skills of a face-to-face group facilitator, we were surprised at how few people have these skills. Too often, beginning facilitators get pulled into separate conversations with each participant. This does not contribute to a functioning group and quickly overwhelms the erstwhile facilitator, which is probably why so many faculty members report that online teaching is exhausting. A good facilitator stimulates conversation within the group and stays out of the middle of this conversation. Hence, we named our course Moving Out of the Middle (MOoM). Done well, we found that facilitating using this approach requires about as much effort as a face-to-face course.

The significance of INTEC is that it demonstrated that sufficiently motivated teachers can learn sophisticated content via well-designed Web-based courses. It helped codify for us the elements of good online course design which include asynchronous communication, tight scheduling, good instructional design, and a central role for well-facilitated online conversations (Tinker, 2001). INTEC also introduced us to high dropout rates, a problem that bedevils many online courses. We found that high motivation was particularly important for teachers to complete this rigorous, yearlong course, because it was so easy to fall behind and then lose the thread of the conversations. We had a final project that involved trying project materials in class and then reporting on the experience. Unfortunately, few completed this, either because they did not need the graduate credit that we offered, or because they were too busy to write up their findings. We are confident that if we divided the INTEC content into shorter courses with stronger motivation, we would have realized very high completion rates.

When other pioneers came to us for help in making their online courses work, we opened MOoM to them and published its notes as a book called "Facilitating Online Learning" that has received critical acclaim (Collison, Elbaum, Haavind, & Tinker, 2000). This was the first of several courses that we named "metacourses" because they are online courses about online courses. Eventually, we decided that offering metacourses required greater focus than we could give at the Concord Consortium, and spun out most of this effort as a separate company under the leadership of Sherry Hsi that continues to offer a range of metacourses in English and Spanish[3].

The Virtual High School

The Virtual High School (VHS) originated in a Concord Consortium retreat in early 1996 where we decided that the INTEC experience could be applied to online courses for students as well as teachers. We joined with Shelley Berman, superintendent of Hudson Public Schools, to propose a collaborative online school. The key innovation in the VHS was the idea of training teachers at collaborating schools to offer their own online courses, rather than hiring teachers who would offer them centrally. By late 1996, the VHS was funded for five years under the direction of Liz Pape at Hudson and Bruce Droste at the Concord Consortium.

We directly applied the INTEC model to the teacher course, which we named the Teachers Learning Conference (TLC). The course was designed to introduce teachers to our model for online courses and to help them create their own course to be delivered online to students from any VHS school. On completion, participants have a course that they will teach the next year, designed to meet a long list of design and content standards. Like INTEC, the TLC is a yearlong course that relies on online collaboration. Unlike INTEC, it requires more time, between 10-20 hours per week, and we had enough confidence to discard the blended design, which was not feasible anyway, because TLC would have participants from throughout the country and the world. The TLC has very strict quality standards for the content and design of the course that participants develop. The only way a school can enjoy the benefits of the VHS is to have a teacher whom they nominate complete the TLC course by designing their own course that meets all the standards. These requirements certainly solved the motivation problem.

---

[3] See http://www.metacourse.com

The TLC has proven to be an overwhelming success. First offered in 1997, it has resulted in the development of over 100 high-quality, online, high school courses on almost every conceivable topic. We cannot keep inventing new courses, so a one-semester TLC was modified into a one-semester course for teachers who will facilitate a section of one of the existing courses, rather than making a new one. We have learned to select teachers who are likely to succeed in these courses and to fail those unwilling to do the work quickly in the first few weeks of the course. As a result, we have over 95% completion rates. Many teachers say that TLC is the most rigorous and exciting professional development that they have ever had and that it improves their face-to-face teaching as well. The TLC is proof that teachers will take and complete a rigorous, 100% online, yearlong course if the motivation is right and the course is well designed and well facilitated.

In the VHS model, a teacher's school reduces their normal teaching assignment by one section so they can teach one section of an online course. The school loses the 25 seats the teacher normally teaches, but is compensated with the same number of seats that students select from any of the 100+ online courses. Thus, to a school, there is no change in the costs of instruction but a huge gain in the variety of courses they can offer. Unlike their response to most virtual schools, the unions love the VHS because there is no loss in local jobs and their members get high-quality professional development that greatly expands their professional options. The VHS was carefully analyzed by an outside evaluation team and pronounced a success (Zucker, Kozma, Yarnall, Marder, & Associates, 2002).

We wanted the VHS to continue post-funding and it was clear that The Concord Consortium was not the right environment for this. The VHS needed a team that had the enthusiasm, financial constraints, and focus of a start-up, not an R&D group that is always studying the next innovation. For this reason, at the termination of the grant in late 2001, we spun out the VHS as an independent nonprofit under the direction of Liz Pape[4]. This transition was difficult, as it required both CC and Hudson to transfer to the new organization valued staff members, intellectual property, and cash. Generous funding from the Noyce Foundation was essential to make this transition feasible. The VHS is now funded primarily from school memberships and continues to offer over 100 teacher-designed courses on a cooperative basis. Many have copied the general idea of online high school courses, but none have adopted the

---

[4] See http://govhs.org

cooperative model or the central role of teacher professional development through the TLC.

Seeing Math

Our practical applications of online collaboration have always been limited by bandwidth available in schools, starting with Kidnet, which pushed the envelope by requiring 1,200-baud modems as opposed to the then-current 600-baud acoustic modems. By early 2000, we expected that most schools would soon have sufficient bandwidth to support short video segments, at least for teachers. Thus, the logical next step for online teacher professional development was to design courses around video case studies, a project we named Seeing Math.[5] We teamed up with Teachscape[6] to produce a dozen video case studies for elementary mathematics. Nine of these are currently available commercially. Each focuses on one math concept and shows one way to address the topic in a real class, not as an example to follow, but as a stimulus for discussion about the content and teaching strategies. The videos are very high quality and the associated materials provide extensive documentation that includes the teacher's lesson plan, examples of student work, the associated standards, and video commentary by an expert mathematics educator. An extensive implementation guide helps school-based trainers design an effective district-wide professional development program that can be based on online or face-to-face discussion groups.

We continue to try to anticipate advances in the technological sophistication of schools and to experiment with combinations of technologies that can enhance teacher and student learning. When we began expanding Seeing Math to secondary mathematics, we decided that it was now feasible to fold in software. Other projects at The Concord Consortium are experimenting with tracking student use of software tools and returning sophisticated assessment data to teachers and researchers. Our goal for our online Seeing Math algebra teacher courses is to combine this capacity with video cases to make compelling courses that will increase student learning. The software and videos both can be valuable stimuli to conversations between teachers. The software can also help the participating teachers brush up on the content, but it will also be available for use with their students. If teachers choose to use the software, it will provide the teachers and us with detailed information about student learning.

---

[5] See http://seeingmath.concord.org

[6] See http://teachscape.com/html/ts/public/html/index.htm

Ultimately, I hope that we can integrate the Seeing Math course for teachers with a course for students linked through the software.

I endorse the recent emphasis on higher-quality educational research. It must not be forgotten that the avoidance by the profession of hard-nosed research has been, in part, an economic issue: it is expensive. We are fortunate to have the resources to study both the elementary and secondary Seeing Math in detail. We are hoping to be able to demonstrate increased student learning as a result of teacher completion of online Seeing Math professional development. We plan a series of very careful tests that will be reproducible and, hopefully, convincing. As part of this planning effort, it has been enjoyable to brush up on statistics and experiment design.

Closing Thoughts

The journey goes on. Technology is not unitary, not all technologies improve education, and technology itself is not the goal of our work, but the evolving capacities of information technologies have much to offer educators. Online collaborative courses represent one of the most exciting new educational resources created by technology. It appears that collaboration is central to the added value of online learning. Without collaboration, the social value of networking is lost and online courses become simply extensions of existing course formats. Effective collaboration comes at a cost, however, because a trained facilitator is needed for each collaborating group, which cannot exceed about 25 participants. In addition, groups need time to build understanding and trust. It may not be too surprising to have discovered that technology does not provide a substantial cost saving for courses, but it does offer many other advantages: quality, integration with other technologies, and the ability to reach thin audiences.

Unfortunately, technology also creates many options for low-quality online courses. This has been a great problem for the VHS and Teachscape, which are trying to compete in an environment where almost anyone can create an impressive-sounding collection of online courses. Many state departments of education and companies have jumped in without the thought and resources to do an adequate job. The result is a plethora of options that have given a bad name to online courses and have created a cacophony that can drown out the few quality sources. Quality is a challenge to measure and difficult to document but the only acceptable goal.

References

Barstow, D., Tinker, R., & Doubler, S. (1996). *National conference on student & scientist partnerships.* Washington, DC.

Berenfeld, B. (1994). Technology and the new model of science education: The Global Lab experience. *Machine-Mediated Learning, 4*(2-3), pp. 203-227.

Cohen, K.C. (Ed.). (1997). *Internet links for science education.* New York: Plenum Press.

Collison, G., Elbaum, B., Haavind, S., & Tinker, R. (2000). *Facilitating online learning: Effective strategies for moderators.* Madison, WI: Atwood Publishing.

Feldman, A., Konold, C., & Coulter, B. (2000). *Network science, a decade later: The Internet and classroom learning.* Mahwah, NJ: Lawrence Erlbaum Associates.

Harasim, L. (Ed.). (1990). *Online education: Perspectives on a new environment.* New York: Praeger.

Romiszowski, A.J., & de Haas, J.A. (1991). Computer-mediated communication for instruction: Using email as a seminar. *The Journal of the Learning Sciences, 3*(3), pp. 265-283.

Tinker, R. (2001). E-learning quality: The Concord model for learning from a distance. *Bulletin of the National Association of Secondary School Principals, 85*(629), pp. 36-46.

Tinker, R. (2003, May 2). *The Karplus lecture: History and the next revolution.* Paper presented at the National Science Teachers Association, Philadelphia.

Tinker, R., & Kapisovsky, P. (1991). *Consortium for educational telecomputing.* Conference Proceedings. Cambridge, MA: TERC.

Tinker, R., & Kapisovsky, P. (1992). *Prospects for educational telecomputing: Selected readings.* Cambridge, MA: TERC.

Zucker, A., Kozma, R., Yarnall, L., Marder, C., & Associates. (2002). *Teaching Generation V: The virtual high school and the future of virtual secondary education.* New York: Teachers College Press.

Index